CONVERSORUM®

CONVERSORUM

They can be a great people, if they wish to be.

Jor El, 1978

Published by Conversorum®
Copyright © 2013 by Revilal Vidyadharan

ISBN: 978-0-9576547-0-9
Draft edition: Limited to 2000 copies

A catalogue record for this book is available from the British Library.
Conversorum® is the publishing subsidiary of Conversorum® Ltd.   Reg No: 08482077

Primary Internet Presence: www.twitter.com/Conversorum   www.conversorum.com

Book design, layout and build:	Revilal Vidyadharan
Front cover design and layout:	Revilal Vidyadharan
Book printing:	Shore Books (www.shore-books.co.uk)
Rear cover author image:	Sourced from movies: 'V for Vendetta' (2005) and 'The Dark Knight' (2008)
	"What does it take to make you people get off the bench and into the game..."

CONVERSORUM®

200 conversation topics
to twitch those curious minds

Larivel Dravidayahn

Contents

Question Topics listed by Order
See Overleaf for 'Topics listed by Subject Area'

Question Topics listed by Subject Area
See Previous Page for Topics listed by Order

~

Introduction

Conversorum… well, that's not even a word!
What could this book possibly be about?
Why didn't I just leave it on this coffee table where it was comfortably accumulating tea rim stains!?!!
Why didn't the author just do an eBook so I can correct the spelling myself?

Granted, the fact that this 'C' word doesn't exist in any dictionary and is likely to give a fair indication of the state of grammar throughout this book. Alas, though I can't, and wouldn't, vouch for the grammar past this page (darn, I still struggle with when, where and why an apostrophe should be used!), I can certainly try and alleviate your worries about the title. Well, in short, the title is an amalgamation of two English dictionary verified words: 'Conversation' and 'Forum'.

Which ties me in nicely into addressing your second concern - the book's primary intention is to encourage conversation in an open forum. This is facilitated by the conversation topics and the (hopefully) adequate background information to get you up discussing and debating subject matter you either knew nothing of a few minutes prior, couldn't care less about or is a topic close to your heart.

Thirdly, it's wasted as a coaster, just too wide and thick… firewood, now there's an idea. Do you know how much warmth burning 450+ pages would provide, not to mention the small fortune you'd have saved by not switching on the central heating (see, you've broken even already by buying this book. Even better financially if you found it discarded next to a bin). Now, go forth and tell all your friends of the benefits of a physical book over those god-damned eBook's.

Finally, onto your point about the virtues of going down the electronic route and embracing an author's dream of zero overhead costs. Well, this author wishes to express his desire for the readership of this book to be ideally those splendid individuals who shun unnecessary digitalisation, preferring to hold and caress the beloved paper book rather than those ghastly unromantic digital mediums. Besides, you'd probably author a whole new book a lot quicker than having to correct the spelling/grammar in here (is digitalisation even a word!).

Conversorum® essentially holds 200 conversation topics on a wide range of subjects, with differing levels of difficulty designed to try and cater for most levels of intellect. Each conversation topic is intended to hold enough information to understand the subject and be able to sufficiently initiate and conduct a two-way forum for debate or ideally, the topics have been conducted in chapter order such that the background information given in preceding chapters had fed enough knowledge and thinking processes to not be fazed by the increasing difficulty and obscurity of the latter topics.

That's not to say the book should be read in order, quite the opposite, actually. Conversorum® is designed to be a 'coffee table' book, one that is picked up and casually flicked, purely for the purpose of wishing to engage in a random debate or as a conversation starter amongst friends. Nevertheless, the book contents are structured in such a way that will allow for either approach to be taken, one lists the topics by page order and the second categorises the topics by subject (to help you avoid all those boring 'Business and Finance' topics). Or if you have some cojones, you could always select a random letter between A-H and a number between 1-25 to arrive at a random topic.

Please bear in mind however, that the entire content of Conversorum® has actually been written with you in mind, in that it hopes the reader ultimately becomes somewhat knowledgeable in anything, questions everything but an expert in nothing. This book alone could clearly never achieve this, but what it hopes to do, is that by embracing the concept of this book and engaging in topics way out of your comfort zone may well clear the path for one's naivety to recede and to also awaken a desire to actively seek knowledge. After all, a fair and stable society is one where the people are empowered to be able to ask any question, demand answers and level criticism of and at any individual, organisation or institution that purports to have any authority, whether it being political, moral or spiritual.

Here's our mission statement which best encapsulates Conversorum®:-

• Master the art of topical conversation and debating;
• Encourage open points of view and thinking freely and without bias;
• Learn to seek out the truth and cross-reference everything you read/hear;
• Expand your mind and your thinking processes (by adopting a counter view to your own);
• To learn to appreciate, as well as becoming more accommodating, of viewpoints which may differ from one's own deep lying (perhaps indoctrinated) opinions.

Authors Note

To get the most out of this book, and before you delve in, please read through and take in the following 'How to Use This Book' section, as this will help you better understand the conventions used, the format of the questions and how each conversation forum is enabled.

Please note that all the views and opinions expressed in this book are purely for the purpose of providing a conversation angle, and does in no way represent the author's feelings, beliefs and opinions on any subject. Besides, my views on almost every aspect of life changes by the year.

I did think about writing about my background, my inspiration for doing this book, my motivations behind the topics etc. but I figured by this stage the book has likely been put down by now, or you've moved straight onto the 'How To Use' section. Therefore, there's no point in wasting both our time, so I'll resort to writing this commentary in the immortal words of George Costanza, and yada, yada, yada... and that is how this book came about. Inspired and flabbergasted... so you should be!

Omissions and Amendments: During my research, I discovered a brilliant book called Soul Pancake® which adopted a similar approach to this book, however realised there were a few topics which seemed to contain some overlapping discussion areas, so decided to remove them altogether from here. So, if you do have the more stylish and better written Soul Pancake® book, you can still go ahead and buy this one and take comfort in the knowledge that you won't be double-dipping.

Additionally, I had to remove almost 40 topics for either being that tad bit too controversial or was too deep a debate topic to contain comprehensively within a single double page spread.

eBook disclaimer: As I've already mentioned, and would like to reassure again, Conversorum® will never be produced in an eBook format. So long as there is a bookshop still standing, a bookshelf waiting to be filled and a library not closing down, our stance will stand loud and proud.

Larivel Dravidayahn

How to Use this Book

As mentioned, the discussion topics can be either selected in order, selectively by subject or completely at random. But once that question is selected, it needs to convey the respective points of conversation in order to stimulate an effective discussion, and this section intends to provide this. Over time, you will likely familiarise yourself with the conventions used, the format of the questions and how each conversation forum is enabled but until such time please refer back to this section when need be.

How to Play
• For each discussion topic, try to split the discussion group evenly in terms of intellect, pertaining to the subject at hand, where the two teams either select or are allocated the 'For' or 'Against' the motion. The group then utilise the information given or their own prior knowledge in order to conduct a healthy and reasoned debate – albeit with no time limit, no winners or losers and the opportunity to change one's own opinion.
• To encourage healthy debate and an open forum, it is anticipated that players opt for the side which goes against their own formed opinions.
eg. If a question topic *Is religion a good thing?* is selected, then all the Atheists will be placed on one team and the Believers on the other, to which they are then allocated the 'For Religion' and 'Against Religion' stands respectively. Atheists will then subconsciously fight their own deep opinions and argue in favour of God and Religion while the Believers forcibly take the stance that Religion has no place in modern society, is evil and there is indeed no imaginary man in the sky.
There's fun, fun, fun to be had by all!

Order of Questions
• The difficulty level of the questions have been ranked from easy to hard and respectively assigned a Chapter, where A is the easiest and H is the most difficult. It is envisaged that Chapter A is used primarily to test and become familiar with the 'conversation forum' format and the question formats and conventions.

• Best effort has been made to evenly distribute the subject areas across the chapters, so as to avoid the feeling of duplication. In some cases, topics have subtly overlapped but only for the purpose of progressively building up specific knowledge or it's simply that the consequent topic debate focuses on completely different lines despite similar subject matter (eg. see topics on *Human Cloning* and *Fractional Reserve Banking*).

• The author expects the more difficult question topics to be repeated whenever one feels they are better researched and equipped to tackle the issue, particularly when a turn of events occur in real life which has particular relevance.

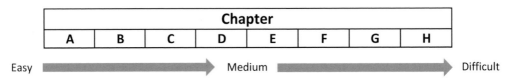

Question Formats

There are two formats (*Forum* and *In Play*) that the discussion topic can be presented in, and this could determine the form of debate that can be conducted.

• *Forum* - The standard question format which contains the question and any background information necessary. In some cases, viewpoints are provided for which to initiate for/against points of view.

• *In Play* - This is in many ways similar to the 'Forum' format except that it provides distinct For/Against viewpoints to stimulate the debate that little bit further.

Please refer to page 8, which illustrates the two formats more effectively.

Types of Question

The majority are straightforward debate topics but occasionally it deviates from this norm, where the concept of a 'classroom exercise' is put forward that attempts to engage all players to fulfil the task at hand, and even more rarely, the topic may be ambiguous enough that it serves only to put an idea in the player's head for one purpose or another.

• *Forum* - Straightforward debate topic.

• *In Play* - Straightforward debate topic, except with suggested For/Against viewpoints.

• *Reform* - Future scenarios where a change in law or a significant development have been hypothetically implemented/proposed.

• *Classroom* - Assumes players are given a classroom exercise in which they must all perform and undertake together or individually, as instructed.

Term Conventions

Honourable/Dishonourable Mentions

These sections came about because of the text constraint found in the 'Forum' question format. Because we had to be very inventive in trying to cram as much essential information as possible and sufficient enough to conduct debate, some of the planned real-life cases pertaining to the topic could not unfortunately be accommodated in its entirety.

Instead, we were left with either doing away with this limitation of this 'double page spread' concept and adding extra pages per question, or we leave it to the players to go ahead and research the clues and pointers given. We opted for the latter because i) I haven't got a clue on how to do a 'multiple page spread dependent on word count' automated action and ii) Google® is everyone's friend!

Discussion Viewpoints

Within questions adorning the 'Forum' format, for/against discussion viewpoints may be provided to help aid the discussion.

Further Discussion Points

This provides further discussion points to the debate at hand, approaching the subject matter from different angles. This should either supplement the main debate topic or alternatively, provide food for thought during the debate to stimulate some creative thinking.

Classroom Exercise

An additional branch for discussion, where once the topic has been adequately debated, players are invited to engage in an exercise, in which participation intends to ultimately magnify the issue at hand.

Wildcard View

This is sometimes added as a random 'out of the box' viewpoint, in order to prompt additional discussion or provoke a different approach to the topic.

Higher Order Architects

A common theme necessary throughout the book is the idea that there is a secretive, sinister cabal of individuals who control, manipulate and orchestrate major policies and events around the globe with the goal of achieving an ultimate ideal. Rather, a high-level hierarchy who are the real architects and puppeteers behind the world's most powerful countries, corporations and institutions, and will be referred to in the book throughout as the *Higher Order Architects* (see below).

How To Use: Question Formats

◦ In Play

Ch No	Question Type	Subject

{Holds the summary of the debate topic or puts forward the debate topic in question form.}

FOR

Holds some suggestions for arguments and viewpoints in favour of the subject matter (to aid the FOR debaters).

AGAINST

Holds some suggestions for arguments and viewpoints NOT in favour of the subject matter (to aid the AGAINST debaters).

Background	Facts and Examples

Provides sufficient background to the debate topic as well as stating the focus of any debate.

Primarily provides any facts, examples or viewpoints pertaining to the topic at hand.
However, could also be used to supplement the 'Background' should there be insufficient room to accurately describe the topic clearly.

Image Area:
Contains either of the following;

• A relevant movie scene capture/caption
• Supporting graphical information
• Dishonourable Mentions
• Supporting factual or fictional information

This section contains further information covering either of the following self-explanatory areas;

• Be Controversial
• Classroom Exercise
• Did You Know?
• Further Facts
• Future Reform
• Wildcard View

◦ Forum

Ch No	Question Type	Subject

{Holds the summary of the debate topic or puts forward the debate topic in question form.}

Background, Facts and Miscellaneous

Provides sufficient background, facts, examples and viewpoints pertaining to the debate topic as well as stating the focus of any debate.

Image Area:
Contains either of the following;

• A relevant movie scene capture/caption
• Supporting graphical information
• Dishonourable Mentions
• Supporting factual or fictional information

The Higher Order Architects (HOA)

In the modern world, conspiracy theorists have ludicrously suggested that a shadowy cabal, compromising some of the wealthiest people on earth, top politicians, the corporate elite and members of the most powerful aristocracies have colluded over the centuries to orchestrate events as part of a plan to take control of the world, establishing a *New World Order* where a fascist government presides over a feudalist state. They have assigned this concept the term *The Illuminati*, and the mere mention of them often accompanies choruses of disapproval from those less paranoid and those quite comfortable with today's society in which people have lost their moral compass, compassion and decency.

Well, not us here at Conversorum®, as such association with imaginary concepts concocted up by conspiracy theory nut-jobs would suggest that we welcome and seek ridicule too. Nope, not us.

We do have, coincidentally, a totally independent non-related term for an imaginary bunch of fellows at the top, coined the *Higher Order Architects*. We merely presume that these architects do indeed orchestrate government policy and manipulate global events, forsaking their ethical, moral and communal obligations, such that ultimately there will no longer be a middle class, just the wealthy elite and the lower classes. And in time, the world may well become just as it is portrayed in this depiction below from the 1987 movie *The Running Man*.

Those who sit at the top of the tree in positions of power and trust, having no moral conscience and driven by one sole ambition (wealth), know it's coming, they know someone is orchestrating it and they all want their bloodline to be assured of a place on that 'mother ship'.

Any similarities our *Architects* have with this *Illuminati* are pure coincidence and unintentional...

Chapter A

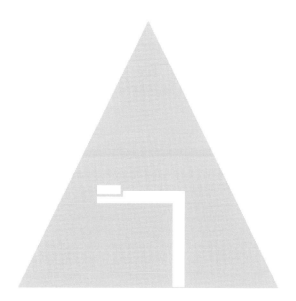

"Nothing puts a greater obstacle in the way of the progress of knowledge than thinking that one knows what one does not yet know."
- *Georg Christoph Lichtenberg*

How would civilisation have panned out if the concept of religion had never existed - Could we have entrusted human nature to naturally prosper and be good to our fellow man without any such given 'guideline' or 'inclination' for good morals?

Background

The term *Religion* is given to what humans regard as holy, sacred, spiritual or divine. It's commonly regarded as consisting of a person's relation to a God, spirits or any other form of supernatural entity. Worship is probably the most basic element of religion, but moral conduct, belief and participation in religious institutions are generally also constituent elements of the religious life as practiced by believers and worshipers and as commanded by religious sages and scriptures.

Today, religion is the most prominent and divisive form of segregation, eventually leading to conflict and war around the globe- prompting many to increasingly ridicule the concept and its place in modern society. Nevertheless, religion does have a positive influence on a great number of people, be it giving a purpose in life or providing a social congregation of like-minded people - but more importantly, providing a framework for good moral and responsible behaviour.

Facts and Examples

• Today, there exists many hundreds of different religions, faiths or cults, worshipping countless different gods, supernatural beings, people and even extra-terrestrial beings. This contrasts to the estimated 1 or 2 religions which existed from day dot.

• Religion helps to regulate our conduct and behaviour in society by providing a set of morals and value-system for a harmonious human existence. It ensures balance in a life where negative social influences can be increasingly disruptive, immoral and corruptive for the human mind.

• *Devadasi* is the practice of hierodulic prostitution, involving dedicating prepubescent or young adolescent girls into a forced ritual marriage to a deity/temple, who would perform functions such as spiritual guides, dancers and prostitutes servicing male devotees.

Dishonourable Mentions:- Thuggee; Exorcisms; Martyrdom; Youcef Nadarkhani; Goa Inquisition.

FOR

Religion still plays an important role in reforming bad characters, even the most violent and depraved. § Morally corrupt individuals have never believed in a god nor truly embraced religion. § Only religion can put forth a *moral code and bill of rights*. Any other entity or organisation could never wield such adherence or authority. § Social Interaction. § Positive and revered role-models.

AGAINST

Some religions actually advocate the use of violence in order to spread the 'word'. § Certain religious scriptures widely mention the acts of violence, rape, incest, murder, oppression and genocide throughout. § Religious based conflict and hatred is prevalent today as it has been throughout history. § Religion is being used to justify and excuse evil practices and rituals.

Image Source:- Movie: Doubt (2008)
Starring: Meryl Streep & Philip Seymour Hoffman

Wildcard View

A Ticket to Ride

Some religions tend to allow one to absolve all their past sins if they ultimately accept their maker into their heart - surely this *small print* then allows anyone to live their life however which way they want, however depraved, knowing full well a full pardon is on its way.

Does this then mean that Religion actually promotes some to lead a 'selfish, irresponsible, self-serving' life rather than a 'good moral' one?

Reading about history always prompts thoughts of 'What if' and 'How close were we to X scenario' - Discuss the following alternate historical scenarios and whether it would have been beneficial or detrimental to todays world?

Background, Facts and Miscellaneous

• Scenario Q1:
If World War II was won by Germany and the Middle Eastern countries became the only region brave enough to offer safe passage and refuge for the chamber-bound British Jews, what would have taken place in that region with regard to peace amongst its many diverse communities?

• Scenario Q2:
If during the moon landings the craft became irreparably damaged, and was bad enough for take-off to be deemed impossible. How would the quest for space exploration have been affected by the witnessing first-hand of three true heroes being stranded alive, and by the fact that every gaze at our Moon (as a mausoleum) served as a reminder of when we take a step too far?

• Scenario Q3:
If former PM *Tony Blair* remained throughout his term of office an honest man of sound integrity and moral character, possessing a backbone and the ability to reason an opinion for himself, could his lone yet powerful voice against the mischievous intentions of trigger-happy presidents have been enough to change the course of history?

• Scenario Q4:
If JFK had not been assassinated, would the many of his reported misdemeanours have eventually led to his impeachment by the House of Representatives?

• Scenario Q5:
If *Operation Northwoods* was given the green light?

Background to the US Governments 'Operation Northwoods' Plan :-

The proposed plan stated intent among the Joint Chiefs of Staff to stage terrorist attacks within the U.S. including killing innocent civilians, to provoke war with Cuba.

The document opposite was signed by Chairman of the Joint Chiefs of Staff *Lyman Lemnitzer* and reportedly presented to Secretary of Defense *Robert McNamara* in March 1962.

This previously Top Secret document was originally made public in November 1997, by the John F Kennedy Assassination Records Review Board, a U.S. federal agency overseeing the release of government records related to the assassination.

The "Appendices to Enclosure A" of the Northwoods document were first published online by the National Security Archive in November 1998 in a joint venture with CNN as part of CNN's 1998 Cold War television documentary series.

The author is so disgusted by this ploy that he'd wished not to put any of it to paper. Only that he would like to state that the thinking behind this scheme is fairly representative of the moral conduct of those in power.

Source:
http://publicintelligence.net/operation-northwoods/

TOP SECRET SPECIAL HANDLING NOFORN

THE JOINT CHIEFS OF STAFF
WASHINGTON 25, D.C.

UNCLASSIFIED

13 March 1962

MEMORANDUM FOR THE SECRETARY OF DEFENSE

Subject: Justification for US Military Intervention in Cuba (TS)

1. The Joint Chiefs of Staff have considered the attached Memorandum for the Chief of Operations, Cuba Project, which responds to a request of that office for brief but precise description of pretexts which would provide justification for US military intervention in Cuba.

2. The Joint Chiefs of Staff recommend that the proposed memorandum be forwarded as a preliminary submission suitable for planning purposes. It is assumed that there will be similar submissions from other agencies and that these inputs will be used as a basis for developing a time-phased plan. Individual projects can then be considered on a case-by-case basis.

3. Further, it is assumed that a single agency will be given the primary responsibility for developing military and para-military aspects of the basic plan. It is recommended that this responsibility for both overt and covert military operations be assigned the Joint Chiefs of Staff.

For the Joint Chiefs of Staff:

L. L. LEMNITZER
Chairman
Joint Chiefs of Staff

SYSTEMATICALLY REVIEWED
BY JCS ON _____
CLASSIFICATION CONTINUED

1 Enclosure
Memo for Chief of Operations, Cuba Project

EXCLUDED FROM GDS

EXCLUDED FROM AUTOMATIC
REGRADING; DOD DIR 5200.10
DOES NOT APPLY

TOP SECRET SPECIAL HANDLING NOFORN

Image Source:- See Appendix for Source

15

Animal Testing -
Though in somewhat justifiable to test the effectiveness and safety of medicines on animals, is it ethical to extend this courtesy to the testing of cosmetic beauty products?

Background

Using animals in scientific experiments has led to many discoveries that have improved the human quality of life. Advocates of animal testing say that the benefits far outweigh the costs, leading to the creation of vaccines, antibiotics, therapies, surgical techniques and medications. However, widespread evidence has shown that animals are not treated humanely and there is the unwavering belief that it is unjust to sacrifice one species for the benefit of another.

Cosmetics testing is usually focused on ensuring that a product does not harm a person's eyes and skin, and is also tested for overall toxicity.

With respect to this, scientists argue that animal testing is necessary and claim (well, they would!) that acute animal suffering is a myth and that animal suffering is limited. They also argue that, although there are alternatives, while useful, these alternatives do not provide the scientific significance required.

Facts and Examples

• Cosmetics testing on animals relates to many aspects of the manufacturing process, and may occur on the full, finished product or it may occur on individual ingredients within a formulation. Another country may even be contracted to conduct the testing within the cosmetic company's homeland or it may be contracted out to a country where animal testing is not currently banned or restricted.

• The European Union (EU) introduced a cosmetics testing on animals ban in 2009, however, it should still be noted that although finished cosmetics products are not tested on animals in the UK, there are still substances that have both cosmetic and medical uses. As such, they are essentially exempt from the regulations around cosmetics testing on animals.

• In the UK, there were nearly three million experiments on live animals in 2002. Animals bred purely for research but subsequently killed as 'surplus' - possibly millions - are not included in statistics.

FOR

There are cosmetics we would not have had, had we not been able to test on animals. § Allergic reactions, sometimes fatal, can only be discovered through adequate testing on real living body matter. § Lab animals are bred for this single purpose, therefore would not even have existed anyway. § Long term use and high doses must be confidently concluded. § Humans > Animals.

AGAINST

Is smelling and looking good really worth the life of a living creature? § Can't we just make do with the ingredients and chemicals that already exist in todays safe cosmetics products without the need to discover newer concoctions. § Experimenting on humans directly (for a generous fee), would be the ideal solution for all. § If animals only knew the macabre reason for their suffering?

Let me make sure I got this right... you want to take us away from our loved ones, pump us with chemicals and then watch us die a slow death.

Sure, where do I sign up?

Image Source:- Movie: Up (2009) Starring: Dogs

Wildcard View

Why is there an irrational obsession with Perfumed Fragrances? A self-regulated industry where selling a bottle of approximately 55-80% ethanol has become a £? billion a year industry. And yet, the number of animals which have endured unbearable pain and suffering to ensure that the 'scent' has no adverse effect on the 'more precious than diamonds' human being is astoundingly and disturbingly high. As unethical as this clearly is, the real pressing concern is why so many idiots spend so much on the damn thing!?!!

Company/Bank Account/Loan Applications - In order to help prevent bank and identity fraud and to utilise effectively the use of facial recognition software as a criminal deterrent, potential company directors and account-holders must have their photo taken in person to accompany any application.

Background, Facts and Miscellaneous

Currently, there are no requirements whatsoever to provide photographic or biometric information to supplement the opening of bank accounts, starting a company or applying for a loan, mortgage or credit card.

In order to address the following issues and to aid prosecution efforts, this law has come to pass;
• Bank fraud is defined as using fraudulent means to obtain money, assets or other property owned or held by a financial institution.
• Identity Theft fraud basically involves obtaining information about an individual, then using that information to apply for identity documentation, accounts and credit in that person's name. Most disturbing is the fact that perpetrators of such crime are content in the knowledge that their ac-

tions could well see the targeted victim ruined.
• Some companies are started by individuals purely for the intention of criminal practices and dishonest gain, lacking any integrity whatsoever.

Discussion Viewpoints:- A simple low-cost deterrent, yet strangely isn't considered viable by government or financial institutions. § Multiple bank accounts for the intention of sinister purposes. § Withdrawing a vulnerable person's savings. § Cheque fraud. § Credit cards imprinted with facial profile. § Fraudulent loans.

Dishonourable mentions:- Todd Davis and confidence; Carousel Fraud; Winston Kabia and residency permits; Chibuikem Uzoma-Ubani and Leonard Nwannenah; Asil Nadir and Polly Peck.

What came first, the Chicken or the Egg?

There's only one answer, so without invoking a circular reference, which is it?

Background, Facts and Miscellaneous

This conundrum has baffled the godfathers of wisdom for thousands of years, including no less than Aristotle himself, who stated:

"For there could not have been a first egg to give a beginning to birds, or there should have been a first bird which gave a beginning to eggs; for a bird comes from an egg."

So, what we have are chickens lay eggs, and these eggs contain chicks, which in turn grow into egg-producing chickens. Hang on!
• So how did the first egg come about?
• Can an egg-producing chicken just theoretically appear or evolve?
• Or was an egg placed beside Adam and Eve?
• How does an egg shell contain the correct attributes to sufficiently protect an embryo but yet allow a newborn chick to hatch effortlessly?

Scientific View: The *theory of evolution* states that species change over time via mutation and natural selection. Since DNA can be modified only before birth, a mutation must have taken place at conception or within an egg such that an animal similar to a chicken laid the first chicken eggs. These eggs then hatched into chickens that inbred to produce a living population.

Theology View: It seems the chicken came first according to the Bible, Genesis Chapter 1;

"And God created great whales, and every living creature that moveth, which the waters brought forth abundantly, after their kind, and every winged fowl after his kind: and God saw that it was good. And God blessed them, saying, be fruitful, and multiply, and fill the waters in the seas, and let fowl multiply in the earth."

Instead of Child Maintenance payments, absent fathers are now committed by law to spend their off-peak time with their natural children.

Discuss the possible benefits or adverse effects to society this new law will generate?

Background, Facts and Miscellaneous

Many absent fathers continue to breed recklessly because they are exempt from making child support payments due to individual financial circumstances, and therefore have had no constraints to undertaking irresponsible random and multiple impregnations. On the other hand, many unmarried mothers who bear children to multiple men do so in order to multiply their revenue streams of child maintenance payments.

In order to stem this callous and immoral approach to a child's upbringing and to promote the importance of being a positive father figure, it will now become mandatory for absent fathers to spend 3 hours per fathered child over the weekend and must be spent in a positively active way (ie. not just babysitting). This would mean an average *lothario* with 4 children must allocate 12 hours EVERY weekend without exception.

Discussion Viewpoints:-
• The more children recklessly fathered, the more hours which must be given up since the time is not run concurrently.
• Mentally disturbed or undesirable fathers.
• Happily married men with settled lives whose wives are unaware of their past.
• Unreasonable mothers and reluctantly absent fathers. Bad mothers and great fathers.
• Reducing benefit payments to party(s) responsible for bad and/or reckless parenting.
• Possible shifts we can see in demographic birth trends, particularly with regard to those from traditionally poor upbringings.

Image Source:- Movie: The Butterfly Effect (2004)   Starring: Eric Stoltz

There is a common trend in Third World countries where billions of dollars are channelled out unashamedly to bank accounts belonging to the very people entrusted with the power to help progress the country forward - Should the net wealth and all personal bank accounts be publicly declared before coming into power?

Background

In the developing countries of the Third World, where the issues of economic development, the environment and people's health are of utmost concern, corruption can greatly undermine them and it is the poorest affected the most by such underhanded practices. But, we've entrusted good honest men with morals to rise above it and the power to ensure the country's wealth and resources are put to good use. Wrong!!!

Corruption is rife at the highest level and it's become evident that many politicians seek office purely for the purpose of personal monetary gain.

Politicians must now publicly declare their complete net wealth holdings and all bank accounts held. In addition, an international agreement will be put in place where financial institutions will disclose any offshore bank accounts showing suspect activity originating from a foreign land. If exile is sought by the account holders, then these will be automatically suspended.

Facts and Examples

• The organisation *Transparency International* undertakes a research assessment called CPI (Corruption Perceptions Index). The CPI assesses the following: bribery of public officials, kickbacks in public procurement, embezzlement of public funds and assesses the strength and effectiveness of public sector anti-corruption efforts. It has consistently found, without exception, that all assessed African countries came at the bottom, globally, on the CPI.

• According to the Nigerian government, almost $4 billion USD in foreign assets have been traced back to their former president *General Sani Abacha*, his family and their representatives.

• In India, as much as $14.5 billion in food aid was looted by corrupt politicians and their criminal syndicates over the past decade in the state of Uttar Pradesh alone, according to data compiled by Bloomberg. The theft blunted the country's only weapon against widespread starvation - a public food distribution system.

FOR	AGAINST
It can be said that no amount of wealth can help some countries, however it certainly can't be allowed to continue to be recklessly plundered. § Will deter many with dishonest intentions to enter politics in the first place. § Stick it to the corrupt banking institutions who shamelessly allow 'daylight robbery' to take place. § Can uncover previous misdemeanours so promotes good practice.	Will deter people of genuine good character who don't wish their financial assets in the public domain for obvious reasons. § Money will be funnelled out regardless of any new laws, ready and waiting for them once the reign is over. § It's the way of the uncivilised world where accumulation of money is above and beyond helping your fellow people and future generations.

Here, give this to them. God knows they need it.

Future Reform

A binding agreement is in place should a candidate decide to accept a place at the top table;
• If corruption is uncovered, then it will be recovered by all means possible. Failing this, any remaining relatives still residing in the country will forfeit their assets to make up the shortfall.
• Net assets will be monitored for 20 years after the position of power has lapsed.
• All corruption payments received during the tenure must be disclosed, of which 20% can be legally kept.

Image Source:- Movie: Midnight Run (1988)
Starring: Robert De Niro and Danielle DuClos

With the perceived low threat of global warfare and little risk of conflict between the superpowers, why is it that in the West, an increasing portion of our tax contributions is still spent on military defence and 'foreign military operations'?

Background

With the unlikely event of long tactical wars between the superpowers, accelerating military technology and the threat of mutually assured nuclear destruction, the need for high military expenditure is no longer deemed necessary, yet we are still seeing what seems irrationally high military spending around the globe.

During the Cold War, countries adopted *nuclear deterrence*, the credible threat of retaliation to forestall enemy attack. Since the cold war end, concern over nuclear weapons has shifted to the prevention of localised nuclear conflicts resulting from nuclear proliferation, and the threat of nuclear terrorism.

The UN was set up to commit to preserving world peace through international cooperation and collective security. Yet for nearly two decades, they have faced financial difficulties and has been forced to cut back on important programs in all areas. As of 2009, its entire budget counts for just 1.8% of the worlds military expenditure.

Facts and Examples

• Despite the global financial and economic crisis of 2007+, 16 of the 19 states of the G20 still saw real-terms increases in military spending.
• US military spending in 2009 is almost 6 times more than China and 12 times more than Russia.
• The UK as of 2010 is the fourth highest spender (in cash terms) on Defence in the world (behind the US, China and France).
• In 2002, the then US Defence Secretary *Donald Rumsfeld* declared North Korea a terrorist state, part of the *axis of evil* and a target for regime change - on the verge of becoming a proliferator of nuclear weapons. It transpired that in 2000, he served on the board of a company which sold light water nuclear reactors to the government of North Korea, which is claimed could be used to produce nuclear weapons.

Dishonourable Mentions:- BAE Systems®; *Dick Cheney* and Halliburton®; $2.3 trillion just slipped by.

FOR

Keeping military companies afloat and in-house requires assurances of reliable and growing revenue streams. § Stimulates the economy with high spending. § Military corporations control western governments and will never stop creating fraudulent excuses to start wars around the globe. § Wars help us rid the stupid people who couldn't get a real job - a brighter future.

AGAINST

No need for war now, we're all grown up and wise enough to know better. § Military spending drains resources from the productive economy. § Spending needs to be tied to GDP and/or credible threats. § Corruption is clearly at play. § High military spending only leads to forming threats, global unrest and creating disharmony. § Allies know they can get away with spending less.

With the defence cuts, the top brass had to decide between their chauffeur driven rides or mission critical defence armoury. On a brighter note, our max speed is now 25% faster.

Captain, we have a message coming through...

Image Source:- Movie: Crimson Tide (1995)
Starring: Gene Hackman, Denzel Washington and Matt Craven

Future Reform

Contribute to war, then you can sure as hell contribute to peace.

Each country is now legally decreed to apportion a % of their military budget directly to the UN to help achieve something in the worlds best interests, global security and peace. Every 5 years, each country's average military spending over the same period must be donated. This will in turn help curb irrationally disproportionate military budgets (and consequently our tax and funeral bills).

Should money-centred, morale lacking, conscious-free defence lawyers be put on an 'offensive low-lifes' register?

Background, Facts and Miscellaneous

Regardless of whether 'the truth' of a situation favours the client or not, the primary role of a legal representative is to protect their client's best interests, by means fair or foul - so long as they are all above board. The Judge's role is to decide the case on what he believes to be 'the truth' (having heard both sides, and in view of applicable statutes and case law).

Discussion Viewpoints:-
• A fair legal system must ensure that guilt must be proven and a full and fair defence is necessary,
• For many of them, it's just about money and to hell with ethics or integrity,
• They are a necessary evil, in order to preserve a democratic, just and civilised society,
• Everyone, regardless of the evidence presented

or the nature of the crime, is entitled to a fair trial.
• Lawyers still unashamedly do their utmost to have their client acquitted even when in full knowledge of the defendants guilt or their past,
• A typical lawyer's reluctance to defend pure scum is correlated only with the fee negotiated.
• What would be the consequences to society if defence lawyers exhibited some morals and refused to defend the indefensible?

Dishonourable Mentions:- Geir Lippestad; Jeffrey Samuels and the Dowlers; Lindeman & Alvarado; Jacques Vergès, a plain b*stard; J Cochran. Honourable Mentions:- Fusaaki Uzawa; The trouble with the legal profession is that 98% of its members give the rest a bad name; Abbas Al Hawi; Where there's a will there's a bill.

Why do so many intelligent grounded men/women fall for the marketing strategy for diamond engagement rings, accepting it as matter of fact and that the rule had been written in stone (pun intended) from the dawn of time?

Background, Facts and Miscellaneous

"You need to spend three months salary on your diamond engagement ring to show her how much you love her and what she really means to you."

Up to half a century ago, diamonds were not even considered as conventional an engagement ring present as they are today. But this simple advertising campaign undertaken in the 1940s by *De Beers*, the diamond wholesaler, has surpassed all their expectations and the slogan has now become not just a rule, but the rule of thumb - a marketing man's dream.

Today, the diamond industry is estimated to be worth a staggering $60 billion but yet provides no real worth except that of a sensible investment, in the form of an asset which can be relied on to hold the majority of its value.

However, to the everyday man, this really is of no ultimate benefit as the 'investment worth' is simply being transferred to a woman who he'll most likely detest within 10 years (if marriage statistics are to be believed).

So, rather than fall for the oldest marketing gimmick in the book, should men re-consider whether slaving away every working hour for 3 months to pay for a gemstone that can be readily switched for *Cubic Zirconia*, be worth the effort?

Further Discussion Points:-
• Why are diamonds so sought after when it requires an expert with a microscopic lens handy to verify its worth to friends and family?
• If you held a rock in your hand worth 200 times your annual wage, what would you do?

Under the 1961 Vienna Convention, foreign officials, their spouses, children and staff are diplomatically immune from prosecution by their host country. Why should they be exempt from ANY crime - particularly with regard to murder, rape, child abuse and fraud?

Background, Facts and Miscellaneous

Diplomatic immunity is a form of legal immunity and a policy held between governments that ensures that diplomats are given safe passage and are considered not susceptible to lawsuits or prosecution under the host country's laws.

The *Vienna Convention* is explicit that *it is the duty of persons enjoying such privileges and immunities, to respect the laws and regulations of the receiving State.* Nevertheless, on occasion, protected diplomats have violated laws of the host country and that country has been essentially limited in their powers only to declaring that those persons are no longer welcome (*persona non grata*).

• Figures released in 2006 revealed that between 1999-2004, 122 serious offences were allegedly committed by embassy staff - including allegations of murder, indecent assault, rape and child abuse as well as relatively lighter offences such as bribery, fraud and firearms possession.

• The age of consent for a person legally allowed to have sex in Hungary is 14, yet in most of the western world it is between 16-18.

• In countries such as Saudi Arabia, the death penalty can be imposed on offences such as drug use and adultery, practices normally considered as standard behaviour amongst people in power.

Dishonourable Mentions:- Traffic violations; Burmese Ambassadors & Pyres; PC Yvonne Fletcher; Raymond Allen Davis and Muhammad Abad ur Rehman; Ralph Leo Boyce Jr; Contradicting laws and punishments between the host and origin country (eg. age of consent).

Image Source:- Movie: Omen III (1981)   Starring: Sam Neill

In order to facilitate a fairer VAT system, it's been calculated that a VAT rate of 25% can be placed on 'luxury goods' so that the standard VAT rate can revert back to 12-15%, without affecting the total VAT revenue. Discuss the implications?

Background

The most important criticism of VAT is that it is a 'regressive' tax, falling largely on the poor and the middle classes, who pay a greater proportion of their income than the rich.

A fairer VAT system would be one that should not deter or discourage spending but one which reflected a person's disposable income and ideally, penalised the excessiveness of 'luxury good' spending. The key behind this reform is that if disposable income can be so callously and recklessly spent, then a similar unforgiving attitude can be taken towards the tax charged.

Luxury Goods will now officially be termed as a product or brand that only the 'filthy rich' or 'those that have more money than sense' will purchase. Unofficially, it is a product which carries a premium price tag hugely disproportionate to the manufacturing costs and which is based purely on taking advantage of its affluent target market and/or their *brand reputation*.

Facts and Examples

• VAT was introduced in 1973 at a standard rate of 10%. In 1979, VAT was consolidated to a single rate of 15%, and in 1991 it was raised to 17.5%.
• Louis Vuitton's® 'Raindrop Besace', a stylish and refined bag available for a mere £1000. In order to counter accusations that it resembles a plastic trash bag, it has a drawstring closure and will be available in green.
• The wife of a legendary luxury designer, the wife, designed one of the world's most desirable computer tablets. Made entirely from 22ct gold, it's worth every cent of its £130,000 price tag. Well, at least until the Ipad2 was released a little over a year later.

Dishonourable Mentions:- Stuart Hughes and the precious metals he has lying around; Fernando Altamirano®; Damien Hirsts 'Art'; Amosu® Phones; Dormeuil® Suits; Linley® Furniture; Birkins;
Honourable Mentions:- LexiCON®, Oppo® and their buddy THX®; Coca-Cola®'s Dasani; Denon® AKDL1;

FOR

Best for everyone that those with more money than sense have their money taken off them. § Rightly penalises the extravagant and irresponsible. § Luxury goods manufacturers and their obscene profit margins. § VAT being an unfair taxation system. § Rich folk like to be seen with bags in their hands from the posh shops, so taking their shopping abroad won't be a realistic consequence.

AGAINST

With the advent of internet shopping and lower shipping costs, people will buy from abroad instead. § Penalising the rich (again!). § Just abolish VAT altogether to encourage spending by all. § This action is just a step towards moving to a VAT system only for the middle/elite classes. § Less and less reason for the affluent to stay in the UK or for premium brands to manufacture here.

Image Source:- Movie: Pretty Woman (1999) Starring: Julia Roberts

Future Reform

A 'tiered' VAT system is proposed where the tier amounts are inflation-adjusted annually, with the lowest tier band being indexed to the cost of an average family shopping basket. Subsequent upper tier bands are indexed to this low band at a fixed factor.

Main perceived benefit would be that this could eventually fester a mutual collective effort by all to try and keep the price of staple items at a reasonable level, helping to prevent undue inflationary pressures.

There are absurd claims that the Fluoride added to our drinking water and to our toothpastes are solely for the sinister purpose of mass medicating the public, in order to become susceptible to being controlled and submissive - Does the high correlation of persistent criminal offenders and their lack of dental hygiene support such theories?

Background

It's been claimed that Fluoride, an extremely toxic substance, can reduce an individual's power to resist domination, by slowly poisoning and narcotising an area of the brain, and thus making them submissive to the will of those who wish to govern.

Though the concept of mass-medication as a means of control is nothing new, there seems very little evidence to actually support the claims that fluoride is effective in this manner. However, opponents against the fluoridation of our drinking water and our toothpastes argue otherwise, stating that moral, ethical and safety concerns are being violated.

It's not hard to disagree with the fact that a high proportion of criminals display poor dental hygiene and this tends to be a constant throughout their criminal history. This begs the question - has the forced use of fluoride in toothpastes actually made society a safer place and should we all adhere?

Facts and Examples

• As one of the strongest anti-psychotic substances known, it's found in 25% of the major tranquillisers.
• A 2003 survey found that the amount of untreated dental disease among prisoners was about four times higher than that of the general population. Some prisoners had endured chaotic lives before coming inside and may not have looked after their teeth.
• In the general US population, 80% of tooth decay occurs among 25% of children aged 5-17 years, primarily in those from minority and low-income families and in those with low educational levels. These are the children who are disproportionately represented in juvenile justice facilities.
• At the United States Penitentiary in Leavenworth, Kansas, White inmates had significantly fewer decayed teeth than did Black inmates, and the number of decayed teeth increased significantly with inmate age.
• The Nazi regime had notoriously researched the concept of mind control through chemical means.

FOR

Indicates such control can be achieved and harnessing it further should be pursued for the greater good. § Increased fluoridation of the prison water system can act as an additional rehabilitation method. § Every cloud has a silver lining - Something good ultimately came from Hitler's mind. § Standard rehabilitation is clearly failing and such thinking should be applauded.

AGAINST

Depriving the rights of citizens to be free from unwelcome mass medication. § Restricting free will. § Many other possible common factors amongst criminals. § Sets a dangerous precedent, especially for communist regimes. § Permits the criminally insane to begin actively avoiding such methods of control. § Only good intentions as Fluoride clearly holds properties beneficial to health.

Image Source:- Movie: Magnolia (1999) Starring: Pat Healy & Art Frankel

Did You Know ?

Richard Foulkes, M.D revealed:

The water fluoridation studies showed only positive results. Studies that did not fit the concept they were 'selling' were either omitted or declared as 'bad science'. Endorsements had been won by coercion and the self-interest of professional elites. Some of the basic 'facts' presented to me were, I found out later, of dubious validity. We are brought up to respect these persons in whom we have placed our trust to safeguard the public interest. It is difficult for each of us to accept that these may be misplaced.

The Home Audio Visual industry and related parties are currently promoting the 'next best thing' (again). Who has the most to gain from the unrelenting push of 3-D technology into the home?

Background, Facts and Miscellaneous

A 3-D presentation is one that enhances the illusion of depth perception and the technology has actually existed in various forms since 1915. In the '50s, 3-D films had prominently featured in American cinema, and had later experienced a worldwide resurgence in the '80s and '90s, culminating in the unprecedented success of the 3-D presentation of James Cameron's *Avatar* in 2009.

But who is most likely the driving force:-
• AV hardware producers: Hot on the heels of selling 'HD-Ready' and then 'Full-HD' audio visual equipment, a 3-D setup at home would require a complete overhaul of equipment from the AV Amplifier to the TV and even to the cables.
• Movie studios and disc producers: Extending the life of the Blu-Ray/DVD industry that little

bit longer, since downloading 3-D movies would require greater storage and bandwidth. Also, would allow a 3-tier retail release strategy to succeed; 1-Disc version, 2-Disc Special Edition and then the must-have 3-Disc Special 3-D Edition.
• Cinema operators: With flagging audience numbers, 3-D would re-invigorate the industry and keep cinemas around for years to come. Not to mention the extra £2 per film and the additional rental charge for 3-D glasses (yes, really).

Further Discussion Point:-
With the inevitable failure of 3-D and with mainstream consumers being quite happy with Full-HD broadcasts (high-definition), what possible innovations are necessary to stave off the impending threat of downloadable (free) content?

Image Source:- Movie: Poltergeist (1982) Starring: Heather O'Rourke

Hospital Acquired Infections -
Should it become compulsory for all persons
(staff/patients/visitors) to wear disposable
medical gloves at all times while on the premises?

Background, Facts and Miscellaneous

Infection with MRSA bacteria mainly occurs with people who are already ill in hospital and can be difficult to treat as MRSA bacteria are resistant to most types of antibiotics. MRSA spreads from person to person usually by direct skin-to-skin contact, and the spread is further exacerbated by touching sheets, towels, clothes etc. which have been used by someone who has MRSA.

Data from the *Office for National Statistics* covering 2004 to 2007 showed a record number of deaths linked to hospital superbugs in England and Wales, with more than 20,000 deaths linked to *Clostridium difficile* and more than 6,000 associated with MRSA. It has been identified that the failure of doctors and nurses to simply wash their hands between treating patients was one of the main causes behind the shocking statistics.

Medical gloves are disposable gloves used during medical procedures and help to prevent contamination between caregivers and patients.

Discussion Viewpoints:-
Additional costs. § Outsourcing and cost-cutting has led to a relaxation of infection controls. § Bad for the environment. § Possibility of cross-contamination caused by laziness to constantly change their gloves. § The weak and dying are normally the ones vulnerable - easier and more cost-effective for the NHS if they were allowed to succumb. § Low pay of nurses have meant that they take less pride in their expected duties. § More nurses from foreign climates where cleanliness and hygiene aren't considered a high priority.

Image Source:- Movie: ER (1994) Starring: Anthony Edwards and Alex Kingston

Judge Judy receives approximately $25m per year from her reality courtroom show - Is it right for a public servant to exploit their (misrepresented) position for celebrity status and does this consequently affect the attitude towards the plaintiffs such that it maintains viewing figures?

Background, Facts and Miscellaneous

Judge Judy is a day-time reality court show featuring former family court judge *Judith Sheindlin* arbitrating over small claims cases. Since premiering in 1996, the show has been the ratings leader in courtroom-themed, reality-based shows. In 2006, the program earned *Sheindlin* a star on the Hollywood Walk of Fame(!)

In fact, her honour is actually only a 3rd party arbitrator, and no longer an actual judge. She however engages in conduct which is materially misleading to the entire viewing population. At the beginning of each show, it's stated "the people are real, the cases are real" and we see a court room with Mrs Sheindlin in her black robe. The fact that litigants must refer to her as they would any other judge reinforces the misrepresentation that she is a bona fide judge.

A 26Nov02 article in the *New Post* and subsequent interviews quoted former Los Angeles Superior Court Judge *Joseph A Wapner* as saying of her: "She's rude, discourteous, abrasive, arrogant, insulting and an absolute disgrace to the profession. She does things I don't think a judge should do - demeaning people constantly."

The respected lawman also commented "If she does it on purpose, then that's even worse. Judges need to observe certain standards of conduct and she doesn't."

Discussion Points:- Her straightforward manner and intolerance of liars/cheats is just what the courts need. § $millions at stake therefore a few intentionally immoral judgements are acceptable. § Who says crime doesn't pay. § Syndi-courts.

Image Source:- Movie: A Few Good Men (1992) Starring: Jack Nicholson

With more and more IT companies going public, the need to dazzle investors with plans for maintaining revenue streams and new initiatives has never been greater - Advanced computer viruses that 'threaten the world' seem to be more commonplace today, but could they be the handiwork of the IT firms themselves?

Background

The viruses of yesteryear were consigned to just being a nuisance, deleting system files and more recently installing malicious software for the sole purpose of stealing personal or confidential data.

However, in recent years we've seen the rise in the *Super-virus*, where the intent is to destroy data permanently, bring down IT infrastructure or more disturbingly, take control and tamper with industrial infrastructure. For countries, governments and corporations, such a threat is becoming all too real and frighteningly dangerous, one whose presence cannot afford to be tolerated or be exposed to.

Today, with free reliable anti-virus programs and the possible shift towards cloud computing, the future of the computer security industry would appear doomed. But has the advent of this new super-virus era secured their longer term and assured presence with an altogether new customer base who have deeper pockets?

Facts and Examples

• It's estimated that the total cost for the work done in preparation for the *Millennium Y2K* bug exceeded $300 billion, yet many suggest with the lack of any significant problems occurring, that the danger(s) had been deliberately overstated. Only time will tell if we'll witness a similar repeat of the level of scaremongering and precautionary measures for the upcoming *Unix Millennium* bug in the year 2038.

• The *Flame* virus was discovered to possess a range of complex espionage capabilities including remotely changing settings on computers and turning on computer microphones to record conversations.

• With anti-virus vendors unable to keep apace with the numerous variants released every year, the loss of the 'virus arms race' has led leading industry analysts to propose better preventative measures such as *whitelisting* or *behavior-blocking* programs.

• Blair/Bush's Dodgy Dossier: "If there's no credible threat to justify the expense, we'll create one."

Scaremongering tactics can be more imaginative (especially when the word *Armageddon* can now be comfortably deployed). § Without the evolution of viruses, these companies would cease to be. § Turnover would be considerably increased with the higher sense of urgency and importance. § Oh, to become a member of the military-industrial complex. One can dream!

Corporate suicide - analysis of virus code could trace its origins back to the antivirus company. § Many criminal elements with legible reasons for creating viruses. § Whistle-blowing. § Political espionage often seems to resort to employing questionable tactics. § Huge financial and logistical commitment required with no guaranteed payoff. § Providing the stick in which to be beat with.

Basically, the internet will crash in 2038, but I the One, can prevent it.

Ok, you win! What are your rates, and I guess you'll need to commence working in 2030, right?

Nope... all I want is the blue pill !!!

Image Source:- Movie: Matrix Revolutions (2003) Starring: Keanu Reeves

Future Reform

With the traditional PC desktop environment, all internet-related activity are downloaded to the 'Temporary Internet Files' folder.

Why, were it possible, isn't all online activity and this folder location quarantined altogether. Quarantined in the sense that it should have absolutely no permissions whatsoever to move files, to execute files or commands or have read-write access to anything other than within itself, effectively acting as a standalone netbook.

What is the optimal path to a fulfilling life - Something you can look back on with total satisfaction and few regrets when you are back n forth on that rocking chair?

Background, Facts and Miscellaneous

Each of us are born with the opportunity of living a happy fulfilled life, treading a path which we feel best fits our strengths, beliefs, interests and morals and one that ideally conforms to our parents' best wishes and hopes.

However, sometimes, events and obstacles frequently interrupt our desired path and most of us reluctantly stray from it, ending up living a mundane unfulfilled existence filled with unhappiness, frustration and stress, holding little optimism for the future.

How should one prioritise what is important in life and do we ever have the level of maturity required in our younger years to appreciate the finer things in life and all the wonderful things around us? Or should society dictate what is best for us?

Classroom Exercise 1:-
You are 10 years old and the following outcomes are available to you in your old age, and you must determine your optimal path to realistically achieve this using the grid opposite:-
• Conventional: Enjoying retirement; Large loving family; Becoming grandparents; Debt-Free;
• Selfish: No meaningful relationships; Living on benefits; Living day to day just waiting to die;
• Free-loving and easy-living: Sitting in a rocking chair with nothing but great memories of adventures and laughs, in a council provided bedsit.

Classroom Exercise 2:-
Which single aspect of your life thus far do you wish you'd lived differently, and how dramatically different would your life be now?

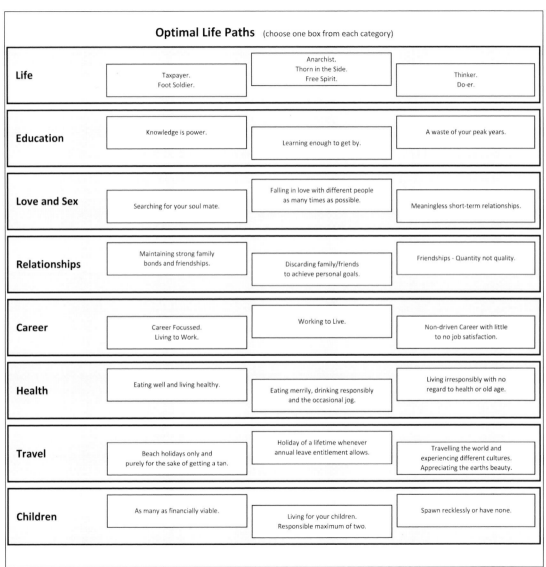

Optimal Life Paths (choose one box from each category)

Life	Taxpayer. Foot Soldier.	Anarchist. Thorn in the Side. Free Spirit.	Thinker. Do-er.
Education	Knowledge is power.	Learning enough to get by.	A waste of your peak years.
Love and Sex	Searching for your soul mate.	Falling in love with different people as many times as possible.	Meaningless short-term relationships.
Relationships	Maintaining strong family bonds and friendships.	Discarding family/friends to achieve personal goals.	Friendships - Quantity not quality.
Career	Career Focussed. Living to Work.	Working to Live.	Non-driven Career with little to no job satisfaction.
Health	Eating well and living healthy.	Eating merrily, drinking responsibly and the occasional jog.	Living irresponsibly with no regard to health or old age.
Travel	Beach holidays only and purely for the sake of getting a tan.	Holiday of a lifetime whenever annual leave entitlement allows.	Travelling the world and experiencing different cultures. Appreciating the earths beauty.
Children	As many as financially viable.	Living for your children. Responsible maximum of two.	Spawn recklessly or have none.

Image Source:- By The Author

When current prison sentence tariffs were initially drafted, it never accounted for or even legislated for the possibility that prisoners could be released 'on licence' halfway through their term, due to a shortage of cell space - Should the tariffs now be revised accordingly, or maybe even doubled to account for this 'early release' loophole?

Background, Facts and Miscellaneous

There are different types of prison sentences in the UK, depending on how serious the crime committed is and the defendant's character.

A 'determinate' sentence is a prison sentence for a fixed length of time. If the sentence is 12 months or more, the first half of the sentence is spent in prison and the second half is spent in the community 'on licence', where one must adhere to certain conditions.

The sentencing guidelines for the minimum prison term for each type of criminal offence were initially evaluated in good faith, such that it would be i) truly consistent with the seriousness of the crime committed, and ii) one a criminal would acknowledge was lengthy enough to receive as penance for their crimes, and finally iii) one that would act as a genuine deterrent.

However, in recent times, the crisis of having a shortage of prison space has resulted in the government introducing a policy of releasing prisoners automatically at the halfway stage. It's therefore reasonable to assume that criminals view prison terms as (ultimately) lenient which would mean they now no longer act as a deterrent.

Q1: Should all sentencing guidelines be toughened up, doubled even, so that the punishment handed down is actually restored to its initial pledge and that the 'licence' acts only as a rehabilitation tool to help ensure convicts stay on the straight and narrow after the FULL term is served?

Q2. Should minimum tariffs for life imprisonment be set by authorised officials rather than at the discretion of out-of touch judges?

Image Source:- Movie: The Shawshank Redemption (1994) Starring: Tim Robbins

Like the rest of Europe, the UK are slowly allowing themselves to become a nation of tenants rather than houseowners, due to unaffordable house price levels. Discuss the long term implications if all residential homes were owned by wealthy individuals or foreign investors?

Background, Facts and Miscellaneous

It is estimated that one in three London houses are now owned by overseas investors looking to take advantage of the high cost of rent and the tax breaks. Non-resident property owners do not have to pay UK Income tax or Capital gains tax meaning that they will not have to pay tax on the rent they receive or on purchasing the property if it is considered a second home.

According to a National Housing Federation's forecast in 2012, home ownership in England will slump to just 64% over the next decade, the lowest level since the mid-80s, with the decline down to huge deposits, combined with high house prices and strict lending criteria. The federation forecast that in London, the majority of people will rent by 2021, with the number of owner-occupiers falling to 44% by 2021.

Discussion Viewpoints:-
• Will money paid in rent ever find itself back into the UK financial system?
• If it simply goes to topping up the savings accounts of the wealthy and the coffers of foreign nations, what are the implications of this substantial negative cashflow on the economy?
• To ensure a permanent stream of revenue, property is never sold. Does this mean that property market valuations become redundant and therefore landlords can eventually charge whatever level rent they like, much like a cartel?
• With high rent levels and consequently less disposable income, could the wealthy and foreign landlords develop a unified conscience and lower it to sensible levels? Or can we rely on a government to impose such well-overdue restrictions?

Image Source:- Movie: Dirty Rotten Scoundrels (1988)
Starring: Steve Martin and Michael Caine

In 2017, a pro-active stance to tackling population control has been initiated and the first tactic to be used will be to rewrite the social security benefits system - A maximum of only two children can be used to determine total social security payments and any housing provisions. Discuss the long term impact of such a policy?

Background, Facts and Miscellaneous

In Great Britain, the social security system is such that those who are unemployed have a financial incentive to have more and more children while those in work are forced to cease having children because they simply cannot afford to or refuse to rely on state handouts.

This has led to some worrying concerns for our time, being i) the population increasing limitlessly, especially amongst the lower classes and ii) growing realisation that there is now little need to work for a decent existence - almost resulting in a culture of entitlement amongst those unworthy.

Couple this with the obvious disturbing trend of the lower classes and the immigrant population out-breeding the working/middle class, the country is perhaps facing a bleak and hopeless future for young and old alike.

Therefore, the social security system will be overhauled with immediate effect so that any children below the second child cannot be taken into account whatsoever when applying for any kind of welfare benefits. This is so that only those self-sufficient enough to bear/raise additional children do so, and those who wish to seek to better themselves can only do so through hard work.

Any appeal can only be taken into consideration if the tax/NI records of the applicant's display an above-average contribution to society.

Dishonourable Mentions:- The Smiths and the medieval act of a single Nintendo Wii; DWP; Abdi Nur, seven children and a £2m Kensington property; Lottery jackpots and Toorpakai Saiedi; Polish Express 'Benefit Hunters'; Sue McFadden.

Image Source:- Movie: The Crow (1994) Starring: Michael Massee and Anna Levine

One Religion, One Faith but oh so many Choices.

Why for a specific Religion when there is one underlying common faith, belief or scripture, are there many sects and rival institutions vying for that 'worshippers' attention?

Background, Facts and Miscellaneous

Despite many protestations of what values religion can provide society, there can be no doubting that it offers the worshipper a sense of belonging, community support and an underlying common faith with his fellow man.

But why, when an institution provides such wonderful contributions and fulfils its purpose as an intermediary or 'gateway', do some feel the need that they can do things better or that their 'truth' is more accurate - proceeding to start a rival offshoot and try to persuade and recruit other followers of the same religion?

Discussion Viewpoints:- Formed in order to excuse criminal intentions. § The desire for power, control and personal adulation. § Personal agendas. § Contradicting interpretations of scriptures.

• There are approximately 38,000 Christian denominations in the world (taking into consideration cultural distinctions of denominations in different countries), with the Roman Catholic Church being the largest.
• There are reported to be more than 1500 different Christian faith groups in America.
• Violent clashes in a New York based Sikh Gurdwara, were started by the recently ousted leaders. It's been cited that the control of power and the privileges it entailed was behind the use of swords and cricket bats!
• Philadelphia Jan12 - Turmoil over a mosque's leadership erupted in violence after its previous imam *Shamsud-din Ali* was convicted of eight illegal moneymaking schemes, in which he used the Islamic school as his headquarters.

Image Source:- Movie: Scarface (1983) Starring: Al Pacino

55

Superman, imagine a world with him in it.
Breathe...
Now, imagine that he has just 24 hours to sort sh*t out?

Background, Facts and Miscellaneous

Superman is a fictional character appearing in comic books published by *DC Comics*®. As a mortal born on a planet with a red sun, he possesses the ability to absorb and store the solar energy from yellow stars, which in turn grants him incredible powers and abilities, including superhuman strength, enhanced senses, impenetrable skin and the ability to defy gravity. Though his weaknesses are limited, one exists in a rare form extremely harmful to him, *Kryptonite*, causing extraordinary pain, the loss of his powers and eventual death.

In an alternate universe, *Superman* has been resident on our planet for the last 20 years, and has been a heaven-sent check on crime and global affairs ever since, with the world's people living in relative harmony and safe from natural harm.

Nevertheless, despite his best efforts, the world is exactly as it is in our real world, suffering from the insatiable whims of modern man, the propensity to be selfish, inconsiderate, corrupt and the desires to seek control and power.

Unbeknown to him, the (real) criminal underworld (those in the corridors of power and whose best laid plans and agendas have been continually flouted by the *Man of Steel*) have conspired to restore the right to rule with free reign, and have decided on a world without *Superman*. He was meticulously tricked into swallowing a *Kryptonite* pill and now has only 24 hours worth of superpowers before he becomes mortal again.

What or whom should *Superman* target within this time frame to make the most effective impact on our chances to become a prosperous world?

Image Source:- Movie: Superman III (1983) Starring: Christopher Reeve

Women have been put on this earth for one reason, and one reason only. So why do they go about f**king it up for everyone else?

Background, Facts and Miscellaneous

The female reproductive system is a series of organs that, together with the male system, combine to initiate the human reproductive process.

As technical and mechanical as this process sounds, there is a significant manual yet essential intervention coming in the form of who the female decides which Man and their set of genes is worthy of passing through to the next and all subsequent generations of the human race. A duty and responsibility that thankfully women have honourably taken on board and undertaken with the utmost vigilance (fulfilling their purpose as being effectively a human screening process).

Sadly, this statement carries the same grain of truth as the story about the pink elephant who engaged in sexual relations with a flying pig!

If women only bred with men of good character, those of a good gene pool or those displaying wholehearted willingness to be a great father, the world would inexplicably be a much better place.

It can be argued that with the state of human society as it is, a large portion of blame should be laid at the door of women who breed so recklessly and callously, with no consideration for mankind. With this in mind, discuss and rank which following types of mother are the worst:-
a) Breeding with 'Losers';
b) Breeding Interracially;
c) Breeding purely for financial gain;
d) Knowingly being unfit mothers-to-be;
e) Stubbornly breeding with inherently evil men;
f) Breeding with men holding physical hereditary disadvantages eg. short or ugly people.

Image Source:- Movie: The Godfather: Part II (1974) Starring: Diane Keaton

In order to promote and encourage the importance of family time and the long-term benefits of de-stressing sufficiently, should it become compulsory for the working week to start at 1pm on Mondays, so that the weekend can be fully appreciated, enjoyed and utilised?

Background

De-stressing is considered to be an extremely important factor to our overall health, as we find that physical and mental health problems due to stress are increasing at an alarming rate. Our lives are consumed by distress and stress from the time the alarm clock goes off, until the time our heads hit the pillow. Stress affects our lives in many different ways and often create undiagnosed health issues that go untreated.

With today's busy lifestyles, many people now appreciate the importance of spending more quality time with their children, partners or friends. However, the work and social pressures put on us in this day and age have found us aimlessly walking into a life of *Living to Work* rather than our desired *Working to Live* mantra. Something, we all realise all too late.

By implementing this new workplace law, this shorter working week could certainly address the imbalance of working against free time, as well as the lack of quality family time in today's day and age.

Facts and Examples

• Stress has become the most common reason for long-term employment sickness, eclipsing strokes, heart attack, cancer and back problems. So widespread is the condition that its been dubbed the '21st century equivalent of the Black Death'.
• France recently dropped their 35 hour working week whereas Finland experimented with a 30 hour week.
• The *New Economic Foundation* recently claimed that a 21-hour working week would reduce power consumption and increase productivity.
• Spain, on the other hand, have plans to increase the working week above 25 hours.
• King Alfred the Great reputedly proclaimed *"Eight hours work, eight hours sleep, eight hours play, make a just and healthy day."* In this, he justified his greatness!
* The author's attempt at a joke!

Dishonourable Mentions:- Presenteeism; Public sector employees; Annual Leave in the US; Darrin Thomas.

FOR

Extra motivation and drive in your workplace effort knowing a well-deserved and sufficiently long enough break is waiting at the end of the week. § An inclination to dedicate spare time to charity work. § Increase in workforce numbers to meet man hours required for operation. § Family-time. § Less inclined to take sick leave. § Hectic lifestyles demand at least 3 lie-ins a week.

AGAINST

Mondays become a burden, and end up being treated like a chore. § Non-competitive. § More employee numbers. § More inclined, and maybe acceptable, to take just an afternoon off sick. § Conflicts with other working cultures and may stem UK expansion under foreign companies. § Can only succeed in the long-term if it became a global policy. § Reluctance for lower pay.

Friday 3:57pm

Wildcard View

With the relaxing of Sunday trading laws, has Sunday now just become yet another weekday.

Should we restore the previous religious based policy of no trading on Sundays so that we can have 'free' days for all again, empty roads and help encourage Sundays to become the Social and Sports day it used to be rather than the working and shopping day it has now become? Or should we be grateful for the extra employee hours this has provided for?

Chapter B

"The foolish and the dead alone never change their opinions."
- *James Russell Lowell*

For the purposes of improving school attendance and focus of those from poorer backgrounds, compulsory 'Careers Advice and Guidance' will be provided for all children for the ages of 6-11 years - such that it motivates parents to help encourage education and progression to that career direction. Could it have a positive impact?

Background, Facts and Miscellaneous

Pupils will now be rigorously evaluated and monitored from the age of 6-11 years old, where measures of their intellectual, physical, mental and social attributes are scientifically assessed to provide them with a reasoned 'best view' career direction based on their suitability and chance of success.

The main reason for this reform to the early years school system is because the *closing the stable doors after the horse has bolted* approach to careers guidance is clearly not working (unsurprisingly), and is slowly having a destructive effect on youth and society. It is envisaged that if young minds were convinced of the well-meaning intentions and provided with a realistic aim throughout their early years, then there could well be less chance for them to become disillusioned with education and instead become wilfully driven and focused.

• The *subject* should only be guided to a career path(s) which are suited to their natural traits, and be collectively dissuaded from those deemed unattainable eg. a shy smart child should be guided away from becoming a banker to a doctor instead.
• The onus should only be on the individual or their parents to support and adhere the expert guidance provided, and those parents who make this effort will (and should rightly so) have a better chance of attaining success for their child.

Discussion Viewpoints:-
• Will nurture amongst youth, a wilful desire to contribute back to society, rather than take.
• It is too young an age to discourage or outline a career path. Let nature take its course eg. a shy kid could become the life of any party.

Image Source:- Movie: The Breakfast Club (1985)
Starring: Emilio Estevez, Molly Ringwald and Anthony Michael Hall

Should good upstanding citizens allow the thought of bringing innocent children into this awful world dissuade them from producing any offspring - Is there actually a moral responsibility and duty for such folk to breed regardless (recklessly even)?

Background, Facts and Miscellaneous

There are many wonderful and practical reasons to have children ranging from parental instincts to love/nurture/raise through to just having someone to leave the family silver to.

But there are also as many reasons why increasingly, loving committed couples are opting out altogether from having or raising children, some being the financial burden, the upheaval in life and the lifelong responsibilities associated.

However, in a day and age which has given us all cause for apprehension - a world filled with hate, corruption and an immoral lack of social responsibility - a disturbing new factor has emerged in that many good honest people refuse to bring children into such a sick society, regardless of the unconditional love and nurturing they would have no doubt received.

Dr Kristin Park, a sociologist at Westminster College of Pennsylvania, found that childfree women (and men) are more educated, more likely to work in professional occupations, more likely to live in urban areas and are less religious.

A cynic would further suggest that such findings highlight disturbing trends for future generations and draw from this the following:-
• The uneducated recklessly breeding,
• More children born into deprived families,
• Other religions observing a faster than expected fruition of their 'outbreeding' plans.

Is there a need, now moreso than ever, for the intellectually gifted, the wealthy, the good citizens in our society to put aside their fears and prioritise an obligation to bear children?

Image Source:- Movie: Batman Begins (2005) Starring: Liam Neeson and Christian Bale

Should 'pit bull' owners be put down -
Why does any respectable society need to tolerate the breeding of dangerous fighting dogs, or allow to roam free those individuals who conduct in such activity?

Background

Fighting dogs were historically bred to be used in war, for hunting and as guard dogs, and are more than capable of inflicting grievous bodily harm.

There are currently 4 classified breeds of dog which are banned in England today, under the *Dangerous Dogs Act*. In contrast, Switzerland have banned 12 dangerous dog breeds and owners whose dogs weigh more than 25kg must hold a valid permit in order to walk them in public.

They say dogs, like children, are the product of the people that care for them - treat them poorly, neglect them, abandon them and the psychological trauma they experience will turn them into hateful and cruel beings. Today, unscrupulous owners are known to try to enhance their dogs' natural fighting instincts by forcing them to fight each other, but have been known to also pit them against badgers, bears, monkeys, horses and even humans.

Facts and Examples

• In England in 2008/09, there were over 5,000 hospital admissions resulting from being bitten or struck by a dog. This total shockingly includes 1,250 children, including many babies and toddlers.
• In 2009, dog attacks on people in England cost the Health Service an estimated £3.3 million.
• The average dog's mouth exerts 150 to 180 lbs of pressure per square inch, whereas the pit bull on average exerts between 1,600 to 2,500 lbs per square inch. To put this into perspective, it requires just 4 lbs of pressure per square inch to break a human's finger.
• Pit bulls are considered by some to be kind, reliable family pets, treated unfairly due to misinformation.

Honourable Mentions:- Jack Ayton (age 2); Toni Clannachan (age 10); Sky Barker (age 8); Rhys Webb (age 5); John-Paul Massey (age 4); Jaden Mack (age 3 mths). Dishonourable Mentions:- Kyle Dyer; Cross-breeding; Operation Navara; Christian Foulkes, Lita & 11 pups.

FOR	**AGAINST**

Fighting Dogs are more likely to snap or display uncharacteristic behaviour when provoked or even played with. § Certain dog breeds have a more innate desire to go feral for no particular reason. § There are hundreds of friendlier breeds, therefore there is no pressing reason why one must opt for a family dog which has such a background and underlying violent tendencies.

Any breed of dog can be deemed potentially dangerous given the specific type of grooming and treatment undertaken. § Labradors, Alsatians and Great Danes are all capable of killing a grown adult but are regarded as ideal family pets. § Maybe a revised law based on the actions of owners rather than specific breeds. § The actual proportion of pit bull attacks for the population is miniscule.

They're the best thing thats ever happened to me. Awww, the little cherubs, they grow up so fast !

Image Source:- Movie: Snatch (2000) Starring: Alan Ford

Future Reform

In 2018, a law is passed that every dog must be muzzled in public. However, dog owners can receive an exemption permit if they are able to prove that their dog is public-friendly - only by way of locking their dog alone in a small room with a child relative under 5 years old and must display no danger towards them. The child's safety is assured as guards will destroy the dog upon the commencement of any attack, to ensure that only confident owners consider the permit application.

If a natural cure for Diabetes was found and was about to be published in a mainstream publication, what sequence of events would take place to ensure that the original article never sees the light of day or that the claims be (officially) debunked prior?

Background

The pharmaceutical companies are in a billion pound industry and treatments for Diabetes have played a large contributory role in their revenues. Diabetics have become dependent upon these revolutionary drug treatments, yet many patients have wondered why drug companies don't spend time searching for a cure instead of just promoting newer treatments, especially as the profits are more than enough to fund studies that help find a cure for their condition.

Somewhat understandably, many drug companies don't push money into research for cures because if one was found, then this would render their lucrative but assured long term revenue stream obsolete. Even moreso is this the case with Diabetes since the same companies provide the same diabetic aids that are recommended in addition to prescription medication, products used throughout the remainder of their lives.

But how far would these capitalists go to preserve it?

Facts and Examples

• This economic interest of the pharmaceutical industry to protect and increase sales of drugs, could indeed be as to why no major medical breakthrough has occurred over the last century and why we are likely to see none in this one. If cures or prevention therapies for diseases are discovered, especially one that is naturally occurring, the industry would use all its considerable power and influence to suppress, discredit and obstruct these medical breakthroughs.

• *Codex Alimentarius* is apparently an international cartel formed by the pharmaceutical industry with the aim of outlawing free access to natural therapies.

• Research scientists at the *Massachusetts Institute of Technology* are developing an antiviral drug called *Draco*, which has so far proven successful against all 15 viruses to which it has been applied in lab trials with human tissue and mice (including H1N1).

• Could vaccines deliberately contain substances which are designed to stimulate the onset of diabetes?

FOR	AGAINST
Pharmaceutical company directors and shareholders will rejoice after being relieved of the burden and cumbersome logistics of providing diabetes treatments to millions around the globe. § Offer an honorary place on the board to the person discovering the cure, to help assist in finding more natural therapies. § A world without illness is what we all want, even the capitalists.	Fellow members of the Freemasons will be contacted, who in turn get the wheels in motion to provide the writer and editor an offer they can't refuse. § The persons involved with the article will meet an untimely death. § The official bodies, PR agencies and distinguished members of the scientific community will pool together to dispel the (valid) claims.

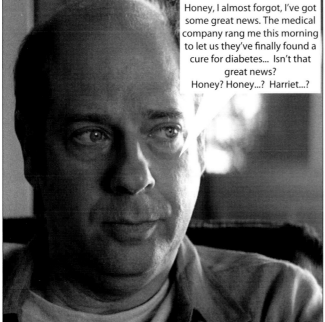

Honey, I almost forgot, I've got some great news. The medical company rang me this morning to let us they've finally found a cure for diabetes... Isn't that great news?
Honey? Honey...? Harriet...?

Be Controversial

Consider the scenario where documented evidence has been discovered, showing that a proven cure for Cancer was actually discovered over 50 years ago but was deliberately withheld from further development or production, purely in the interests of profit maximisation.

How should the general public react to such news, knowing loved ones have unavoidably suffered so much and died before their time?

Image Source:- Movie: Memento (2000) Starring: Stephen Tobolowsky

State Pensions will now be based on a stockmarket investment fund which the public can themselves actively help grow. Every 10 years, a committed 30 year investment is made and the general public are then informed of these investments, encouraging them to henceforth conduct business with these corporate entities.

Background

The existing state pension is a government-administered scheme, funded by NI contributions, to provide those who have reached the government-defined retirement age a guaranteed weekly income. The state pension age is currently between 60 and 65, however, due to an ever increasing life-expectancy levels, these levels are being constantly re-evaluated.

To be less of a drain on the country and to improve retirement income, it has been proposed that a government controlled state pension investment fund (SPIF) be initiated. The key strategy of investment is for high-potential companies to be invested in and whom business and success can be heavily influenced by the adult working population of the age 30+. This would provide an element of mutual benefit and active control for the people and would encourage more investment, ethical purchasing, better pension returns and possibly earlier retirement.

Facts and Examples

Case Study:- In 2015, a new investment cycle for the SPIF begins, for a fixed investment of 30 years. It's been decided that the Supermarket sector will be injected with this substantial investment because *Tesco*® hold too much of a monopoly on the high street and the adverse affect on local shopkeepers has been wholly unethical and inconsiderate. Of all the floated supermarkets, *Morrisons*® is the smallest but most effective target for potentially high growth.

In 2016, persons between 25 and 35 will be informed of the detail of investment in the hope that they and those nearest and dearest, will do their utmost to improve the share price.

A recent Treasury report revealed that of the £2.1 trillion assets under management in the UK, £67.2bn a year went on management charges - with the most being spent on wages and bonuses for traders and fund managers. We are in it together then!

FOR

Less need for private pensions. § Maintaining a static retirement age. § Less moving in and out of stock means less accumulation of fees. § Little chance of unscrupulous activity by pension fund managers/traders to line their own pockets at the expense of the naive investor without a face or voice. § Ethical or sensible investment in companies beneficial for the country's well-being.

AGAINST

Would conceivably be the death knell for traditional private pensions and the adverse knock-on effect on the economy. § What happens to these companies when the 30yr commitment ends and stock investment is realised by selling all SPIF backed stock. § Retirement becomes lucrative even for those not contributing positively to society. § No need for pensioners to hold a bulk of wealth.

Happy 65th Birthday Mortimer.

Randolph, we're back!

Image Source:- Movie: Coming To America (1988) Starring: Don Ameche

Further Facts

Currently, the amount of State Pension received is not means tested, and depends mainly on how many qualifying years of National Insurance payments you have made, not on savings or previous salary levels.

At the point of payout, all those eligible for the new SPIF pension must pass a fairly easy 'eligibility test', which determines if they have made at least some positive contribution to the UK. Those who fail will receive the mandatory NI based state pension.

In order to help reverse disturbing trends in gun crime, should the second amendment, protecting the right of US citizens to keep and bear arms, be amended as follows; 'Being necessary to the peaceful harmony of a free state, the right of the people to be free from gun-wielding maniacs, shall not be infringed'?

Background

The Second Amendment to the United States Constitution provides citizens with the following right;

A well-regulated militia, being necessary to the security of a free state, the right of the people to keep and bear arms, shall not be infringed.

The actual meaning of the Second Amendment has drawn much debate over the years as to what the actual right is. The *National Rifle Association* (NRA) insists quite predictably, that the Amendment guaranteed the right of individuals to possess and carry a wide variety of firearms, however, advocates of gun control contend that it was only meant to guarantee to States the right to operate militias.

In 2008, the Supreme Court issued two decisions ruling that the Amendment protects an individual's right to possess a firearm, unconnected to service in militia and to use it for traditionally lawful purposes, such as self-defence within the home.

Facts and Examples

• The second amendment along with the rest of the Bill of Rights was originally adopted in 1791, an era when the country was still reeling from the end of the American Civil War.

• The NRA is widely recognised today as a major political force and as America's foremost defender of Second Amendment rights.

• In 2010, there were 12,996 murders in the US, of which, 8,775 were caused by firearms.

• Based on production data from firearm manufacturers, there are roughly 300 million privately owned firearms in circulation.

• Based upon a 2012 US survey, an estimated 40-45% of households own a gun.

• Thomas Jefferson once famously said:

"No man shall ever be debarred the use of arms. The strongest reason for the people to retain the right to keep and bear arms is, as a last resort, to protect themselves against the tyranny in government."

FOR	**AGAINST**

Deters lawyers from abusing this right to absolve the use of firearms. § The legal right to use firearms are out of place in modern society and should certainly not be encouraged. § The statistics alone suggest that an overhaul of the law is necessary to curb gun crime. § Paves the way for appropriate punishment for firearm possession and the ensuing falls in gun-related incidents.

In todays world, it's become human nature to put material things before your fellow man, and any revision would make no change to such attitudes and behaviour. § Everyone should be assigned the right to lawfully defend their homes and loved ones. § Level playing field for law-abiding citizens and criminals, weapon-wise. Such laws have curbed violent crime over the decades.

Image Source:- Movie (Dialogue): Ben-Hur (1959) Starring: Charlton Heston

Did You Know ?

A used car dealership in Florida, launched a promotion recently, providing a complimentary AK-47 assault rifle with every purchase of one of its used trucks.

The general sales manager of *Nations Trucks*®, a Mr Ginetta, insisted the dealership was merely allowing customers to assert their rights under the Second Amendment of the Constitution. "You have the right to buy an AK-47 as long as you meet all state and federal laws. So it's just a promotion"

With property booms inevitably ending with busts, and the only individuals really benefitting from such trends being those property speculators lucky enough to buy at the bottom and sell at the top, why does it seem that almost everyone has a vested (unhealthy) interest in seeing property prices escalate beyond sensible market levels?

Background, Facts and Miscellaneous

The young estate agent saving up for a mortgage deposit makes good commission on selling a knowingly overvalued property to a couple with a young child who, being first-time buyers were offered a generous 100% mortgage at 6 times their joint annual salary, and does so because they believe that property prices can only go up because the mainstream media say so, on the basis that the 'smartest people in the room' have factored this upward trend as the only possible scenario in their risk assessments with their business strategy reflecting this viewpoint to justify such generous lending.

One-way rising prices leading to increasing property wealth, means its win-win for all of us, as well as future generations! Surely...?

But what of our children who'll need to buy one day, the couple who'll need to trade-up, the elderly wanting to downsize, the endowment mortgage holders with no provisions made for a shortfall, the estate agent whose minimum deposit requirement kept running away from him and the banks with unsustainable bad debts!

When even the most simplest spreadsheet model could have illustrated the only possible outcome of a triple-fold property market increase accompanied by record debt levels, why did so many entities insist on promoting the untenable notion that 'property prices can never go down'?

Discussion Viewpoints:- The general public are dumber and more naive than we give them credit for. § The sudden refusal to 'forecast' house prices when the market turned. § An increasing desperation to keep the bubble inflated. § Front page scaremongering by leading papers.

Class Exercise:

Guess in which order these articles were published on the front pages of UK mainstream newspapers, and also when on the curve it took place. (Answer below the chart).

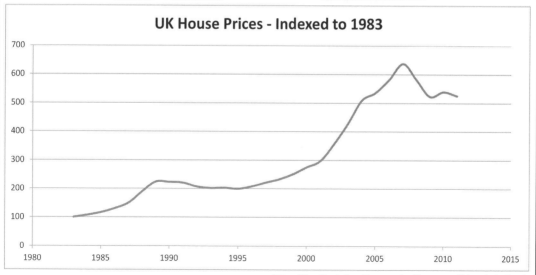

Answer: When they believed the general public were a gullible and naive bunch.

Image Source:- House Price Data:- Halifax House Price Index
1. All(SA): All Houses (All Buyers), Seasonally Adjusted - Quarterly Data

With so many folk pushing for the Islam way of life, could it really be so bad. Should we just embrace it?

Background, Facts and Miscellaneous

Islam is a religion of peace which actively promotes good living, encourages good moral virtues, a prosperous afterlife for the worthy only and provides an invaluable blueprint for a balanced and fulfilling life.

However, some misguided individuals over the years have tried to besmirch the name of Islam for their own purpose and this has resulted in a flawed somewhat volatile view on this religion and its followers. With these 'crusaders' doing more harm than good, have we allowed them to unfairly distort the benefits of a single religion presiding over the world population - with that religion being Islam.

If we assessed without bias what life could be like based on original teachings and not the skewed interpretations, is Islam the way forward?

• Consider that Islam is the worlds fastest growing religion and that folk tend to only seek out religion to either become a better person or for the great things it can provide them (or promise!).
• Though the author considers this to be a major disadvantage, there are many benefits for men/women alike for the man to have many wives.
• Clear distinction that only those who have lived by God's word will reach the heavenly paradise.
• An outright condemnation of evil acts towards your fellow man justifies an *eye for an eye* form of justice. Painful retribution is appropriate yet swift.
• No alcohol/drugs means a responsible society.
• A financial banking system where no interest rate charges on loans or savings can be made, could well facilitate a move to a fairer and stable global monetary system.

Some of the benefits to be earned and enjoyed by those who wish to become Muslim

according to the president of the 'Foundation for Islamic Knowledge': Dr. Ahmad H. Sakr, Ph.D

◦ You will be able to communicate with your Creator at any time and through this, you will be able to know your origin, your roots and the wisdom as to why you are on this planet.

◦ As your loyalty, allegiance, and obedience will be to the Creator himself, you will transcend yourself from all types of allegiance for this world. This means that if there is a conflict of interest between your boss, your job, your government, your system or any worldly relationship with the Creator, you will undoubtedly put your trust in Allah, the Creator of the universe. You will follow Him before you follow anyone else.

◦ You will be able to acquire peace, harmony, tranquility and happiness within yourself, with your family, with people of the world, with the environment and with the universe.
One has to remember that the source of peace is Allah, and one of his beautiful names is that He is The Peace.

◦ You will get rid of the extra electrostatic charges from your brain and the central nervous system by performing the daily Salah. As a result of this act, you will get rid of many of the neurological diseases from your body.

◦ As a result of Salah, you will acquire a pleasant personality, being friendly and amicable. You would not need to drink alcohol, to use drugs or to get involved in vulgarity or immorality.

◦ Through the experience of fasting in Islam, you will be able to have self-control, self-restraint, self-discipline, self-education, self-evaluation, and self-obedience to Allah the Creator. You undoubtedly will be able to improve health, personality, character, and behavior. As a result you will be able to control your lusts, selfishness, desires, greed, ego, and conceitedness.

◦ You will be generous and hospitable; you will try to purify yourself and your mistakes by sharing your happiness and your wealth with those who are less fortunate than you. Your rewards will manifold, compounded daily until the Day of Judgment.

◦ By performing pilgrimage to Makkah, you will transcend yourself from being nationalistic, sectarian, or denominational into being universal. You will be part and an essential constituent of the rainbow of Islam, being part of the brotherhood of Islam with those who already submitted themselves to the Creator.

◦ In becoming a Muslim, you will do your best to stop all types of exploitations in all their forms: economic, biological, mental, spiritual, psychological, political, etc.. You will also work to liberate people and give them freedom of worship, freedom of speech, and freedom of expression. You will be a leader and help lead people to peace, tranquility and happiness.

◦ In accepting Islam, you will help to reduce all types of social ills in the society: juvenile delinquency, child abuse, domestic abuse, incest, homosexuality, sexual promiscuity, premarital relationships, extramarital relationships, and other vices.

◦ Finally, when you die, you will die at peace. You will have a happy life in the grave and later, eternal happiness. Angels at the time of death will comfort you. They will also show you your place in paradise. On the Day of Judgment, you will be able to see and meet all the prophets and messengers of God to mankind including Noah, Abraham, Moses, Jesus, and Muhammad. You will be able to see and meet any and all of your friends and relatives and you will live an eternal life of bliss in paradise.

Should criminal judges who cannot pass a tougher sentence due to legal limitations be allowed to submit their informed opinion on what level of punishment should have been given? To aid rehabilitation, this opinion becomes a legal pending sentence if the perpetrator commits a similar or worser crime in the future.

Background, Facts and Miscellaneous

Something disturbing is taking place in our justice courts. Murder is regularly reduced to manslaughter, concurrent sentencing, inconsistency, overriding legal legislation such as the *Human Rights Act*, low conviction rates but most seriously, we are observing all too often that the punishments rarely seem to fit the crime(s). Lenient sentencing for the most criminally depraved is almost becoming almost back page news.

Because of clearly inadequate sentencing guidelines, acquittals based on legal technicalities and where there is a clear and high likelihood of reoffending, judges have now been granted the power to act in an immediate court of appeal role. But only where they deem the sentence isn't strong enough for the seriousness or circumstances of the crime that has been committed.

Dishonourable Mentions:-

• *Aso Mohammed Ibrahim* had knocked down a 12yr old girl and then abandoned her, dying six hours later. He was sentenced to just four months imprisonment, despite previous convictions!

• Described as 'evil and depraved', *Alan Webster*, who raped a 12 week old girl, was sentenced to a minimum term of six years in jail.

• 16 year old *Amina Filali* killed herself after the courts forced her to marry her rapist. This was in accordance with Article 475 of the Moroccan penal code, allowing for the 'kidnapper' of a minor to marry his victim to escape prosecution.

• Curtis Lutterloh; The Wonderland Club; Cherie Blair and Lee Williams; Sharia Law; Mark Hobson; Jake Ormerod of Devon; Robert Hathaway; Roger Keen QC and 'good-natured horseplay'.

Image Source:- Movie: The Untouchables (1987) Starring: Robert De Niro

Vaccines are wonderful advancements in medical science - However, is the push to promote vaccinations on children for various illnesses too aggressively forced?

Background

A vaccine is a biological preparation that improves immunity to a particular disease. It can typically contain an agent that resembles a disease-causing microorganism, which stimulates the body's immune system to recognize the agent as foreign, destroy it, and 'remember' it, so that the immune system can more easily recognise and destroy any of these micro-organisms that it might later encounter.

Though the benefits of preventing suffering and death from serious infectious diseases greatly outweigh the risks of rare adverse effects following immunisation, disputes have arisen over the morality, ethics, effectiveness and safety of vaccination.

Opponents argue that children's immune systems can deal with most infections naturally, and that the possible side effects of vaccination including seizures, paralysis and death are not worth the risk of safeguarding against non-life threatening illnesses.

Facts and Examples

• Illnesses including rubella, diphtheria and whooping cough which once killed thousands of infants annually are now gratefully prevented by vaccination.

• Famed neurosurgeon *Dr Russell L. Blaylock MD* stated: "the present crowded vaccine schedule is extremely destructive on the developing brain. Health authorities are of the opinion that they can give an unlimited number of vaccines to young children without risk. Our neuroscience proves that this stance is insane".

• Ingredient classes found in vaccines: Neurotoxin (acts specifically on nerve cells), Infertility Agents, Carcinogen (directly involved in the exacerbation of cancer), Immunotoxins and Nephrotoxins.

• It's been strongly claimed that the principle cause of *encephalitis* (inflammation of the brain affecting the central nervous systems) in the USA is their childhood vaccination programme.

• During illegally administered laboratory vaccine trials conducted by GSK in Argentina, 14 babies died.

FOR

Adequate research takes place to ensure ingredients used are tested satisfactorily to prevent the said 'disease/condition' and have no long term adverse effects. § By definition, pharmaceutical companies have only our best health interests at heart and would have of course verified that the cumulative effect/combination of ingredients used in vaccines pose no danger whatsoever.

AGAINST

The big pharmaceutical companies hold no concern in breaking something down the line, just pocketing the vast profits to be made when vaccines are approved. § Difficult to disprove that vaccines can disarm and unbalance the immune system. § Immoral exploitation of the poor and illiterate people in the third world for vaccine testing. May even be encouraged by authorities to *cleanse*.

Image Source:- Movie: Outbreak (1995) Starring: Kevin Spacey and Dustin Hoffman

Be Controversial

If long term adverse effects are known/discovered by the pharmaceutical companies, it is in their best interest to promote the vaccine use and possibly heighten the combination of ingredients which causes the adverse condition IF they market the medicine which treats this condition.

eg. Vaccine for Swine Flu has a 10 year delayed effect of giving the patient narcolepsy. But the vaccine company also develops and licences the sale of the only proven narcolepsy treatment.

Mediums and Clairvoyants claim to either hold knowledge of the future or can reach out to the spirits of the deceased - Is it time for this profession to become classed under the criminal offence 'Conspiracy to Defraud'?

Background, Facts and Miscellaneous

Are they all simply charlatans, poor excuses for human beings who look to deceitfully earn cheap and illegal income, undue prestige and shameful fame? Do they feed on the feeble-hearted and exploit the misery of the human condition? Do they flourish on the weak? Are they parasites giving false hope and stirring false fear into their victims? (See also *Religion*).

Or should we not dismiss so lightly the possibility of the dead walking amongst us, after all, as much as the existence of God cannot be disproved, the same can be said about how we cannot truly know what happens to our bodies (and souls) after death.

Is there indeed survival of ones consciousness after death? And would we prefer to believe that no-one is looking out for us from above?

In recent years, there's actually been increasing acceptance from the scientific community too. Professor *Gary Schwartz* of the University of Arizona stated "We've proved it experimentally. Some mediums are real and they're getting accurate information. We've convincingly ruled out every one of the conventional sceptical explanations." Dr *Peter Fenwick*, a neuropsychiatrist at Kings College London, agrees: "It's difficult to see another reason for the effect other than there is genuine communication with the deceased going on. This is the most logical interpretation."

Dishonourable Mentions:- Peter Popoff healing, for a small nominal fee; Marks exploiting a mark. Honourable Mentions:- Raonaid Murray and Diane Lazarus; Christine Holohan & Jacqui Poole.

Some conspiracists believe that rogue elements in the Royal Family decided 'Princess Diana' had become a real threat to the throne and the stability of the 'Establishment'. With some aspects of the theory gaining credibility, should the death of Princess Diana and Dodi Fayed be re-investigated as a possible 'honour killing'?

Background

Diana Spencer married the heir to the British throne, *Prince Charles*, in 1981. They had two sons but sadly divorced in 1996. In Aug 1997, Princess Diana died in a car crash after trying to escape the paparazzi in Paris.

The main motive for alleging 'murder' included suggestions that Diana was pregnant with Dodi Fayed's child and the couple were to be engaged. Additionally, the idea of a non-Christian within the British Royal Family meant such a relationship between the mother of the future king and a prominent Egyptian Muslim family would not have been tolerated.

Honour Based Crime involves the dishonourable act of violence against family members, committed by people who want to protect or defend the reputation of their family within the community.

Such violence occurs when the perpetrators perceive that a relative has shamed the family and/or community by breaking their strict honour code.

Facts and Examples

• In 1997, during a private walk, the then Prime Minister Tony Blair allegedly told Diana that he felt her relationship with Fayed "was a problem".

• It's claimed that Diana had many lovers during/after her royal marriage, including James Hewitt and allegedly, a soon to be wife-less Will Carling and the supposed love of her life, Dr Hasnat Khan.

• In 2004, a special Metropolitan Police inquiry team, *Operation Paget*, was established and headed by the then Commissioner Lord Stevens to investigate concerns of possible royal involvement. It's noted that prior to the investigation, Lord Stevens had been knighted by the Queen and had received other royal honours.

• The man who carried out the controversial embalming of Princess Diana's body, Jean Monceau, admitted that the procedure was illegal as he went ahead without official written consent from her family. Dodi's father claims the procedure was ordered by MI6 to obliterate chemical traces of a pregnancy.

FOR	AGAINST
Foiling the ultimate coup. Advancement of a family or community by way of association. § Shamelessly flaunting lovers in front of ex-husband. § Prince Harry's ginger hair follicles. § In some countries, adultery is punished by the stoning of a woman in front of her lover. Diana was with her lover when they piled into a Stone Pillar. § The Royal Family and their privileged *Royal Prerogative*.	A car accident by a drunken driver, pure and simple! § Diana and the Royal Family had already severed all ties with each other. § The Royal Family were very fond of Diana and above all, knew she was the real victim in the marriage. § She was well aware of the consequences of conducting behaviour considered disgraceful and shameful to 'the establishment'. § Losing a fanbase.

Be Controversial

Assuming this tragedy didn't happen and Diana and Dodi had eventually married, Diana would have had to convert to the Muslim religion, as per Islamic custom.

Is it conceivable that Dodi would have inevitably succeeded in converting his beloved step children to Islam, leaving the UK with a non-Christian King-In-Waiting.

What sequence of events could have possibly occurred, followed this scenario?

Image Source:- Image Source: British Royal Family Coat of Arms

In 2018, a new directive has passed and will be implemented at every prison, regardless of security level - Every inmate must endure a daily morning ritual of receiving a 'water cannon' to the naked body. Discuss the implications, particularly with regard to punishment, reoffending and remorse?

Background, Facts and Miscellaneous

In modern Britain, the generally held view is that prison is not working for the majority of inmates either as an effective punishment and deterrent nor more importantly, rehabilitation.

Its been decided that, short of re-instating capital punishment and within the confines of the *Human Rights Convention*, prison must become and be regarded as an institution where;

i) criminals never ever want to go to or endure any time in whatsoever,

ii) having experienced a custodial existence, the chance of reoffending becomes very low,

iii) provides a daily ritual of humane suffering, one that inmates will remember,

iv) to help the inmate over time display true remorse for the crime(s) committed.

As such the following daily routine will be implemented for all inmates except those who have committed a true victimless crime:-

• Every morning at 6am, all inmates will be rounded up and each inmate must endure three bursts of a high-pressure stream of freezing cold water towards them, each lasting 15 seconds,

• To exacerbate the shock to the body and the discomfort to the prisoner, this will take place in an extremely warm climatised environment and each inmate must be forced to wait approximately 20 minutes such that their body acclimatises to the tropical temperature,

• Paedophiles and child abusers get a special treat in that their middle burst will instead be replaced with only a 7 second duration one, albeit with borderline legal hot water.

Should the 'inflation rate' take into account only REAL factors with respect to the average family and their average conservative spending habits?

Background, Facts and Miscellaneous

Inflation, in the UK, is calculated through measuring changes in the cost of living. The official method is the *Consumer Price Index* (CPI), and measures the annual % change in price level.

The 'shopping basket' of items that make up the CPI are reviewed every year. Some items are taken out of the basket, some are brought in, to reflect changes in the market and to make sure the indexes are up to date and representative of consumer spending patterns.

However, with constant year on year inflation-busting price increases of staple items and mandatory living expenses, the government will now introduce a new *Actual Prices Index* (API), to ensure that these items are not outweighed disproportionately by non-essential and luxury items. It is expected that this new API will be-

come the new index of choice for media reporting and for consumers when assessing a real price or wage increase.

The API basket of goods will contain only essential items, those which do not come under the spending jurisdiction of 'disposable income'.

These spending patterns and the disposable income element are based on the average family unit (1.5 working parents and 1.8 children) and the average national salary, which is then used to revise the CPI weightings in order that they best reflect REAL inflationary pressures.

Dishonourable Mentions:- Fuel poverty; Squeezing the middle class; Low interest rates and increasing money supply being Partners in Crime.

The Actual Prices Index (API)

Consumer Price Index Basket of Goods 2012	CPI % Weighting	API Basket Weightings			API Factor Notes
		API Adjustment Factor	API Non-Standardised % Weighting	API Standardised % Weighting	
Food and non-alcoholic beverages	11.2	1	11.2	15.1	
Alcohol and Tobacco	4.2	0.2	0.8	1.1	Tobacco is excluded altogether.
Clothing and Footwear	6.5	1	6.5	8.8	
Housing and Household Services	14.4	0.9	13.0	17.5	Domestic cleaning and gardening services are now excluded.
Furniture & Household Goods	6.1	1	6.1	8.2	
Health	2.4	1	2.4	3.2	NB: API Factor will triple if NHS Privatisation takes place.
Transport	16.2	0.8	13.0	17.5	Fuel costs for inefficient cars are excluded eg. 4x4s. Penalty Fares are added (£80!!!).
Communication	2.7	0.8	2.2	2.9	Excludes the retail purchases of expensive smartphones.
Recreation and Culture	13.4	0.7	9.4	12.6	Excludes extortionate theatre productions, gadgets and 5 Star package holidays.
Education	1.9	0.4	0.8	1.0	Private and international schooling is excluded altogether.
Restaurants and Hotels	11.4	0.2	2.3	3.1	Unessential.
Miscellaneous Goods and Services	9.6	0.7	6.7	9.0	Non-essential items are excluded.
	100	1.347	74.26	100	

Source: "Consumer Prices Index and Retail Prices Index: The 2012 Basket of Goods and Services" by the Office for National Statistics

Note: All items which can now be replaced by the internet freely is now excluded from the basket. Eg. Newspapers and Music

If Science eventually manages to invalidate the genesis and creation theories put forward in the Holy Bible - should the Bible then be officially referred to as a book of fiction? Consequently, should all other texts which refer or cross-reference to its teachings and characters as factual, by association, also be regarded as fiction too?

Background

Generally, there are two views of the origin of the universe and the origin of Man:-

• The biblical position set forth in the book of *Genesis*, affirms that God created the heavens and the earth on the first day of creation. Subsequently, during the remaining periods, attention was directed to this planet, the abode of man - who was uniquely fashioned in the image of the Creator. The sun, planets and stars were then created to facilitate a sustainable existence.

• The second view of the beginning of the universe is wholly materialistic. Sciences' current inclination is known as the *Big Bang Theory*, which alleges that all of the matter in the known universe was tightly packed into a microscopic cosmic 'egg', which then in a sense 'exploded', randomly resulting in this marvellously ordered universe. The theory of evolution fills in the gap by suggesting that all living creatures evolved from an initial spark of life that accidentally generated itself from inorganic components a few billion years ago.

Facts and Examples

• Scientific research is based on the idea that everything that takes place is determined by the laws of physics and nature. Therefore the idea of spiritual or supernatural influences are not tolerated.

• In recent times, achievements in modern science seem to regularly contradict religious 'facts' and undermine the faith of all but the most devout.

• At last count, around 5+ mainstream religions including Judaism and Islam regard the main 'Jesus' character in the Christian Bible as real and is extensively referred to in their respective texts. This is also the case with Noah and his Ark.

• The Bible, according to some religious scholars, states that the earth is around 6,000 years old. Advocates of the widely accepted *Big Bang Theory* puts the age of the universe a little older, at approximately 14 billion years.

• The Jehovah Witnesses' scriptures *New World Translation* are effectively, only around 100 years old.

FOR

With the numerous contradicting views across the main religions on the universe origins, gods and life after death, have the religious scriptures already effectively brought themselves into disrepute? § Science has already supported their views with evidence of evolution and the earths age. § Scriptures were written by mortal men, not placed here by gods or angels.

AGAINST

If something was eventually discovered or proved in support of the Christian biblical view, what knock-on effect would this have on the readership of rival religions? § The Science community respond unfavourably to any supernatural evidence, such is their agenda or motivation. § Many unexplained gaps in the theory of evolution and the 'something out of nothing' big bang theory.

Image Source:- Movie: Misery (1990) Starring: Kathy Bates and James Caan

Did You Know ?

"The religion of the future will be a cosmic religion. It should transcend personal God and avoid dogma and theology. Covering both the natural and the spiritual, it should be based on a religious sense arising from the experience of all things natural and spiritual as a meaningful unity."

~ *Albert Einstein*

With a privileged upbringing, generous living allowance, squatting rights in palatial residences and being able to hold taxpayer-funded garden parties, is it fair to acknowledge that members of Royal Families have never had or have lost all sense of the value of money?

Background, Facts and Miscellaneous

Royal monarchs tend to have vast personal fortunes (garnered through inheritance or frugal saving of plundered bounty) yet have all their upkeep and expenses covered as well as being provided with generous living allowances, all provided by the taxpayer or other public means.

With such an indifference to wealth or money (as savings can conceivably remain untouched), is it through no fault of their own that members have known no different as they were deprived of one of the most essential parts of growing up, learning to live within your means.

Or has this attitude been borne out of the misguided belief that the family line were key to the nations current prosperity and fortune, and are therefore entitled to be kept in luxury?

• In 2012, the King of Spain *Juan Carlos*, embarked on a £27,000 elephant hunting expedition to Botswana just as the country's economy teetered on the brink of collapse.
• Under UK constitutional law dating back to medieval times, the Duchy of Cornwall (being the Prince of Wales) is entitled to the estates of people who die without a will in Cornwall.
• In 2012, a Saudi princess tried to stroll out of the exclusive *Shangri-La®* five-star establishment in Paris without paying her $5 million hotel bill. The rather brazen act was foiled probably because of the 60 servants in tow, the mountain of suitcases and the awaiting limousines.
• In 2012, RM520,000 (around $200,000) was spent by the *Sultan of Johor* to secure ownership of the car registration number 'WWW1'.

Image Source:- Movie: Coming to America (1988) Starring: Frankie Faison & Eddie Murphy

The responsibility of safeguarding the future of the Human Race from an impending global catastrophe has been put in your capable hands, yet this time the rules have been tweaked ever so slightly as to who you can bring with you onto the Ark. Discuss and argue out the ideal optimal selection for the best chance of a harmonious future?

Background, Facts and Miscellaneous

You, being Noah, have been chosen as the patriarch who, because of your blameless piety, must perpetuate the human race after your wicked evil contemporaries have perished on this doomed land, one bereft of compassion or decency and rife with selfishness, corruption, greed and evil.

God has solely provided you with a divine warning of an impending global disaster and has made a covenant promising to save you and your family. You have been instructed to follow directions to a hidden cavern in the holy land of Jerusalem which houses a sophisticated spaceship able to travel at the speed of light and has built-in the co-ordinates of a far-away paradise, a habitable sustainable planet only a few light years away.

To comply with your divine purpose, you must instruct in accordance with God's instruc-

tions which cross-section of society you wish to select as fellow passengers, those from which the human race can be replenished via this manipulated yet much advantaged gene pool.

From these instructions, a random balanced selection of individuals who have displayed relatively good morals and which conform to this cross-section will be made. These individuals will then be provided the same instructions to rendezvous at the cavern at the chosen date.

From there, you will undertake the authority of being the *intellectual superbeing* in God's absence. Henceforth, you will outline your divine mission to start a new human race, promising to learn from our mistakes and will look to live and prosper together in unity for the rest of days.

Noahs Ark

Between yourselves, select two items from each section to bring with you on the Ark. Confer with each other and make the case for/against that selection to come to an informed decision.

Distinguished Professionals

Doctors/Nurses

Charity workers

Psychiatrists

Priests

Scientists

Descent

African

Asian (Chinese etc)

Jewish

Latin

Middle-Eastern

South Asian (Indians etc)

White

Layabouts

Poets

Artists

Writers

Socialites

Housewives

Criminals

Murderers

Paedophiles

Fraudsters

Drug Dealers

White Collar

Undistinguished Professionals

Defence Lawyers

Politicians

Evangelists

Estate Agents

Bankers

A worked example of the 80 individuals chosen based on the following choices;
{Priests, Scientists, Poets, Artists, Fraudsters, Murderers, Bankers, Lawyers, African, White}.
10 persons of each of these 4 non-descent buckets will be randomly chosen from the Earths population but will also satisfy an equal male/female split plus a further equal split for White/African descent.
eg. 20 White Females/20 African Females/20 White Males/20 African Males

Is the Cyberdyne Systems 'Skynet' Global Defence Network an accident just waiting to happen?

Background, Facts and Miscellaneous

Being in the midst of revolutionary advances in *Artificial Intelligence*, an emergence in exploiting algorithmic programming and an ever-increasing reliance on computers as an efficient and cost-effective alternative to manual responsibilities, it's reasonable to assume that it will only be a matter of time before humans are eliminated altogether from the decision-making process or absolved from any duty wherever possible.

• *Artificial Intelligence* (AI) - systems technologically endowed with the intellectual processes characteristic of humans, such as the ability to reason, discover meaning or learn from past experience.
• *Algorithmic Programming* - involves the translation of a strategy into computer form such that the computer undertakes all the remedial steps.

In the 1984 movie *The Terminator*, Cyberdyne Systems' *Skynet* was a computer system developed for the U.S. military. Based on an advanced AI framework and utilising state of the art 'algorithmic' foresight, this 'Defence Network' was given command over all computerised military hardware and systems including America's entire nuclear weapons arsenal. The strategy behind *Skynet's* creation was to remove the possibility of human error and slow reaction time to guarantee a fast, efficient response to enemy attack.

Being merely a matter of time before such sophistication becomes commonplace, can it be envisaged that one day the authorities would be stupid and ignorant enough to handover complete automation and control of its nuclear armoury?

Image Source:- Movie: The Terminator (1984) Starring: Michael Biehn and Linda Hamilton

Scientists are now able to produce sperm cells using stem cell technology, and such developments mean that the main reason for a male's existence now come into question, with no recognised role in the longevity of our species - With women's increasing independence and confidence, will Man become a useless and unnecessary 'burden'?

Background, Facts and Miscellaneous

In 2010, Japanese scientists at Kyoto University used stem cells from mouse embryos to create primordial germ cells, which drive the production of male sperm. The experiment involved transplanting these cells into the testicles of infertile mice, who were then able to produce normal fully-functioning sperm. This was then implanted into female mice which then gave birth to healthy offspring, but more crucially, these babies were able to reproduce naturally.

With stem-cell technology advancing at an alarming rate, it's reasonable to presume that we are merely baby steps away from generating standalone human male testicles. And with such developments, the critical importance that the male possessed in the reproduction cycle and to be amongst us, suddenly becomes redundant.

Further Discussion Points:-
• What possible untold long term consequences from a child bred in such a way await their single unmarried mothers?
• Will the act of sex ultimately die out or even become considered a 'deviant' activity in a sole female population? Or will women through the generations evolve to develop a natural sexual attraction to the same sex?
• In 2098, due to their incompatibility with an all-female utopia, male abortions have become compulsory. However, for males not aborted in time, is it conceivable that they instead be raised as animals, a 'womans best friend' perhaps?
• Will womens football ever be worth watching?
• Women, what will you most miss from men once they are a distant memory?

Image Source:- Movie: Enter the Dragon (1973) Starring: Ahna Capri
ps. Looks like the ghost of Bruce Lee in the top right hand corner of the photo.

Stoning -
Do the individuals who undertake the stoning of defenceless women and childen, genuinely believe they are carrying out God's duty and don't expect their cruel actions to hamper their chances of entering Paradise?

Background, Facts and Miscellaneous

Stoning is a form of capital punishment whereby a group of individuals, mainly adult men, throw stones at a person until he/she dies, a practice borne from religious texts. No individual among the group can be identified as the one who delivered the incisive blow, yet everyone involved bears some degree of moral culpability.

Today, it is accepted practice in the laws of seven countries including Saudi Arabia, Pakistan, Sudan, Iran, Yemen and United Arab Emirates. Iran's Penal Code prescribes execution by stoning and dictates that the stones are *large enough to cause pain, but not so large as to kill the victim immediately.*

"He that is without sin amongst you, let him cast the first stone at her."
~ Jesus Christ

In Somalia in 2008, 13 year old *Aisha Ibrahim Dhuhulow* was stoned to death in front of 1,000 spectators. Fifty men from *al Shabab militia,* a radical Islamist group that controlled part of the country and enforced the Islamic Sharia as the law, carried out the brutal act. Aisha was charged with adultery which according to them is a violation of the Islamic law and is punishable by death (though her father had an altogether different story, in which he claimed that Aisha was in fact the victim of a violent gang rape). According to eyewitnesses at the stoning, the girl screamed and pleaded for her life as she was dragged and forced against her will into a hole dug in the ground, buried up to her neck and then tactically pelted with stones until she died (at the second time of asking). God is indeed, merciful!

Image Source:- Movie: The Stoning of Soraya M. (2008) Starring: Mozhan Marnò

Afghanistan has been shot to shreds and the international community are now questioning the need of rebuilding a country, one which borders a hostile region on all fronts. Is it feasible to 'retire' a country and if so, how should the repatriation of the people be decided?

Background, Facts and Miscellaneous

Afghanistan has been the battleground for modern warfare for the last 30 years, and the once beautiful landscape has been more or less destroyed for good. The country today now suffers from a poor infrastructure, lawlessness, widespread corruption and there is little hope for the people other than just surviving.

With its susceptibility for internal and external conflicts, there is real concern that rebuilding the country would just be a futile exercise.

Therefore, a novel solution has been proposed instead that the country as a habitable region will now be 'retired'. Instead, the land will be designated a resource mining area where all proceeds will go towards the *United Nations'* efforts to help the Third World. Discuss the benefits and drawbacks of such a move.

The following considerations have also been put forward. Discuss the merits of each:-

• Repatriate all its people proportionately to the countries held ultimately responsible for the destruction bestowed upon them. Alternatively, requests will be taken for a move to a country where an Islamic state is already established.

• Leave it be and let the country rebuild itself - allow Afghanistan to become a lasting symbol for what becomes of military rule or undemocratically elected power. Allow the struggles and the long road to restore the beauty of this country be a lasting reminder of the mistakes of the past and be an obligation to retain its serenity.

• Internationally administered opium cultivation, proceeds of which go directly to the UN or directly to its repatriated people thereafter.

Image Source:- Movie: Black Hawk Down (2001) Starring: Josh Hartnett

105

In a musical genre traditionally dominated by black artists, what reason could it be that 'Eminem' became one of the most successful rap artists of all time (when only a handful of white artists had only just barely managed to break into the genre)?

Background, Facts and Miscellaneous

Eminems' The Marshall Mathers LP became the fastest selling hip hop album in history, following increasing popularity and critical praise. Other rankings have included #9 on MTV's list of *The Greatest MCs of All Time*, #13 on MTV's *22 Greatest Voices in Music* and #83 on Rolling Stones prestigious *The Immortals* list.

• Beastie Boys *Licensed to Ill* became the best selling rap album of the 1980s and the first rap album to go to #1 on the US Billboard album chart.
• Vanilla Ices' *Ice Ice Baby* became the first rap single to reach #1 on the US Billboard Hot 100.
• Snow's *Informer* was #1 on the US Billboard charts for 7 consecutive weeks. It has been recorded twice in the *Guinness Book of World Records*® as the best selling reggae single in US history.

Discussion Points:- Because he's above average and white. § Produced by a revered black legend in the hip-hop world (Dr Dre), so the 'project' managed to bridge different races, thus overcoming any prejudices. § Other popular rap artists of the time tended to be ego driven and often saw no shame in flashing their gaudiness. § Just down to being lyrically superior. § Historically, black artists have been tremendously successful across all genres, so prejudice surely can't be at play here. § Racism, the most juvenile of prejudices, is now only the refuge of the lower classes (the social demographic most likely to be Hip Hop fans).

Dishonourable Mentions:- Kanye West & award ceremonies; Hard Knock Life; A must-tell Hollywood story; 50 Cent, wads and hotel rooms.

If trends were to continue, future generations of children will totally immerse themselves online, practically living a virtual existence - With the market for Virtual Goods booming, can we expect this to be the no-brainer entrepreneur opportunity of the future?

Background, Facts and Miscellaneous

Virtual goods are non-physical objects which are purchased for use in online communities or online games. Therefore, as they exist only in cyberspace, they have no intrinsic value and are intangible by definition.

Though these virtual objects are nothing more than a series of digital 1s and 0s stored on a remote database, there is an emerging market for them and it's slowly becoming big business. In 2009, revenue derived from the sale of virtual goods reached a staggering $7 billion worldwide.

But is it really so shocking? With no investment outlay necessary or manufacturing costs, these products can literally appear out of thin air and instantaneously hold a market value which meets the expectations of those who wish to engage within such communities or alternate 'existences'. Market value that can provide a firm with an instant 100% profit at the swipe of a button.

But to many of us, the notion of people spending their real hard-earned cash on 'objects' that have absolutely no tangible substance (or perhaps any real sell-on value) is one many of us can never grasp. However, it can be said that many of us never grew up in a world surrounded by computers, let alone the *world wide web* and its infinite possibilities for total immersion.

Dishonourable Mentions:- Second Life® Marketplace; Farmville®; Facebook® Virtual Gifts; Asian Gold Farmers; Virtual Currency bought with Real Money(!); Club NeverDie - For those who don't like socialising, dancing, perving or drinking.

Image Source:- Movie: Star Wars (1977) Starring: Carrie Fisher & Alec Guinness

Why is it that water is the only thing that evaporates, providing the most critical stage in the water cycle?

And is it just pure sheer luck that this coincides with the human requirement for clean water?

Background, Facts and Miscellaneous

Earth is a truly unique planet in terms of its abundance of water. As well as being necessary to sustaining life on Earth, water is essential to the survival of all organisms, being a crucial component of metabolic processes and serves as a solvent for many bodily solutes. Water also helps tie together the Earth's lands, oceans, and atmosphere into one integrated system.

Precipitation, evaporation and condensation are all part of the hydrological (water) cycle - a never-ending global process of water circulation from the lands and oceans to the clouds, and back again. This cycling of water is intimately linked with energy exchanges among the atmosphere, ocean and land that determine the Earth's climate and cause much of the natural climate variability. All seems a rather fortunate scenario for our race?

Discussion Viewpoints:-
• With all our advanced technology, we create countless tons of unrecyclable toxic waste annually. Yet, with the Earth's natural recycling systems (water, carbon, oxygen and nitrogen), the Earth manages to recycle all its wastes perfectly, using ingenious chemical engineering methods.
• Is it conceivable that the earth's ecosystem had evolved by chance alone, over billions of years and come to exist in an almost perfect level of environmental harmony?
• With the manual process of water purification being an exhaustive one, what would transpire if some kind of environmental or man-made disaster disrupted the water cycle?
• Chickens and Eggs: What came first, organic life or the water cycle?

Image Source:- Movie: Waterworld (1995) Starring: Kevin Costner

With increasing costs, inconsiderate drivers, constant traffic delays, environmental factors and parking limitations, the love of driving has all but disappeared from 'getting around town' - Should a city law be introduced that allows only electric SMART cars to be driven freely within its city limits?

Background, Facts and Miscellaneous

With what was once an enjoyable pastime, feeling the wind in your hair has now become an opportunity to pay through the nose to inhale the fumes from fellow congestors.

Together with the fact that fuel, taxes and insurance now take up a substantial proportion of disposable income, and traffic becoming unmanageable in over-populated areas, one can no longer genuinely enjoy using the car to zip around.

In the year 2017, a proposal has been put forward by the Mayor of London that only electric SMART cars can be driven within the M25. All other non-commercial vehicles will be subject to a £250 congestion charge per day.

Such a measure is expected to ease congestion and allow the easy implementation of an infrastructure able to cope with high populations - due to the dimensions of a significantly smaller car, parking spaces can effectively double and more lanes can be marked from existing road.

Further Discussion Points:-
• Aside from the obvious, why do drivers go out of their way not to give way !?!!
• Road planners being the intelligent equivalent of a toll booth operator.
• That awkward moment when your adult child asks how you could have possibly wasted $50,000 on a blasted car all those years ago!
• Why don't car manufacturers just cap the maximum speed, so not to exceed 80mph?

Dishonourable Mention:- BMW X6;

Image Source:- Movie: National Lampoon's Vacation (1983) Starring: Dana Barron & Chevy Chase

Chapter C

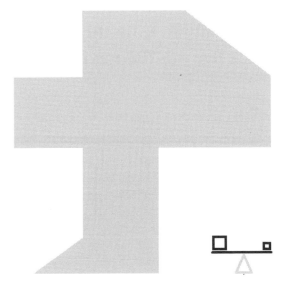

"Reputation is what men and women think of us;
Character is what god and angels know of us."
- *Thomas Paine*

It is the year 2080 and scientists have now verified that the '1999 RQ36' asteroid is indeed directly on course with Earth and will collide in exactly 20 years time, causing mass destruction and wiping all life from the planet. How would the human race live out their existence?

Background, Facts and Miscellaneous

The '1999 RQ36' asteroid was first discovered in 1999 and experts calculated a 1:1000 possibility of a catastrophic collision with our planet in the late 22nd century, based on best measurements.

Subsequent mathematical calculations by amateur physicists in the year 2040 not only suggested a considerably higher possibility of collision at 1:50, but also that it was travelling much faster than previously calculated. These supposedly 'outlandish' claims were quickly dismissed by leading space agencies around the globe.

Today, in the year 2080, the *Global Space Agency* announced that mathematical models and observations had actually verified the accuracy of the 'speculated' 2040 estimations, but a collective decision was made in the public interest not to publicise this in order to avoid any undue panic. It has also now been revealed that subsequent significant 'pushes' due to the *Yarkovsky Effect* - where an asteroid gains momentum from thermal radiation that it emits - have caused not only an increase in velocity but also for the asteroid's orbital path to directly coincide with ours, for a collision date of January 1st, 2100.

Our unavoidable Armageddon.

With little reason for long term planning, wealth accumulation, social cohesion or legal adherence, it would be understandable to suggest that only anarchy can ensue, resulting in social disorder and flagrant lawlessness. Or should we give human nature more credit when the pursuit of wealth, material possessions and relationships can no longer be a distraction. Discuss?

Discussion Points:-

General
- What will become the most sought-after commodity?
- What parts of the world are most likely to become irretrievably lawless?
- Could people live in peace and harmony for 20 years?
- For the purposes of openness, will the *Higher Order Architects* reveal their tactics over the decades and what ultimate 'plan' had they hoped to achieve?

Travel and Leisure
- Will travelling the world become the only feasible pastime?
- Will there even be supporting infrastructure to support a global travel industry?
- The scramble to guess the actual time of the impact and correctly pre-booking the Space flights that will have ringside seats to witness the doom of humanity?
- With order crumbling, major sporting events will become difficult to maintain and will slowly die out. Life without sport?

Religion
- Which cult or religion was spot on?
- Is the need to believe in 'God' and a 'Life after Death' inexplicably brought forward?

Leadership
- Will the government continue to be obeyed?
- What would become the government role(s) in an anarchic society or a society-driven environment?
- Should the government cease all medical related activity (hospitals, vaccinations etc) and allow 'survival of the fittest' see the light of day, albeit briefly?

Children
- How will parents plan for their young children now?
- With childhood potentially being the most enjoyable part of a persons life, will people start having more in the knowledge that their child can enjoy life's little pleasures with no concern for future responsibilities and aspirations?
- With career aspirations all but redundant, how will young teenagers even start to begin revising their life plans?

Love and Relationships
- Will people leave their unloved ones and seek a loved one?
- Is 'free love' the key to living out a happier, more fulfilled, cohesive existence?
- With little to no punishment likely, will non-consensual sex become an accepted occurrence?

Career
- Will people try to continue in their profession in order to maintain an orderly society?
- With the value of 'money' all but diminishing, how many medical doctors will leave their posts to leave the sick to fend for themselves?
- Will the 40 hour week become a distant memory?

Law and Order
- Would aspects of Sharia Law work effectively for controlling order for this short-term period?
- Would we live out selfish lives with the only objective being self-preservation?
- Will serious crime become more commonplace as the impact date draws closer?

You sure about this son ?

Image Source:- Movie: Deep Impact (1998) Starring: Frank Whiteman

Fast food chicken menu prices have remained relatively constant in times when wholesale food prices have soared, indicating a cost-cutting exercise somewhere in the chain - Even as a nation of animal lovers, do we conveniently sidestep our conscience just to save a few pennies?

Background, Facts and Miscellaneous

For those eating establishments that sell meals on a per chicken basis (such as *Nandos*), it would stand to reason that they would likely have supply contracts in place with 'poultry farmers' to purchase whole chickens on a 'units per cubic volume' basis, in order to help manage costs and assess menu pricing effectively.

A recent rise in food costs globally saw many restaurants and supermarkets revise pricing levels, however the likes of *Nandos* and *KFC* saw no such changes, which meant great news for the vegetable hating consumer.

However, if firms felt no pressure or inclination to raise prices to maintain the profit margin, then this would suggest that adverse global food costs made little to no difference and thus the average cost of each chicken remained the same(?).

A common ploy by food manufacturers to increase or maintain profit margins in light of an increasing cost base is to repackage a product such that the consumer does not realise they are paying the same price for a lot less.

Bearing this practice in mind, could it well be that in order to keep prices the same to avoid consumer dissatisfaction, the firms and the poultry farmers have colluded to provide a larger number of chickens than had normally been supplied per cubic shipment. This would mean that battery farms now slaughter chickens at a younger age so that more units could fit per shipment.

Are we morally excused in allowing a chicken to be killed at 5 instead of 6 weeks old because we feel the need to have more disposable income?

Movie: Planes, Trains & Automobiles (1987) Starring: The Legend 'John Candy'. RIP

Your Economics tutor has assigned you the exercise on the opposite page - So, do Billionaires really have billions in the bank?

Background, Facts and Miscellaneous

Supporting Notes:-

Opening Balance March 2016:

MWH Loan Book	$0
MWH Bank Account	$0
Bill	$10,000
Donald	$1,000
Mark	$1,000
Warren	$1,000

Closing Balance June 2016:

MWH Loan Book	$200,000
MWH Bank Account	$0
Bill	$10,000
Donald	-$99,000
Mark	-$99,000
Warren	$201,000

Closing Balance August 2016:

MWH Loan Book	$0
MWH Bank Account	$50,000
Bill	$10,000
Donald *(Liquidated)*	$0
Mark *(Loan Written Off)*	$0
Warren	$201,000

Bank Financial Position as of January 2017:

Legally Binding Bonus Payments;	-$50,000
Physical money in bank vault;	$13,000
Account Balances;	$261,000
comprising of;	
- MWH Loan Book	$0
- MWH Bank Account	$50,000
- Bill	$10,000
- Warren	$201,000

Economics GCSE Exam Paper

Question 3 - Fractional Reserve Banking & Accountability   (10 points)

A prestigious new bank '*Maddof Withit Hall (MWH)*' has opened in the year 2016 and encourages individuals to bank and save with them. It currently has only four customers holding savings accounts; Warren, Donald, Mark and Bill.

March 2016:
Bill deposits $10,000 real hard money to the bank, with the rest depositing just $1000 each. At this point, $13,000 is all the bank holds in its vaults.

June 2016:
- Donald takes out an unsecured loan of $100,000 from the bank. He places all of this money on a sporting bet with Warren, wiring the whole amount directly to Warren, who just happens to bank with the same bank, MWH.
- Mark takes out a mortgage of $100,000 from the bank in order to buy a nice house from Warren, who has owned the house outright and also just happens to conduct business at the same bank.
- Warren anticipates a property crash and will rent until he is ready to buy again sometime in 2020. He therefore deposits the proceeds of the sale of his house in a MWH well-marketed fixed period high interest account until 2020.

August 2016:
- Donald inevitably loses the bet and with pressure mounting to start repaying the loan plus interest, he commits suicide. He sadly left no surviving relatives or friends.
- Mark unfortunately realises he has bought at the top of the market and after a property fall of 30%, he decides to bail out of his property investment and hand the keys into the bank, thus ending the loan agreement.
- The bank are able to auction off the repossessed property at 50% the loan value, $50,000, resulting in a net book loss of $50,000 from the bad loan.

January 2017:
- Banking bonuses paid out based on loan book activity and realised profits of $50,000.
- With low interest rates and an impending financial crisis looming, Bill and Warren decide to withdraw all of the money from their accounts and move abroad. Therefore, these accounts will need to be liquidated and assets physically returned to the account holder.

Question:
Who of the banks employees will be given the task of breaking the news to Warren?

With our inevitable transition to a Cashless Society, what possible eventualities can transpire with regards to criminal activity?

Background

A 'Cashless Society' is a policy that eliminates the use of physical money by providing alternative channels and means for executing financial transactions.

A compelling new world awaits where cumbersome notes and coins are replaced with safe electronic transactions initiated and completed with the touch of a mobile handset or the swipe of an *Oyster* card.

This widely expected onset of a 'cashless society' raises concerns, not so much because of the idea itself, but because of the increasing ease at which criminals have already been able to conduct electronic fraud and commit identity theft. Unfortunately, aside from those wretched bankers, there is an element of society who have absolutely no morality or remorse when it comes to the acquisition of money, and are willing to deal with the consequences given the potentially lucrative monetary payoff (assuming one can be identified by their IP address).

Facts and Examples

• Fraudsters use cloning devices to copy a credit or debit card's electronic data, which is then used to recreate an exact copy of the card to gain access to the money. One victim, former deputy PM *John Prescott*, explained away some expenses due to a (ahem!) cloned government credit card.

• *Carl Scheible*, managing director of PayPal® UK, stated: *"By 2016, you'll be able to leave your wallet at home and use your mobile as the 21st century digital wallet."* PayPal®, the company which managed to somehow become the superfluous commission-happy middleman between purchasing an item online and paying by credit card.

Dishonourable Mention:-

Once cashless transactions are embedded in society and paper money and coins are no longer produced, how long will the operating companies bide their time before they introduce their *pièce de résistance*, the mandatory 0.5% admin charge for every single transaction?

FOR	**AGAINST**
Cash transactions facilitate illegal activity such as drug dealing and corruption. Without it, it becomes an almost untenable activity. § Financial dishonesty can be easily tracked, end to end. § No more ATM's, therefore harder for cheating partners to cheat in style. § The logistical restrictions on money supply are removed, so more money in our pockets (wait, hang on!).	A move to virtual money requires no physical reserves to start a bank or credit card company. § All numbers now exist in cyberspace only, therefore prone to all threats digital data currently suffers from, such as computer viruses and database manipulation. § Card cloning means there'll no longer be a need to work for a living. § Increase in petty thefts of 'cashless' enabled devices.

Wildcard View

The Heist

Bank heists will now take place behind a computer and no longer on the high street.

However, the instantaneous nature of cyber-transactions are so quick that subsequent account transfers of the stolen money can be conducted many many times, eventually becoming lost amongst the many legitimate transactions. Almost beyond reasonable investigations or outside an investigative authority's financial jurisdiction.

Image Source:- Movie: Pretty Woman (1990) Starring: Julia Roberts and Richard Gere

Does it make us a lesser person to want to see certain folk fall so spectacularly and to still revel in their descent?

Background

There are many of us who pride ourselves in working hard and living responsible lives, free from immoral behaviour and thoughts towards our fellow man.

But what if this fellow man, who has no discernible talent, drive or the energy to work hard for a living, is someone who has now become rich, famous and revered. Some would argue that it defies human instinct to not feel some animosity or envy towards such folk, but then, you can also argue one shan't hold ill-feeling towards or concern themselves with those who can barely deserve your respect or your time.

But is there something that just does not sit right about that person who channels their whole energy into pursuing avenues of life which can grant not only an easy living but one that allows oneself to gloat and to hopefully be revered - the 'talentless' celebrity.

Is it morally honourable to actually object and protest to this way of life, and your moral duty to help stem these disturbing narcissistic attitudes?

Facts and Examples

Classroom Exercise A:- If such ill-feeling were not to affect your conscience, how would you prefer for these non-entities to live out their lives post-fame?
i) Dead within 10 years;
ii) Entire middle age spent depressed and lonely;
iii) Feeling absolute disgust and unfulfilled by 40;
iv) Ambled along in their prime in a futile existence before realising that life had inexplicably passed by;
v) A newfound sense of adulation as the years go by, more acceptance and more reverence.

Classroom Exercise B:- Fill in the respective pairs?
"X, famous for being Y, as well as... hhmmm, that's it" where X can be selected from:-
Katie Price; Paris Hilton; Imogen Thomas; Kerry Katona; Farrah Abraham; Mark Wright; Kim Kardashian; and Y can be selected from:-
Sex tape star; sleeping around; role model for Chavs; reality TV star; talentless; budding sex tape star.

FOR

Sets a disturbing precedent when mainstream media can openly encourage and embrace these types. A counterbalance is necessary to nullify the threat. § Short term exploitation by agents. § Long term unhappiness and an oncoming spiral of descent is almost always assured. § Revelling in the misfortune of those who categorically deserve some can always warm the cockles of your heart.

AGAINST

Envy is an unattractive quality. § Not everyone has been blessed with the required intellect or abilities to achieve their social or financial ambitions They should in fact be applauded for recognising and acknowledging their deficiencies, and having the drive to explore any avenue which helps them attain their goals. § Better to have realisable ambitions than none. § Self-serving society.

Excuuuse me! I'm an actress, honey...

Honey, we know. We've all seen the tape!

Image Source:- Movie: Disaster Movie (2008) Starring: Kim Kardashian

Further Facts

Scripted reality is a type of television series featuring real people who talk naturally but are actually put in pre-arranged structured situations likely to invoke certain reactions or paths of conversation. The dialogue may not be scripted but the tone has been engineered. Today, these talentless individuals are the envy of todays' youth and the toast of the celebrity tabloids, regularly featuring on the popular 'Daily Mail Sidebar of Shame'.

Dishonourable Mentions:- TOWIE; Living TV; The Hills.

Assuming the discovery of Cold Fusion becomes reality and it's proven beyond doubt to be a safe, reliable and abundant energy source, discuss the impact this would have on current global political and economical affairs?

Background, Facts and Miscellaneous

Cold Fusion is a theoretical form of energy source, derived from nuclear fusion reactions that take place at relatively low temperatures with, crucially, no radioactive by-product.

If proven successful and employable at room temperatures, the possibilities would be limitless allowing inexpensive small portable power units to provide energy on-demand at any location. This potential game-changer could conceivably render all other conventional sources obsolete.

Now, putting aside any cynical thoughts dismissing such discoveries and applications, speculate how the dynamics of world politics, global economics, conflicts and everyday life would be impacted upon the proven discovery of this reliable, safe, cheap and abundant source of energy?

Discussion Viewpoints:-
• Demand for oil and fuel falling dramatically and consequently, vested interests in the regions that supply the majority of it will likely recede;
• In this capitalist world, will the technology be permitted to progress and be shared. Or will protecting the bottom line take utmost precedence, even above the best interests of humanity, with the secret being discreetly placed in the vault;
• Conflicts borne primarily from the hidden desire to exploit a regions natural resource riches;
• Cheap energy would alleviate all worries about paying bills whatever the financial circumstances.

Classroom Exercise:- Can you foresee a future that has fully embraced Solar Power, with solar panels factory-built onto vehicles, mobiles etc?

127

In 2015, it has become law for the DNA profile to be taken from every single person at the point of birth. This database of DNA identification samples can only then be used during investigation of the most serious of crimes; murder, rape and child abuse.

Background

DNA profiling is a technique employed by forensic scientists to assist in the identification of individuals solely by their respective DNA profiles.

Currently, the law is that only anyone arrested on suspicion of a recordable offence must submit a DNA sample - which is then stored on the DNA database as a permanent record. This *National DNA Database* has thus far provided police with a soundly effective tool in the prevention and detection of crime since the development of fingerprint analysis. From 1998-2008, more than 400,000 *crime scene* to person matches had been detected with the aid of the database, highlighting the clear potential of DNA aided crime fighting.

In 2015, with strict protocols established and followed throughout the collection, submission and analysis of DNA samples, to minimise the possibility of administrative or analytical error and contamination, the authorities have ratified a full mandatory rollout of DNA collection for the benefit of forensic analysis.

Facts and Examples

• An investigation into the murder of *Sally Anne Bowman* failed to track down the culprit. The following year, a *Mr Mark Dixie* was arrested after a fight and swabbed under standard procedures. The database subsequently alerted officers of a match to a DNA sample taken from the scene, and he was consequently jailed for 34 years - yet, he may never have been caught had it not been for the DNA profile held on file.

• In a study conducted by *Nucleix* published in *Forensic Science International: Genetics*, scientists found that an 'In vitro' synthesized sample of DNA matching any desired genetic profile can be constructed using standard molecular biology techniques without obtaining any actual tissue from that person.

Dishonourable Mentions:- Phantom of Heilbronn; Dr John Schneeberger; Harry Davey and a victim.
Honourable Mentions:- Peter Hamkin and Annalisa Vincenzi; Sean Hodgson and Teresa De Simone.

FOR	**AGAINST**
Convicting people earlier than would have been obtained by traditional investigative methods. § Less likely for lawyers to contest indisputable DNA evidence. § Would be criminals less likely to commit an offence with little to no possibility of not being caught. § Only a person with sinister intentions would be against such a positive initiative. § Exoneration of the innocent.	DNA database tampering. § Hacking databases to target innocent individuals. § Commercialising the database for other initiatives eg. selling DNA codes of individuals with good genes. § Being an IT function, how long before the database is outsourced to foreign lands. § Fabrication of DNA evidence - engineering a crime scene. § Violation of Human Rights.

Peter Parker, I'm arresting you because we have you at the scene of more than 30 murders and multiple scenes of criminal endangerment, not to mention damage to public property.

Be Controversial

Prevention Better than the Cure.

Statistical Analysis of the DNA profiles of criminals can help identify strong patterns or strains common amongst certain types of offence or the type of criminal. This can then lead to pre-emptive rehabilitation of children whose DNA display such patterns. Alternatively, pre-emptive incarceration of individuals before they have a chance to commit their crimes or to become the person they will most inevitably become to be.

Image Source:- Movie: Spiderman (2002) Starring: Tobey Maguire

In 2022, this blasé attitude to taking control of a vehicle while under the influence of alcohol or drugs has been tolerated for far too long, concluding that the punishment (however appropriate) has never gone far enough, thus the law will now be revised such that it does indeed deter - Immediate confiscation and destruction of the vehicle.

Background

Amidst rising cases of uninsured vehicles and a perceived relaxed attitude to driving while inebriated, the law has been adjudged to have never been strong enough to act as a conscious deterrent while a subject is under undue influence.

Because many drink drivers point blank dismiss the thought that they could possibly cause an accident or that they are even worse for wear, coupled with the fact that if convicted would result in just a few points on the license, a small fine or a suspended sentence, it's no wonder why violating the drink-driving law has become so rife and an accepted norm in Britain.

To stem this, the UK authorities have finally acted to revise the punishment to be hard-hitting enough such that it can consciously register as a deterrent at any stage of one's inebriation - a no-quibble and no re-course immediate confiscation and complete destruction of the vehicle. This will take place in addition to any court proceedings as a result of the offence.

Facts and Examples

• The owner will however receive a slow-motion HD 1080P recording of the act, packaged in a lovely Blu-Ray Steelbook case for the preserving of the memory.
• In 2020, breath-testing technology had arrived which ensured a 100% accurate reading at roadside.
• According to the UK Department of Transport statistics for 2008, 8,620 road accidents happened when a driver was over the legal limit for alcohol. 2,020 people were killed or seriously injured as a result.
• Nearly one in six of all deaths on the road involve drivers who are over the legal alcohol limit.
• In the UK, the law states that anyone caught and convicted of drink driving will be banned from the road for at least 12 months, and fined up to £5,000, with a possibility of also being sent to prison for up to six months. If the driver is convicted of causing death by dangerous driving, they could then receive a prison sentence of up to fourteen years.
• Penalties for drug driving are the same as for drink.

FOR

Confiscation and destruction of weapons are in keeping with other offences where unnecessary injury has occurred. § The owner is aware of the potential a car accident can have to other road users, thus fully comprehends that the car could be deemed a weapon if the driver is over the limit. § Drink/drug driving statistics leave no other option. § The only functional deterrent.

AGAINST

It is too harsh a punishment for a simple human right. § Alcohol is so embedded in our society that drink driving laws should be relaxed. § Being under the influence adversely affects our perceptions, therefore one really does believe that their altered state is no different than their sober state. § Live by the sword, die by the sword. § A booming market in lower priced vehicles.

Wildcard View

Why is driving under the influence of drugs handled with such indifference and even neglected by the authorities in this day and age. It can be argued that drugs (especially those of the hallucinogenic variety) are considerably more detrimental to a person's senses than is alcohol, yet today, there is inadequate verification of a driver's 'drug' limit. This has arguably, in turn given licence to many drivers to opt for irresponsible drug use rather than be limited by the confines of what is actually monitored - alcoholic blood levels.

Image Source:- Movie:The Hangover (2009)
Starring: Zach Galifianakis, Ed Helms, Justin Bartha and Bradley Cooper

The year is 2032 and the authorities have introduced a public approved policy of mandatory euthanasia for all persons aged 65 or over. The principle aims being to relieve pressure on existing infrastructure and to encourage people to lead a focussed life within the shorter lifespan. Discuss the benefits and other implications?

Background, Facts and Miscellaneous

After decades of suffering at the hands of an inadequate infrastructure for a growing population, elderly care and rising fees, strains on medical resources and unsustainable national pension deficits, the general public have grown increasingly accustomed to the idea that elderly folk are a luxury that we can well do without.

In 2032, these feelings finally came to fruition with the passing of a universally agreed '*Euthanasia the Aged*' law which decrees that all persons aged over 65 are subject to an execution order.

Legally, the last will and testament for all remaining assets must be submitted by the age of 64 with financial provisions set aside to fulfil the personal objectives of their last living year. All net debts will be inherited by their children.

Discussion Viewpoints:-
• Will there now be an era of 'living life to the fullest' rather than 'saving for the future'?
• Can the housing market become fairly balanced by virtue of the elderly now being removed completely from the house dwelling population?
• To what extent will the strain on the national health service be relieved by?
• Will the short lifespan now encourage good living and an appreciation of family?
• As with most who near the end of their lives, the tendency to be concerned about the afterlife becomes more prominent. Will there be a greater embrace and adherence to religious faiths?
• What is the wider impact for loved ones knowing that their parents end is nigh?
• Is finding your soul mate the key to a good life?

In light of overwhelming evidence that a persons origin can lead to genetically superior sporting attributes, should the main power events of the Olympic Games be split accordingly, by way of ethnicity? ie. Two versions for the 'Mens 100m Sprint'; one for native Africans and one for everyone else.

Background

There is increasing evidence to indicate that human biodiversity is present and can somewhat explain why certain races are physically and genetically superior to the average white person in the field of sports, which consequently leads to an outright advantage.

Recent research suggests the reason why black athletes largely outperform athletes of other races in running events is because of distinct physical differences in the length of the limbs and the structure of the body means that the centre of gravity tends to be higher in the bodies of black people, both considered major advantages in the art of faster sprinting.

From a physics perspective, the legs do the work of running and the torso being just extra weight that the legs must carry, so the race tends to go to the runners with longer legs and shorter torsos. By contrast, whites tend to have the advantage in swimming, where a longer torso allows for faster speeds.

Facts and Examples

• Black athletes hold world records in all of the seven major sprint events.
• Of the top 200 official times at 100 metres, not one has been run by a white athlete. Only black sprinters have (officially) run under 10 seconds.
• Underneath black skin, there is more muscle and less fat than those with white skin.
• Research by the *Copenhagen Institute of Sports Science* show distinct genetic characteristics which help Kenyans store oxygen in the body and reduce fatigue. At the 1988 Seoul Olympics, Kenyans won the men's 800, 1500, 5000 and 3000 steeplechase titles.

Consider the case where a 6ft tall man with long legs runs 0.01ms faster than a 5ft tall man with short legs. Who would you consider to be the *better* athlete?

Dishonourable Mentions:- Jean-Phillipe Rushton; The mutual exclusivity of athleticism and intelligence;

FOR

Individuals who've harnessed their skills and are unrivalled in ability will succumb only because of a genetic disadvantage such as height. § In sports where even the smallest differences matter, segregation of the originating race can and must be the inevitable future. § Talented white runners would be unfairly discouraged from harnessing any natural skills or determination.

AGAINST

Olympics should always be one unique event for the ultimate athlete in each field. § Potential champions would strive to achieve the right balance of skill, focus, graft and abilities. Any physical advantages merely complement these. § Next, we'll have shorter athletes requesting competition by height class. § Physical disadvantages can provide motivation to drive people on harder.

Image Source:- 1988 Olympics 100m Final feat. Carl Lewis and Ben Johnson

Future Reform

In 2022, with public and scientific acceptance of the genetic advantage theory, alarming trends in the origin of top-tier footballers and a shocking fall in white parents encouraging their children to become footballers, the European football leagues have acted to stem this by breaking-up their respective leagues in the same manner, one for native-africans and one for everyone else.

What would transpire in terms of spectatorship and would underlying prejudicial tones play a part ?

George Costanza is a philosopher for our age. With his wise perspectives on life, does he have a voice to be heard and a point to be made with his uncensored 'life' quote?

Background, Facts and Miscellaneous

George Louis Costanza is a character from the American TV comedy series 'Seinfeld' (1989-98), played by the hilarious Jason Alexander.

Known for his quirkiness and nuggets of advice, he once stated in an episode: "*It became very clear to me sitting out there today that every decision I've made in my entire life has been wrong. My life is the complete opposite of everything I want it to be. Every instinct I have, in every aspect of life - it's all been wrong.*"

Due to the pre-9pm watershed, one of Costanzas' famous philosophies on life (shown in the next column) had to be hastily rewritten to avoid causing any controversy. It can now be unveiled in its original format, seen on the opposite page. Was 'Georgie Boy' unfairly censored and if so, does he actually make a good point?

"*The most unfair thing about life is the way it ends. I mean, life is tough. It takes up a lot of your time. What do you get at the end of it? A death. What's that, a bonus!?!?! I think the life cycle is all backwards. You should die first, get it out of the way. Then you go live in an old age home. You get kicked out for being too healthy, go collect your pension, then, when you start work, you get a gold watch on your first day. You work forty years until you're young enough to enjoy your retirement. You drink alcohol, you party, and you get ready for high school. You go to primary school, you become a kid, you play, you have no responsibilities. You become a little baby, you go back, spend your last 9 months floating with luxuries like central heating, spa, room service on tap, then you finish off as an orgasm! Amen.*"

~ George Costanza, Seinfeld

George's Uncensored Rant :-

"The most unfair thing about life is the way it shits all over you. I mean, life is tough, and what do you really get at the end of it?

Lying on your deathbed knowing that almost all the money you earned was grabbed back in taxes, family who want you to die so they can fight over what you have left, a life of failed dreams and unexplored opportunities but yet you're able to draw some comfort because you are leaving a scorched earth where young people full of promise have no desire to fulfill it, people who refuse to speak up or take action, and declining moral standards in every crevice you look.
What's that, a bonus(!), knowing you leave the earth
in a worse place than when you found it?!?!

I think this way of life where all we think about is the 'here and now' is so corruptive, people need to start viewing things and starting to behave in the knowledge that you will one day look back on it retrospectively and want to be happy you made that decision.

When you get married, you need to know that the person you'll be spending the rest of your life with is someone you can do so when all their looks and youthful attributes are slowly stripped away. When you encounter upon a career, you'll need to know that it's something you wished you hadn't swam against the current for 40 years. When you raise your children, you treat them knowing that this is going to be as good as it will ever get for them and have endeavoured to make the most of it for their sake. When you have billions in the bank, you'll need to be wary that all the people you trampled over to get it would most likely not have been worth the conscience you will reluctantly harbour. When you commit that sin which causes physical or emotional pain, stop and think of the repurcussions that will resonate over time.

Then maybe we'll die with a smile on our face, tears on our families cheeks and to be able to bask in the comfort that you helped leave the earth for your loved ones a better place than when you found it. After all, that's surely the whole point!"

Should we defy God's Will -
Do we accept that God has a divine plan for humanity and our lives are just 'cogs in the wheel' in helping to ultimately accomplish his purpose OR should we continue striving to overcome obstacles to achieve our personal desires?

Background

The Christian Bible informs us that we were created by God, in his image, for a purpose, thus has a co-ordinated plan for each of our individual lives.

Specifically, this means that God has equipped us to do what he calls us to do. If we aren't gifted in a certain area, God has probably not called you to minister in that area (according to Romans 12:6-8, 1 Corinthians 12:1-11 and Ephesians 4:11-13).

God's ultimate purpose for all of us is that He would be glorified (1 Corinthians 10:31) and that the gospel and God's kingdom would be advanced (Genesis 50:20 and Philippians 1:12).

By this reckoning, all our abilities, talents, deficiencies and disabilities are divinely bestowed upon us to serve a particular role and nothing more. Should we stick to this path and accept our limitations in order that we achieve our ultimate purpose or should we selfishly deviate from it to meet our personal desires?

Facts and Examples

Now, if I was a religious man:-
• Klara Hitler suffered numerous miscarriages and sadly, all three children who had survived pregnancy died in their infant years. Despite these unfortunate events, she continued to try and bear children and eventually succeeded, with a beautiful baby boy called Adolf. Now, one could suggest that God tried and failed for her offspring never to survive but failed to counteract the strength of the human spirit.
• Famine in Africa is almost a common occurrence resulting in millions of starving children. Now, one could suggest that people in the region just stop having children so that the people die out so the land could become farm land for the rest of God's people.
• Aborted foetuses as result of being raped. Now, one could suggest that a 'forced' merging of DNA strands was required in order to conceive the human saviour.
• Curing diseases. Now, one could suggest that we'll introduce a new strain eradicating the human race.

FOR

What a load of horsesh*t. § If God is so powerful, why engage in such a pointless exercise. Jump straight to it. § Hard to comprehend why the worlds suffering is orchestrated such that it achieves the ultimate good. § The bible states a plan for our life, yet this is directed only at the Jewish population, the chosen ones. § Reason to denounce Religion. § Fate and Destiny!

AGAINST

The human race needs to prove themselves worthy of the most wonderful of purposes. Suffering and sacrifice should be endured by the collective all. § Having the bigger picture in mind. § The greater the sacrifice and suffering, the greater the reward. § The talents and remarkable traits afforded to us are all gifts from God, and we must harness them in the way it was intended.

You know, I'd love a baby sister...

For the last time, no means no....

Be Controversial

"All part of God's Plan"
Are mental or physical disabilities at birth down to divine intervention by a higher power, as part of a pre-emptive strike against those born evil or morally corrupt.

If so, as honourable as the intentions are, does this suggest that God practices the work of the Devil in burdening a young innocent defenceless child with untold suffering? With this in mind, can your Soul really enter paradise with a clear conscience?

Image Source:- Movie: My Sisters Keeper (2009) Starring: Sofia Vassilieva and Cameron Diaz

Instead of pursuing a ban on the Muslim veil, would it serve better to empower women by actually doing the opposite and try to encourage women of all walks of life to embrace the idea of a 'hijab', to wear standard muslim attire whenever they feel to, despite wishes of the wider general public and the average gentleman?

Background, Facts and Miscellaneous

Western countries have been wrestling with the issue of the Muslim veil (various forms include the body-covering *burka* and the *niqab*, which covers the face apart from the eyes), and the debate has taken in issues such as religious freedom, multiculturalism, female equality, secular traditions and even fears of terrorism.

To date, there are varying bans of the wearing of the niqab across Europe including France and the Netherlands, on the basis that it oppresses women or exists to protect a countrys' way of life and culture, as well as security reasons.

However, if we were to take away the religious influence and if some look past their bigotry towards anything 'Islam', can an accepted covering of the face or body actually be empowering?

Some possible benefits could include:-
• Slipping one on when walking home alone late,
• When the looks are long gone and your loving husband doesn't like being seen with you,
• Relaxed - not wanting to be seen with the man or woman on your arm,
• Less stress - to be able to get up to no good, and have extra-marital affairs in peace,
• Improving your love life - not being blessed with looks but your personality is top notch,
• Living with bad hair days and make-up breaks,
• Body like Baywatch but Face like Crimewatch,
• Putting the slimy paparazzi out of business,
• A smaller wardrobe and shoe collection.

Further Discussion Point:-
Does it seem *Islam* is just ahead of the curve?

Image Source:- Movie: Se7en (1995) Starring: Morgan Freeman

Hindus and Climate Change -
Was it divine intervention which forbid the Hindu
population through the ages from eating beef?

Background, Facts and Miscellaneous

Scientists claim that while it may already be too late to prevent global warming, reducing greenhouse gases could still limit the impact. Currently, carbon dioxide accounts for more than 60% of the enhanced greenhouse effect caused by the increase of greenhouse gases.

According to a 2006 report by the *Food and Agricultural Organisation*, entitled 'Livestock's Long Shadow', the world's cattle population are responsible for a remarkable 18% of the greenhouse gases that cause global warming.

Seems we are very fortunate that the appetite for beef hadn't been higher, otherwise it's quite conceivable that we may have been in a state today where the global warming effect would have been irreversibly catastrophic for humanity. But then, should we also be grateful to religion?

In Hinduism, the cow is considered a sacred animal and its protection is a recurrent theme in which it is a symbol of abundance, of the sanctity of all life and of the earth that gives much while asking nothing in return. As such, the consumption of beef is strictly forbidden.

• There are currently 900 million Hindus worldwide, making up almost 13% of the population.

• The world cattle population is around 1.3b, with India holding the largest proportion at 280m.

• Cows are estimated to release between 70-120 kg of methane per year. Methane is a greenhouse gas like carbon dioxide (CO_2), but the negative effect on the climate of methane is 23 times higher than the effect of CO_2. Therefore, the release of about 100kg methane per year for each cow is equivalent to about 2,300 kg CO_2 per year.

Projected Estimates of Cattle Based CO2 Emissions Accumulated

Decade	World Population	Hindu Population	Cattle Population	Based on Hindus Not Eating Beef			Based on Hindus Eating Beef			
				Methane Emissions from Cattle (CO2 Kg equivalent)	Cumulative Methane Emissions from Cattle (CO2 Kg equivalent)	Additional Cattle	Additional Methane Emissions from Additional Cattle (CO2 Kg equivalent)	Cumulative Methane Emissions from Additional Cattle (CO2 Kg equivalent)	Cumulative Methane Emissions from ALL Cattle (CO2 Kg equivalent)
1900	1650	215	330	7590000	7,590,000	215	4933500	4,933,500	12,523,500
1910	1750	228	350	8050000	15,640,000	228	5232500	10,166,000	25,806,000
1920	1860	242	372	8556000	24,196,000	242	5561400	15,727,400	39,923,400
1930	2070	269	414	9522000	33,718,000	269	6189300	21,916,700	55,634,700
1940	2300	299	460	10580000	44,298,000	299	6877000	28,793,700	73,091,700
1950	2519	327	504	11587400	55,885,400	327	7531810	36,325,510	92,210,910
1960	2982	388	596	13717200	69,602,600	388	8916180	45,241,690	114,844,290
1970	3692	480	738	16983200	86,585,800	480	11039080	56,280,770	142,866,570
1980	4435	577	887	20401000	106,986,800	577	13260650	69,541,420	176,528,220
1990	5263	684	1053	24209800	131,196,600	684	15736370	85,277,790	216,474,390
2000	6070	789	1214	27922000	159,118,600	789	18149300	103,427,090	262,545,690
2010	7000	900	1500	34500000	193,618,600	900	20700000	124,127,090	317,745,690
2020	8050	1047	1610	37030000	230,648,600	1047	24069500	148,196,590	378,845,190
2030	9258	1203	1852	42584500	273,233,100	1203	27679925	175,876,515	449,109,615
2040	10646	1384	2129	48972175	322,205,275	1384	31831914	207,708,429	529,913,704
2050	12243	1592	2449	56318001	378,523,276	1592	36606701	244,315,130	622,838,406
				378,523,276	2,133,046,651		244,315,130	1,377,855,323	3,510,901,975

Estimated Cattle Based CO2 Emissions Increase due to Hindus Eating Beef = **65%**

Key :
- All numbers are in 000,000s
- Fields in Grey are projected population numbers.

References :
World Population stats from: http://commons.wikimedia.org/wiki/File:Population_curve.svg

Assumptions :
- World Population has grown 15% over the last two decades so this will be used to project population figures for 2020-2050
- In 2010, the hindu population made up 13% of the whole world population. This rate will be assumed to project hindu populations before and since.
- Will assume that cattle has the same ratio to people throughout history. The rate based on 2007 numbers is around 20%.
- A single cow releases 100 kg of Methane per year, equivalent to 2300Kg CO2.
- Additional Cattle is based on the assumption that every member of the hindu population eats 1 cow every 10 years.

Image Source:- By The Author

If the knowledge and memory portion of the human brain can be identified and somehow be cloned as a blueprint, is it conceivable that human clones could be implanted with this blueprint - If so, could the world of tomorrow justify it as ethically acceptable?

Background, Facts and Miscellaneous

Replacement human cloning is currently a theoretical possibility combining the therapeutic and reproductive cloning methods, and entails the replacement of an extensively damaged, failed or deteriorating body through cloning, followed by whole or partial brain transplant or harvesting the internal organs of the clone.

Our ventures into space, the final frontier, will inevitably require manual roles that either the human body will struggle to fulfil or is too strenuous to accept. However, since human limitations have hardly stood in the way of progress, this hurdle will no doubt be overcome, at whatever cost.

A 2009 film starring *Sam Rockwell* explored one such possibility, depicting brilliantly the effective solution of deploying battle-ready clones.

If indeed scientific advancements in Human Cloning technology were to progress, then the opportunity certainly opens up to try and identify and map the components of the brain sufficiently enough to be able to apply selective copying to the brain during the cloning process.

If so, the ability to implant a 'knowledge set' blueprint that is optimally respective to the task they are assigned to fill (clones rebooted with a start-up program), would bring about a wealth of deployment opportunities to employers/authorities alike. Roles such as sewage workers, foot soldiers, long term space travellers, planet colonisation settlers etc. would now no longer need to call upon the native naturally-occurring human race but instead from ready made, primed, able and willing clones. Surely, a good thing?

Image Source:- Movie: Prometheus (2012) Starring: Noomi Rapace & Michael Fassbender

If a global pandemic was to wipe out the Human Race, would it actually be the best thing for our beloved planet?

Background, Facts and Miscellaneous

The threat of a global pandemic, be it natural or man-made, has sadly become a terrifyingly real one. So, imagine a scenario where a virus caused the human species to become totally extinct.

With humans absent from the evolutionary cycle and no longer causing an artificial environmental imbalance, does the animal kingdom now have a realistic chance of living in harmony, food cycle permitting, till the end of days? (Did God not count on Humans to intelligently evolve?)

Consider the following in your evaluation:-
• No more fishing/hunting for food/medicine,
• No adverse environmental impacts from the manmade industrial 'human support system' - a collection of factories, energy power plants etc,
• The recovery of a depleted ozone layer,

• Rainforests and trees allowed to remain the critical component of the natural carbon cycle,
• Human race stopped in their tracks from unintentionally creating an irreversible global catastrophe affecting every living thing on earth, be it a virus, radioactive levels or mass destruction.

Classroom Exercise:- With Flu mutating continuously in a never ending game of tit-for-tat, has the time come to change tact and cease trying to fight the various flu strains and let it be?

The underlying premise behind such thinking is attributed to the theory of evolution. The laws would suggest that mutation would no longer be necessary and thus would remain in a stationary state, since there is now no longer an opposing force (flu vaccines and medicine).

Image Source:- Movie: Moon (2009) Starring: Sam Rockwell

147

Human Rights Act -
Should the UK abandon it and instead rely on Judges and Lawyers to fight it out on whether someone's human rights have been violated?

Background

The Human Rights Act (HRA) of 1998 gives further legal effect in the UK to the fundamental rights and freedoms contained in the European Convention on Human Rights. These rights not only impact matters of life and death, but they also affect the rights we have in our everyday lives: what we can say and do, our beliefs, our right to a fair trial and other similar basic entitlements.

Most rights do have limits to ensure that they do not unfairly damage other people's rights, however, certain rights - such as the right not to be tortured - can never be limited by a court or anybody else.

The UK Home Secretary *Mrs Theresa May* warned in Oct '11 that the Act was hampering the Home Office's struggle to deport dangerous foreign criminals and terrorist suspects (Article 8, which specifies the right to a family life, tends to be the one used and abused by some mischievous lawyers).

Facts and Examples

• There are now at least 2,000 HR lawyers in the UK. Compensation claims under the HR legislation cost around £7 billion a year and legal fees arising from HRA cases are estimated at £250 million a year.

• A convicted sex attacker, asylum-seeker *William Danga*, raped and violently molested two young girls (one as young as 4yrs old) as he fought deportation on human rights grounds. The judge remarked it was 'remarkable' that the sex attacker was not thrown out of Britain after being jailed for ten years for raping a 16-year-old girl a decade earlier.

• A dangerous rapist, *Rohan Winfield*, was allowed to cheat deportation because of his 'right to family life'- even though he'd abandoned his wife. Despite him being a clear danger to women, an immigration judge allowed him to stay, ruling "The human rights of the rapist appear to trump society's interest."

Dishonourable Mentions:- Hesham Mohammed Ali; Raja Mohammed Anwar Khan; Akindoyin Akinshipe.

FOR

It's become a law for the unlawful. § Those who violate other peoples human rights should automatically be exempt from an act advocating Human Rights. § Maybe constantly refine and replace parts of the act with legislation that's better fit for purpose. § Constant abuse of human rights laws and the meddling by often ill-qualified European judges needs to be urgently curbed.

AGAINST

Lawyers will always look for loopholes. § Taking rights away from the people would allow governments to easily become more authoritarian. § Human Rights should not be perceived as a radical ideology, it is a right we are all born with and should be protected at all costs. § What about those individuals who have genuine cases against deportation or have been saved from legitimate concerns?

Your honour, I've found the wonders of 'Homosexuality' while I was on remand.

Classroom Exercise

What atrocities and injustices would we have seen if there was NO charter for Human Rights?

Consider the following historical events in your answer:- Guantanamo Bay; Religious intolerance in Godhra, Gujarat 2002; Abu Ghraib; The Lord Resistance Army and Slavery; Unit 731; Treatment of refugees after the ceasefire between the Angolan government and UNITA in 2001; Vietnam and the 'high risk behaviour for contracting HIV' groups.

Image Source:- Movie: Harold & Kumar Escape from Guantanamo Bay (2008) Starring: John Cho and Kal Penn

Though Greece has in recent times been under enormous economic strain due to much of its own doing, should the people actually deserve credit for their relaxed attitude to paying government taxes?

Background, Facts and Miscellaneous

As of 2012, Greece's debts totalled around €350 billion - or around 165% of the country's GDP. This unmanageable level of debt followed years of living beyond its means with public spending having soared and public sector wages doubling over the past decade.

The ensuing deficit was as a direct result of tax income being hit due to an inherent culture of widespread tax evasion by all, from regular citizens right through to high-ranking officials.

But with such practices regularly and unashamedly undertaken by the wealthy elite and large corporations, all complicit in actively avoiding their rightful tax liabilities, are the Greek people in good company by adopting similar reluctance and if so, should they be applauded?

Classroom Exercise:-

A UK citizen has received an average gross salary of £100,000 over a period of 20 years and now outright owns property worth the same amount at which it was bought 20 years earlier, £1m. Sadly, he unexpectedly dies and leaves the house and any remaining wealth to loved ones.

Q. Between yourselves, estimate what proportion of the £2m earned ultimately went to the taxman, after inheritance tax is accounted for?

Assume the following in your answer;

- There is no inflation, no interest on savings and no possibility of tax avoidance.
- The interest rate on his mortgage was 0%.
- The income tax rate remained at 50% throughout his career; inheritance tax rate is 50%; VAT rate remained at 20%; Stamp Duty was 10%.

I've heard you pay no tax whatsoever on your income... I'd like you to show me how.

Image Source:- TV Series: Battlestar Galactica (2004-09) Starring: Katee Sackhoff and Edward James Olmos

In order to curb excessive pay/bonuses and encourage fairer remuneration levels across the workforce, the PAYE taxation system has been overhauled to now accommodate a tiered approach with progressively increasing tax rates. Discuss the implications of such a measure on workforce morale and the economy?

Background, Facts and Miscellaneous

There seems to be a disturbing trend in today's business world where it's become almost accepted practice that executives receive inflation busting pay rises and bonuses while the pay for lower level workers can remain relatively stagnant.

To stem this immorality, new legislation to the income tax is proposed, the key points being:-
• Low taxation levels for the low paid and higher taxation levels as one progresses salary levels.
• Facilitating a reasonable disposable income where possible by way of a higher tax-free allowance and a lower starting tax rate.
• At a certain salary point, employees will pay more tax than receiving net. Conversely, companies will become sensitive to this 'tipping point', hopefully appreciating the efficiency in allocating fairer pay levels across the whole organisation.

Discussion Viewpoints:- The only legitimately fair way of taxation. § Talented people would just go and work abroad instead. § If the higher paid threaten to work abroad, then let them. Plenty of applicants lining up and more than happy to pay their fair share of tax. § Shareholders want the best, and will happily remunerate adequately as long as it brings value to their investments. § Salary remuneration won't be in line with talent. § Exceptions made for commission based roles. § Talented people like to see acknowledgement of their 'talent' in the form of large variations in take-home pay against that of lesser subordinates.

Dishonourable Mentions:- RBS makes room for a £800m bonus pot amidst a £2bn loss in 2011; Qantas chief executive Alan Joyce; Windrush.

Increasing Tax based on Tiers/Buckets

Minimum Living (Tax Free) Allowance £		10,000
Tax Income Required Target £000s		122,896,200
Incremental Tax Rate per Tier %		1%
Multiplier Factor to attain Tax Reqd Target		**6.48**

(Use Excels 'Goal Seek' Function - Cells AL84=G6 Changing G9)

Column	C1	C2	C3	C4	C5	C6	C7	C8
Math;			AVG (C1,C2)		See Brkdwn	C5 / C3	C5 x C4	C6 / SUM(C7)

Salary Tier	Salary Range			No. of Taxpayers 000s	Summary Tax Income			% TaxPayers Allocation
	Min	Max	Average		Tax per Salary Tier	Effective % Tax	Total Tax Income	
A	4,745	6,000	5,373	1,440	-	0%	-	0%
B	6,001	7,000	6,501	1,160	-	0%	-	0%
C	7,001	8,000	7,501	1,590	-	0%	-	0%
D	8,001	10,000	9,001	2,950	-	0%	-	0%
E	10,001	12,000	11,001	2,760	65	1%	179,031	0%
F	12,001	15,000	13,501	3,650	324	2%	1,183,455	1%
G	15,001	20,000	17,501	4,950	1,005	6%	4,974,860	4%
H	20,001	30,000	25,001	6,000	2,788	11%	16,727,917	14%
I	30,001	50,000	40,001	4,090	7,326	18%	29,964,934	24%
J	50,001	70,000	60,001	859	14,458	24%	12,419,549	10%
K	70,001	100,000	85,001	410	25,156	30%	10,313,866	8%
L	100,001	200,000	150,001	300	57,897	39%	17,369,073	14%
M	200,001	500,000	350,001	89	171,356	49%	15,250,704	12%
N	500,001	1,000,000	750,001	16	420,967	56%	6,735,467	5%
O	1,000,001	3,000,000	2,000,001	6	1,296,224	65%	7,777,344	6%
				30,270			**122,896,200**	**100%**

Breakdown of Tax Calculation:-

The Banking Crisis of 2007 - How did it ever come to this! Banking recruitment in the 1980s included a wave of unscrupulous characters of no discernible intellect - Is it this irresponsible and unmonitored recruitment policy, which led to such folk now running these banks, the real reason why the industry has become so undistinguished?

Background, Facts and Miscellaneous

Though initially only intended as a short term appointment for their market-trading savvy and hard-living ethos which encapsulated the culture of a successful trading floor, the uneducated 'wide-boys' and 'barrow boys' grew accustomed to the hard days slog of liquid lunches, fancy dinners and corporate perks to just give it up and walk away without a fight. And fight they did!

Using all their brash confidence, charisma, scheming and interpersonal skills they'd harnessed on the trading floor, they managed to manoeuvre themselves into roles which contained promising career paths thus providing an avenue for longevity within the organisation.

They then muscled and bullied their way to the very top (taking friends with them), meaning that eventually these personality traits would become commonplace across the breadth of the upper tiers of management.

Once in position, they recalled all the underhand, dishonest and primitive tactics from their trading desk days, the same ones used to make lots of money with little adherence to economic understanding, rules, standards or ethics. This, unfortunately, was the grounding for all their business knowledge and their way of working.

With the senior bankers of yesteryear (those who upheld honest ethical banking based on strong economic foundations) finding themselves to be outnumbered, intimidated and shoved aside, the new breed of bankers and their business 'know-how' would become the basis of future business strategies, ethics and practices. Discuss?

Further Information :-

○ In 2012, Britain's biggest bank, HSBC, stood accused of fostering such a 'polluted' culture that it became a conduit for criminal enterprises, allowing rogue states and drugs cartels to launder billions of pounds through its branches.

Evidence in the Senate report showed that HSBC staff sought to get round sanctions that prevent American firms from doing business with Iran. It stated: "From 2001 to 2007, HSBC affiliates sent almost 25,000 transactions involving Iran worth over $19billion (£12billion) through HBUS and other US accounts, while concealing any link with Iran in 85 % of the transactions."

To conceal the transactions, HSBC affiliates used a method called 'stripping,' where references to Iran were deleted from records. They also characterized the transactions as transfers between banks without disclosing the tie to Iran in what the Senate report called a 'cover payment'.

○ Barclays was fined a record £290million in 2012 for its part in rigging the LIBOR lending rate, which affected millions of homeowners and borrowers.

Recent revelations showed that not only did the Barclays compliance department fail to act on three separate warnings about conflicts of interest but in fact, senior executives were comfortable in the knowledge such activity was taking place.

○ In 2012, charges laid against 'Standard Chartered' by US financial regulators depicted it as a 'rogue institution'. Standard was, its accusers claim, motivated by sheer greed into immorally chasing business from corrupt regimes including Iran, Burma and Sudan.

The New York state department of Financial Services claimed the bank plotted with Iran to conceal more than 60,000 illicit financial transactions amounting to £160bn over nearly a decade, which allegedly "left the US financial system vulnerable to terrorists and corrupt regimes".

○ Honorable Mentions:- Mr G Smith, GS of GS; Greg Smith;

○ A common complaint of those resistant to ethics training and legislation is that an increased focus on doing the right thing could have a negative impact on profits.

"When I would talk about ethics, especially to people directly in the Wall Street community, I would typically get a response, 'What do you want, Darcy? Do you want ethics or profits?'" he says. "I would always say, 'I want both. This is not an either/or proposition. I want the highest possible financial outcomes for our organizations at the highest possible standards.' They're not mutually exclusive".

~ *Keith Darcy*, Executive Director
Ethics and Compliance Officer Association

○ *Hector Sants*, the fomer chief executive of the Financial Services Authority (FSA), used his departing speech to call for integrity to replace greed in the banking sector; "Should there not be some level of expectation that people entrusted with the leadership of financial services organisations ultimately are driven by the desire to do the right thing. It shouldn't solely be about how much we earn but also how much we care for the market's users and their well-being".

○ The FSA's report in Dec 2011 explaining the demise of RBS stated that one of the key factors was the management, led by Sir Fred Goodwin (of £340k pension a year fame). It said: "The multiple poor decisions that RBS made suggest that there are likely to have been underlying deficiencies in RBS management, governance and culture which made it prone to make poor decisions".

○ A recent study showed that though the wealthy may think of themselves as the more respectable and upstanding members of society, they are in fact more likely to lie, cheat and break the law than those who have less.

The researchers suggested that the rich's view of the world may be clouded by self-absorption and greed. As a result, they have fewer scruples than those who have less money.

Why would the US authorities steadfastly refuse to undertake a reconstruction of the supposed 'lone gunman' theory using their finest marksman?

Background

After decades of silent whispers and insinuations, there is now a growing desire to put this dark chapter of the 'JFK Assassination' firmly behind, put to rest.

In 2014, a TV production company have submitted a proposal to the US authorities for their approval and assistance, which aims to finally debunk the 'JFK' conspiracy theory once and for all. The approval is necessary primarily for legal reasons but also sheltered a fool's hope that it might help avoid any unnecessary 'dissuading interventions' that could be co-ordinated by folk in the upper echelons of power.

The idea is to broadcast freely to the world a live re-enactment of a strict reconstruction of the events of 22nd Nov 1963, in accordance with the widely embraced official 'lone gunman' theory. Since much of the doubt rests in the fact that *Lee Harvey Oswald* was an inexperienced gunman and who had supposedly perfected two long range shots at a moving target, it is this premise that the proposal will focus on.

Facts and Examples

• Reconstruction: Will take place when the exact conditions of that day hold with regard to weather, essentially the wind factor and visibility. Aside from this, the same type of car, the crowds, the number of vehicles, the sniper and a human stand in for JFK will be primed and ready for the 'event of the century'.

• Sniper: Will be one of the US Army's most experienced marksman and will use a state of the art sniper rifle. He/she will be randomly independently selected.

• JFK: A person of similar build will be employed, ideally a conspiracy theorist nut job who believes so vehemently that there was no single shooter that he be willing to risk his own life. Failing that, a serial paedophile will be sedated and placed in the convertible.

• The Vow: The US authorities will grant a promise that should the marksman fail to hit the target twice from three shots within 7 seconds, then all classified documents pertaining to the event and the investigation shall be released immediately to the public.

FOR

By formally assisting such practices, authorities give further credence to the theories. § No interest in entertaining conspiracy theories of any kind. § It's in the past, leave it be. § The real powers in the USA supersede that of the official lines, and they have their own reasons to decline. One dares not question their best intentions. § Proving the 'lone gunman' theory will change nothing.

AGAINST

Could discredit undoubtedly the theory that LHO was the shooter. § Concludes that such accurate shooting, trajectory paths and exit wounds would only be possible with scattered synchronised shooters. § Chance that a realistic reconstruction would spawn more questions than answers, fuelling even more outlandish theories. § Declassification of documents would implicate the CIA.

I can't get a clear shot. Get to the knoll NOW!

Be Controversial

In 2017, to finally halt all the accusations that the great ole' USA killed their own President, the documents have been granted de-classification without objection. If however, they prove that the CIA were indeed clearly complicit (as a means to extend financial support for the Vietnam war), then is it not inconceivable that the same powers-that-be could have co-ordinated the Sep 9/11 attack, especially considering the significant military funding that would have been made available on a justifiable 'war on terror'.

After the Holocaust atrocities of WWII, we like to believe that the human race has learned lessons and such acts would never be allowed to happen ever again - But why is there so little perceived condemnation or military action against the regimes who shamelessly undertake the massacres and atrocities in this day and age?

Background

Todays conflicts tend to arise mainly due to either the pursuit of power, the control of natural resources or tensions due to the differences in religious or cultural beliefs. Those conflicts taking place within the borders of a country amongst its own people is normally termed a Civil War, and therefore understandably requires little to no external intervention.

However, when one-way oppression towards the minority takes place, terming this (incorrectly) as a Civil War has virtually permitted external entities to adopt similar policies, and thus absolve themselves of any involvement or intervention.

Genocide, as stated in International Law means acts (such as murder, physical harm and preventing births) committed with intent to destroy, in whole or in part, a national, ethnical, racial or religious group.

Yet, constant violations throughout the last half century has yet to see any *Knights in Shining Armour*.

Facts and Examples

• Genocide bodycount based on upper-end estimates:- Bangladesh 1971 (3m), Sudan (400,000), Rwanda (1m), Cambodia 1975 (3m), Bosnia (8000 Muslims).

• In Sri Lanka, the government created 'protected' zones, duping the remaining Tamil population into thinking they were now safe from harm. Herding them into an ever-confining space and then bombing them was a fast-tracked version of the gas chambers used by the Nazi's, just quicker and more efficient. It seemed that disease, starvation and infection that was already decimating the Tamil population wasn't.

• USA played a controversial role supporting the rule of *Lon Nol* during the Cambodia civil war, however were nowhere to be seen when the *Khmer Rouge* won control and began undertaking mass executions.

"The world is a dangerous place to live, not because those who are evil but because of those who don't do anything about it".
~ Albert Einstein

FOR	**AGAINST**
Each to their own. § No financial incentive to intervene. § Allowing the third world or the non-white ethnicities to self-implode. § Population reduction strategies to be applauded and not discouraged. § Powerless against the madmen of the world, who never listen to reason. They believe what they are doing is right for the sake of their country and its people. § We have the UN.	*With great power comes great responsibility.* With all the military might the powers of the world possess, what use is it if the little people aren't looked after. § Sanctions that are too little too late. § A sense of responsibility and pro-active action should always be prevalent. § UN's priority is to prevent the persecution of a civilian population first and foremost. It's currently misplaced.

Be Controversial

It is 2020, and the extreme right wing party, the *British National Front* has finally come into power with the key manifesto item of 'ethnic cleansing' being the deciding factor in victory. However, to the public's dismay, it turns out that the leadership had always meant to systematically execute those persons immediately instead of the expected repatriation route. Would any country or the UN attempt to intervene or is it futile to stop a military might such as Britain from doing what it likes within its own borders?

Image Source:- Movie: The Lord of the Rings: The Two Towers (2002)
Starring: Karl Urban

If David Koresh had existed over 2000 years ago, could it have been conceivable for his cult to have stood the test of time, with Koreshtians being todays majority?

Background, Facts and Miscellaneous

For some, *Jesus Christ*, was not the son of God but simply an entrepreneur who saw a gap in the faith market and exploited it. Or rather, he was groomed as the front for the made-up notion of *Religion* by well-meaning individuals who had the sole intention of honourably trying to curb depressing trends in immoral and depraved behaviour, lawlessness and non-conforming attitudes.

As you've no doubt observed, there is little difference here to what is commonly defined as being a *Cult*, where manipulative and charismatic folk band together to perpetuate the idea of a superbeing and the ways he wishes people to live, conform and be bound by their actions.

David Koresh, was the charismatic spiritual leader of the notorious *Branch Davidians* cult. He believed himself to be an angel and final prophet of God, or more accurately, he was able to convince the gullible and naive types normally susceptible to these self-serving cults, of the perception he wished to project and used his newfound reverence to lead them into a wasted existence.

Religious Studies Classroom Assignment:-
It is 100 AD and you have decided to start a new religion, but realise that you need to entice people away from the currently well established faiths. Begin writing your scriptures with sole emphasis on the incentives for its followers, of 3 gifts awaiting them in heaven, a sanctuary for your soul in the afterlife. The group then needs to confer on whose religion they would have likely followed. The participant who has the most followers can then go forth and start a collection box.

Image Source:- Movie: Boiler Room (2000) Starring: Vin Diesel & Others

If we can't rely on scientists to have a moral and ethical code, who then can we trust?

Background, Facts and Miscellaneous

We expect our scientists to be impartial, observant and diligent, and as science is dependent on observation, they must be vigilant enough to pick up on any data which can possibly place doubt on any conclusions made.

It is this strict set of principles that cements our faith their work is both innovative and sound.

In 2012, the supposed but much disputed prospect of 'climate change' was dealt a blow when the very scientists who advocated the idea (yet never provided any credible evidence) hoped to seek immunity from prosecution for their actions.

The *United Nations Framework Convention on Climate Change* (UNFCCC), the organisation responsible for managing a global cap-and-trade system worth billions of dollars for carbon emissions projects around the world, were for some reason or another seeking diplomatic and legal immunity from challenges such as possible conflicts of interest in their duties.

Aside from the vast money-making potential in perpetuating this long term state of fear, it surely is not the remit of this revered profession - but why look to seek protection unless of course dishonest practice is knowingly taking place.

When even scientists who wish to work for an organisation which promotes world peace and unity can be swayed by political or personal agendas, the question must be asked that when even the morally incorruptible and intelligently superior individuals amongst us can set aside the greater good, is there anybody left we can trust?

Scientists and the Art of Marketing

The late Stephen Henry Schneider (1945 - 2010) was the Professor of Environmental Biology and Global Change at Stanford University and served as a consultant to federal agencies and White House staff in the Richard Nixon, Jimmy Carter, Ronald Reagan, George H. W. Bush, Bill Clinton, George W. Bush and the Barack Obama administrations.
His research included modeling of the atmosphere, climate change, and "the relationship of biological systems to global climate change".

In 1971, Schneider was the second author on a Science paper with S. I. Rasool titled "Atmospheric Carbon Dioxide and Aerosols: Effects of Large Increases on Global Climate". The paper concluded:

"However, it is projected that man's potential to pollute will increase 6 to 8-fold in the next 50 years. If this increased rate of injection... should raise the present background opacity by a factor of 4, our calculations suggest a decrease in global temperature by as much as 3.5 °C. Such a large decrease in the average temperature of Earth, sustained over a period of few years, is believed to be sufficient to trigger an ice age. However, by that time, nuclear power may have largely replaced fossil fuels as a means of energy production".

Schneider had previously commented about the frustrations and difficulties involved with assessing and communicating scientific ideas. In a January 2002 Scientific American article, he wrote:

"I readily confess a lingering frustration: uncertainties so infuse the issue of climate change that it is still impossible to rule out either mild or catastrophic outcomes, let alone provide confident probabilities for all the claims and counterclaims made about environmental problems. Even the most credible international assessment body, the Intergovernmental Panel on Climate Change (IPCC), has refused to attempt subjective probabilistic estimates of future temperatures. This has forced politicians to make their own guesses about the likelihood of various degrees of global warming".

In 1989, Schneider addressed the challenge scientists face trying to communicate complex and important issues. This citation below had sometimes been used by critics to accuse him of supporting misuse of science for political goals:

"On the one hand, as scientists we are ethically bound to the scientific method, in effect promising to tell the truth, the whole truth, and nothing but - which means that we must include all the doubts, the caveats, the ifs, ands, and buts. On the other hand, we are not just scientists but human beings as well. And like most people we'd like to see the world a better place, which in this context translates into our working to reduce the risk of potentially disastrous climatic change. To do that we need to get some broadbased support, to capture the public's imagination. That, of course, entails getting loads of media coverage. So we have to offer up scary scenarios, make simplified, dramatic statements, and make little mention of any doubts we might have. This 'double ethical bind' we frequently find ourselves in cannot be solved by any formula. Each of us has to decide what the right balance is between being effective and being honest. I hope that means being both".
(Quoted in Discover, pp. 45–48, Oct. 1989)

See Appendix for Sources.   Image Source:- Movie: Back to the Future (1985) Starring: Christopher Lloyd and Michael J Fox

163

There has been an accelerating upward trend of 'women in the workplace' and it's somewhat inevitable, given their superior work ethic and drive, that women could soon outnumber men in professional careers. Discuss the long-term consequences of a female-dominant workforce?

Background

Recent studies have shown that young males are feeling increasingly insecure about their roles in society and their future in the workplace, and as such, many are putting their careers on hold to stay at home. The number of so called 'house husbands' according to analysis by the *Office of National Statistics*, has seen numbers almost triple to 62,000 between 1996-2011.

In contrast, 50 years ago women were still considered second class citizens in the workplace, where they had very few rights and could be dismissed from their job simply because of the natural demands of pregnancy. Women were then only seen as mothers and housewives and certainly not business professionals.

In the US, a Department of Labour study showed that in 1950, about one in three women participated in the workforce. However, by 1998, nearly three of every five women of working age were in the workforce, and this looks to be an irreversible trend.

Facts and Examples

• The need to switch/share primary responsibilities for home and family matters means there will be an adverse impact on work attendance. Employers will be challenged to provide family-friendly solutions for working men/women who need flexibility for childcare and care for the elderly.

• A survey by the *British Association of Anger Management* revealed that an increasing number of women in positions of power are bullying colleagues and employees. It was commented that "high-flying women are now encountering the psychological problems that have historically blighted the lives of men at the top. The main reason for an increase in anger is their inability to deal with stress."

Honourable Mentions:- Dr Julia Harris DDS; Lewis Asquith, a jacuzzi and some colleagues.
Dishonourable Mentions:- Admiral Helena Cain; Naomi Campbell, Dr Glenda Stone and her 27 PA's.

FOR

Equality. § Oppressed women tend to endlessly spawn children just to keep themselves occupied. § Women tend to be more hard-working and loyal. § Mutual respect between partners. § Extra-marital affairs are good for the soul. § Workplaces would become warmer and caring places to be. § Sympathetic and understanding of family commitments. § Nicer to look at.

AGAINST

Increasing importance of a full-time female role model for very young children. § Office politics and hissy-fits over nothing. § Long absences due to pregnancy and maternity. § Man's sexist refusal to accept a female superior. § Sexual tension. § House husbands. § Each hive has only room for a single Queen bee. § Women are more susceptible to stress and depression. § That time of that month.

I can't make head nor tail of this credit card statement. I don't remember getting any refunds last month.

That's the end of year accounts dear !

Be Controversial

• The most intelligent amongst us tend to be those who are uncomfortable in the company of women, or reluctantly feel intimidated by beautiful women.

• With only so many jobs to go round, unemployment can be solved overnight if all the happily married women resigned.

• Conceivably, children would be more grounded, happier and turn out better if they had their father caring for them from a young age.

Image Source:- TV Show: Arrested Development (2003) Starring: Portia de Rossi and Jessica Walter

Chapter D

"Have nothing to do with the evil deeds of darkness, but rather expose them."
Ephesians 5:11

Developments in Food Science have now formulated a new form of Alcohol which is neither detrimental to health nor does it trigger a hangover -
With a 'drinking culture' now generally practiced by all, would the world now become a less stressful place?

Background, Facts and Miscellaneous

Alcohol is a drug that has the immediate effect of altering mood. It can make people feel relaxed, happy and even euphoric, but ironically, alcohol is actually classified as a depressant.

Drinking too much can leave you with a hangover the next day, but regularly drinking more than the recommended intake can also cause long-term damage to the body's organs.

Discussion Viewpoints:-
Letting your hair down with no adverse effects can certainly destress your mind and give the daily release the mind needs. § People never realise the importance to destress and will always let things simmer or get on top of them. § Will just make existing moderate to heavy drinkers consume more. § Better social lives. § If alcohol didn't exist as a 'vice', then people would look for something else to feed their rebellious channel. Thus drinking would become less attractive to young adults and will instead crave an alternative 'vice', and drug-use may well be it. § Declining family-time. § Could such advancements just be harbouring adverse long-term physical and mental health build-ups - short term profits being the company remit.

Future Reform:- Such is the propensity for humans to abuse resources, that a weekly non-transferable ration of alcohol units has been assigned to each adult. By introducing such a restriction, it is hoped would make persons aware of the health/mind benefit allocated to them and will be more open to utilising it rather than allowing it to expire - leading to a less stressed population.

Image Source:- Movie: The Mist (2007) Starring: William Sadler and Marcia Gay Harden

With the thousands of Disappearances and supposed Alien Abductions around the globe every year, rather than being outrightly dismissed, do the high numbers tend to suggest that there's indeed some systematic and controlled extraction of some kind under way?

Background, Facts and Miscellaneous

Of the 250,000+ missing persons reported every year in the UK, many are never heard of or seen ever again. The figure stands at around 16,000 persons currently missing without trace, though admittedly, a proportion were either abducted, killed or had voluntarily left a life behind, but the number still appears extraordinarily high.

So where do they go? What happened to the bodies? Why are so many disappearances out of character and out of the blue? Are there more serial killers and paedophile rings out there than we care to imagine?

All valid questions, but let's think out of the box and speculate the far-fetched theory that a persons body is extracted from the world via supernatural forces, disappearing without trace.

Possible Scenario:-

With many seemingly credible accounts of abductions, there is a widespread belief amongst a certain community that supernatural beings travel here to undertake human experiments or abduct them back to their worlds. Is it conceivable that persons are randomly selected for assessment, where their personal memories are scanned to determine their *goodness* factor, and only those who've lived honourably or possess a good soul are permitted to leave these 'evil lands'?

Further Discussion Points:-
• Should abductees who lived to tell their tale feel aggrieved that they were not deemed worthy enough to be one of the 'chosen ones'?
• Do some humans prove alien impregnation?

Image Source:- Movie: Independence Day (1996) Starring: Randy Quaid

With bribery and illegal commission payments coming in many forms, is the 'Backhanded Backhander' the most devious and cunning of them all?

Background, Facts and Miscellaneous

Modern humans have long had this obscene craving for money and when an opportunity comes up to wring any last cent for themselves, even moreso when the *little people* can be trampled on.

This behaviour exhibits to such an extent that it has unfortunately infringed on almost every facet of our lives and has even become accepted practice in the world of business where the clamour to offer or receive bribes/commission has become the norm rather than the exception.

The idea that corruption exists at every level of an organisation is indeed widely and openly accepted around the globe yet there have been ever-improving measures to try to curb such practices in light of the growing discontentment amongst the law-abiding society and the unfair consequences on the poorest in society.

Though all's well and good in having watertight measures to eradicate corruption but what if corruptive acts take place where no legitimate contractual relationship exists and individuals have concocted up sophisticated methods to plunder from their own employers?

If you were to take a cynical look at any regular business transaction that takes place involving large amounts, there is a decent chance you'll be able to identify an angle which could have been exploited to facilitate a 'backhanded backhander' (remember, we can be an ingenious bunch when we need to be).

To put this to the test, evaluate the real-life cases opposite and assess whether the fictional scenarios put forward were a missed opportunity by the parties involved?

Missed Opportunities for the Backhanded Backhander

Sex, Lies and Telephones

Sotirios Hatzigakis, the former Greek justice minister, admitted in 2010 that while in office he gave 30 friends and relatives free mobile telephones which were subsequently used to call premium-rate sex lines. With some clocking up to £10,000 a month in calls to the sex lines, the scandal once uncovered was found to have eventually cost the taxpayer up to £20 million.

A Fictional Scenario:- Mr Hatzigakis had made a secret agreement with the sex line operators informing of a method to legitimately extort large sums of taxpayers money, with the potential of making unqueried and unchallenged millions. The agreement constituted that a substantial volume of calls be made to a custom designated premium phone line (setup with minimum initial cost and almost no overheads as there would be a mute response). The premium rate for these calls will be set at the maximum possible and all revenue would be split 50:50 between the operator and the phone holders.

Thus, it was in the interest of Mr Hatzigakis to procure as many government phones as possible and recruit as many 'commission-loving friends' as possible.

Pension Pots

In 2009, it was revealed that former RBS boss Fred Goodwin could have been awarded just half of the £16 million pension pot he was eventually given. It transpired that some of the award was discretionary, despite RBS giving the government a false impression that the amount was an unavoidable legal commitment. The entitlement to an undiscounted pension from the age of 50 stemmed from a decision of RBS that he should be treated as retiring at the request of the employer. Had those concerned decided instead simply to terminate the contract, as RBS could have chosen to do with 12 months' notice, the right to an undiscounted pension would not have applied.

A Fictional Scenario:- Fred the Shred had made a secret agreement with those deciding on the final package of a method to legitimately divert some of the bank bailout funds directly into their pockets too.

The agreement stipulated that the person at the very top (Sir Tom McKillop) would request he retire and the respective government minister (Lord Myners) would sign it off, as long as the additional £8 million be split equally between Fred, Tom and Myners. It was further agreed that all parties would feign ignorance and blame each other to the extent that an investigation would prove futile.

The finest biscuits money can buy

It was revealed that the Department of Health spent over £100,000 on tea and biscuits in just three months. The huge amount spent is understood to have been spent under a pre-arranged Private Finance Initiative (PFI) contract.

A Fictional Scenario:- The PFI agreement actually privately stipulated that any public official spending extortionate amounts on perishable items and/or those that can prove difficult to track, would receive half of the profits in return for the deliveries be falsely verified as being complete.

This potential £400,000 profit per annum proved lucrative for the poorly paid public servant.

Authors Note:-

The author wishes to reaffirm the fact that these are all fictitious scenarios and have been merely conceived to illustrate the financial opportunity that was missed had both parties been corruptible.

Branching Off

In 2012, the Lloyds Banking Group agreed to sell hundreds of branches to the Co-operative Bank when it accepted their bid, which could be for as little as £350 million. This was despite a rival offer just a year earlier for around £1.7billion. As part of the extraordinary deal, Lloyds were also giving the Co-op £1.5billion in capital meaning that the bailed out bank could end up taking a loss of more than £1billion from it.

A Fictional Scenario:- Despite the correct market valuation of £1.7 billion, Lloyds and Co-op executives entered into a secret agreement of making the transaction at a value of £1 billion. This meant a paper loss of £700 million for Lloyds and a saving of £700 million for Co-op and its long suffering shareholders.

However, not one to pass up the opportunity of raiding the bottomless pot of a banking bailout, the bank bosses decided to publicly sanction the deal at £350 million. With the official transaction completed at this level, the remainder of the concealed level of £1 billion, £650 million, would eventually find its way scattered evenly amongst the offshore coffers of the Lloyds banking executives.

The Fergie Bebes

In 2010, the great Manchester United signed the player 'Bebe' from Portuguese first division club Vitória having only played six pre-season friendlies, for the astonishing sum of €9m. Astonishing not only because he had only played competitively in the Portuguese third division but that he moved to Vitória on a free transfer just months earlier.

A Fictional Scenario:- Sir Alex Ferguson began to get fed up of finding great players and then selling them at a huge profit, only for the proceeds to top up the owners accounts or go towards paying off the huge debt commitments the club is currently under.

Therefore, liaising with a crooked football agent, they orchestrated the transfer of a player well above the market value with the proceeds being split 50:50 between Sir Alex and the agent - with the extortion taking the form of the agents fee being a remarkable 40%.

With the agents fee amounting to €3.6m and being duly split accordingly, it effectively meant that the owners paid Sir Alex an under the counter €1.8m (for which he rightly believed was his due anyway) and the agent the same amount for a player they should have got on a free transfer.

Risk-free Strategy

In 2011, Kweku Adoboli, was accused of gambling away £1.4bn while working as a trader for Swiss bank UBS. At one point, his trades are alleged to been at risk of causing the bank losses of up to12 billion US dollars (£7.5 billion).

A Fictional Scenario:- A regular trading counterparty for Adoboli was Goldman Sachs and their head of Equity Trading was 'Mr Bankstain' who advised Mr Adoboli that the short position the UBS trader had undertaken against GS would soon result in a £300 million profit for UBS (Mr Bankstain/GS had just become party to information of an upcoming cycle and an upturn in the stocks fortunes). Mr Bankstain then proposed that if Adoboli not only cancelled out his position (and consequently any profit) but also took up a reverse long position of greater magnitude and risk against GS, his employers GS have agreed that 50% of the profit made from this new position will be passed to Adoboli discretely.

Therefore, depending on the timing of the pre-meditated upturn, the closing price of the position could mean a profit to GS of between £1 and £4 billion if Adoboli traded up to the same limits he'd have been previously.

With lives literally in the palm of doctors hands, should the GMC appreciate their civic responsibility to serve and protect the public, and afford themselves the luxury of applying a 'guilty until proven innocent' mantra when overseeing tribunals of those medical professionals suspected of not being fit to practice?

Background

The purpose of the *General Medical Council* (GMC) is to protect, promote and maintain the health and safety of the public by ensuring proper standards are adhered to in the practice of medicine.

One of the main functions is to 'deal firmly and fairly with doctors whose fitness to practice is in doubt'. Any doctor that fails to meet these standards, powers can be enforced to protect patients from harm - and when necessary, by removing the doctor from the register and their right to practice medicine.

However, recent disclosures of many that have continued to practice despite overwhelming evidence to the contrary, have raised serious concerns about the system of regulating doctor's conduct. With the high risk of highly incompetent doctors or those of a sinister disposition being able to cause long term harm to a patient, is it time to adopt a safety first approach and assume guilt unless proven otherwise?

Facts and Examples

• *Dr Navin Zala* sexually abused female patients over a 20-year period but was able to carry on as a GP despite facing at least nine different complaints, a series of police investigations and four criminal trials.
• *Mr Richard Neale*, a gynaecologist whose botched operations in the UK left a trail of women with life-long complications and recurring pain, was revealed to have been previously struck off in Canada for serious professional incompetence leading to two deaths. Disturbingly, the GMC were informed of this 12 years before he was finally struck off but remarkably took the decision to take no action.
• After being suspended in both 2004 and 2006, the GMC saw it fit to suspend *Dr Arun Rauniar* again in 2008 after finding him guilty of multiple failings.
• The GMC are currently considering proposals to allow fitness-to-practice hearings to take place behind closed doors. Such a system would mean doctors would escape public exposure unless struck off.

FOR	**AGAINST**
Will encourage doctors to be more vigilant in their treatment of patients, resulting in ultimately better responsible care. § Current system is clearly inadequate and prone to abuse. § Old boys club allowing suspects to walk free and continue with an unblemished record. § Innocence can be easily proven rather than trying to prove guilt beyond reasonable doubt.	Will end up with no doctors on the rota. § Dream scenario for dishonest or disgruntled patients. § Defies the basis for all fair legal systems if guilt is assumed foremost. § Doctors unfairly suspended will sought career moves or foreign shores. § System as it is currently functions well and such measures will discourage future budding doctors if injustice becomes rampant.

Now, let's lift that top up and see those bad boys...

Image Source:- Movie: The Cannonball Run (1981) Starring: Jack Elam

Be Controversial

Wearing the Cloak of Invincibility

Should a person who has obtained a medical degree automatically afford them the right to be eternally held as intelligent, open minded, upstanding professionals. Or are they like the rest of us, susceptible to acting dishonestly or giving into our desires, when opportunity arises.

Should a deep probing 'fitness to practice' psychological test be undertaken during the medical school application procedure?

Why is Banking Fraud (Online/Loan/Credit Card) allowed to brazenly continue and even flourish, encouraged by the banks perceived blasé and relaxed approach to it?

Background

As technological advancements have supposedly made online banking and payments more secure and with millions of pounds invested in ensuring the security and safety of online banking, one would have assumed that banking fraud would by now have been a relic from our financial past.

The reality, it seems, is rather different where the increased ease of accessibility, virtual cash movements and online banking have opened up all new avenues for the criminal underworld to plunder from under, in other words, to be able to steal from unsuspecting victims and then casually walk away (from their PC).

But are we missing the bigger picture here - do banks purposely allow such fraud to take place as they are in fact insured against fraud. Or are our banks under 'instructions' from external entities who fund the lax effort - these entities being governments who stimulate spending in this creative way?

Facts and Examples

• Consumer spending is the most critical element of a growing economy, but when this fails, government initiatives are in place to ensure that it is given a push in the right direction. Recent examples have included economic stimulus packages (payments, tax relief etc) and Quantitative Easing (printing extra money, albeit electronically).

• With the move to smartphone use, the banks have already jumped over hoops to provide loosely guarded online banking apps, before the security of such devices can even be assessed or safely determined.

• In 2010, a gang were charged over an online banking fraud netting tens of millions over the space of just a few months using the infamous *Zeus* trojan.

• Credit card fraud in the UK in 2011 reached £341m, a fall from the 2008 figure of £610m.

• Online banking fraud was put at £59.7m in 2009.

• Before pin-enabled cards, why weren't the customers photo printed on the back of a Credit Card?

FOR

Fraud is so widespread that it's impossible to monitor and secure effectively. § Procedures are constantly reviewed and measures put in place to try and stay one step ahead. § Banking and international transactions are considerably different and more complex from 10 years ago. § The internet generation will insist on ease of access and everything online - shunning overly secure means.

AGAINST

Banks have insured themselves from fraud, so have very little interest, if any, in prevention of fraudulent activity. § Fraudulent activity means more transactions and more money (be it virtual) freely flowing through the economy and in bad times, banking fraud in any form is actively encouraged. § An organised systematic transfer of financial stock away from the western world.

Image Source:- Movie: Batman & Robin (1997)

Future Reform

• Should we move away altogether from online banking activity and not run blind into a world of online banks, virtual money, direct debits, smartphone banking and countless passwords, passcodes and memorable questions/answers which are anyway duplicated elsewhere?
• Should international banks pool together to monitor and alert when there is an abnormally high activity of incoming funds into a certain bank account, especially from multiple sources, indicating live dishonest activity?

How did Man ever get convinced that the concept of 'marriage' would make their lives happier, despite women naturally craving commitment and men being the opposite. Has the original pledge been conveniently forsaken with Man now wondering how and why they were hoodwinked into something so unnatural for them?

Background, Facts and Miscellaneous

Many centuries ago, men and women lived together in blissful unity and society was happy and joyful, with each gender having clearly defined roles and also distinct desires.

Then one day, Woman collectively managed to convince Man that something was amiss from their lives and eventually the concept of lifelong commitment and marriage was born, and so it was that everyone lived happily ever after.

But with the emergence of feminism, Woman now desire equality in the workplace as well as the home, and Man has duly given in to them.

But has Man forgotten about the *deep magic from the dawn of time* or has Woman conveniently allowed it be forgotten - with Man now giving up their freedom to be stranded in an equal roles relationship without any of the pledged benefits?

In the renowned CS Lewis tale *The Lion, the Witch and the Wardrobe*, it tells the story of a Man who ruled the land in peace but was exiled to death due to the deep magic with the Woman exclaiming *"And so that human creature is mine. His life is forfeit to me. His blood is my property..."*. But the Man had forgotten about the *deeper magic* and as such its revelation would eventually lead to Man's resurrection and peace across the lands.

If we were to draw parallels to this text, one could say that marriage is the *land*, feminism being the *deep magic* and the original pledge (see opposite) was the *deeper magic*. Discuss?

"No matter how good she may look you can be sure that somebody, somewhere is sick of putting up with her sh*t"
~ A famous philosopher, perhaps Aristotle

The Original Pledge

Dear Man,

Thy knows thou are designed to procreate and are not wired to commit to a single physical relationship for the rest of your lives, but hear us out.

If thou commits to thee for the rest of your days, thy will care for thou, never argue with thou, take your word as gospel, bear and raise your children, cook and clean and keep a good home and generally be subservient to your needs.

For thou, I merely pledge thee in return for thou taking this burden off my parents hands and putting up with my monthly cycles and irrational mood swings, that thou promises to keep a roof over our heads, provide us with an household income and pledge unwavering commitment to our happiness and wellbeing.

And thy further pledge that thy will never have a headache and thou will always be rewarded with your favourite slippers and a warm home cooked meal at the end of your hard working day.

Yours Forever,
Woman

Honourable Mention :-

"Why... I don't get it. Even if the p*ssy was great and sparks shot out the woman's ass and cannons blared and the mountains crumbled and the seas roared, no p*ssy is worth committing the rest of your damn life to!"
~ Eddie Murphy, Raw

Source: By the Author   Image Source:- Eddie Murphy Raw

Are the lower castes of Southern India accurately representative of the dumbest people in the region, therefore justifying the ethos of the Hindu Caste System and why such folk hold the degrading classification and fully deserving of their low social status and treatment?

Background, Facts and Miscellaneous

The *Hindu Caste* system is a rigidly enforced class structure that has lasted for well over 2000 years, where a person's caste was determined by birth only and traditionally dictated their role in society. But is it fair to classify groups in such a way or is it unjustly based on primitive principles to create, preserve and force a social order regardless of wealth, integrity, intellect or professional status?

For example, take this case in point:- examine the structure opposite and what seems evidently clear is how easily such a forced name-based social structure could break down, and allow one to free itself from its shackles. Well, evident to most anyway, and therein seems to lie the whole justification for a caste system perhaps. It correctly distinguished the intelligently inferior from those blessed with an ounce of it*.

Further Discussion Point:-
Could this *Caste* system conceivably be considered an early proponent of an applied Eugenics ideal, based on the fact that such systems assume genetic traits are inherent through the generations and remain so throughout the family line.

By identifying these traits centuries earlier and then establishing a system to mark the distinction between groups, it allowed for an ability to efficiently discriminate against the exponentially increasing population of the *inferior* people. Sound familiar!?!!

* If you're of one of the lower caste denominations, then you'll probably need spelling out that by 'it', the author was referring to the word 'intelligence'. Don't mention it!

The Confines of being Lower Caste

The Traditional Caste System of India

◦ The *Hindu Caste System* is comparable to class structures in other countries, except that the Indian system has been rigidly enforced throughout the subcontinent until the adoption of the Indian constitution in 1949, which outlawed the caste system. However, it remains a deeply ingrained social structure, particularly in rural India.

◦ It is a system where people are divided by family and birth into certain social and economic positions.

◦ Traditionally, the system would have dictated your occupation, choice of spouse and many other aspects in life.

The Caste System in Kerala

If we were to simplify the caste system existing in Kerala to that of just the highest caste (Nair) and the lowest 'untouchable' caste (Ezhava), we are able to illustrate how the 'Surname' of a person was used as the only distinguishing factor. The upper castes would all have the surname 'Nair' whereas the lower castes would have traditional low-caste names but also had to conform to the rule that children would adopt their fathers' first name as their surname (which meant family lineage as an Ezhava was negligent or was perceived to be an wholly inappropriate privilege).

Therefore, citizens of Kerala could comfortably conclude those that belong and were descended from the superior higher caste and those deserving of disdain and ill-treatment by distinguishing them quite easily from the surname. A quiet efficient foolproof system, one would say, one that makes all that hard work centuries ago of putting these distinctions into law a worthwhile one.

The Exodus

Now, as Indians left these shores to settle abroad in more prosperous western countries, there was a single distinct difference from the one Ezhava families had to conform to back home, the need to assume the fathers' first name as the surname. Across the western world, there was a single well-heeled convention that all immigrants were expected to adhere to and that was that the Surname was an essential means to help identify family members, encourage family cohesion and identify possible heritage.

Maintaining Order

Now, unfortunately, the upper castes didn't take too well to the idea that a caste system was not accommodated for in legislation and was legally unenforceable, therefore were subject to the same treatment as any other citizen. Not taking this lying down, they managed to main-tain through the decades a continued shunning of the lower castes, affording themselves an artificially elevated social status (albeit only amongst the Kerala Hindu community).

And thus, the Nair and Ezhava communities lived in peace side by side, with Ezhavas content with their mistreatment and the look of disdain from their Kerala brothers.

And so it should come to pass, that it can and always will remain this way (or see below for the blatantly obvious).

"...what you said about structures becoming shackles? I know what you mean now but I'm going to go ahead and blindly and ignorantly accept it"
~ John Blake, 2012

Answer: Now, as 80% of the readership of this book have no doubt gathered, that by simply naming a child 'Nair' and then adhering to the first name=surname tradition one last time, would then ensure that a child born into an Ezhava bloodline now has the upper caste symbol, the Nair surname. And without question, the children brought up under western influence and upbringing with no real romantic sentiment to Kerala tradition, would adhere to the western tradition of keeping the surname as is. This would therefore mean that the 'Nair' surname would forever also be associated amongst lower caste families as well and with the distinction now blurred, the caste system that simmered under the surface in western countries would slowly disappear.

Similarly, if centuries ago in Kerala, the 'Nair' name became the most popular first names given by Ezhava parents two generations in a row, then a spate of individuals going by the name of 'Nair Nair' would have eventually rid the society of this caste distinction and its degrading policies.

Image Source:- Movie: The Dark Knight Rises (2012) Starring: Joseph Gordon-Levitt
Source: By the Author

With the emergence of 'virtual' points of reference and a consequent decreasing reliance on physical sources of information, can we expect over time that disinformation and the pseudo-sciences (mumbo jumbo) will eventually become matter of fact?

Background

Disinformation is defined as intentionally false or inaccurate information that is spread deliberately, the act of feeding deceptively false statements to convince someone of untruth(s). It aims to manipulate audiences by either discrediting conflicting information or supporting false conclusions.

Information had almost always been the province of mainstream media and the information published had to be credible as their stock in trade was accuracy. These institutions always upheld strict procedures and protocols in place for verifying that accuracy.

An internet age later, suddenly anyone could publish anything. The careful and cultivated control of information devolved into 'information anarchy'.

The dangers we now face are that the people of tomorrow will only know the internet as the source of reference and they will likely never discriminate or question the source or cross-referenced sources.

Facts and Examples

• The WikiLeaks Cable leaks of 2011 took place during the famed Middle East uprising. Were some deliberately leaked (or even altered) by the US government in order to stoke the fires of discontent in the Middle East region?

• A quote floating around the internet attributed to Lord MacAulay in a speech to the British Parliament in 1835 seems to have no authoritative source whatsoever. Though authentic looking, together with some native language, the format can only be described as a feeble attempt at a mock-up article from a newspaper of the time. Its viral success has, however, since served the political views of certain elements well.

Dishonourable Mentions:- Some sources used in this book; Loose Change; Alternative Medicine; Boiler Rooms and the websites of 'investable' companies.
Honourable Mentions:- Uncyclopedia; John Seigenthaler Sr.

FOR	AGAINST
Past events in the public domain known to be just far-fetched conspiracy theories may actually be based on fact, but government tactics have ensured that the truth will be lost over time. Todays internet age means these counter-truth tactics wouldn't succeed as easily. eg. Roswell actually occurred but the public were manipulated into believing it was just an outlandish conspiracy theory.	Future generations will be more tech-savvy, being more aware of cross-referencing sources, ascertaining any bias and scrutinising any attributed quotes. § Over time, we will be using a core base of credible internet sites and less reliant on the random google search. § E-Books should never be allowed to replace physical books as the former is susceptible to tampering.

LORD MACAULAY'S ADDRESS TO THE BRITISH PARLIAMENT 2 FEBRUARY, 1835

"I have travelled across the length and breadth of India and I have not seen one person who is a beggar, who is a thief such wealth I have seen in this country, such high moral values, people of such caliber, that I do not think we would ever conquer this country, unless we break the very backbone of this nation, which is her spiritual and cultural heritage, and, therefore, I propose that we replace her old and ancient education system, her culture, for if the Indians think that all that is foreign and English is good and greater than their own, they will lose their selfesteem, their native culture and they will become what we want them, a truly dominated nation."

Be Controversial

There is an excellent book by Damian Thompson called *Counterknowledge* which outlines the dangers and ease of accepting fictional 'truths'.

However, is the book itself actually commissioned by the higher powers as a knee-jerk reaction to the fact that the general public are no longer readily accepting false truths which had been previously been packaged as actual truths. The book's real intention actually being to effectively countering counter-counterknowledge!?!!

Why did the Vatican withhold the 'Third Secret of Fátima' until the year 2000, despite Lúcia's declaration that it should be released to the public after 1960?

Background

The *Three Secrets of Fátima* consist of a series of visions and prophecies allegedly given by an apparition of the Blessed Virgin Mary to three young Portuguese children, Lúcia, Jacinta and Francisco in the year 1917. The apparition, also known as *Our Lady of Fátima*, is said to have entrusted the children with three secrets.

The first two secrets prophesied the two world wars and also provided a vision of *Hell* awaiting the sinner or the non-believers. However, one should note that this foretelling only took place after the second world war had commenced(!).

The Third Secret was finally revealed in the year 2000, more than 50 years after the secret was first written down by Lúcia declaring at the time that it could only be disclosed after 1960. However, rather than releasing it, the Vatican published an official press release stating that it was "most probable the Secret would remain, forever, under absolute seal."

Facts and Examples

• The four-page handwritten text of the Third Secret proved to be not much of a revelation at all as no mystery or future apocalyptic event was unveiled. Considering the speculation it had stirred throughout the decades and the Vatican's own press release supporting such, the mind boggles as to why the Vatican had withheld it for so long.

• Critics have noted that the Third Secret had always been associated with being written on a 'single sheet of paper'. This apparent inconsistency could suggest that the actual secret remains "under absolute seal."

• There is documented evidence that the secret was written in the form of a signed letter. The text released by the Vatican was not in the form of a letter.

• The then *Cardinal Joseph Ratzinger*, commentated that the purpose of the vision is not to show a film of an irrevocably fixed future: it's meant to mobilise the forces of change in the right direction.

• Embedded was a call to conversion and penance.

FOR

No actual big revelation and therefore would not have met the public expectations, exonerating believers of Christianity. § A secret so macabre and disturbing that it must never be revealed. Even today, the true secret remains. (What could it possibly be?) § There were only honourable intentions to delay so humans absorb the other secrets and submit to God's will, for the good of humanity.

AGAINST

Typical of religious institutions to promise acts of divine intervention but never deliver. Where is this indisputable proof that the world is craving? § Waited for a world war to begin before releasing a version predicting it, thus cementing the existence of the Virgin Mary and the only 'Truth'. § Why was it kept in the possession confines of a religious institution, who had no legal jurisdiction.

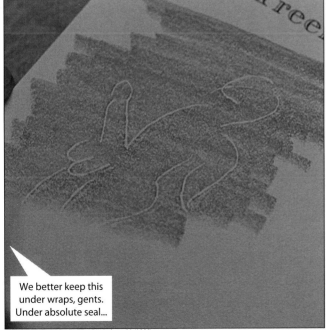

We better keep this under wraps, gents. Under absolute seal...

Image Source:- Movie: The Big Lebowski (1998)

Wildcard View

Is it conceivable that the the Third Secret was to reveal that it was all just one elaborate hoax, admitting it was concocted up by her parents, under directions from the Church.

A famous hoax of the 20th century, the *Cottingley Fairies*, also involved two young cousins and the appearance of supernatural entities. When did this take place, well, only the same year as the one *Our Lady of Fátima* supposedly graced us with her presence! The confession came a mere 5 years before the conspirators died.

Many of us would feel pity if law-abiding citizens thieved food in the course of 'desperately needing to feed the kids'. But what if a new legal precedent was set, whereby granting an exemption from prosecution for such crimes - discuss the long term implications and if the foundations of law will be undermined from such a courageous stance?

Background, Facts and Miscellaneous

The year is 2025 and with the developed western nations in serious economic turmoil, the real threat of long term unemployment and financial struggles have become all too real, with many young families suffering more than most.

As is expected with any society/economy falling into disarray, crime and disorder has been on the rise. But what the authorities have had to confront ever more prominently in recent years is the moral dilemma about punishing those who steal food primarily only to feed their children.

To the surprise of all the emerging nations, the UK government announce an unprecedented move in the field of law - a proposal that prosecution for crimes of this nature will be waived. Should the House of Lords ratify this exemption or outright refuse to condone this act of lunacy?

All these conditions for the waiver must be met:-
• Only basic essential food (eg. Bread, milk, pasta etc) and clothing items (eg. nappies, winter items etc) are permitted to be stolen under this scheme;
• The theft took place within a multinational supermarket (where possible) and that had posted >£10 million net profit* in the previous tax year;
• Short of selling their habited property, all avenues to generate enough cash flow are exhausted;
• Family assistance has already been maximised;
• Salary or state aid has not been frittered away recklessly on non-essential items (such as gambling, private education, cigarettes, alcohol etc).
* All shoplifting crimes will be considered exempt from being investigated/prosecuted if said victim (corporation) had displayed an immoral act of corporation tax avoidance the previous year.

Image Source:- Movie: True Romance (1993) Starring: Dennis Hopper

187

With Human Cloning now being a trusted medical concept and Human Evolution proving not to be necessarily 'progressive', should we proceed to undertake mass re-cloning of the minds and bodies of those individuals who have proved to be exceptionally good human beings and/or are intelligently superior to the average person?

Background

• Human cloning technology is the creation of a genetically identical copy of a human. *Somatic-Cell Nuclear Transfer* (SCNT) is the laboratory technique for creating a clone embryo from a donor nucleus, potentially allowing the creation of endless copies.

• *Devolution* is the notion that a species can change into a more 'primitive' form over time, a degenerate form of their ancestors.

Recent technological advancements have allowed for a clone to develop within an artificial womb under controlled laboratory conditions, effectively removing the last barrier permitting large scale reproduction.

In order to address the pressing concern of devolution, an active programme to 'multiply good genes' is proposed, where human clones will be mass-produced from 'perfect' donors. These clones will then only be placed with those deemed to have the capability of being loving caring parents.

Facts and Examples

• The criteria for being considered as a donor for 'multiplication' is extremely challenging, focussed and very strict. The process is optimised such that only those with an all-round good set of genes are admitted.

• There is no minimum number for successful candidates (as just one person can be re-cloned many times) therefore the selection process need not be compromised. However, to ensure a diverse clone population and avoid potential future inter-breeding issues, long term success of the project requires a significant number of diversified candidates to proceed.

• Candidates put forward for the selection process must also possess the following attributes; Good looks, above-average height, well proportioned body and a healthy attitude to sports and well-being.

• It is envisaged that at least 20% of the next generation will be born the 'perfect human specimen'.

Honourable Mentions:- Sylvester Stallone; Anthony Jay Mahavorick; Mélissa Theuriau; Éowyn of Rohan.

FOR

Gene Pool has to be aided in order to counter human devolution. § Can push future generations to do better in all aspects of life, to fit the criteria. § Can help to maintain a healthy contingent of the 'indigenous' people. § Solves the heartache for those not able to have children. § Clones becoming sperm-donors. § Counters the rampant overbreeding by the lower classes.

AGAINST

Conventional pregnancies and normal babies soon become a thing of the past. § Clones have an unfair advantage over regular persons. § Such high-level intervention can inspire other countries/regimes to adopt similar approaches for bad intentions. § A man's role is diminished further. § A dormant but yet undiscovered 'evil' gene. § The mothers' bond. § Ticking timebombs.

So... Where do I sign up?

Be Controversial

With its general dislike of dark skin and a perceived negative perception from the rest of the world, India will undertake a programme to eradicate dark skin from its gene pool. Targetting the predominantly 'dark' state of *Kerala*, women will be banned altogether from having children and an even ratio of light-skinned male and female clones will then be placed with willing parents. Decades from now will see the fruition of these plans, with the superior fairer skin adorning *Gods Own Country*.

Image Source:- Movie: American Psycho (2000) Starring: Christian Bale

Do we need a radical rethink on how a free National Health Service can sustain itself and how best it can continue serving the general public, encouraging good responsible healthy living - Should all self-inflicted diseases and conditions now be turned away outright?

Background

Professor *Tim Evans*, lead fellow at the Royal College of Physicians', stated in 2011: "*All hospital patients deserve to receive safe, high-quality, sustainable care delivered in an appropriate setting by respectful, compassionate, expert health professionals. We must act now to make the drastic changes required to provide the care they deserve.*"

The truth in that statement is abundantly clear and though the NHS is overstretched and in financial disarray, a revolutionary hard-hitting approach is certainly necessary to preserve such ideals in a service provided for free - a service becoming open to abuse and where a sense of entitlement has slowly arisen.

To counter this, it has been proposed that all self-inflicted conditions and preventable diseases will be refused treatment forthwith such that the free health service is only available to those who deserve to be treated and aims to relieve long term pressure on services by discouraging irresponsible lifestyles.

Facts and Examples

• National Insurance contributions are compulsory and non-refundable, regardless of lifestyle.

• Alcohol and drug abusers will be denied treatment for conditions directly resulting from prolonged abuse. In addition, crash drivers found to be under the influence will be afforded only secondary care at the scene of accidents which were of their own doing and any post-care must be personally funded.

• Clinically obese individuals will be banned from all national health care due to the rather obvious fact that if one cannot look after the basics themselves then one cannot expect someone else to neither.

• Smokers will be refused free treatment for conditions arising from the disgusting habit – including emphysema and more critically, lung cancer.

• All failed suicide 'attemptees' will be turned away at the door regardless of their physical state.

• Genuine accidents which result in physical/mental injury will continue to receive full free treatment.

FOR

Saves money and frees up beds. § Staff work in a safer environment. § Long term health of the NHS is assured. § People sway away from becoming addicted to harmful substances knowing no treatment will ever be forthcoming. § Doctors no longer have to treat people they feel do not deserve their time or pity, let alone medical assistance. § Win-win for all concerned.

AGAINST

Needless loss of life. Defies the very notion of 'healthcare'. § Unethical for doctors to turn away persons in dire need of medical help. § Human nature means people will naturally always crave what makes them happy. § An illegal precedent is surely set where contributions are taken knowing personal conditions are not met. § Relatives (if any) will need to treat the rejected.

Why God... why do all the good ones die so young?

Future Reform

With the practice of turning away sick patients being considered an immoral act, should the NHS alternately put forward a mutually beneficial agreement. In return for free care and treatment, self-inflicted patients must agree to become human guinea pigs for medical research - which otherwise would have been reliant on animal testing - win win for all.

eg. A heavy smoker with lung cancer will receive care in the form of extensive testing of a possible cure which had previously stood up to successful animal tests.

With natural resources on the wane, humanity will have no choice but to turn to the stars for our resources. But with 'land' ownership practically unenforceable, can we envision star wars within our own galaxy in order to assume control over the lands and regions for their untold riches and their strategic importance?

Background, Facts and Miscellaneous

Today, plans are already underway to mine near-Earth asteroids for their precious resources. Asteroids are fabulously rich with valuable elements that are rare on earth, such as platinum-group metals, rare minerals and even water.

With such an abundant source of rare earth metals - crucial to all kinds of modern industrial applications, from solar panels to fuel cells, it's clear to see the financial motives for such plans as well as the benefit to humanity overall.

Companies currently involved envisage our immediate space territory to be one-day littered with fuel depots, mining points and water filling points, which effectively paves the way for deep space exploration. However, military outposts and weapon bases also seem feasible and represents a more sinister factor in the equation.

The Outer Space Treaty, an agreement ratified by all spacefaring nations in the year 1967, established amongst other things, that no nation or legal entity may claim sovereignty over space, the moon or celestial bodies. Though this is open to interpretation, it's hard to see how such a 'property law' can ever really be established or enforced.

With natural resources being cited as the main reason for many of today's conflicts, is it conceivable that the future will be no different?

• It has been estimated that a 500 metre space rock could yield more platinum than has ever been mined throughout human history.
• Of the roughly 9000 known near-Earth asteroids, approximately 150 are water-rich and easier to reach than the surface of the moon.

A long time ago in a galaxy not so far away...

James Bond's Demise -
Having survived all manner of elaborate assassination attempts by some of the worlds most evil criminal masterminds and henchmen, what would be the most fitting way for James Bond to meet his end?

Background, Facts and Miscellaneous

Try and be imaginative in your answer, perhaps using modern interrogation techniques or macabre murderous inventions:-

• consider the kind of torture and slow death he would endure if he had been captured by some of the murderous regimes in todays world,
• or should he die in an honourable manner?
• or will he die by a means which makes him regret every single henchman whose children he left fatherless (though, they were likely absent ones)?
• Or one where he'll get to ask you *"Do you expect me to talk?"* to which you'll gladly respond to?

The person with the most imaginative, ingenious or appropriate method worthy of 007 wins a date and a 5* hotel night stay with the Bond girl, the 'girl at the pool' from *For Your Eyes Only*.

Some important considerations to help feed your macabre imagination:-
• Up to Pierce Brosnan, Bond had racked up 195 kills, kissed 54 women and bedded 23,
• Never returned calls for:- Fiona Fullerton, Denise Richards, Ursula Andress, a young Honor Blackman, Diana Rigg, Jill St John, Lana Wood, Jane Seymour, Britt Ekland, Barbara Bach, Maud Adams, Kim Basinger, Tanya Roberts, Rosamund Pike, Famke Janssen, Sophie Marceau, Halle Berry and Gemma Arterton.

Some previous attempts which failed:-
Poisoned martinis; Forced off-piste by Russian spies on skis; Being chased by the cousin of Sheriff JW Pepper; Abandoned cremations; Tarantulas in beds; Drugged horses.

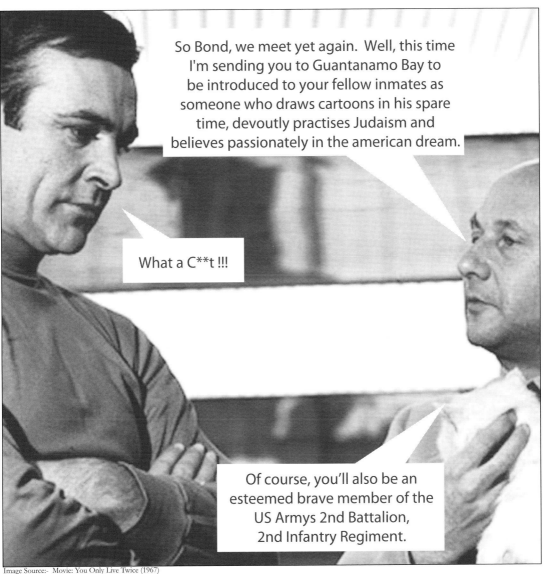

A world without criminal defence lawyers - a good thing surely?

Background, Facts and Miscellaneous

Lie-detection based on MRI 'brain-imaging' has become so advanced and reliable that they are now considered to be 99% accurate, in spite of the subject's best efforts, however ingenious, to fool it. So much so, that in the year 2030, after relentless lobbying by law enforcement agencies, the use of 'involuntary confessions' via lie detection evidence from such methods were finally admitted into the UK legal system.

Together with the advancements in DNA supported evidence, the pairing have become impenetrable in a court of law, giving defence lawyers absolutely no room for manoeuvre in the light of such overwhelming cognitive and scientific evidence against their client(s).

Consequently, this particular field has seen a dramatic decline with many forsaking their much toiled skills/talent as the 'defender of the guilty', and these trends have continued to the point that in 2060 the profession has all but practically died out. Those who have however continued in this now pointless and fruitless exercise fully acknowledge that they are of no discernible 'investigative' talent nor do they do it out of some misguided loyalty to a fair and just legal system based on an *innocent until proven guilty* mantra.

Discuss the following such developments bring:-
Q1) Does everyone deserve a fair shot at beating the system and getting away with murder?
Q2) Should we handover the court system to a bunch of zeros and ones. Or should the law courts stand as the 'last bastion' for human input and judgement, to be preserved at all costs?

Image Source:- Movie: A Few Good Men (1992) Starring: Tom Cruise

To safeguard the innocence and welfare of young children as well as preventing any long term anguish and psychological effects from sexual abuse, should an unforgiving hard-line approach be taken towards those who engage in such depraved sexual practices?

Background

It can be argued that an adult's sexual attraction towards young children is an unavoidable state of mind and that they cannot help but crave and ultimately give in to this unwanted deviant form of attraction.

However, a look at recent cases would suggest that many *Paedophiles* actually transcend this psychological reasoning for their behaviour (society's attempt at being understanding), and that many are truly evil in every capacity - with child abuse being just one manifestation of their deeply ingrained depravity and immorality, selfishly fulfilling individualistic desires.

Bearing this in mind, that *Paedophiles* are likely to be of this predisposition, should we finally put the safety of our children foremost forsaking any understanding to their plight(!), and adopt a hard-line uncompromising stance to punishing these lowlifes. Should we cease to bestow any more trust in them, take away their rights and liberties and force them to undergo surgical castration and life imprisonment?

Facts and Examples

There are probably three distinct classes of *Paedophiles*:
i) Those who acknowledge that they harbour this disgusting affliction and consciously recognise and accept the immoral nature of it. Regularly fighting their inner demons, trying to stem and contain it, their deep lying inclination proves futile to resist forever and they eventually submit to it, with genuine remorse. In every other sense, they have upheld a good moral life;
ii) Those who knowingly infringe, neglect and disregard a child's ultimate right to protection. That one can do anything they want as long as it does not hurt anyone else and thus allow it to excuse them forcing themselves on, hurting and damaging children who are too young to understand what's happening;
iii) Those child abusers that are the very epitome of evil and are very adept at concealing attitudes, manipulating psychological analysis and displaying remorse.

Should and would the i)'s take one for the team?

FOR

A child's rights are forsaken, so they should naturally forsake all of their own. § To violate a child's innocence is truly worthy of the most extreme punishment. §Instead send them involuntarily to War as human bomb disposal experts (on-the-job training). The UN and both sides will encourage planting bombs in civilian destinations with prior warnings and providing GPS co-ordinates.

AGAINST

A state of the mind, where one does not willingly engage in having sexual thoughts about children. As goodness is pre-wired, so can the idea that evil can be, therefore they should be considered innocent of their actions. § Human nature to fulfil desires. § Paedophilia is so widespread and accepted that it festers underground. Society needs to accommodate this inherent affliction.

...but to have you mingle and stroll amongst us, now that I can't abide!

How about a big ole 'P'?

Image Source:- Movie: Inglourious Basterds (2009) Starring: Brad Pitt and B.J. Novak

Be Controversial

i) A Victimless Crime
As children are unable to recall memories from a very young age, do they regard acts as victimless.
ii) Corridors of Power
Is the act of paedophilia so naturally receptive to the human psyche, that it actually lingers in all of us. Until at which time that we are in a position of power, insulated from society's norms and constraints that we can finally indulge without guilt - hence the increasing evidence of such immoral behaviour being exhibited by those we hold in high regard.

It is 2017 and a critical time has arrived for this country to establish long term economic superiority and standing. As such, manoeuvres have begun in order to maintain the intellectual strength required for the decades ahead - Immigration is only permitted on an exchange basis, where an incoming person must be offset by an outgoing inferior.

Background

With decades of unmanned borders, insufficient deportation procedures and a Home Office 'unfit for purpose', the cost of uncontrolled immigration to the long term economy has considerably outweighed the initially perceived benefits.

Add together the distinct absence of any kind of political recourse over the years to stem the symptoms of such policies, many of our brightest and intelligent folk concluded that the country was now in decline and had actively sought not only employment abroad but also permanent residence.

Some of the concerns aiming to be addressed by such drastic action is as follows:-
Brain drain; EU movements with no criminal checks; White flight; Almost standard protocol for asylum seeking criminals falsely claiming to be Gay or converting to Christianity in order to avoid deportation and being granted permanent stay; Benefits culture.

Facts and Examples

With Third World countries needing to offer their children an incentive to educate themselves by offering real prospects of a brighter future, and the developed world needing to urgently attract the brightest from around the world, treaties will be signed between participating countries allowing a citizen exchange to take place, with persons fitting certain criteria.

Here, the long term unemployed are automatically selected for 'repatriation', but disillusioned benefit claimants or those looking for a fresh start can also sign up for exchange candidacy as long as they fit the criteria of being 'of below average intelligence'.

Potential immigrants on the other hand, must have excelled in education or displayed entrepreneurial talents, as well as no history of dishonest behaviour.

Successful 'exchangees' will be provided with accommodation and a generous settling in grant, but must revoke all rights to residency to their countries.

FOR	AGAINST

FOR

Encourages folk to seek employment in any capacity and not live off the state. § Possibility of a fresh start with no social or peer pressures. § Allowing those who will work on a minimum wage with a smile on their face to walk through the border, was always destined for failure. § Economic superiority back on track. § Win-win for all concerned. § Racists could now encounter racism.

AGAINST

Third World countries effectively signing the death warrant on their own economic development. § As is consistent throughout history, the western nations plunder with a sleight of hand. § Reducing opportunities for the native well-to-do western citizens. § Unlawful restriction of movement and forced revoking of birth rights. § Unlimited exchanges would have a detrimental effect.

Its win-win for all really. This hot-shot financial whizzkid called *Patrick Bateman* will be coming to take your benefits scrounging good for nothing place here... Now, Miss JK Rowling, please take your papers and leave this paradise asap.

Image Source:- Movie: The Terminal (2004) Starring: Stanley Tucci

Classroom Exercise

Q1. UK Immigration. An irrecoverable demographic deficit has taken place that has changed the landscape forever, resulting in a true multicultural community. Though deemed a negative, surely diluting the inferior indigenous population can only be a good thing, right? Q2. If Hadrians Wall had existed around London and remained intact surviving through the ages with strictly controlled exit/entry points, how different would London be today with regard to social classes and races.

If the rein of Saddam Hussein had not been curtailed, would the potential alliance between Iraq and Iran (given their common animosity towards the West) and the chance to collaborate together on nuclear weapon development been a slightly more dangerous proposition - Should this 'pre-emptive' strike be applauded?

Background, Facts and Miscellaneous

In 2003, the term *Weapons of Mass Destruction* was concocted up by those in the higher echelons of the Western power hierarchy in order to manipulate the commencement of an illegal and unjust attempt to overthrow the leader of Iraq, President *Saddam Hussein*. The operation would act under the guise of establishing a functioning democracy for the people of Iraq.

The plan worked, with the people as well as the international entities hoodwinked by the idea that an Islamic state led by a psychopathic dictator, which had previous history of unprovoked aggression as well as remorseless use of biological warfare, were soon to be in an unfathomable position of being able to deploy biological weapons to anywhere in the world.

But was the real intention really the much touted reason being 'Oil' or was it actually something which would have been universally unacceptable, wouldn't be sanctioned by the UN and the likely possibility of condemnation by rival nations coming in the form of military retaliation - a pre-emptive strike to ensure a certain scenario detrimental to global security never panned out?

If the facts are taken into consideration, with regard to *Mr Hussein* being a law unto himself, a trigger happy *Mr Mahmoud Ahmadinejad*, an active pursuit of nuclear weapon technology, a supposed religiously based calling to eliminate the *infidel*, the scenario of collaboration between the two countries and expedited nuclear capability was certainly feasible. With this in mind, discuss the outcome if no pre-emptive action took place?

Image Source:- Movie: Hot Shots! Part Deux (1993) Starring: Jerry Haleva

The last 100 years has seen dramatic and evolutionary advances in all areas of engineering, technology, medical science and space exploration - With our newfound expertise, freedom, know-how and intellect at an optimum, does the expected exponential advancements make for a rosy future?

Background, Facts and Miscellaneous

We are extremely fortunate to be living in an era that seems to be on the cusp of greatness - a time when the final frontier is being breached. Practically moments away from manipulating pre-birth DNA, finally embracing solar energy that had been here all along, portable computing, recreating the conditions of the *Big Bang* (albeit within a collider) being just some of the milestones indicating how far we have come since that first telegraphy machine over 170 years ago.

These amazing advancements would suggest that we are probably now at the pinnacle of discovery and there seems little else remaining worthy by comparison. Alas, the human mind is an inquisitive one and in the desire to help advance mankind to a better place, any new territories that can be tapped into, will be explored.

Needless to say, like all aspects of invention and development, one man's perception of what is beneficial to mankind is another man's idea of progressing to self-destruction or self-implosion, foreseeing the possible havoc that could ensue.

With this in mind and fully appreciating the rate at which we are advancing in each field, can the 22nd century be such that we can look at our grandchildren with envy or with pity?

Further Discussion Points:-
On the opposite page are some predictions of what could possibly come to pass in various fields of discovery. Assess between yourselves the possibility of such developments coming to fruition and whether any of them would ensure that the 23rd century never sees the light of day?

The World Reaping the Benefits of Curiosity, Invention and Discovery

If we think rationally without any romantic sentiment about the future civilisation, does it look good?

Space Exploration
○ Supersonic travel to other planets within our Solar System.
○ Terraforming other planets and moons.
○ Powerful telescopes providing us with the ability to see activity real-time on planets within close proximity.

Poverty and Disease
○ Most diseases will be eradicated but the sudden need to 'adapt and evolve' will result in a super-disease lying dormant until the right sequence of events coincide to release it.
○ Third World Poverty will be a distant memory as weather is able to be manipulated and coordinated in order that famine-stricken countries now observe the minimal amount of rain required to have a self-sustaining food and water supply.
○ Food substitute pills become reality and an immediately affordable solution for poverty-stricken families.

Bio-Science and Genetics
○ Understanding every facet of the DNA code including the unknown parts, can have unlimited applications.
○ Made to Measure children become standard practice with certain traits being outlawed when manipulating DNA. Human Deformities reaching new extremities due to amateur DIY attempts.
○ Remote genocide - The pollution of a groups DNA which conform to a certain pattern, in order that the target is destroyed (die out quicker and unnaturally).

Medicine
○ Reboot of the immune system will become possible, restoring its main components back to a young refreshed state.
○ Risk-free stasis chambers will become commonplace for patients who wish not to live through normal ailments such as flu, hay fever etc through to longer term cases of suffering such as the Chemo-therapy treatment period for treating Cancer.
○ Nano biotechnology will mature to a point that nanobots permanently reside in our body from birth as a helping hand to our natural immune system (See 'Outer Limits' TV episode *The New Breed*).
○ Robotic artificial limbs capable of extraordinary energy output - and its application in the fields of crime and sport.
○ The ability to recharge the heart of a dead person such that it can completely revive the physical body of someone who has not died of natural causes or irrecoverable injury, but effective only within a few hours of them being declared dead.

Information Technology
○ Miniature Hard Disk Drive body implants holding personal files, accessible only via a Bluetooth type technology.
○ Fully functional computers held as a tiny implant underneath the skin with a touchscreen permanently implanted across the left forearm (if right-handed). Or even projected on the surface of the eye pupil.
○ Finding solace and joy only in virtual existences (See *Rate of Advancement* topic)

Physical Appearance
○ Laser procedures progress to the degree that it can be conducted at home. Fat or excess skin can be lasered away, haircuts can be done based on a 3-D picture and even manually eroding bone/cartilage slowly to converge to a persons desired bone structure.
○ Post-food diet pills will be available which breaks down food immediately - effectively providing anyone instantly with an artificially fast metabolism.
○ Cosmetic procedures will be so advanced that almost any appearance can be attained effortlessly - its accuracy success will be largely based on the age at which it is commenced.
○ Ivory-based replacements of the front part of the skull also become a riskier alternative to traditional cosmetic facial procedures.

Science and Discovery
○ How the Big Bang actually really started.
○ The full understanding (and global acceptance) on how human evolution took place, and whether Intelligent Design had a part to play.
○ Clean source of alternative energy sources, such as nuclear fusion.

War and Peace
○ Chemical/Biological Warfare has been determined as the most effective deterrent, therefore sophisticated dispersion technology and facilities become commonplace across the globe's military mights.
○ Robotic military frontline personnel.
○ EMP based weapons only in development meaning electronics and computer reliant combat weapons become redundant.
○ Military weapon installations on satellites.

Business and Finance
○ Financial Trading no longer takes place since algorithmic trading undertaken by every party cancelled out any possible significant gains to be made.
○ Due to software, careers such as 'Accountants' no longer exist.

Image Source:- by the Author

Why does the Banking industry so vigorously pursue the path of 'repossession' and then attempt selling the property preferably via traditionally undervalued channels, when it can so clearly exacerbate the dire financial situation for the already distressed borrowers?

Background, Facts and Miscellaneous

Repossessed properties have traditionally been the bargain to be had for the cash-rich, able to realise a healthy paper profit almost instantly.

Property which had likely witnessed a hasty exit and had previously harboured an harmonious existence of a young family and their precious memories - thus the reason why it is oft discreetly offered to individuals who bear no guilt in profiting from the misfortune of others.

By sparing distressed families the indignity of selling, it is perhaps a final gesture of kindness from a bank who dutifully showed little restraint in lending and displayed great patience when their trust was betrayed and repayments begun not to be honoured. But why is the process done in a dishonourable and inconsiderate manner, delivering a final financially debilitating insult?

Which of the following is likely the reason(s):-
• Help expedite the rich-poor divide;
• Penalise the stupidity of those who overstretch;
• Auctioneers/estate agents paying backhanders;
• Bankers' stupidity and the lack of know-how in doing basic math;
• Genuine bona fide business reasons to sell the property via the quickest method possible;
• Best for the UK housing market in the long term for there to exist an avenue for under-pricing property, for the purposes of providing a sobering benchmark for accurate market price levels as well as to provide downward pressure;
• Customer are always last, profits are priority;
• To encourage renting rather than buying;
• Maintain borrower as a long term profitable entity by burdening them with avoidable debt.

Worked Example of treading the 'Undervalued' Path :-

Example Case:
2007 - House Purchase with 10% Deposit

Assumptions:

- Interest Only Mortgage @ Rate	Variable
- Interest Rate between 2007-2012 =	0%
- Auction House Typical Discount =	20%
- Kickback from Auctioneer/Buyer to Bank =	0

Specifics:	£
Market Value	300,000
Purchase Price	-300,000
Deposit Paid	30,000
Opening Mortgage Balance	-270,000
Market Value	300,000
Real P&L	0

Scenario A - House Repossessed when Market Value has increased by 10%

Market Move %	10%		Market Value	330,000
Mortgage Outstanding	-270,000		Auction House Sale Value	264,000

	Estate Agent Route			Auction Route		
	Buyer	Seller	Bank	Buyer	Seller	Bank
Sale Price	-330,000	330,000	-330,000	-264,000	264,000	-264,000
Outstanding Mortgage		-270,000	270,000		-270,000	270,000
Net Value Assets	330,000	0	0	330,000	0	0
Assets Current P&L	0	0	0	66,000	0	0
Bank Liability	0	60,000	-60,000	0	-6,000	6,000

The Distressed Seller is now left with no home and a loan to be repaid at an annual compound rate of 5% = **-6,000**

	Estate Agent Route			Auction Route		
Deposit Forfeit		-30,000	30,000		-30,000	30,000
Real P&L	0	30,000	-30,000	66,000	-36,000	36,000

	Amount	**-66,000**
Additional Liability to Seller when Bank selects Auction Route	% of Price	**-22%**

Scenario B - House Repossessed when Market Value has fallen by 10%

Market Fall %	-10%		Market Value	270,000
Mortgage Outstanding	-270,000		Auction House Sale Value	216,000

	Estate Agent Route			Auction Route		
	Buyer	Seller	Bank	Buyer	Seller	Bank
Sale Price	-270,000	270,000	-270,000	-216,000	216,000	-216,000
Outstanding Mortgage		-270,000	270,000		-270,000	270,000
Net Value Assets	270,000	0	0	270,000	0	0
Assets Current P&L	0	0	0	54,000	0	0
Bank Liability	0	0	0	0	-54,000	54,000

The Distressed Seller is now left with no home and a loan to be repaid at an annual compound rate of 5% = **-54,000**

	Estate Agent Route			Auction Route		
Deposit Forfeit		-30,000	30,000		-30,000	30,000
Real P&L	0	-30,000	30,000	54,000	-84,000	84,000

	Amount	**-54,000**
Additional Liability to Seller when Bank selects Auction Route	% of Price	**-18%**

Further Background:-

- As of 2012, approximately 3000 repossessions are taking place every month.

Royal Families enjoy a god-given right to the allegiance of the people, authority over the conquered lands, magnificent stately properties and a 'working wage' - What unique trait(s) did the founding member of a Royal Family hold in order for him and his future dynasty to be afforded such unrivalled extravagance?

Background, Facts and Miscellaneous

At the point a Royal Family was first conceived, with such privileged existence on offer to the eventual winner, you would think that one must have really stood out as an extremely talented individual or held some unique 'magical' ability, either of which would be hereditary, satisfying the pre-requisite for a superior lineage.

Or was it simply the wisest person deemed to have had the highest morals, was religiously faithful, incorruptible and would always have the peoples' concern and welfare at heart regardless.

Or are we thinking too romantically about the origins. Could it be that, as history seems to support, that the power-hungry, manipulative and egotistical type will tend to exploit the weakness and naivety of the people to conjure up positions of power and control.

Further Discussion Points:-
• Did they have superpowers!?!!
• Are the people behind the 'Royal Family' concept of a sinister undertaking and the family actually just a 'front' for the goings on which discretely take place behind the scenes?
• Is the 'Royal Family' concept the only notion feasible enough to be accepted wholly by the public in allowing for the control of power and the influx of legitimate* working budgets? In other words, would an alternative proposal of a 'Royal Council' have lasted to this day?
• Did *one* spin the "Visions came to me" line?

* In the absence of a Royal Family, the US instead simply and unashamedly siphoned off $ billions from defence budgets. See *Donald Rumsfeld*.

In order to curb existing remuneration practices, the authorities hope to encourage fairer salary distribution by placing a cap on the total accumulated remuneration an employee can receive from a single employer - Will the outcomes be realised or will corporations just look to exploit any loopholes to avoid their moral duty?

Background

Today's world is one where fair *wealth distribution* isn't practiced, but rather to the contrary, where it is actively discouraged - a stubborn willingness to attain and hoard extreme wealth steadfastly remains amongst the wealthy, and by hoarding their vast riches through the generations means ultimately that a significant proportion of wealth will, never again, see the light of day. These self-serving attitudes and lack of distribution can clearly become disintegrating and slowly destructive to society and the economy as a whole.

With such disastrous scenarios inevitable, the authorities have decided to finally try to curb such attitudes and will look to instil legally enforced guidelines and practices that will alter attitudes and behaviour not conducive to a better and fairer society. The first area is that of curbing extravagant pay and bonuses in the private sector, reasons for it being addressed first stemming from the total disregard and indifference shown by bankers during the 2007+ recession.

Facts and Examples

From 2016, authorities have implemented a new company law that forbids employees from accumulating more than £7m in remuneration from a single firm or parent company, after tax. Thereafter, it is expected, though not enforced, that the employee will then forsake any continued paid employment with the firm or its affiliated companies.

The expected outcomes are that ultimately, promotions occur more frequently, salary distribution across an organisation no longer remain top-heavy and bonus pools are spread more evenly.

Other aspects of this guideline are as follows:-
• Continued remuneration with the same employer beyond the £7m mark incurs an 80% income tax rate,
• If tax avoidance schemes are in use, then a blanket assumption of 0% tax obligations were enjoyed,
• The initial £7m figure will be revised annually with regard to inflation and its effectiveness.

FOR

Encourages fairer pay practices across an organisation as it is in the firms interest to keep a good employee. § Motivation and employee satisfaction would become less of a pressing concern. § The attitudes of the selfish need to be reined in, regardless of the apparent unfair restriction on genuinely talented individuals. § Early retirement no longer a viable option for the decadent.

AGAINST

Loyalty and commitment will suffer. § Always a loophole to conveniently exist and be exploited. § Gifted individuals depart for sunnier, less pay-restricted, climates. § It can be argued that the distribution of salary is consistent with intelligence, drive and ambition. This would prove that the system does not need rectifying, and any such interference would hinder ambition.

Did You Know ?

In 2009, at least 4000 anarchists, anti-capitalists and environmental- ists moved into London's financial district to peacefully demonstrate against the scourge of *Capitalism*, and the resulting global financial crisis that has adversely affected millions of innocent folk. Bankers had long been lambasted as being greedy, selfish and blamed for the recession that had made the jobless figures soar. Amidst growing tension and a state of unrest, what do the city workers go and do - only go and taunt them further by waving £50 notes at everyone!

Has the time come for a global 'French Revolution'?

Background, Facts and Miscellaneous

The French Revolution of 1789 was caused by:
1) the increasingly prosperous elite of wealthy commoners - merchants and manufacturers, often called the *bourgeoisie* - produced by the 18th century's economic growth resenting its exclusion from political power or positions of honour;
2) the peasants were acutely aware of their situation and were less and less willing to support the anachronistic and burdensome feudal system;
3) the philosophers who advocated social and political reform were being marginalised and suppressed more widely in France than elsewhere;
4) participation in the American Revolution drove the government to the brink of bankruptcy;
5) crop failures in much of the country in 1788 coming on top of a long period of economic difficulties, made the population particularly restless.

Potential reasons for a 21st Century Revolution:
1) the increasing trend of morally corrupt or privileged members of society holding the upper hand in the higher echelons of power, with those well intentioned being suppressed by any means;
2) the lower classes becoming increasingly aware of the long term consequences of a widening divide, and are now less willing to support the unbalanced distribution of wealth and privileges - especially those exempting the wealthy elite from moral responsibility, taxation and civil justice;
3) the revolutionaries who advocate free speech, democratic societies and social reform, are being increasingly hounded by military/political means;
4) Western financial support for a Capitalist ideal had driven the global economy into turmoil;
5) The people's concern for future generations.

We take the World from the corrupt, the rich! The oppressors of generations who have kept you down with myths of opportunity, and we give it back to you... the people. The World is yours. None shall interfere. Do as you please. Start by freeing the oppressed. Step forward those who would serve, for an army will be raised. The powerful will be ripped from their decadent nests, and cast out into the cold world that we know and endure. Courts will be convened. Spoils will be enjoyed. Blood will be shed. The police will survive, as they learn to serve true justice. This great civilisation, it will endure. Humanity will prosper!

If conventional punishment and torture methods are an ineffective deterrent against preventing those who are inherently evil from playing out their depraved fantasies, can a simulated presence in a Virtual Reality environment prove to be an ingenious and gratifying alternative?

Background, Facts and Miscellaneous

The year is 2040 and with crime rates reaching epidemic levels and the degrees of depravity plumbing depths never before envisaged, realisation has struck that a new elevated form of *evil amongst men* is now prevalent throughout the wider society - one in which remorse or a moral compass seems to be totally lacking within.

How it became so isn't immediately obvious, but factors such as inadequate deterrents and uncensored internet exposure through childhood have been cited as possible catalysts for this seismic shift in criminality. With this in mind, authorities have reasoned that with an emergence of a new level of immorality present, a radical rethink is necessary to determine what adequate retribution would best fit and effectively act as a deterrent sufficient to contain and stem this trend.

Advances in neuroscience and nanotechnology have led to a new form of simulation known as *Full Immersion Virtual Reality* (FIVR). This proven technology can provide astounding realism and detail, and users now have the ability of actually being in and experiencing any virtual environment, affecting all our senses in a manner that is wholly indistinguishable from the real world.

The authorities have now ventured to utilise this FIVR technology for the idea of punishment via *virtual reality* - providing a means for the most evil of perpetrators to be submitted to environments and scenarios not normally accessible or imaginable, but those which can prove mentally distressing. These FIVR sentences shall be confined only to those committing the most heinous of crimes.

Sentencing Options

Victims or their loved ones have the option of committing the perpetrator(s) to permanent stasis, where the body and mind is locked in a virtual reality environment of their choosing, where the perpetrator shall 'live' this same simulated day for the rest of their physical lives.

Slot A: Hell on Earth

Utilising scenes and re-enactments from the film *Necronomicon: Book of Dead* and *HellRaiser II,* you will undertake the role of an evil soul banished to Hell, to burn for eternity (well, for a 12 hour day at least, and then you get 12 hours respite before resuming the next day).

Slot B: Nazi Concentration Camp

Utilising scenes and re-enactments from the film *Escape from Sobibor,* you will undertake the role of a young 8 year old boy who has to witness firsthand the degradation, torture and execution of his beloved parents and much adored younger sister. Then live out the rest of the day aimlessly digging the scorched earth with your bare hands.

Slot C: Starvation

Utilising scenes and re-enactments from past archived news footage, you will undertake the role of a 32 year old mother of 4 children living through the Ethiopian famine of 1983-85. Starving yourself, you witness your beloved children suffer from unrivalled starvation and watch them fight over the smallest of food scraps with no water available. Then live out the rest of the day swatting away flies.

Slot D: Child Abuse Victim

Utilising characters and re-enactments from the film *Bastard Out of Carolina,* you will undertake the role of the young girl abused and raped. Then live out the rest of the day wallowing in disgust while waiting for the bathroom to be free.

Slot E: Frontline Soldier

Utilising characters and re-enactments from the film *Platoon,* you will undertake the role of a 19 year old soldier sent into the heat of battle on the very day of arriving in Vietnam. You will have received completely inadequate training and will spend some of the day hiding in the jungle with your whole batallion dead and the Viet Cong closing in. The rest of the day will be spent being dragged to a POW camp.

Slot F: Stoned to Death

Utilising scenes and re-enactments from the film *The Stoning of Soraya M,* you will undertake the role of a young innocent woman sentenced to death by stoning. The day will begin with the punishment event, witnessing around 100 small rocks hurtle towards you. The rest of the day you will be spent up to your neck in soil and stones, barely alive but enduring the slowest and most agonising of deaths.

What will you most miss in 50 years time when the internet/digital revolution is well and truly embedded into society?

Background, Facts and Miscellaneous

If we begin to think how quickly the InterNet has moved along and the revolutionary impact it has had on almost everything we do, it can only be thought of fondly. With the InterNet here to stay and developments in cyberspace accelerating rapidly, we can be rest assured that it will intrude upon any commercial/social domain it can find some solace - for the betterment of mankind.

Of the many benefits witnessed (such as the advent of online commerce, social networking, free porn, instant connectivity, knowledge at your fingertips, digital media, interactive banking, thesis plagiarisation, multiplayer gaming), it can also be said that the dark side has overshadowed its growth with many of the irresponsible and immoral online and digital activities taking place and in full view (technically).

The unregulated InterNet led to inadequate control of access and anonymity, enabling activities such as the following to not only prosper but to become mainstays of the world wide web; virtual existences, child abuse, the spread of misinformation and fear, fraud, copyright violation etc.

Fortunately, this dark and deeply tangled web has kept the tech-shy amongst us on our guard, fearing for the future of an unregulated playing field for online endeavours. But is it too late?

After all, the children of tomorrow will grow up knowing only of living an online existence and its many *ahem* benefits, whereas in the physically interacting environment we grew up in provided us with a benchmark on what is right and what is wrong, allowed us to learn how to discern any online dangers and corruptive influences.

The World Reaping the Benefits of 50+ years of the InterNet

If we think rationally without any romantic sentiment about the future environment, does it look good?

Digital Media
∘ All movies, music and books made throughout history will be stored online on a remote server, accessible by anyone at anytime for a small annual fee. Therefore, as there is no need for locally stored media, a commercial market for media is no longer viable (also partly due to copyright infringement and illegal sharing).

∘ Movies will no longer be made as cinemas go out of business due to decades of online streaming, and a customer base now more use to experiencing cinema on their HD mobile devices.

∘ eBooks with its low carbon footprint and low production cost will see an end to the physical book. The popularity already today amongst those of us who grew up reading physical books is astounding but when we consider the children of tomorrow who'd have attended schools that have (irresponsibly) long abandoned their book libraries and have had free access to any book available, they would only baulk at the thought of physically turning a page themselves.

∘ All types of new media that can be digitalised will die out, as artists acknowledge only negligible profits can be made from such risky and time-consuming endeavours.

Online Dating and Pornography
∘ Matter of time before dating websites open up for schoolchildren.

∘ Virtual Dating will encourage people to become accustomed to conducting multiple relationships.

∘ Access to the many free porn sites from a young age, will now deem even the most deviant activities as normal sexual behaviour and this will manifest itself in what one expects or is expected of them in the act of love making (constant exposure eventually desensites).

∘ Amateur sex tapes will become the norm and be used as a grooming tactic (sending potential sexual partners a web link or even one to a facebook video album).

∘ Merry Go Round of casual relationships due to social connectivity and the loss of innocence and romanticism at a young age.

High Streets and Out of Town Shopping Areas
∘ Will consist only of stores selling perishable items and food eating establishments.

∘ Banking will be done wholly online as money will no longer exist in a physical form.

∘ With the sheer volume of online shopping, delivery and logistics may become so sophisticated that it can be optimised for same day deliveries, effectively ending the need for any customer-facing premises at all.

Schooling
∘ Physical buildings for schools will slowly be sold off as classes reduce in size due to home schooling and online tutorials. Remote schooling will become the norm once 3-D webcam technology is realised, and online virtual environments can help project the feeling of being part of the school environment.

∘ Social and other interpersonal skills will suffer as a result. As there will be no physical school friends, a child's social circle will be confined only to those who live in the neighbourhood.

∘ In the absence of physical buildings and grounds, physical education could be irresponsibly entrusted to the parents to ensure that they are followed. This could also mean that any natural sporting abilities or talents are never noticed or harnessed.

∘ Much of the coursework students undertake today is already heavily plagiarised. 50 years of archived thesis' from all the hundreds of universities around the world would mean that it will become impossible to isolate and identify if cheating has taken place. The inevitable move to >90% coursework based assessments can only result in young adults ill-equipped for the rigours of a skilled professional career.

Travel and Leisure
∘ Google StreetView will become 3-D enabled and will eventually capture every part of the world, especially tourist hotspots and hard to get to scenery.

∘ As children grow with the internet, by the age of 16 they'd have already visited the wonders of the world from the comfort of their lap, experiencing 3-D scenery as if they were actually there. The desire to visit those places in person later in life will hold little attraction, if any.

∘ Online gaming becomes social entertaining experiences that fulfills all social and leisure needs.

War and Conflict
∘ Propaganda becomes more difficult to orchestrate. Similarly, suppressing information originating from outside the borders will become difficult to enforce.

∘ Conflicts can be resolved via online public live dialogue, avoiding the lies and deception we have experienced in this day and age by those who wish to engage in or incite a war.

∘ Civil injustices can be communicated quickly and easily, resulting in international organisations convening unexpectedly earlier, potentially saving thousands of lives and preventing future unrest.

∘ Alternative cyber wars take place.

Image Source:- by the Author

Chapter E

"Of all the manifestations of power, restraint impresses the most."
- *Thucydides*

If abortion became restricted for the good people amongst us, albeit with genuinely honourable intentions, will the positive implications allow them to reluctantly accept it?

Background, Facts and Miscellaneous

Poring over social demographic trends and the adverse pattern observed amongst birth rates between the different social classes, the authorities have decided to intervene by instilling some legally-enforced measures to somewhat attempt to offset the diminishing gene pool inevitable by unchecked rampant and reckless breeding by the lower classes as well as the growing reluctance by the middle classes to bear children.

Frustrated from being legally and ethically refrained from forcing abortions on non-consensual parents, the authorities have instead introduced a radical new legal precedent with regard to Abortion - the stated aim being to avert the abortions of babies that could possibly harbour genes and traits beneficial and rare enough to be considered critical for preservation.

Specifically, abortion is now only permitted if either biological parent is of questionable moral character or background, in other words may have had inherited genes or traits that the authorities wish to contain. Additionally, mothers forced to carry their child to full term are invited and openly encouraged to immediately place their unwanted baby onto a fast-track government-sponsored adoption scheme, with the added assurance that their child will be taken care of and be placed with parents willingly wishing to provide a stable, loving and nurturing environment.

Is this type of class based social discrimination an effective tool in trying to craft the population of tomorrow, and if so, will it have the desired effect or will it instead force the middle class to subconsciously seek out unworthy partners?

Image Source:- Movie: The Omen (1976) Starring: Gregory Peck and Lee Remick

Alternative and efficient vaccination routes - inevitable, unavoidable and necessary?

Background

Bioscientists are currently busy making advancements in the field of vaccine and medication delivery, paving the way for medical treatment to be transmitted effortlessly, efficiently and in a cost-effective manner. Breakthroughs such as *nanoparticle vaccines* could in theory, be administered without consent or knowledge.

And though the ethical violations of such practices are clearly evident, it seems future possible scenarios of virus contagion would justify this approach. For instance, upon an emerging threat of a deadly or debilitating virus mutating into an airborne pathogen, the race to find a vaccine before the spread takes hold is a nervously strained one, and yet even if the race was won, what follows would be an even more anxious race to vaccinate the entire global population in time, or god forbid, mutates further.

Clear cut it may appear, but does the potential dangers of covert mass medication outweigh the benefits of having this arsenal in our armoury?

Facts and Examples

• Since 1951, the concept of airborne immunisation and vaccinations has been developed by US Scientists, a technique referred to then as 'aerogenic immunisation'. *Dr Gardner Middlebrook*, a hospital research director, stated "mass immunisations by the airborne technique could be used theoretically to fight any infectious disease. The big problem now is developing highly infective but non-disease producing vaccines".

• Developments have recently been made in the idea of covert mass-sterilisation, specifically using sharp blasts of ultrasound directed against a man's scrotum to render him infertile for up to six months.

• Developments have also occurred in the form of *nanoparticle vaccines*. The particles would penetrate skin through hair follicles and burst upon contact with sweat to release vaccines, therefore can conceivably be administered via skin cream or the water supply.

• Both of these beneficial technologies have been kindly funded by the *Bill and Melinda Gates Foundation*.

FOR	**AGAINST**
DNA tweaks made easy. § The government always knows best, trust in them. § Time is of the essence when an airborne virus is 'live'. § Population control. § No other feasible solution for a next generation virus/disease. § Automatic scheduling of vaccine booster shots. § Countries can have a permanent immunisation surround zone, preventing all known viruses from entry.	DNA tweaks made easy. § Selective administration based on race, colour or even gender. § Mass involuntary sterilisation programmes. § Involuntary vaccination tests. § Terrorist organisations dishonestly obtaining the means to disperse via air, a disease or virus instead. § Inadequately tested vaccines which cause long term side effects. § Impossible to trial its safety sufficiently.

Image Source:- Movie: American History X (1998) Starring: Edward Norton and Fairuza Balk

Classroom Exercise

An airborne trial of a permanent male sterilisation treatment is secretly taking place in a controlled laboratory environment, at the epicentre of America. Unfortunately, a leak occurred causing a release into the atmosphere, dispersing in all directions - and disturbingly, the dose was enough that it had a 'blast radius' of 1300 miles, reaching the breadth and width of the entire country. One finding of the test was that it was successful only on those of White/European origin! Speculate on the future of the US?

Is there something fundamentally insane about conjuring up a $Trillion a year market out of thin air (albeit polluted). Did the capitalists become envious of the 'Virtual Goods' success story and for not thinking of such a scheme first, and therefore introduced the Carbon Emissions Trading Market to redress the balance?

Background, Facts and Miscellaneous

Carbon credits and carbon markets are a component of national and international attempts to mitigate the growth in concentrations of greenhouse gases (GHG's).

A carbon credit is a generic term for any tradable certificate or permit representing the right to emit one metric tonne of carbon dioxide or equivalent gases. GHG emissions are capped and then markets are used to allocate the emissions among the group of regulated sources.

The goal is to allow market mechanisms to drive industrial and commercial processes in the direction of lower emissions.

Virtual goods are purchased for use exclusively in cyberspace, therefore have no intrinsic value and are intangible by definition.

• Since 2005, policymakers have distributed these allowances to emit carbon to utility companies and heavy industrial polluters (initially for free). Any allowances not used or extras required can be traded on the open market, as each country gradually reduces the amount of available credits and begins to auction them.

• The scheme has acted as a huge subsidy for some of the biggest polluters in Europe, with a handful of energy companies making billions of profit without having to reduce their emissions. This suggests its only effect has been to redistribute wealth among companies and traders.

• The banks are doing with carbon what they've done before with tangible products: design and market derivatives that will help client companies hedge their price risk over the long term.

Image Source:- Movie: Revenge of the Pink Panther (1978) Starring: Tony Beckley, Peter Sellers and Robbert Loggia

225

In light of increasing dubious business practices amongst the big corporations and an almost blasé attitude to ignoring ethical principles - Every FTSE-100 corporation will extend courtesies to a government-assigned 'Ethics Director', permitting identical status and security as other board directors.

Background, Facts and Miscellaneous

Ethical issues include the rights and duties between a company and its customers but primarily a fiduciary responsibility to its shareholders. With regard to relations between different companies, this includes hostile take-overs, contract negotiations and industrial espionage.

Today, major corporations promote their commitment to non-economic values under guises such as ethics codes and social responsibility charters but many executives believe their compliance only lies in achieving business objectives and making as much money as possible for their shareholders. With increasing numbers of companies/executives paying little attention to ethical business conduct, it seems that 'doing the right thing' even though it has a negative impact on profits is deemed 'doing the wrong thing'.

The government have now implemented a mandatory requirement that every FTSE-100 member must allow for a rotating *Ethics Director* who will review company strategies and must be present at every high-level board meeting.

• Any possible breaches of the government ethical code will be recorded with the Central Ethics Committee who will review and undertake appropriate measures within their power.

• ED's will be rotated frequently and at random considering their susceptibility to accept bribes.

• Any deliberate concealment of practices will result in an immediate withdrawal of the license to conduct business in the UK.

Dishonourable Mentions:- ST Equity Options; BP, the Labour Party and Al Megrahi; Xigris;

With all the numerous religions available to choose from, what possible motive is there to go through all the hassle of starting your own religion or cult - the paperwork, the ridicule, the recruitment drives, the expense and of course, the eternal disdain if it doesn't quite work out as planned?

Background

Cults are most often religious or spiritual groups that use teaching and social structures to exhibit strong and/or controlling influences over its members' financial, material and social circles. The beliefs are typically driven by a single cult leader and a specific set of religious beliefs unique to that group.

Many people join because they have a longing to belong to a community in which they have an identity, one which existing religions may not quite fulfil. Religion or cults provide such an avenue to make people feel better about themselves in being part of something especially if it fills a spiritual void in their lives.

Though the term 'cult' is oft used in a denigrating manner, they must hold honourable qualities and intentions, otherwise they would surely cease to exist.

"Beware of false prophets, who come to you in sheep's clothing, but inwardly they are ravening wolves".
~ The Holy Bible: Matthew Chapter7, Verse15

Facts and Examples

• The *Fundamentalist Church of Jesus Christ of Latter-Day Saints* teaches that a man having multiple wives is ordained by God. The then prophet, a *Rulon Timpson Jeffs*, obliged and promptly went on to have an estimated 60 wives and at least 60 children.

• Jones' *Peoples Temple* had a vision of a communist community, one in which everyone lived together in harmony and worked for the common good.

• The late *Sri Satya Sai Baba* commanded a following of millions, believing him to be an Avatar or an incarnation of God in human form. However, allegations of sexual abuse towards children clouded the life of the self-proclaimed 'God-man'.

• How many more members would Scientology have had, had the 'Internet' not come along and ruined the ending for everyone?

Dishonourable Mentions:- Reincarnated messiahs; Breatharians; Amma; Flirty Fishing; David Koresh.

FOR	**AGAINST**
A honest belief in the visions they have experienced or their mission to better humanity. § Privileged to being solely granted by a higher power the wisdom to lead humans to spiritual fulfilment. § All existing religious versions of history have been discounted by science and condemned by the intellectual amongst us - a new forward thinking approach is necessary.	Oh, to be as revered as the Pope - Adulation and Obedience. § Money, pure and simple. Once the realisation dawns that one does not possess the intellect to succeed in business or life and is destined to be just another 'foot soldier'. § Unlawful sexual relations. § Unlimited lawful sexual relations with the opposite sex. § A con-artists ultimate trick. § Teach the gullible a valuable bankrupting lesson.

HUBBARD COMMUNICATIONS OFFICE
Saint Hill Manor, East Grinstead, Sussex

HCO POLICY LETTER OF 16 FEBRUARY 1969
ISSUE IV
REISSUED 24 SEPTEMBER 1987

TARGETS

The vital targets on which we must invest most of our time are:

T1. Depopularizing the enemy to a point of total obliteration.

T2. Taking over the control or allegiance of the heads or proprietors of all news media.

T3. Taking over the control or allegiance of key political figures.

T4. Taking over the control or allegiance of those who monitor international finance and shifting them to a less precarious finance standard.

T5. Generally revitalizing the societies in which we are operating.

T6. Winning overwhelming public support.

T7. Use all other similar groups as allies.

These, of course, are very long-range targets. But it is what must be done to continue the longevity of our organizations.

Our only justification for doing these things is that Scientology is the only game where everyone wins.

Wildcard View

How much % of the revenue or profits do 'celebrity ambassadors' receive in commission by marketing the tax-exempt *Scientology* 'religion'. Or do celebrities like *Tom Cruise*, *Anne Archer* and *John Travolta* do so purely due to their undying devotion to their galactic overlord *Xenu* and because of the state of *Clear* that has been bestowed upon them by stepping on to that 'The Bridge to Total Freedom'.

NB: The revenue for 2008 stood at an estimated $500 million.

Image Source:- Official Document revealed by:
Frank Oliver, former agent of the Scientology's Office of Special Affairs

Drug Dealers convicted of 'possession with intent to supply' for a second time MUST now disclose all information about their suppliers. Otherwise, an automatic non-negotiable 10 year jail term will be handed down.

Background

With huge profits to be made in the supply and distribution of illegal drugs, it's indeed a worthwhile risk and too attractive a venture for individuals to be deterred by short prison sentences or large fines.

With traditional deterrents clearly failing, a new bottom-up approach to minimising drug use will be adopted, by targeting and imposing sanctions on the *street dealers* instead of the traditional import routes and/or wholesalers.

All drug enforcement agencies will now shift their focus to infiltrating the low-level drug supply networks and apprehend those guilty of supplying drugs to end consumers. Those convicted of this offence for a second time will require the court judge to immediately offer the no-quibbles plea agreement, to which there is no recourse. Acceptance of the plea agreement must include providing credible evidence and taking the witness stand if necessary.

Facts and Examples

• Currently, the maximum penalty in the UK for 'possession with intent to supply' depends on both the trial venue and the class of drug:-
Magistrates Court:
    Class A/B: £5000 fine and/or 6 months prison,
    Class B: £5000 fine and/or 6 months prison,
Crown Court:
    Class A: Unlimited fine and/or life imprisonment,
    Class B/C: Unlimited fine and/or 14 years prison.
• Based on 2001 Heroin figures, a kilo of Opium can be bought from a farmer for $90 and it would ultimately have a street value (at 40% purity) of $290,000, a mark-up of over 3000%. Not to be sneezed at!
• From 2009 statistics, of the 6,394 people sentenced for drug dealing in England and Wales, just 56% were imprisoned. The other 44% received either suspended sentences, community sentences or discharges - rather incredibly, the figure included one in four found guilty of peddling Class A drugs.

FOR

Dealers will be less inclined to get caught thus will only look to provide to a limited customer base of trustworthy individuals. § Discourages 'grooming' of potential drug users. § Drug use will become prevalent only amongst the lower society, hence, dealing becomes a less lucrative pastime leading to less dealers which in turn will lead to an eventual decline in drug use.

AGAINST

Suppliers could resort to otherwise more sinister measures to silence the individual. This could quite conceivably involve violence, murder or kidnap. § Drug use should be considered a basic human right, and must therefore not be unfairly restricted. § Penalising foot soldiers instead of generals. § Fall in drug supply affects the poor farmers who help to cultivate the raw form.

Wildcard View

This directive strikes at the heart of drug delivery therefore if no dealing channels exist then suppliers are forced to provide direct to the consumer wholesale amounts only.

This could lead to heavier use or more worryingly, consumers engaging in more frequent levels of criminal activity in order to afford the larger quantities. On the other hand, the more expensive an outlay required each time can encourage users to cease any personal use altogether.

Image Source:- Movie: Pulp Fiction (1994) Starring: John Travolta and Eric Stoltz

Invasive species and the manipulation of the ecosystem - Discuss the effects on the delicate ecosystem if we eradicated the entire mosquito species?

Background

The ecosystem can be described as the complex of living organisms, their physical environment, and all their interrelationships in a particular unit of space.

The principles underlying the study of ecosystems are based on the view that all elements of a life-supporting environment of any size, whether natural or man-made, are parts of an integral network in which each element interacts directly or indirectly with all others and affects the function of the whole.

Mosquitos serve important functions in numerous ecosystems, yet kill more than a million people across the globe every year through the transmission of dangerous viruses and parasites. There is no evidence that mosquitoes can transmit the HIV virus (yet).

The Butterfly Effect - the theory that something as small as a butterfly flapping its wings can produce long-term effects on a dynamical system.

Facts and Examples

• Of the 3,500 different species of mosquito, only a small fraction interfere with humans. However, they are responsible for more human deaths than any other living creature.

• One female mosquito may lay 100-300 eggs at a time and averages 1000-3000 offspring during her life span.

A Case Study:-

The removal of all feral cats from Macquarie Island took place in order to save the native seabirds.

This however allowed the rabbit population to explode and, in turn, destroyed much of its fragile vegetation that birds depended on for cover.

Dr Dana Bergstrom wrote in the British Ecological Society's Journal of Applied Ecology: *"There had been widespread ecosystem devastation and decades of conservation effort compromised. The unintended consequences of the project show the dangers of meddling with an ecosystem - even with the best of intentions."*

FOR

Mosquitos serve absolutely no useful purpose and are only a nuisance and a spreader of disease. § The Earth is a resilient system and not a delicate one where everything is just about holding together in balance. § The ecosystem hasn't exactly been in turmoil since the last Dodo died (Any ecological scar would be fulfilled). § It's time to pro-actively fine-tune the ecosystem.

AGAINST

Keeping every cog and wheel intact (no matter how pointless they appear) should be the first precaution of intelligent tinkering. § Starting down this path, can you rely on these *scientific terrorists* stopping there, or will they continue to eradicate other 'pointless' organisms (such as bats, dolphins, vultures and ducks) until at which time the damage or effects are irreparable.

So basically, the person who invented CGI was inadvertently killed before he had a chance to invent those ground-breaking techniques.

Wildcard View

Could mosquitos evolve a defensive tactic to the human threat - for example passing live blood from one host to another, without having digested any dangerous viruses such as HIV?

The Theory of Evolution certainly suggests that defensive tactics are indeed a progression stage, therefore this scenario certainly does seem plausible. If so, the consequences for the human race could be disastrous (or beneficial, depending on your point of view).

Image Source:- Movie: A Sound of Thunder (2005)   Starring: Ben Kingsley and Edward Burns

With luxuries and privileges granted throughout their childhood, is it fair to still extend 'toffs' safe passage through the legal system unharmed - Do 'friends in high places' set a damaging precedent for the sanctity and grounds of criminal law?

Background

The privileged elite, the ones through sheer hard work and dedication, have elevated themselves into a deserved status of an upper class in society where they are rightly revered. A class that sets a benchmark for society to reach through similar endeavours.

The many accomplishments such talented individuals have achieved, and helped to progress the world to a better place, means there is little justification for any resentment or envy. This courtesy also extends to descendants of such pioneers, as it's only right their lineage should also be afforded the fruits of their labour and the respect from the general public.

However, there exists within this group a deep-rooted mindset of a divine right (or a self-granted privilege) that the upper class elite should be immune from the criminal legal system, a system they genuinely believe was only put in place by their forefathers to keep the underclass in check and to maintain order.

Facts and Examples

We are now seeing disturbing trends amongst regular folk who find themselves in authority or power, who delusionally believe that this elitist 'privilege' is now extended to them and as such, these 'pardons' are now assumed or will be forthcoming. This is evident in the self-serving actions of many men today who have undertaken senior roles in politics, banking and law.

Is this new growing attitude a manifestation of the decades of dismissive concerns about legality by the upper echelons, and which have now found allies amongst those further down the food chain?

Dishonourable Mentions:- Bo Guagua and the Three; Freemasons and favours; Enron Executives; Lord Lucan; Lehman's Dick; Eva Rausing and the ill-fated decision not to prosecute; The Mitterrands and Arms; Tony Blair; Murdochs and their merry band of hackers; Pippa, Paris and Pistols; The case of Pamela Werner and horny dentists; Maxwell Pension Funds;

FOR

Everyone has their rightful place in society and this should be safeguarded at all costs.

The wealthy, well educated and intellectual must remain on the fringes of normal society looking in, ensuring the system ticks over as architected and that their own position is never compromised. § The need for a systematic implosion of the underclasses has never been more pertinent than today.

AGAINST

Symptoms of unchecked corruption, particularly in times of austerity. § An uprising is being fuelled and anarchy can be the only outcome unless a level playing field is observed. § This sense of invincibility will ultimately lead to one's downfall. The lower classes are just biding their time to pick up the pieces. Then what? § Any legal system must have unshakeable foundations.

Past the US Border Control, you say... Hhhmmm!

Be Controversial

Has such thinking led to the wealthy elite voluntarily absolving themselves of further distractions, anything which they deem cumbersome, or beneath them?

Paying taxes is now unashamedly avoided at all costs (see *Jimmy Carr*). Perhaps the most immoral examples are those already having benefitted from a lifetime of creative tax avoidance and offshore tax havens, and are now bypassing generations of inheritance tax by placing property assets into trust.

Image Source:- Movie: Inception (2010)
Starring: Ken Watanabe & Leonardo DiCaprio

With Darwin's 'Theory of Evolution' all but removing the need to believe in a 'divine' concept of human origin, the ideology of Pragmatic Atheism was born. But did we sleepwalk into this new era without addressing the gaps, resulting in this corrupt, immoral, selfish world via the manifestation of a faithless generation?

Background, Facts and Miscellaneous

• *Pragmatic Atheism* defines those individuals who live as if there are no superior intellectual beings and look to explain natural phenomena without resorting to the divine or supernatural. The existence of a God isn't wholly rejected, but may be deemed an unnecessary view since they neither provide purpose to life nor influence it.

• Religious teachings for children have traditionally projected notions such as karma, life after death and spirituality. This guidance effectively helped one to establish and maintain a good, morally responsible base, particularly when parents and guardians showed no such interest.

• A *Gap Analysis* would ultimately involve identifying the differences between the current and the previous environments, and then implementing the means to address these gaps.

However, with rising trends in children deprived of these 'moralistic' teachings (because of their parents' spiritual dismissals), are we seeing this manifest in the young people of today, where they lack any sense of moral duty and are more concerned with selfish and materialistic gain.

Future Reform:-

In order to address this decline in moral standards and the evident lack of appropriate parental guidance on benchmarks for social responsibility, the school curriculum will now; i) resume the role previously held by the religious institutions in providing a moral compass for children to know the right from wrong, as well as ii) adopting the role of traditional parenting, sadly lost in this era of the digital age and two working parents.

Gap Analysis: 10-yearly breakdown comparing the trends of Faith vs Indiscipline

Assumptions and important events:-

○ Charles Darwin's *Theory of Evolution* was proposed in the year 1859.

○ The 'God-Fearing Index' is the % of the population that is deeply religious or fearful of a superior intellectual being.

○ The 'Indiscipline Index' is the % of the child population aged between 7-13 who regularly exhibit behavioural difficulties or disturbing behaviour not normally expected from an average child in a modern developed and disciplined society.

○ The index rates over time has been completely projected by the Author and has taken into account the likely consequences from an increasing faithless society on indiscipline in the classroom.

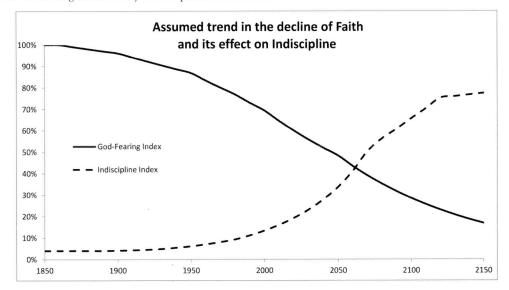

Supporting viewpoints for forthcoming topics:-

○ See topic E14: *Nature vs Nurture*

The resultant plateau at 80% between 2120-2150 infers that ultimately only a disturbing 20% of human society did not require any form of Religion nor a God to live, follow and honour a good moral life. Intruigingly, this would suggest an *evil gene* could well have been present and dormant in 80% of the population through the ages and religion/god helped to suppress it.

○ See topic H7: *Dark Energy*

In 1917, when *Albert Einstein* applied his theory of general relativity to the universe as a whole, he added a 'fudge-factor' to explain away a mysterious force at work which defied the observations of that time. Did Darwin inadvertently prevent Einstein from making the greatest discovery ever made?

Image Source:- By The Author

Should we so easily dismiss the eccentric amongst us as being 'mad' or 'insane', with the ridicule it entails automatically discrediting their 'rants' or 'claims'. Or are they merely forward thinkers who can think out of the box, see past the rhetoric and/or are party to knowledge the rest of us aren't?

Background

When one presents outlandish ideas, without a support network to back them up, they tend to be immediately dismissed as the rantings of a mad man. Especially, when these ideas go against conventional thinking and beliefs.

In a similar way that some conspiracy theories are readily dismissed by the deceitful, meaning to divert attention away from what is actually the truth, are we too easily allowing ourselves to accept the label society has given people who display an intelligence or alternate thinking that we mere mortals can't quite comprehend yet.

Couple this with the fact that those who don't refute these rantings also be labelled with negative connotations, there seems little choice but to dismiss outright their thoughts by similarly and ignorantly labelling them what society has already allocated them to be. But are we letting the 'truth' slip us by?

Facts and Examples

• *Empedocles*, a Greek scientist and philosopher, is amongst the most revered geniuses in history, with some of his famed discoveries including the earth was round, light travelled at a speed, a (crude) theory of evolution and centrifugal force. One would think that this occurring in a time 500 years before baby Jesus was born, the claims alone would have the masses exclaiming the 'screw loose' somewhere in him, alas not. An extremely smart fellow and lest we forget, someone who also believed he was God!

• *David Icke* was a well known BBC sports presenter before a psychic told him he was a healer who had been placed on Earth for a purpose, and that spirits were going to pass messages to him so he could educate others. Years of public ridicule followed after being mocked shamelessly on the *Wogan Show* in 1991, but today he is an author of 19 books and has attracted a global following. Laugh when you're ready at his wild claims of a 'global fascist state' in control!

FOR

Many claims are disprovable or have an apocalyptic theme, which many would not want to embrace or face. § Through the ages, many conspiracy theorists have been proved correct in some form. § The 'truth' can be disturbing. § A spirit world exists around us, however only few have the ability to channel. Apparitions and hearing voices shouldn't be dismissed as the manifestation of an ill mind.

AGAINST

Intelligent young adults develop delusions of grandeur about their intellectual standing amongst others, feeling they should have been elevated higher or away from the average person. To have the same thinking would be to imply that their intellect was always similar or that one was not able to harness their talent. This results in the proactive desire for alternate thinking.

No...! She's the dummy!

Image Source:- Movie: Mannequin (1987) Starring: G.W. Bailey

Wildcard View

The sheer scale and volume of individuals who claim to hear voices, and even when cross-examined or interrogated under duress would always stick to their stories, suggesting something untoward could well be going on.

"*Your honour, I'd like to call a new witness to the stand*".

In court cases where the 'criminally insane' pitch their defence as 'voices in my head made me do it', can the *Ouija Board* be used by both sides to help corroborate the testimonies of the defendant?

With video gaming becoming ever more realistic and 3D/virtual technology finally being realised, will there ever be a need to leave the house when daring adventures, a sporting career or fighting crime as a superhero is literally at your fingertips?

Background, Facts and Miscellaneous

The future of Video Gaming is in safe hands, assuring a promising future to all who embrace it. Or is it?

• The term *Virtual reality* applies to computer-simulated environments that can simulate physical presence in the real world as well as an imaginary one. Increasingly, simulations are beginning to include additional sensory information.

• Developments are already underway for brain-driven video gaming in which controllers aren't necessary. By utilising *electroencephalography* (EEG), cerebral data nodes and wireless technology, electrical activity from the brain can now be registered and translated into a playing decision.

• 3D gaming has yet to take off but with the technology evolving steadily, the industry will no doubt see a resurgence in 3D gameplay.

Typical scenarios for 21st Century Gaming:-

• Playing football with friends at the Nou Camp. Or rather adorning a virtual headset with a 360 degree view and wired into your brain senses allowing you to control the body and legs of an immensely talented sportsman, basking in the adulation for a worshipped hero.

• Experiencing the harsh reality of war as a front-line soldier. Or rather wear a specially fitted all-over body suit which mimics the exact pain experienced from a gunshot or a grenade blast.

• To witness first-hand and savour every blow the capture, torture and killing of a man responsible for the death of 3000 innocent civilians.

• Fly on rooftops; Grasp the falling helicopter; Throttle the Orange Man; Know where to get all those wonderful toys; Be worthy of Anduril.

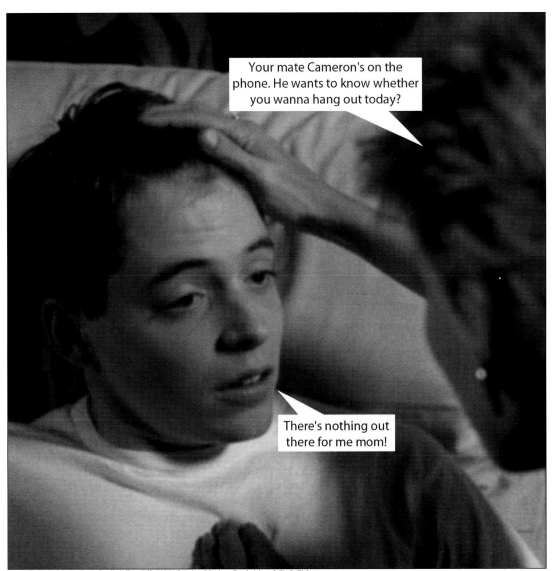

Image Source:- Movie: Ferris Bueller's Day Off (1986) Starring: Matthew Broderick and Cindy Pickett

When the penny finally drops that the extortionate and unbalanced expenditure on IT is no longer justified, will the eventual fallout be catastrophic for the world economy?

Background, Facts and Miscellaneous

There will come a point in time (sooner than we think) when we experience a dead end in the field of *Information Technology* infrastructure - when systems, databases, software and technology will be at an ultimate optimal point (at a level discernible by the human brain) in terms of speed, self-diagnostic maintainability and technology that the need to upgrade, evolve and keep up with technological developments becomes a futile exercise.

When realisation finally dawns that the cumulative benefit of decades of installs/upgrades etc. have amounted to no 'real' speed or efficiency because of the relatively negligible increment, the policy of blind over-spending in IT should come to a sudden and shuddering halt.

If this fallout occurs in a synchronised manner, in that organisations simultaneously realise that IT requirements had already been largely fulfilled for some time now and this stance having a knock-on effect around the globe, could it lead to the onset of a Great Global Depression, albeit a longer more sustained one?

• The 'Trading Floor' of the future will embrace and encompass the practice of *algorithmic trading*, rendering state of the art IT systems unnecessary if such trading becomes commonplace, minimising any speculative trading opportunities.
• Super-durable smartphones with embedded computers and lifetime energy cells will soon be upon us, phone development will soon die(?).
• Microsoft®'s *Windows Vista* OS was universally rejected by corporations/industries alike, primarily because it provided little incentive for upgrade.

Image Source:- Movie: Honey, I Shrunk the Kids (1989) Starring: Marcia Strassman and Rick Moranis

243

To encourage responsible living, the government pension scheme has been revised such that only those deserving receive it and the amount paid becomes leveraged to the life that has been lived - Will a life-linked pension be enough to alter attitudes?

Background, Facts and Miscellaneous

The year is 2030 and a revision to the government state pension policy has been proposed which aims to provide a fairer pension entitlement while simultaneously acting as a guideline for good living and the importance of working for a living and saving for the future.

The idea behind it is that the system will no longer rely on National Insurance contributions or credits to determine the entitlement but rather reflects on the life that has been led and the type of character you may have been.

What should now appear evident to the people is that there is absolutely no entitlement to any pension provisions in old age. Similarly, good people or hardworking members of society will be aware of the potential financial rewards that will be bestowed upon them in later life.

Specifically, each person is assessed against a number of criteria and 'pension points' will be added/subtracted depending on the nature of the criteria eg. positive points are assigned for an indication of a good or a hardworking life.

The higher number of points accrued would then equate to a higher payout, but critically, the maximum pension entitlement isn't fixed. Rather, the total pension pot is unchanged regardless of the points distribution and is split accordingly - which means in a society where good morals are prevalent throughout then the pension entitlement is more or less similar for most. On the other hand, in a society which has decayed to a point where only a small proportion live a good life, then the large pot will be split generously amongst the do-gooders.

Life-Linked Pension: Worked Example based on a population of 8 Persons

Citizen's Name → Main Profession → Character	Pension Points	Aaron Doctor Law-abiding Honourable		Bradley Doctor Dishonest Greedy		Charles Unspecified Lazy Directionless		Delroy Criminal Wayward Poor Morals		Eleanor Nurse Law-abiding Giving		Frank Labourer Hard Working Uneducated		George Teacher Convicted Paedophile		Hercule Banker Wealthy Poor Morals	
Assessment Criteria	**Pension Points**	Y/N	Points	Y/N	Points	Y/N	Points	Y/N	Points	Y/N	Points	Y/N	Points	Y/N	Points	Y/N	Points
Starting Position	100	Y	100	Y	100	Y	100	Y	100	Y	100	Y	100	Y	100	Y	100
Criminal Record with >1 convicted offence	-80			Y	-80			Y	-80					Y	-80		
Criminal Record includes; Rape, Murder or Child Abuse.	-200													Y	-200		
Assets over £10 million	-120															Y	-120
Distinguished Healthcare Professional	20	Y	20	Y	20					Y	20						
Academic Professional	20													Y	20		
Has Undertaken Considerable Unpaid Charity Work	40									Y	40			Y	40		
Been employed or actively seeked employment from the age of 25-65	30	Y	30	Y	30					Y	30	Y	30	Y	30	Y	30
Unemployed for more than 30% of the employment availability period	-60					Y	-60	Y	-60								
Points Accumulated - Pre Adjustment		150		70		40		-40		190		130		-90		10	
Points Accumulated - Post Adjustment (If Negative, apply Null)		150		70		40		0		190		130		0		10	

Total Adjusted Population Points	590
Annual Pension Fund Available for Population	£100,000
Pension Amount Payable per Points Accrued	169

Pension Calculation Summary

	Aaron	Bradley	Charles	Delroy	Eleanor	Frank	George	Hercule
% of Pension Pot	25%	12%	7%	0%	32%	22%	0%	2%
Annual Pension £	25,424	11,864	6,780	0	32,203	22,034	0	1,695

Human extinction is upon us due to a virus that resulted in the world's population to suffer permanent and hereditary infertility. Modern science has come to the rescue with one shot at saving mankind by cloning fertile humans from the preserved DNA of a pre-virus era human. Unbeknown to anyone, the unwilling donor is 'Jeffrey Dahmer'. Discuss?

Background

The year is 2048 and the world has been ravaged by an airborne virus affecting human beings which caused the immune system to slowly deteriorate and crucially, also affected the reproduction system in both males and females - causing permanent infertility and all un-born children to inherit this destructive genetic code.

This 'symptom of infertility' discovery came too late with disastrous consequences as scientists worked with no real urgency or co-operation to find a cure as existing drugs could already be utilised to deal with the immune deficiency.

By the time the complete set of symptoms was finally discovered, not only was the cure to eradicate the virus (and all its strains) just months from wides-cale production but the world's population had already been completely inflicted. A cure that could now only be considered ultimately futile for the human race as future generations would no longer exist.

Facts and Examples

Scientists have finally harnessed a cloning technique which can be attempted only once and would require the preserved Human DNA of someone who died before the virus is believed to first lie dormant, 1996.

On 6th June 2066, with global population decline already scarily evident, a well-preserved sample of Human DNA was finally found in the science labora-tory of a prestigious university famous for its research on genetics and DNA analysis.

Though the source of the sample is not known, the official go-ahead has been given with no regard to the identity or character of the donor or to the long term implications of cloning a new human race from a single strand of DNA (and the supposed argument that an 'evil' gene could be present in the code).

Discuss the possible scenarios for generations to come in the context of hereditary genetics and the possible futility of a good solid upbringing?

FOR	**AGAINST**
No such thing as an 'evil' gene, otherwise humanity would never have progressed to this point that mankind is ever so proud of. § A good loving upbringing can overturn inherent genetic traits. § Adverse and irreversible circumstances occurred at a critical time of the young persons development which coupled with inadequate psychological care led to reverberating repercussions.	You cannot fight nature, and a person is born a certain way, with genes dictating the tendency to be good, bad or neutral. Only in the case of a neutral gene base, can an upbringing actually affect the person he/she will become. § We undoubtedly inherit many of our parents physical characteristics and personality by way of the DNA genetic code downloading this 'data'.

…and it's these 'Midichlorians'…

Oh no you didn't…

Further Facts

- *Dahmer* (1960-94) was a notorious serial killer and sex offender who murdered 17 males by various means involving rape, dismemberment, necrophilia and cannibalism. He was raised by two loving parents in a stable home.
- Some think that people behave as they do according to genetic predispositions while others believe that people think and behave in certain ways because they are taught to do so. Greater understanding of the human genome has recently made it clear that both sides are partially right.

Image Source:- Movie: Star Wars: Episode I - The Phantom Menace (1999)
Starring: Liam Neeson & Pernilla August

With so many cross-rivalries and hatred between nations, are we facing an altogether more disturbing scenario than that of Mutually Assured Destruction (MAD) - Are we now in an era of nuclear deterrence where the idea of CHARRED now overshadows every political conflict?

Background

The concept behind CHARRED (*Connected Hostility Amongst Rivals Reassures Even Destruction*) lies the idea that there is so much long standing interconnected hatred between nations that a nuclear attack originating anywhere in the world would cause a chain reaction of unprovoked attacks on rivals, resulting in a scenario where no continent will escape unscathed from the effects of nuclear conflict.

With a growing trend of less distinguished and trigger-happy individuals taking up the most powerful positions in nuclear capable countries, threatens a personality likely to be susceptible to the notion of an ungracious "*If we're going down, then we're taking them with us*" reactionary instinct at the point of defeat.

Therefore, unlike MAD which assured only those parties engaged in war would be mutually destroyed, CHARRED would ensure global annihilation and an end to mankind if the use of nuclear weapons were ever initiated in any continent/region.

Facts and Examples

Consider the hypothetical scenario where an unbalanced former war general has successfully led a coup, overthrowing the leadership of Iran, a country which had amassed a considerable nuclear weapon stockpile.

Two years on and with a war initiated by the new leader against Israel now on the brink of a humiliating defeat, he authorises a nuclear attack against them. Israel then immediately counter with their own nuclear attack meaning that both countries and immediate regions are now just 30 mins from complete destruction.

With both countries now having a finger on the trigger for 90% of their remaining stockpile, and it being futile to use on each other again, they both decide to take out other lifelong enemies/rivals as a parting shot under a misguided sense of patriotic duty.

Classroom Exercise:- Draw an interconnectivity map which sequences the knock-on attacks required to draw in the regions: India, N Korea, US and China?

FOR	**AGAINST**
Misguided religious fanatics who believe in a duty to initiate conflict may begin to pay more regard to the consequences of such actions. § More responsible attitudes to the procurement and control of nuclear armament will take place. § Destroying an enemy becomes a more far reaching consideration. § Chemical weapons provide nuclear incapable nations to be covered by CHARRED.	The people would never allow unbalanced individuals to ever assume power let alone grant them financial/political backing in pursuit of a nuclear deterrent. § There is always honour in defeat. Such a scenario could never occur as leaderships would never tread such childish and immoral paths. § ElectroMagnetic Pulse technology will eventually render such armoury useless.

Be Controversial

Is it feasible that the superpowers have already configured the GPS co-ordinates for an all-out global destruction strategy - not relying on a CHARRED deterrent ideology to take place as suggested. Such a revelation that the superpowers foremost reason for stockpiling may not just be 'nuclear deterrence', doesn't seem too outlandish when you consider that just 1000 warheads would be required to destroy each other (today, the US have almost 10,000 nuclear warheads while Russia possess over 12,000).

Image Source:- Movie: Indiana Jones and the Kingdom of the Crystal Skull (2008)
Starring: Harrison Ford

Are 'plants' Earths last line of defence against the destructive force of Mankind?

Background, Facts and Miscellaneous

The 2008 film *The Happening* put forward an idea that plants can collectively launch a counteroffensive against the human race by releasing airborne toxins that rewire the human brain - the neurotoxins triggering a reverse-survival instinct by prompting people to commit suicide.

An absurd concept surely, primarily because plants don't have brains and are therefore obviously unable to exhibit the intelligence required to tackle problems that it may potentially face, let alone consciously perceive a forthcoming threat.

But is it really inconceivable? After all, plants, like humans, have evolved over time, have constantly adapted to their changing environment, and have exhibited remarkable defence strategies that the human body can only dream of possessing. Such trends would suggest that there may

well be the possibility of intelligence present throughout the plant cycle. Adding to the fact that evolutionary theory states that survival is paramount in the upgrade process and the threat to the ecosystem posed by mankind is a pressing concern, the idea that plants can initiate a defence tactic doesn't seem so far-fetched. Or do we restrict the assumptions of *Evolution* and *Intelligent Design* just to the Human and Animal species?

• *Red Tide* is a phenomenon which indicates that marine plant life have begun releasing toxins in response to changing environmental conditions;
• When attacked, the *sagebrush* plant broadcasts a predator's presence by releasing chemicals into the air, effectively warning others to increase production of a defensive agent.

Privatisation of the state owned transport and utility institutions - Was it really just an alternative method to charge a head tax (a fixed tax per adult resident) on the people, thereby sneakily helping to shift the tax burden from the rich to the poor?

Background, Facts and Miscellaneous

The attempt to levy a *Community Charge* tax, based on the number of persons living in a house rather than its estimated value, became deeply unpopular resulting in its almost immediate abandonment. However, rather more disturbingly, almost immediately afterwards, a push to privatise state owned firms that provided the core transport and utility services gathered apace (British Gas®, British Petroleum®, British Rail®, National Power®, PowerGen® and the Regional Water Companies all took place in the 90s).

While it's perfectly reasonable to suggest that energy and travel costs are proportionate to the number of people living in a house, its also reasonable to expect that everyone pays the same for travel/services regardless of their financial cir-

cumstances. However, it must be noted that the spectre of rising prices and those which exceed inflation will obviously affect the poorer more.

Recently, we've observed little to no action on the regulators part to restrict or control the inflationary price increases seen year on year. Predictably, profits have escalated to obscene levels while the government quite happily turns a blind eye in order to take their cut of it (head tax anyone?).

Further Discussion Points:-
• Should the government nationalise those industries which should naturally be government owned and restore fairer price levels and salaries?
• Is the privatisation of the NHS inevitable? If so, what are the consequences?
• Privatising highways a license to print money?

Miscellaneous Facts and Examples

◦ In 1999, BT chairman Sir Peter Bonfield received a 130% pay rise, putting his salary at £2.53m.

◦ In 1998, a survey revealed that directors of the water, gas and electricity utilities enjoyed pay rises averaging 18%. In some cases, chief executives received pay increases of up to 40% while boardrooms demanded pay restraint among staff. Typical boardroom salaries at British Gas and Centrica were in excess of £300,000, while in the electricity sector the average package was up 9%, to £241,000.

◦ In 2006, the national passenger watchdog announced that the railways are becoming the 'preserve of the rich', after train companies announced fare increases above the rate of inflation for the fourth year running. The total amount paid each year by passengers had doubled to £4.5 billion since privatisation a decade earlier

◦ In 2011, Ignacio Galan, the Chairman and Chief Executive of Scottish Power, had his annual salary increased to £10.5 million, including a performance-related £6 million bonus. This came amidst Scottish Power raising its prices to UK consumers by 10% for electricity and 19% for gas - a second round of major price rises in a year.

◦ All the large utility firms have continued to report bumper profits since the early days of privatisation.
In 2011, British Gas reported a profit of £742 million, while its parent company Centrica saw its profits mushroom to £2.4 billion. Scottish Power, meanwhile, posted core profits of £1.2 billion.

◦ OFWAT, the water regulator, have instructed water companies to keep prices broadly stable until 2015. After which, we will undoubtedly expect increasing payrises and bills (watch this space!).

◦ Three executives at Thames Water, Britain's largest water supplier, were handed £2m in bonuses in 2011. Meanwhile, with an estimated 300 million gallons of water lost every day due to leakage, a staggering £500m was handed to shareholders (amongst them being large investment banks and foreign-led consortiums).

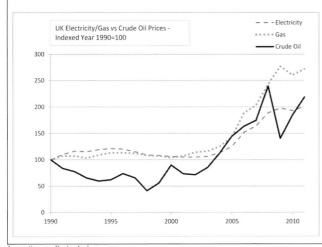

UK Electricity/Gas vs Crude Oil Prices - Indexed Year 1990=100

- - - Electricity
• • • • Gas
—— Crude Oil

Graphic Data Sources:

Electricity and Gas Prices: (www.castlecover.co.uk)
The Castle Cover Utilities Index demonstrates the growth of electricity and gas bills across the UK over the last 20 years. It normalises prices at the same point on the scale at 1990 (100 on the graph) in order to show the rises and (rare) falls in the average utility bill.
Electricity and gas - the two most-used household energies - have nearly doubled over the last seven years of the index, owing to their ties with oil prices, as well as a number of other factors.

Crude Oil Price: (http://inflationdata.com)
Annual Average Crude Oil Price from 1946 to the present. Prices are adjusted for Inflation to December 2012 prices using the Consumer Price Index (CPI-U) as presented by the Bureau of Labor Statistics.
Prices are based on historical free market (stripper) prices of Illinois Crude as presented by IOGA (www.ioga.com).

Image Source:- By the Author

The year is 2055 and a scientific solution for living long lives free from age-related illness has been realised, perfected and now long been practiced. Discuss the impact of a widespread and reckless distribution of this 'gift' applied overnight to the entire global population?

Background, Facts and Miscellaneous

In 2010, scientists discovered a specific gene (*FOXO*) played an important part in determining the rate of ageing and the average lifespan of humans. This led to progressive government-led research through increased funding and relaxed regulations, eventually leading to the discovery of a chemical compound that permanently slowed down the ageing process plus increased a persons immunity and resistance to stress.

The year is now 2055, and the government have been successfully prolonging peoples lives for over 3 decades now, resulting in an average lifespan of 120 years old and more critically, observing age-related illnesses and body deterioration only from an average age of 118 years. With such benefits, the authorities have been understandably strict in who is offered 'preservation',

with the main prerequisites for selection being aged between 30-35, law-abiding and displayed unwavering decent and good morals thus far.

Unfortunately, a secretive terrorist organisation with previous known history for anarchist endeavours and intentions have stolen the chemical formula and have announced their non-negotiable plan to manufacture and disperse it into the global water system within the year.

Discuss the impact this will have on the global populace who banked on a regular lifespan:-
• those who saw an end in sight for all their suffering, hardship and abuse they have endured;
• those who have long harboured unbearable guilt, personal loss or unshakeable grief;
• Hindu's hoping for or dreading *reincarnation*.

If all Religions had entered into a 'cartel' from day one whereby they all synchronised their stances on the back story and the afterlife (together with what kind of life would need to be led for a harmonious one), would we been in a state of religious harmony today with almost no religious based conflict occurring through the ages?

Background, Facts and Miscellaneous

A *cartel* is a formal unwritten agreement or understanding amongst competing entities in order to meet individual or collective intentions. A typical commercial *cartel* would agree on such matters as price fixing, allocation of territories etc.

Today, even without the advent of science, the contradictory mutually-exclusive 'answers' across the different scriptures have allowed the very credibility of religion to be questioned, with increasing discontent and rejection of it globally.

When the various religious scriptures were first written, where a writer's focus was to attract as many members as possible while discouraging and discrediting other scriptures, would a cartel agreement have been advantageous over the course of history - secretly engaging with each other to attain the long term common intention of promoting the following of a religious path and maintaining longevity/unity in the event of reasoned or scientific contradictions of its texts.

With the idea that commonality provides a sense of credibility, could such an agreement have ensured overlapping consistency on their respective backstory and the afterlife as well as encouraging people live a good moral life by agreeing on the notion of Karma tying in with the afterlife?

Further Discussion Point:-
Is it indeed the conscious awareness of these wide inconsistencies and there being no co-operative relationship in place, that forced religious institutions to try and forcibly suppress each other over the centuries, at any cost, even human?

With the emergence of the Islamic community comes the opportunity for some to promote Sharia Law to be the foremost underlying legal grounding for a revised UK legal system - With their steely determination, unfaltering and undying belief that it is for the betterment of society, is Sharia Law inevitable?

Background

Even as recently as 20 years ago, the mere mention of introducing new laws based on a minority's religion would have been outright dismissed and ridiculed. However, today we discover that not only is it even being allowed to be practiced amongst certain communities (clearly flouting British law) but also there being an increasing sense of public declarations for aspects of Islamic 'Sharia Law' (particularly with regard to punishment) to be permitted into UK law.

With the Muslim population in Britain ever expanding, the growing concern is why the idea is not dismissed out of hand and why rather the prospect of it transitioning into British Law is being pro-actively allowed to simmer under the surface.

With the effectiveness of DNA analysis proving reliable in helping to establish guilt, is there indeed a valid case for DNA supported Sharia Law being the only viable and optimal method to mend our broken society as well as acting as a true deterrent?

Facts and Examples

• Judge has discretion to use his hunch on whether the accused is innocent. Conceivably, past criminal history can be considered and there isn't an onus on the detective to uncover irrefutable proof.
• Quran verse 2:282 establishes that a woman's testimony is worth only half that of a man's in court.
• Rape can only be proven if the rapist confesses or if there are four male witnesses (google *Article 308*).
• Punishments for serious crime can vary from prison terms, corporal punishment, stoning or amputation.
• Sharia law in theory sees no homicide as 'justifiable homicide', and if homicide is carried out, the person either forfeits his own life or pays for the blood of the murder victim. Traditionally, the next of kin of the victim would carry out the execution, or the victim himself/herself would inflict the injury.
• Sharia courts traditionally do not rely on lawyers; plaintiffs and defendants represent themselves. Trials are conducted solely by the judge, with no jury.

FOR	AGAINST
Eye for an eye justice. § The low crime and reoffending rates in existing Islamic states which practice Sharia Law. § Impossible for a person to be convicted of committing theft for a third time. § Stadiums filled with the general public thirsty for the blood of scum to be shed - to be able to revel and listen first-hand to the cries of murderers, rapists and (illegal) child abusers.	Child abusers can attempt to cite the various interpretations of verse Quran 65:4 to excuse immoral acts with prepubescent girls. § A first step to moving to an all-Islamic state, with Islamic fundamentals applied to Law, Human Rights, Equality, Commerce etc. § Guilty until proven innocent. § At a judge's discretion! § Inhumane execution and mutilation. § Womens rights.

...I take thee,

...I take thee,

Image Source:- Movie: The Accused (1988) Starring: Jodie Foster

Classroom Exercise

In 2009, a 67 year old grandfather, *Ekram Haque*, was attacked in front of his 3 year old granddaughter. Sadly, the traumatised toddler cradled him as he died.
Two teenagers (with a long history of violence and petty crime) finally admitted to killing him during an orgy of violence against vulnerable and elderly people, filming much of the 'happy slapping' attacks on their mobile phones.
Speculate as to how the UK legal system punished them and how different would it have been had it occurred under Sharia Law?

It's now possible for neurological analysis to accurately determine whether an individual would excel in careers requiring intellectual talent or that of a physical capacity. As such, children are now assessed in their early years to decide their optimal schooling path, one which the child and school system must legally abide to. Discuss?

Background

Younger children display widely varying rates of learning ability, so when a child falls behind the rest it can lead to a premature belief that they are intelligently inferior or lacking. For those that evidently are, the struggle to keep up gets to such a point that they finally let go and allow themselves to sink.

This untended disillusionment with education and eventual lack of hope for their future finds children looking for solace in social subcultures, such as delinquent behaviour, gang membership or substance abuse. Alternatively, children can become depressed, drop out, lose interest in living and maybe even attempt suicide to renounce a life that to them is beset with unrelenting frustration, emptiness and failure.

The year is 2019 and recent studies have proven that analysing a young child's brain accurately determines their intellectual, practical and physical potential. With this, the authorities intend to revolutionise schooling.

Facts and Examples

The main aims for the reform is to stem the growing disillusionment amongst the young as well as help channel individuals towards their natural calling.

There are now two curriculums which schools must now support, an Intellectual (Science and Maths) and a Physical (Sporting/Practical) one. Both curriculums would also contain the same core base which takes up around a fifth of the school week, covering the mandatory element of any satisfactory education.

In order to determine the school curriculum that will be followed throughout their whole school life, the brains of children will be analysed at the age of 7 to assess brain 'quality'. Those unfortunate who display indeterminate optimal potential, will instead need to follow a balanced curriculum, as per the case today.

Understanding that education is now tailored to their natural abilities, enthusiasm for school attendance and compliance is expected to exponentially increase.

FOR	**AGAINST**

Less chance of children losing interest in school and consequently, life. Those who do so are only those comfortable with life defeating them or those exhibiting abnormal levels of laziness or entitlement. § Higher chance of success and fulfilment of potential. § Contentment in the knowledge that potential was pro-actively explored and encouraged by authorities that 'gave a f**k'.	Discrimination. § A child's free will as well as the development of aspirations. § A generation of either dumb or smart adults. § Fiercer competition will result that would not have been observed in a level-playing field. § Enough career opportunities do not exist to satisfy the highly tuned graduates and their expectations. § A balanced society needs non-aspiring and talentless members.

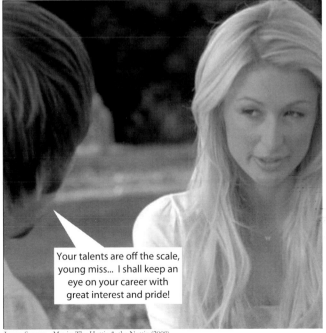

Your talents are off the scale, young miss... I shall keep an eye on your career with great interest and pride!

Future Reform

Champions are Bred.

The secondary aim is to identify those who harbour extraordinary potential with the intention of harnessing these talents for the advancement of the nation.

A child identified with extraordinary natural traits to likely be successful in a certain field (be it science minded or sporting talent), should have personally tailored curriculums drawn up solely with the aim of achieving that goal.

Image Source:- Movie: The Hottie & the Nottie (2008)
Starring: Joel David Moore & Paris Hilton

Do the 'Knights Templar' know the religious prophecies to be true and are aware of the threat a Third Temple would bring, thus why they guide the 'Higher Order Architects' to ensure the Western nations stubbornly stand aside Israel, as a means to assure no such scenario can ever transpire?

Background, Facts and Miscellaneous

The *Temple Mount*, a 35-acre landmass in the Old City of Jerusalem beside Mount Zion, is a place that holds enormous relevance for Judaism, Christianity and Islam alike (they believe it to be where *Abraham* offered his son *Isaac* in sacrifice to God). It is arguably the most coveted archaeological, religious, historical and cultural plot of ground in the world, and furthermore, it is also sadly, the epicentre of the conflict in the Middle-East between Jews and Muslims.

To Jews and Christians, it is thought to be the site of the First and Second Jewish temples, home to the fabled *Knights Templar* and which held the *Ark of the Covenant* and the *Ten Commandments*. For Muslims, the site is associated with *Muhammad's* Night Journey, in which he ascended to heaven into God's presence and then returned to *Mecca*.

Critically, Jewish traditions maintain that it is here that the Third and Final Temple, as prophesised in the *Book of Ezekiel*, will be built. However, a hurdle currently stands in the form of one of Islam's holiest shrines, the *Dome of the Rock*.

The *Bible* refers to a seminal event known as the *Abomination of Desolation*, as a key milestone to the 'end of days' events, which supposedly requires a Jewish Temple to be built upon the *Temple Mount*. The *Book of Revelations* speaks of an end-time battle taking place in Israel, in the hills of Megiddo, better known as *Armageddon*.

Collectively, this appears to prophesise a forthcoming conflict between Islam and Israel, with the *Bible* referring to this as possibly the *War of Ezekiel 38-39*, the battle of *Gog* and *Magog*, a conflict greater than any conflict yet to occur.

Should TV license payers have an 'opt-out' option so that their license fee does not contribute to the 'time of their lives' for the 'Top Gear' presenters?

Background, Facts and Miscellaneous

Top Gear® is a British television show about motor vehicles, primarily cars, and lays claim to be the world's most widely watched factual television programme. It regularly features challenges and long-distance races.

Since the BBC is a publicly funded organisation, legitimate concerns have understandably arisen about the lavish salaries earned by its presenters. But they have been rightly dismissed due to its immense success, much of it largely attributed to the persona of the presenters.

However, should we restrict funding of such 'adventures of a lifetime' to the select few only, conceivably for the rest of their TV careers?

"Fun? I must look that up in a dictionary".
  ~ Jeremy Clarkson

Jaunts include fact-finding missions such as:-
• Road trips along the east and west coasts of the US in high performance prestige cars,
• Road trip quests to find the greatest driving roads in Europe and across the World,
• Riding high performance sports coupes across the Isle of Man and the Pendine Sands,
• Being dropped deep into the Bolivian rainforest armed only with three 4x4 off-roaders,
• Racing hatchbacks on the Monaco GP Track,
• Discovering whether a battle tank could lock its main cannon onto a Range Rover® Sport,
• Middle East road trip - Presenters pass themselves off as 'three wise men' while recreating the famous journey following a star to Bethlehem,
• Undertaking a road test (including a chase through a shopping centre and a beach landing).

Image Source:- TV Series: Arrested Development (2003) Starring: Jason Bateman

With instant justifiable retribution and the feelgood factor associated with exacting appropriate revengeful action, should 'Vigilantism' now be actively encouraged instead, especially with regard to the insufficient policing levels and inadequate punishments that are all too often handed out?

Background

A vigilante is an individual or a group of individuals who undertake law enforcement or acts of vengeance without any legitimate legal authority.

Vigilante justice is rationalised by the idea that adequate legal mechanisms for criminal punishment are either non-existent or insufficient. Vigilantes typically view the authorities as ineffective in enforcing the law; and such persons often presume to justify their actions as fulfilling the harboured wishes of 'the victim'.

However, as vigilantes are not bound to any given protocol in terms of establishing guilt, the likelihood of targeting innocent people is deemed a risk that cannot be encouraged or tolerated, therefore any form of vigilantism is currently outlawed.

Should authorities permit citizens to exercise reasonable force/retribution in instances when the legal system has failed them and where any appropriate punishment is now beyond any official recourse?

Facts and Examples

• *Ken Rex McElroy*, regarded as the town bully of a small town in Missouri had over the course of his life been accused of dozens of crimes including assault, child abuse, arson, burglary and rape. In all, he was indicted 21 times but escaped conviction each time except for when he was finally convicted for attempted murder - to which he subsequently appealed and was later released on bail. Collective retribution ensued.
• Recently, even with serious crime rates on the rise, widescale budgetary pressures to cut police spending (will) have resulted in a significant drop in police numbers across the breadth of England.
• What state of harmony or anarchy would *Gotham City* be in without the masked vigilante, the watchful protector, the silent guardian?

Honourable Mentions:- Giuseppe Munciguerra; Xiaopeng Wang; Rodrigo 'The Punisher' Duterte; Roy Allison - A fathers love; Cyber Vigilantes;

FOR

Criminals less likely to commit crimes knowing unrestricted retribution could be carried out by the person scarred. § Inadequate and corrupt justice system. § Reduces workload for police and the whole criminal justice system. § No legal punishment fit enough for child abusers. § An 'eye for an eye' the only means of providing real closure. § Human primal instincts.

AGAINST

Backfiring - A criminal with no morals versus an upstanding citizen would yield only one eventual winner. § Tit for tat. § Unproved guilt. § When committing sins becomes lawful, the advocation of this can only lead society on an irrecoverable downward spiral. § The initiative to frame someone. § Criminals now alter behaviour to ensure no retribution possible.

Be Controversial

Would it be beneficial for those young male adults who have excess testosterone and are naturally strong to channel their aggression in a positive form rather than living directionless in what would inevitably lead them down the wrong path, one which would likely prove ultimately unfulfilling.

To inspire them to believe they can be a positive effect on society, they are offered to become upstanding 'guardians' of the community, receiving the respect and gratitude of their peers and their elders.

Image Source:- Movie: Once Upon a Time in the West (1968)
Starring: Henry Fonda & Charles Bronson

In an alternate universe, England has had strict tightened border controls and restricted welfare benefits, such that in the year 2020, England is 99% indigenous White English - Are they genetically well equipped to fend for themselves?

Background, Facts and Miscellaneous

The notion that the lower classes are breeding exponentially more than the middle classes is a common theme presented throughout this book, used at points to convey the reasoning behind future scenarios or present issues facing society.

However, it must be said that if a naive simpleton like myself can foretell how this can only end badly, then you can imagine how unfathomable he thinks recent policy has been to open our previously rigid borders and let anyone in. He's also fully aware that the policy makers know full well that this strategy can only exacerbate the problem, what with endless child-correlated welfare benefits and protective human rights legislation also helping to preserve the longevity of their residence and satisfy their desire to stay. He can only conclude that decision-makers are idiots!

But is the Author actually a little too naive to genuinely believe that the authorities would ignorantly sell the soul of this country down the river, in that the bigger picture hasn't been considered.

Is there a deeper agenda at work, where the *HOA* recognise better underlying qualities in the average non-Englishman, that *natural selection* can no longer be left to chance. Are they fully aware of the 'white chavvy' element and that a systematic changing of the wider UK demographic is considered essential to the longevity of Britain as a revered and prosperous nation, as well as to help with foreign business relations, in respect of the everchanging shift in the economic landscape.

How would England's fortunes of transpired in the long term if only the indigenous English people lived here and the lower classes outbred?

Image Source:- Movie: Snatch (2000) Starring: Alan Ford, Dave Legeno and William Beck

Chapter F

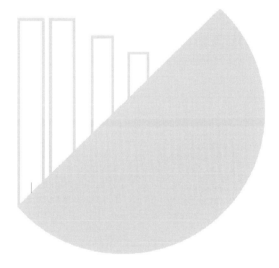

"Honesty is the mother of confidence; it unites, combines and solidifies society. Dishonesty is disintegration; it destroys confidence; it brings social chaos"
- *Robert Ingersoll*

If the United Nations shifted focus towards 'Global Security' solely, can a UN governed 'assassination squad' actually prove beneficial to society as a whole, assuring the people of this world of a brighter and safer future?

Background

With the *United Nations* considered no longer fit for purpose, with its mission irrelevant in a world facing unprecedented conflicts and dangers, the UN are looking to abandon (already neglected) duties and responsibilities to the wider world and instead purely focus on a more prominent objective: 'standing guard' protecting the world from internal threats.

By this, the *UN Security Council* now recognises that their influence and power command very little respect in corrupt regimes or unstable regions, while also appreciating that there are clear and present dangers in the form of individuals who potentially threaten global harmony or harbour harmful yet realistic intentions. Therefore, the UN have secretly ratified, with the agreement of select member states, a formation of an highly-equipped and globally-assisted 'Assassination Squad' to uphold their 'security' directive.

The principal aim being to assassinate individuals who cannot be curbed by conventional legal means.

Facts and Examples

Consider this scenario:-

In an alternative version of historic events, in the year 1994, the middle east uprisings have recently taken place across the region, notably in Saudi Arabia where the rein of President *Hosni Mubarak* ended in disgrace.

Presidential elections are now currently taking place and the *'Muslim Brotherhood'* party seem to be heading for a popular victory with their presidential candidate, a wealthy and distinguished Saudi Arabian resident, *Osama Bin Laden*. He has proudly declared to the voting public that he will employ its vast resources and wealth for the betterment of the region as well as to spread the word of *Islam* by whatever means necessary - for this, he will grant himself unlimited powers to protect the nation and the power to legislate without judicial oversight or review of his acts.

Should the UN intervene with their 'Assassination Squad' at the ready for what it perceives as a real potential threat to global security?

FOR

Pre-emptive strikes can only be beneficial for mankind if correctly administered and co-ordinated, and as long as the initial mandate can never be compromised. § The world is a sick place and only by sinking to this level can true justice be delivered and for peace to be allowed to finally prosper. § The UN can now answer your prayers. § Silently overrules the abuse of authority.

AGAINST

The UN has long been held up as a standard for all human beings to try and live together peacefully. § A slippery slope for international law and enforcement. § Initial mandate can be easily exceeded over time. § Disputes amongst the world leaders arising from differences of opinion in what constitutes 'potential danger' - repercussions that could easily lead to war or lengthy hissy fits.

In such a situation, you have no time to think - instinct takes over. It's either kill or be killed.

Image Source:- Movie: Trading Places (1983) Starring: Dan Aykroyd

Future Reform

Being answerable to a Higher Power.

Should the UN publicly reveal this change in tact, publishing a roll call of who has thus far been targeted as well as those on the hitlist, including full reasons why and the supporting evidence for each case.

Can this PR exercise act as a sobering benchmark for those with dishonourable intentions - to really evaluate their actions, while acknowledging the wider repercussions in an honest and unbiased manner.

Have legitimate charities lost their way so much so that their mission statements no longer hold true and are now simply a cover for otherwise sinister purposes - A vehicle for the corrupt to live lavishly, the wealthy to avoid taxes and the immoral to steal from the generous?

Background

A charity is a voluntary organisation that is set up to benefit the public in a way the law says is charitable eg. helping to improve education or relieving poverty.

Charities are run by volunteers, known as 'trustees', and are subject to charity law, which places strict conditions on how they are run and what they can do. Because they benefit the public, they receive tax breaks and many other benefits.

As there are no legal caps or guidelines on what reasonable salary levels or expenses for trustees should be, has this been open to abuse for too long now that individuals began to exploit this win-win situation.

If trustees appointed have no real genuine concern for the charitable purpose but rather what they can get out of it, should we all be worried that not enough pennies in the pound ever reach the intended target or that we unknowingly fund champagne lifestyles for the truly undeserving?

Facts and Examples

• In 2011, French president *Nicolas Sarkozy* pledged £900 million of taxpayers' money to the Global Fund, a charity set up to fight killer diseases in developing nations. How much of it actually went towards fighting the cause is unknown, but what is known is the financial irregularities surrounding large payments from the fund to certain individuals, persons who regard the charity ambassador a very close friend, and one who also happened to be the French First Lady.
• 'Foreign Aid' being the process whereby poor people from rich countries transfer money to rich people from rich or poor countries. 'Non-profit' being the status allowing almost all profits to be paid as wages.
• Some would say the wealthy would go to any lengths to avoid paying any tax. One such ploy is to setup bogus charity organisations abroad.

Dishonourable Mentions:- Black Tie Charity Fundraisers; Common Purpose; Atlantic Bridge; Plan3t;

FOR	AGAINST
One would not appoint an atheist as the local vicar! § We all expect charities to not behave in a manner which would shock and appall the very people they expect to help. § Tax havens aren't enough for the wealthy, they try to absolve themselves of any guilt by giving to charity (tax-free). § Deplorable to abuse those who donate their time and money, as well as mocking its own ethos.	Law may not be stringent enough but charitable intentions always remain foremost. § Salaries need to be competitive to attract the talent who have the ability to reach the fundraising targets, especially when many are fighting to be the recipient of that single donation. § The wealthy would not sink so low. § The plush offices are a necessity when entertaining the corporate givers.

Salaries well worth every penny of your Year 2008 donations:-

Barnardo's: Chief Executive, *Martin Narey*
£166,532

National Trust: Director General , *Fiona Reynolds*
£165,000 approx

British Heart Foundation: Chief Executive, *Peter Hollins*
£153,000

Action for Children: Chief Executive, *Clare Tickell*
£135,000 approx

Greenpeace: Chief Executive, *John Sauven*
£65,000

Wildcard View

Could it be that those who seek senior employment at charitable organisations do so because it's the easiest most efficient step into a position of power and control, that would have otherwise not have been achieved in private/ public employment. Especially when one lacks the complete suite of interpersonal skills, deviousness and hard work ethic necessary. Positions also grant access to the world of high salaries, pampering, non-fixed working hours, kick-backs and more importantly, the daily pressure to make NO profit.

Image Source:- The Independent Newspaper UK
Report by Robert Verkaik & Eleanor Harding 10Nov09

With Cyber Warfare being a clear and present threat, how would we cope with moving to a world where technological influences are stripped away?

Background, Facts and Miscellaneous

Over a short space of time, we have taken huge strides in the field of computer technology, such that in the near future, it's inevitable that all our interaction, infrastructure, processes, transport etc will be fully enabled and completely dependent on IT, and likely networked to some degree.

Today, we are already heavily reliant and submerged in the internet, and the breadth of unrestricted possibilities it has boundlessly provided, that maybe the clamour has caused us to overlook our increasing dependence and ignore any thought to a contingent and cautious approach.

The TV series *Battlestar Galactica* (2004-2009) portrayed a scenario where cyber warfare ultimately initiated nuclear annihilation and rendered the military battleship armoury defenceless due to its networked connectivity. Though mired in science fiction, the reality is actually closer than we'd feared with the infamous *Stuxnet* virus employed to infiltrate and destroy an Iranian nuclear facility in 2010. Therefore, its perfectly conceivable to envision complex computer viruses sparking waves of industrial and diplomatic cyber warfare, threatening political instability with potentially catastrophic consequences.

If this type of warfare were allowed to become widespread and highly sophisticated, could it get to a point where there would be no choice but to indefinitely shutdown all computer networks and IT based operations. With IT effectively disbanded and almost every aspect of our lives and infrastructure disabled overnight, could our future society cope with going back to a technologically restricted, non-IT dependent world?

Image Source:- Movie: Battlestar Galactica (2004-09) Starring: Michael Hogan and Edward James Olmos

277

As human civilisation matures we are seeing surprising new depths of human behaviour becoming more commonplace around the world, with immoral criminality, depravity, greed and selfishness everywhere you look. According to the 'The Book of Revelations', the Devil will soon walk amongst us - but is he already here?

Background, Facts and Miscellaneous

Over the past century, we have witnessed a steady yet dramatic shift away from traditional moral values which have resulted in epidemic levels of violent crime and morally corrupt behaviour - standards which wouldn't be out of place in a primitive society that lacked any sense of brotherhood, love, responsibility or compassion.

But markedly, in recent decades these levels seem to have grown exponentially as well as in volume and depth, even beginning to exhibit itself in wider forms (ethic-free Capitalism; rampant child abuse; unjustifiable war and conflict).

Yet, we now consider this distorted human psyche so commonplace and widespread that we could soon be in danger of it soon becoming the accepted norm for our species. But is this occurrence consistent with Gods' warning?

According to the Holy Bible, the Devil and his angels will at some point walk amongst us, looking to deceive us and lead us into temptation (Revelations 12:9). This declaration is complemented by many other verses but of particular relevance here is the Bible verse *"and evil will befall you in the latter days"* (Deuteronomy 31:29).

With this in mind, and assuming you hold an adherence to the Christian religion, could it be conceivable that the widespread moral decline coincided with the Devil's presence and his plan set into motion? Are the Devil's angels all in place as architects of this plan, placed in the upper echelons of government, authority and society to ensure that evil deeds and immoral behaviour goes inadequately unchecked, eventually festering into lawlessness and an ethically depraved society?

The Devils Finest Minions

Some candidates which would have probably received a warm pat on the back from Satan himself

Lalit and Preeti Balhara
∘ Forced their infant child Shaurya to consume insecticides.
∘ Enacted mental and physical abuse throughout the poor young boys life, causing numerous broken bones, bruises, burns and malnutrition.
∘ Broke his teeth and caused mouth ulcers which would go untreated by inserting a stick into the mouth as a form of punishment.

Nkosinati Mabanda
∘ Being aware that he was HIV positive, he went onto knowingly and callously engage in unprotected sex with at least eight women.
∘ What is known is that at least one of the women has been diagnosed as HIV+ and secondly, the number would have been much larger had he been blessed with some good looks or a personality.

Carl Whant
∘ Raped a 19 year old girl, who happened to be eight months pregnant and also the girlfriend of his own cousin.
∘ Stabbed her in the abdomen to kill her unborn baby.
∘ Yawned on the dock while sentencing was passed.

Ed Gein
∘ Murdered at least two women and dug up graves for the bodies of at least thirteen other women.
∘ Primarily engaged in acts of necrophilia and cannibalism.
∘ Upon capture, various body parts were discovered around his property, some used as household items such as skulls made into bowls, jewellery made from human skin, lips hanging, chair seats with human skin upholstery, facial skin that was well preserved and used as masks, amongst other disturbing and horrific finds.

Dishonourable Mentions:-
Greg Skidmore, Brandon Lacoff and Tim Davidson; Johann Kuehberger and a four-year-old Adolf Hitler; New Delhi Gang Rapists;

Bryan Clay
∘ Invaded the family home of Mr and Mrs Martinez and inflicted 17 head fractures in the severe beating of the husband.
∘ Raped their 10 year old innocent daughter as well as killing both her and her mother with a claw hammer.
∘ Until he was caught in an unrelated sexual assault case, he shamelessly allowed the surviving husband to endure suspicion and become the prime suspect in the case, so subjecting the two surviving 5 and 9 year old petrified sons to be placed into temporary foster care.

Adam Gordon
∘ While in the process of conducting a burglary, the vulnerable lonely female resident discovered him and tried to raise the alarm. However, Mr Gordon proceeded to brutally punch the woman in the stomach up to 11 times.
∘ She also happened to be heavily pregnant at the time!

Mr Michael Rafferty and Ms Terri-Lynne McClintic
∘ Abducted an eight year old girl from outside her school, sexually assaulted and raped her multiple times and then finally bludgeoned her to death with a hammer.
∘ After the first rape, the little girl who was bleeding and crying, pleaded with her fellow female Ms McClintic "Just don't let him do it to me again". At which point, she calmly brought the little girl BACK to Mr Rafferty so he could commit the heinous crime again.

Grigoriy Bukhantsov
∘ Brutally murdered a woman in her 20s. Also carried out the murders of her two young children, a three year old and a two year old, who suffered severe trauma prior to their death.
∘ The sequence of events and the sheer brutality suggest that it is highly likely that the two young boys witnessed their mother enduring such pain and suffering.
∘ All the while, a six month old baby was left to cry alone in a crib throughout the ordeal.

With IT fast becoming the most efficient legalised avenue for extorting corporate money, are IT Managers now the most rewarding role in a company?

Background, Facts and Miscellaneous

Expenditure on IT within a company has increased dramatically over the last few decades, emphasising the importance of the function and the need to keep apace with the latest emerging technologies and cost-cutting innovations.

This has led to somewhat generous budget allocations where IT managers find themselves suddenly thrust into a position of overseeing the responsible spending of millions of pounds in order to meet the company's IT requirements. There is also the additional pressure of maintaining the level of budget year on year, which leads to irrational and irresponsible spending of the full allocation to give the perception that every last cent is needed, budgetary pressures exist and that the role is being responsibly handled.

Couple this with the simple fact that tech-nology is 'alien' to many in authority, with the IT domain harbouring an air of mystery and intrigue (especially when technology professionals exhibit the strategic deployment of fancy long buzzwords), IT managers have more or less been given *carte blanche* to do what they want and manage the budget any which way how they like.

As with any financial opportunity which comes to pass, comes the chance to exploit it.

Further Discussion Point:-
With the numerous kickbacks on offer to IT directors, what reason can you speculate as to why they all insist in dressing up head to toe in clothing normally found in a jumble sale or enjoy being seen regularly driving to work in a vehicle normally associated with the 'PC support' intern?

Golden Opportunities presented to 'Directors of IT'

Unnecessary System Upgrades

This simply involves the encouragement and pro-active push to upgrade an existing software or hardware implementation, but one that knowingly isn't in the best interests of the company or the end users. Critically, it's an event that would have quite easily have never been considered unless internal intervention were to occur.

The agenda of the IT director is to initiate and maximise the 'variable kickback' promised by the vendor if they can secure a lucrative upgrade contract for them. Where the variable element really comes into it is how big a project can be wrung out - and this is where an IT Directors' technical knowledge and persuasive skills come to use, in convincing key decision-makers of the (apparent) dangers of not upgrading, such as the wonderous life-changing enhancements awaiting end-users, the scenario of a revoked support agreement and the oh so catastrophic ramifications of not keeping apace with the latest technology.

A Fictional Scenario:-
Vendor Sales Director: "Hey, so how's our software been treating you?"
IT Director: "Yeh, good, it's nicely bedding in. Finally!"
Vendor Sales Director: "Good, good, that news warms my heart. Hows the wife and kids anyway - they must be rinsing you dry?"
IT Director: "Haha, you betcha. Could really do with a payrise actually."
Vendor Sales Director: "And my god, you deserve it more than anyone, with your talent and all those hours you put in."
IT Director: "You know, I was thinking... well, we're not due an upgrade for a good while yet."
Vendor Sales Director: "Hhhmmm, go on..."
IT Director: "Well, if I was to initiate and seek approval for an wholly unnecessary upgrade for your software....?"
Vendor Sales Director: "Funny you should say that, because I'm sure we can come to some kind of arrangement which would be beneficial to both of us."
IT Director: "Excellent, I'll need you to give me a list of the up-to-date technobabble associated with the new version?"
Vendor Sales Director: "Sure, will do. We'll talk next week... by the way, say hi to the wife for me."

Income Supplementing Contractors

This is where a prior agreement has been reached with an external associate, to provide them with a lucrative temporary contracting opportunity in return for a kickback based on the percentage of the gross monthly income.

For his part, the IT director ensures that this associate is internally perceived to be the best person for that role and exhibits the skills and extensive knowledge required for the role in a way which is beneficial to the company in the long term. It would be in his best interests to also extend the contract as long as is possible and to try and screen some individuals from any prying eyes by constantly elevating their invaluable(!) contribution to the IT department.

A Fictional Scenario:-
IT Worker: "Damn, my lack of skills have been found out again."
IT Director: "Out of work again. Whats your skill set?"
IT Worker: "Bit of this, bit of that."
IT Director: "Impressive. How about I get you a contract but you give me 10%?"
IT Worker: "That's just plain wrong. If I refuse, can I still apply?"
IT Director: "Nope?"
IT Worker: "Ok fine. Can't believe someone of my calibre has sunk so low!"

Secret Partners in Outsourcing Firms

This is much like the concept of *Pre-meditated Power Placement*, discussed in a previous topic, whereby a person is placed in an IT department with the sole intention of attaining a position (IT Director) that would enable them to have the authority and power to provide lucrative IT projects to their chosen outsourcing vendor, garnishing them with preferential treatment throughout their 'secondment'.

The underlying intentions are clear, not to make a quick buck but the bigger picture, primarily to expedite the growth and expansion of their new venture as well as establishing a firm foothold and presence in their chosen IT field which otherwise would have been difficult to generate through regular legal means and channels (resulting in slow business and eventual inevitable failure).

A Fictional Scenario:-
IT Geek 1: "We're too big and smart for this small outfit. You talk the talk and I can walk the walk, yet we stumble along supposedly happy and content with this barely competitive salary, the odd bonus and expenses paid trips to clients."
IT Geek 2: "You're right, we should be the ones at the top, yet we're still here. But then, we should really be grateful that they gave us a British passport and pay for our flights back to India once a year to see our loved ones."
IT Geek 1: "True. But, I mean, it can't be too hard to start an outsourcing firm."
IT Geek 2: "It's the contacts man, its all about the contacts outside India!"
IT Geek 1: "Hows your English coming along?"
IT Geek 2: "It's ok, it is being almost as good as my native Punjabi."
IT Geek 1: "Ok, brush up on your English boy, Ive got a proposition."
IT Geek 2: "This better be good!"
IT Geek 1: "And you'll need to learn to wear a shirt for no more than one day."

Authors Note:-

The author wishes to reaffirm the fact that these are all fictitious scenarios and have been merely conceived to illustrate the notion that illegitimate opportunities are possible.

Dishonourable Mentions:-

Accenture The U.S. Department of Justice announced that technology services and consulting company *Accenture* agreed to pay $64 million to resolve allegations that it participated in a large-scale kickbacks scheme involving government contracts. The 2004 lawsuit accused Accenture of receiving kickbacks from IT vendors, inflating prices and rigging bids on federal IT contracts.

Royal Bank of Scotland In 2012, RBS said it was increasing its spending on IT, as it delivered a tough set of annual results that saw losses nearly double to £2 billion. According to an internal IT fellow, the IT investments are crucial in meeting regulatory changes - including meeting US governance and risk management requirements, while improving customer service and launching new products.

Public Spending Indifference A new £9.5 million system at the UK's High Court complex has been shut down because it simply did not fulfill the basic requirements. So, the Civil Servants in charge of IT have decided to replace it with an all new system expected to cost taxpayers another £9.5million. The project was originally tendered for the delivery of a system to simply speed up the flow of data across the Royal Courts by removing outdated manual tasks.

It is well-documented that the 'Eugenics' movement influenced Nazi ideology, resulting in the 'cleansing' on a mass scale for the efficient pursuit of the 'master race' - But is 'Eugenics' simply a rehash of the common religious principle that only followers are the chosen ones and all other 'inferiors' must be purged from existence?

Background, Facts and Miscellaneous

The concept of *Eugenics* can be described as the applied science of using genetics ostensibly to 'advance' the genetic composition of mankind.

It was widely practiced in the early 20th century, encouraged by governments, influential individuals and institutions. Its advocates regarded it as a social philosophy for the improvement of human hereditary traits through the promotion of higher reproduction of certain people and traits, and the reduction of reproduction amongst lesser people and traits.

Adolf Hitler had only begun to study its principles after the immense success of the US sterilisation campaigns (*eugenicide*), legitimising his anti-Semitism by medicalising it and wrapping it in the palatable pseudoscientific facade of *Eugenics*.

But had the early pioneers of *Eugenics* simply been sub-consciously inspired by their deeply rooted religious beliefs(?):-

• The Bible and other popular religious texts do generally tend to consider nonbelievers as subhuman or deviants.

• *"they will have no mercy on infants, nor will they look with compassion on children."* ~Isaiah 13:15-18

• *"If there be found among you, hath gone and served other gods which I have not commanded; Then shalt thou bring forth that man or woman, and shalt stone them with stones, till they die."* ~Deuteronomy 17:2-3,5

• *"For you are a holy people to your God, and God has chosen you to be his treasured people from all the nations that are on the face of the earth."* ~Deuteronomy 14:2

• *"I will establish My covenant between Me and you and your descendants in their generations"* ~Genesis 17:7

Image Source:- Movie: Bachelor Party (1984) Starring: Brett Baxter Clark and ?

If the Tamil Tigers had adopted a 'cutting off the head of the snake' strategy to achieve their aim, estimate how many high-end officials would have been allowed to die before the Heads of the Sinhalese authorities started to sit up, listen and be ready to negotiate with them?

Background, Facts and Miscellaneous

On 20 July 1944, an attempt was made to assassinate *Adolf Hitler* and his leading lieutenants, followed by a meticulously planned military coup d'état. The failed plot was the culmination of the efforts of the German Resistance to overthrow the Nazi-led German government - yet this strategy was rightly considered to be both an ingenious and efficient ploy to end the war, by attempting to cut off the 'head of the snake'.

Had it been successful, there can be little doubt that the *Third Reich* and the principles held would have crumbled in the absence of their charismatic and inspirational leader, and an unconditional surrender to allied troops would have inevitably taken place a lot sooner.

If as the old adage goes, *all is fair in love and war*, then why in the face of relentless barbarism and overwhelming odds has this efficient strategy rarely ever been deployed in modern conflicts. After all, human nature is such that powerful people who make decisions only see the bigger picture, showing no regard for the *little people* - but once they become acutely aware their own lives may be in danger, they'll likely become more inclined to reach a more humane fair solution.

Consider the situation in Sri Lanka:-

If the *Tamil Tigers* had adopted a different approach to liberation rather than terrorism, instead targeting the higher echelons of government, would we have witnessed a speedier mutually diplomatic compromise? And indeed, would there have been a well-stocked Tamil community still left to live in harmony with?

Sri Lankan Civil War - Killing Fields of View

After their senseless assassination of a good man in *Rajiv Gandhi*, the Tamil Tigers finally realised the act, as immoral as it was, served no benefit whatsoever to the cause. With the world united in utter condemnation for this sinister act, it was clear that the 'rallying for the Tamil cause' would never again be an item on the agenda and the Tamil Tigers knew then they would fight alone.

The Proposal

In 1992, the Tigers publicly announce a change of tact in strategy: stating that civilians from both sides will no longer be targeted but emphasis will now switch to those in higher levels of authority in the Sri Lankan government who will be systematically targeted for assassination in turn, bottom-up. This strategy can only be revoked if the Sri-Lankan Government can agree to formal discussions with regard to the plight of the Tamil people plus a complete ceasefire until an amicable agreement can be reached. The detailed schedule for the targeted assassinations are as follows:-

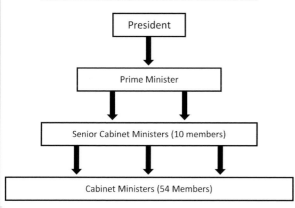

Sri Lanka Government - Hierarchy of Authority

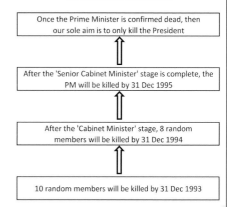

Assassination Strategy

Further Background on the conflict:-

The Sri Lankan Civil War was a conflict fought on the island of Sri Lanka. Beginning on 23 July 1983, there was an intermittent insurgency against the government by the *Liberation Tigers of Tamil Eelam* (LTTE, also known as the Tamil Tigers), a separatist militant organisation which fought to create an independent Tamil state called Tamil Eelam in the north and the east of the island.

° After a 26-year military campaign, the Sri Lankan forces finally defeated the LTTE in May 2009, bringing the civil war to an end.
° The civil war caused significant hardships for the population, environment and the economy of the country, with more than 100,000 people killed during its course, majority of which being innocent civilians.
° The tactics employed by the LTTE against the actions of Government forces resulted in their being listed as a terrorist organisation in 32 countries, including the United States and the member nations of the European Union.
° The Sri Lankan government forces have also been accused of human rights abuses, systemic impunity for serious human rights violations, lack of respect for habeas corpus in arbitrary detentions and forced disappearances.

Image Source:- By The Author

With growing dissent amongst the indigenous population and a fast growing political shift to the far right parties on the horizon, the House of Lords have introduced a new 'Immigration Charter' which aims to stem the uncontrolled influx, the disregard to UK law and the abuse of social security rules. Is this enough to change attitudes of many?

Background, Facts and Miscellaneous

Concerns about immigration have regularly been at the top of the political agenda, and some political parties are now exploiting this animosity amongst the general public towards immigrants (legal or otherwise) for their own means. This 'preserving the indigenous population' stance forms the most important but critical component of the ideology of the far-right.

The year is now 2022 and with decades of unmanageable immigration levels trailing behind, a clear political shift has unfortunately taken place where for the first time in history, an extreme far right party are in a dominant position to assume power in a western democratic society.

The powerful media empires, being instrumental in influencing and shaping opinions on almost all major societal and political issues, had been secretly recruited as far back as 1999 to help in orchestrating this shift. This tactic slowly and surely drew the general public to initially sharing the same views progressing now to a position where there is almost a collective disdain and hostility towards immigrants.

With a General Election taking place in 2025, the House of Lords have uncharacteristically intervened to fast-track an 'Immigration Charter' into UK law. It represents a binding pledge that new and existing immigrants agree to abide by, should they wish to remain part of the UK community.

Will such intervention be strong enough to change opinions or will its good intentions be distorted by the media empires to preserve opinion?

The 2022 Immigrants Charter

The applicant agrees that any single violation of this charter permits a revoking of UK citizenship/residency and invokes immediate repatriation to their originating country. Any legal challenges can only be presented in the UK courts and this charter holds the legal framework that the judge must use to evaluate the case.

○ Thou will learn to fully converse, read and write the English language.

○ Thou shalt not commit any type of crime which causes physical or emotional pain to another human being.

○ Thou shalt only bear children if financial circumstances permit and forsee no reliance on state benefits.

○ Thou can only claim a maximum of 7 years social security support in the first 20 years of residence.

○ Thou can only send a maximum of 50% of their savings to foreign lands, unless they wish to revoke their granted citizenship.

○ Thou accepts that the UK has an underlying Christian/Catholic ethos in its legal and academic foundations and thou will not undertake any attempt to change this. Should you not accept this, then please re-locate yourself to other regions which already practice the underlying faith you so desire and crave.

○ Thou shalt embrace local communities and learn to integrate as well as one can.

○ Thou shalt always try to become a positive contribution and to help encourage the present population to approve a policy of positive net migration.

Small Print: Individuals possessing foreign criminal records need not apply.

Image Source:- by the Author

Does the workings of the Human Waste System prove that 'Intellectual Intervention' in the human evolutionary process did indeed take place, proving to be a crucial alignment necessary for the longevity of our species?

Background

The two well established theories regarding the origins of life, *Evolution* and *Creationism* offered distinct and conflicting ideas: *Evolution* represented science's explanation while *Creationism* offered the religious.

However, concerns slowly arose amongst evolutionists as to how far-fetched it was to assume that random natural processes could have possibly developed into the complexity and diversity seen today.

With the theories being mutually exclusive, there was little room for the evolutionists in which to manoevre in trying to explain this whereas the creationists would simply shrug off any concerns with their standard yet tiresome response that *"God is all powerful"*.

As a result, a new 'Intelligent Design' theory arose addressing this gap by bridging the two theories, in universally accepting the scientific theory of natural selection but accepting that the guidance of an intelligent power must have been present at critical stages of the evolutionary cycle.

Facts and Examples

Victor J. Stenger, a renowned and revered atheist (read evolutionist), once put forward the question to counter the 'intelligent' argument: *"Why would anyone put a recreational area between two waste disposal sites?"*.

There's no denying the old fella has a point and indeed, the most obvious design would have been to utilise the already implemented waste passage (anus) as the means to pass urine rather than proceed to complicate the sexual organs with additional trickery. But has this observation instead provided advocates of 'Intelligent Design' more credence:-

• With the human body in a relatively optimal state, it would be reasonable to assume that *Natural Selection* would have undoubtedly dictated the anal passage to be assigned for the disposal of ALL waste,

• Not passing urine through the sexual organs would have rendered them disfunctional (through lack of any clear function, lubrication or lack of care) by the time young adults figured out the use of them.

FOR	AGAINST
A single passage dedicated to solid/liquid waste, though seemingly a perfect design, would have been anything but. § A high possibility of sexual organs becoming permanently disfunctional, would conceivably have led to the human race prematurely dying out. § The Science community always stubbornly refuse to legislate for any kind of 'spiritual' or unexplainable factor.	Incorrect assumption. Natural Selection would have eventually realised the *two birds with one stone* solution for 'urine' and a prepubescent function. § The ID theory no different from the religious view. A lame attempt to stem the growing atheist movement plus maintain the idea of a 'God' amidst an ever increasing rise in the acceptance of scientific evidence to the contrary.

Enrich you with the ability to populate the earth, your forefathers weep from their graves knowing the future of their bloodline ends with you here tonight.

You may as well just chop the whole thing off... darn load of use it is!!!

Image Source:- Movie: Immortals (2011) Starring: Mickey Rourke

Classroom Exercise

You are a *Higher Being* with a hand in tweaking the engineering of the human species and the time has come for you to make a single configuration update. Confer and then select from the following:-

a) Men and women are now assigned identical sex drives,
b) A drawn out deep migraine is triggered whenever an immoral act is knowingly carried out,
c) Women only have the ability to bear children from the age of 35,
d) Men can only produce sperm until the age of 30.

If market cycles are not a natural result of market dynamics but are actually co-ordinated by the powerful, are we able to analyse the 'instructions' that they have strategically drip-fed out there sufficiently enough to identify the investment area that the next boom and bust cycle has been planned to take place in?

Background, Facts and Miscellaneous

There is a common idea cited by conspiracy theorists that the investment markets are rigged, manipulated by *Higher Order Architects* to engineer a systematic transfer of wealth to the select few.

Specifically, the theory encapsulates the notion that market cycles are meticulously co-ordinated, facilitated by a cabal of powerful and influential entities (bankers, politicians, lobbyists and media moguls) instructed to help ensure the boom and bust take place exactly as planned.

As unlikely, implausible and infeasible such a process to deliberately puppeteer fluctuations and crashes is, it's certainly an accusation which recent events have suggested is no longer one we can so easily dismiss outright anymore, despite the best efforts from those in-the-know to (soundly) debunk any such indication.

If we were to analyse the best performing investment areas over the last 20 years, we are able to observe that major cycles have indeed occurred independently and consecutively, with cycle peaks seemingly almost perfectly coinciding with the start of a boom elsewhere. As the illustration shows, a perfectly timed investment strategy would have yielded a 5000% return for those either very lucky or party to insider knowledge.

Assuming the latter is true, coupled with the fact that the wealthy elite have only one lame aim in life (to get richer), then the beginning of another in-out cycle is imminent (once Gold peaks). Is it possible to highlight patterns or trends in government policy and media opinions over the last two years to pinpoint exactly the next market in which the boom is planned?

Investment Account P&L Statement (1992-2011) for the Higher Order Architects

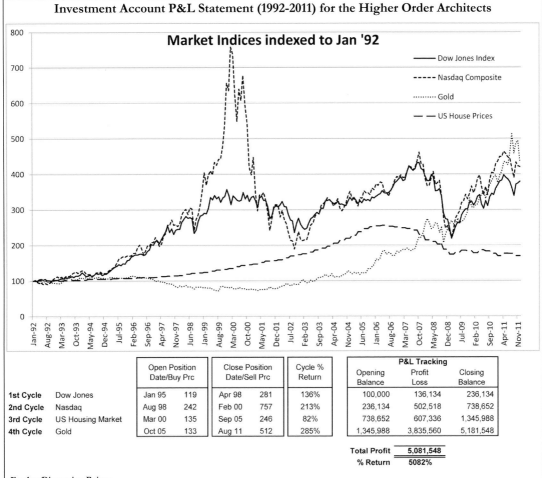

		Open Position Date/Buy Prc		Close Position Date/Sell Prc		Cycle % Return	P&L Tracking		
							Opening Balance	Profit Loss	Closing Balance
1st Cycle	Dow Jones	Jan 95	119	Apr 98	281	136%	100,000	136,134	236,134
2nd Cycle	Nasdaq	Aug 98	242	Feb 00	757	213%	236,134	502,518	738,652
3rd Cycle	US Housing Market	Mar 00	135	Sep 05	246	82%	738,652	607,336	1,345,988
4th Cycle	Gold	Oct 05	133	Aug 11	512	285%	1,345,988	3,835,560	5,181,548

Total Profit	**5,081,548**
% Return	**5082%**

Further Discussion Points:-

Q1: Speculate as to when during the period the following occurred:
    i) Loosening and Tightening of Lending Restrictions, ii) Gold begun being touted as a safe haven, iii) Internet/Dotcom media speculation.

Q2: Were 'endowment mortgages' only designed at a time when they could be implemented at the optimal time policies would start to expire exactly when the HOA wanted the housing market to begin or sustain falling (coinciding when the stockmarket investment was likely not to have covered the outstanding amount resulting in a mass sell-off) and an eventual housing crash (just in time for the next housing boom)?

Image Source:- By The Author

If we do encounter extra-terrestrial beings in our lifetime and it turns out they look and function exactly like human beings, would it immediately debunk all 'evolution' and 'religious' theories while ironically confirming the existence of a 'higher being'?

Background, Facts and Miscellaneous

In recent decades, we've witnessed the childish bickering between *Religion* and *Evolution* over who is right, yet could both one day be cowering in the same corner, pummelled into submission.

If the same 'species' has existed in opposite spectrums of the universe, then it stands to reason that a conscious entity of some form placed a 'human' at these points for a specific reason.

Would such a conclusion dismiss outright the 'theory of evolution' (for obvious reasons), as well as invalidate all mainstream religions for their failure to mention other worlds and/or the existence of 'man' in multiple places?

Additionally, we find ourselves in the strange juxtaposition of a world now devoid of religion but a belief and desired allegiance to a higher being!

• Scientific evidence supporting 'human evolution' has shown that the physical and behavioural traits shared by humans originated from apelike ancestors, evolved over a period of 6 million yrs.
• The sacred religious texts of the world stress God's special concern for humanity within the confines of this world only. One must also note that these scriptures were written in a time when the concept of worlds other than our own or that of extra-terrestrial life was unfathomable.
• The chance of alien life evolving in identical fashion (taking into account the billions of possible permutations) would be practically zero.

Further Discussion Point:-
How will the sudden transition away from a 'religion' adhered existence affect the world?

Marriage has long been the basis for seeking and preserving long term relationships and having children - However, with less and less people believing in marriage, religious institutions have now rewritten the marriage vows to reflect modern society and values.

Background, Facts and Miscellaneous

Marriage is the only institution that allows two people to establish a strong and enduring relationship that is backed by the law and society as a whole. This is the main reason why the Church should and would not countenance the perception that it is becoming an outdated concept.

Therefore, to reflect modern society and to preserve its longevity, the marriage vows have now been rewritten for the following reasons;

• With marriage rates at an all time low and religious beliefs faltering, the institution of marriage is certainly in crisis,

• The main causes of marriage breakdown are due to infidelity, a breakdown in communication and physical or mental abuse,

• Marriage vows in the current form have been recited at UK church weddings since 1552.

In the long term, any system that allows itself to be treated with disrespect and contempt faces extinction.

Discussion Viewpoints:- Marriage must be preserved in todays wayward society. § Provides a base for committed relationships which otherwise may founder under normal relationship pressures. § Marriage just doesn't fit in todays society. § Children have proved to prosper under single-parent families. § Makes people stray who otherwise would never have. § Affairs are good for the soul. § Adapt and Evolve to Survive.

Honourable Mentions:- Linda McCartney; The Church; Charlton Heston;
Dishonourable Mentions:- Paul McCartney; YaVaughnie Wilkins; Earl Partridge;

I, Groom/Bride, take thee, Bride/Groom, to be my lawful wedded wife/husband, to have and to hold from this day forward, for better for worse, for richer for poorer, in sickness and in health, to love and to cherish, till death us do part, and thereto we plight thee;

- ◦ Thou will make each other laugh everyday,
- ◦ Thou will always be presentable and will not live under the view of "*Thy is married now*",
- ◦ Thou will peacefully accept if the relationship is mutually over and assets will be split fairly,
- ◦ Thou will grant each other social lives outside of marriage,
- ◦ Thou will acknowledge physical attraction to others is natural, and will grant each other three '*Infidelity Privilege Passes*' *,
- ◦ Thou will pro-actively share a regular hobby or pastime,
- ◦ Thou shalt not tolerate abuse towards loved ones, nor to oneself.

* The Adultery Clause:

Throughout marriage, thou will grant thy partner the opportunity to wilfully engage in sexual relations with a maximum of three other persons, those of whom must also have undertaken a vow of marriage. These passes can be used from impulsive one-night-stands through to full blown affairs, but it is imperative that this is communicated at the outset of the indiscretion.
- Partners who violate the adultery clause in any way will either invalidate any pending passes or forfeit 75% of all assets in any resulting divorce action.
- An additional discretionary pass is allocated if the other partner has not maintained the same sexual practices that occurred before marriage.

———————————————

Small Print: Same Sex Marriages are now permitted but must revert to the outdated set of vows.

Image Source:- by the Author

In 2076, the ruling World Council has announced a new global decree whereby all natural resources will now become the property of the country's citizens - and all proceeds will be evenly distributed amongst its population as well as helping to improve the country's infrastructure and the lives of its inhabitants. Why did it take so long?

Background

Royal families, dictators, shareholders and other self-serving entities are up in arms at the announcement that their revenue stream derived from the sale of naturally occurring resources will now cease, and the entire infrastructure and facilities to enable extraction including those installed by external companies will now be taken over by the national government (despite assurances of a generous one-off payment covering all infrastructure costs).

In addition to this drastic yet overdue return to the correct ownership, in order to provide global benefit for the worlds natural resources, a mandatory 30% of proceeds must be reinvested back to its originating country of consumption for the purposes of securing long term economic prosperity for itself.

The remaining 70% will go towards improving its own infrastructure, educational and recreational resources, as well as an even financial distribution of the wealth amongst all its law-abiding citizens.

Facts and Examples

Worked Example:-
Consider this fictional scenario where the USA has spent $2 Billion on the oil reserves from the nation '*United Qatari Arabia* (UQA)' resulting in a net operating profit of $1 Billion. UQA has a royal family of 10 members and a population of 200,000 citizens (of which half have criminal records).

• Pre-2076:- Due to its authoritarian rule, the UQA Royal Family simply regard natural resources as a family asset, therefore all proceeds ($1 Billion) will be received wholly by the 10 family members. As a token gesture, a partial amount ($100 Million) will be generously redistributed on a voluntary basis back to its people and for the countries development.
• Post-2076:- Under the new rule, Royal Family members will receive an identical amount to each of the other 100,000 qualifying citizens. A total of $300 Million will be responsibly reinvested back in the USA.

FOR

Major shareholders get a sharp shock to their dividend laden lives. § The only legible and legitimate way to handle the proceeds from a country's natural environment. Should never have even been considered to go into the hands of the few to live immorally luxurious lives. § The financial markets for oil, gas and coal become untenable therefore fairer energy prices will prosper.

AGAINST

A guaranteed two-way financial covenant means more room for ingenious corruption practices. § Creative accounting will ensure that the people still get short-changed. § The heritage of the royal family dynasty is sacred and should not be treated in such a disrespectful manner. § Money corrupts and is the root of all evil, hence why the honourable deliberately withhold the riches.

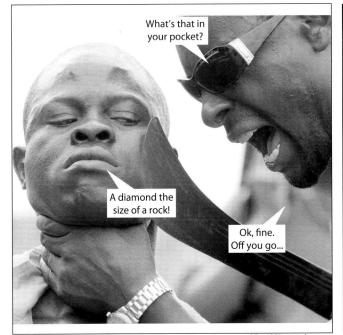

Did You Know ?

Zakat, one of the Five Pillars of Islam, is the giving of a fixed portion of one's total wealth to charity.

The Qur'an views *zakat* as a way to redistribute wealth, thus increasing the role of charity in the economy with a particular interest in the poor and the needy. However, it is considered more than charity - one must give *zakat* for the sake of one's own salvation, the means of purifying one's wealth and one's soul. Knowingly neglecting to will result in damnation in the afterlife.

Image Source:- Movie: Blood Diamond (2006) Starring: Djimon Hounsou and David Harewood

With the world population growing at an alarming rate, in the interests of humanity, would it really be considered immoral to take remedial action?

Background, Facts and Miscellaneous

The year is 2030, and with the world population currently standing at 8 billion people, the *United Nations* have projected the population will reach an unprecedented and unsustainable 12 billion by the year 2060. This conservative estimate is based on the respective birth rates of each region as well as adjusting for some recent developments that occurred in emerging nations (China abolishing their one-child policy; India successfully outlawing the ruinous and detrimental *dowry* system; and the AIDS virus all but eradicated).

Consequently, regardless as to how wonderful these progressive developments have been, the scourge of over-population has now become a foremost concern. With natural resources at breaking point, the *World Council* have concluded that an interception tactic is necessary to preserve the harmony and longevity of a self-sustaining future global population. The decision has been made to undertake an immediate 'vaccination' programme that aims to 'cleanse' select countries or regions, achieved via the deployment of a trusted biological agent which effortlessly renders females instantly and irreparably infertile.

Selection will be based on the following criteria: i) War-mongering nations; ii) Non self-sufficient nations; iii) Uncontrolled birth rates; iv) Lawlessness levels; v) Futile, pointless existences.

Why did it ever have to come to this (?) - by the mere fact that billions more women will now live reluctantly child-free and die unfulfilled than was necessary, for their sake, should remedial measures have been undertaken many decades earlier?

Image Source:- Movie: The Football Factory (2004)

With Hollywood in turmoil, and prequels, sequels and remakes all but exhausted, a new tactic has been proposed aimed at reviving the industry - The 'Requel' – the concept of editing and overhauling movies using existing footage and CGI advancements to effectively create new movies which fit revised visions.

Background, Facts and Miscellaneous

The year is 2020 and Hollywood have finally run out of ideas having exhausted the lame strategy of remaking classic movies under the selling points of them exhibiting either better CGI, extended/alternate endings or better looking actors! And with profit as the bottom line being the only consideration amongst the industry's bigwigs, good writing, imaginary thinking and visions have sadly fallen by the wayside.

Hollywood was now in urgent need of reviving itself, having been completely overtaken by the infinitely superior Korean and Japanese makers (Bollywood had self-destructed years earlier with their trusted formula of 3hr movies which either followed the same template or contained an unworthy payoff, fleshed out dance sequences, incomprehensible plots and ludicrous violence).

Finally, in 2021, a radical approach has been put forward and unsurprisingly embraced, whereby recently released movies will now be remade and/or rehashed from existing footage but utilising CGI and voiceovers etc. to conform to re-imaginings, better endings, new stories, miscasting, dialogue rewrites etc.

With the potential to release movies with significantly lower production costs, the industry has now received a well-needed shot in the arm.

Discuss potential movie ideas, given the ability to make unbound improvements to casting, storyline or dialogue, that could well have the potential to be a box office hit (again)?

Dishonourable Mentions:- Due Date; Psycho; No Riding Dunedain; The alluring Medusa;

Contractual Agreement for WETA to re-engineer the 'Star Wars' Prequel

The Star Wars Original Trilogy will now be renamed Star Wars II-IV, while the much-admired prequels (I-III) will now be condensed into one 4 hour installment, primarily focussing on Anakins slow but orchestrated betrayal to the Dark Side. The main purpose of this trilogy structure is so that while the whole Star Wars trilogy charts the journey of Anakin Skywalker, the original trilogy should remain the bulk of the story with the prequel install-ment purely to provide background to Anakin's character and time as a revered and much respected Jedi Master.

Episode I The Power of the Sith   **Episode II** A New Hope   **Episode III** The Empire Strikes Back   **Episode IV** Return of the Jedi

Scope Directives:-

◦ Solely charts the seduction to the Dark Side - from Jedi Knight to Sith Apprentice. A seduction that was wholly sinister and sophisticated, yet a deci-sion that *Anakin* could not have taken lightly and one which ultimately viewers can sympathise with, holding this underlying affinity with his character through the whole series.

◦ There will be no romance or love interest in the new re-imagining but there will be a single subtlest hint at a possible 'friendship' between *Anakin* and *Queen Amidala*. Subtle as in only making sense once the complete story is known and one that does not hint at the slightest of the startling revelation coming in Episode III (ESB).

◦ The prequel representation of the *Anakin Skywalker* character must now completely conform to the image of the man projected by *Obi-Wan Kenobe* during Episode II (as a good friend and a cunning warrior).

Specific Change Requirements:-

◦ Miscasting: Liam Neesons' *Qui-Gon* character will be recalibrated to be recast as *Anakin Skywalker*. Ewan McGregor' *Kenobe* will not remain intact either with his face and voice being replaced by (a CGI enabled) Jimmy Smits.

◦ *Obi-Wan* and *Anakin* have been Jedi's for a considerable amount of their lives, guardians of peace and justice in the Old Republic, before the dark times... having risen up through the ranks together as well as displaying friendly rivalry yet unquestionable loyalty towards each other.

◦ The prequel story must preserve the 'Code 66' betrayal, the 'Clone Wars', the character of 'Mace Windu', the 'Prophecy' and the 'Duel of the Fates'. This duel between the *Sith Darth Maul* against the Jedi Master *Anakin* and his Padawan *Obi-Wan Kenobi* will now take place as part of the Prequels' final act and the demise of *Darth Maul* is to be rewritten as pivotal to *Anakins'* estrangement from the Jedi movement.

◦ It is imperative that the defining image of *Anakin* (pre *Darth Vader*) is symbolised by the scene when *Anakin* (originally depicted as *Qui-Gon Jin*) and *Darth Maul* are separated by a laser shield during the lightsabre fight. The notion that *Anakin* quietly and confidently meditates while *Darth Maul* paces nervously while pondering an advantageous strike, is to sum up all things Jedi/The Force/Anakin.

◦ There will be no scenes depicting the birth of the twins nor of *Amidala's* death. The prequel will conclude with *Anakin's* path to the Dark Side com-plete, standing by the *Sith Emperors* side.

Requirements that don't need mentioning:-

◦ Weapon/armour technology has not regressed therefore CGI must be in keeping with the technological CGI levels observed in the Original Trilogy.

◦ No 'little Ani', Binks, Chewie, Jabba, Boba, cradle snatching or trade treaties. Additionally, there will be no attempted killing of the very same people for whom you turned to the Dark Side to in the first place in order to save(!).

◦ No midichlorians. Subtle references that Jedi ability comes only from a variety of courage, skill, talent and genes but foremost from the unexplain-able entity referred to as the 'Force'.

Nice to Have Requirement:-

"You refer to the prophecy of the one who will bring balance to the Force. You believe it's this....man?" ~ Mace Windu to Yoda, referring to Anakin Skywalker

The Prophecy outlined in the original prequels prophecises about 'the Chosen One' who can bring peace to the galaxy. During a significant point in the story, in Episode III (ESB), *Obi-Wan* despairs that *Luke Skywalker* is not yet powerful or mentally strong enough to face *Vader* and could therefore succumb to the Dark Side like his father before him, emphasising that he is their 'only hope'.. But *Yoda* tries to allay his concerns by stating that there is 'another', revealing the fact that there is another 'Skywalker' who might also step up to fulfill this prophecy, *Princess Leia*.

This new Prequel must now serve to change this impression upon that scene: What *Yoda* is actually referring to is not that there is another 'Skywalker' but that there is another 'hope' still – a glimmer of faith *Yoda* still holds that that *Anakin Skywalker* is indeed the prophecised 'One' and may yet coura-geously redeem himself to fulfill his true destiny.

Image Source:- Source: By the Author

The Irresponsible Lending that led to the property price boom and its eventual adverse consequences have led to a new legal directive - Income Tax and Inheritance Tax will be abolished in favour of a fairer 'Property Tax', based solely on the net property asset worth.

Background

The irresponsible lending over the past decade has led to a disastrous set of events with the world on the brink of a depression type era, many house-owners in debt or foreclosed on, bank bailouts, corporate victims and disgruntled priced out first-time buyers.

With no confidence in the banking industry adhere to stricter lending guidelines, together with their uncanny knack of developing complex products to conceal any deceit, the focus of regulation will no longer be on the banks themselves but rather on the hope that the people self-regulate to the point that a fair and stable housing market being born.

The key to this objective is to align annual tax commitments with the property assets owned and then pegged against the average annual income. The long-term aim of this being two-fold, overseeing an organic growth/decline in the property market as well as instilling an underlying shared civil responsibility in increasing the average wage.

Facts and Examples

All property will be annually valued and indexed to the average national salary level. Upon this valuation, the deed owners will be directed to pay the tax equivalent of the total value of the property assets owned. (See figure opposite for a breakdown of the calculation).

Additional notes:-
• Foreign owners are not exempt and though there is the question of whether non-UK residents should pay UK tax, it will be a blanket rule.
• Owners who refuse to pay will be offered the choice of either selling the house to avoid the tax burden or will automatically become government owned after 5 years of non-payment.
• Hopes to encourage owners to move frequently in keeping with their financial/family circumstances.
• Wealthier property owners would prefer this type of taxation because the tax burden is more evenly distributed as well as being able to manage it.

FOR	**AGAINST**
Fairer taxes leads to citizens feeling genuinely better treated. § 'Inheritance tax' is only paid if inherited property is not sold. § Advantages of increased disposable income. § Unoccupied or oversized properties encouraged to be sold, rather than be held as an investment. § Difficult for the housing market to become overpriced or experience artificially-driven booms/busts.	Will encourage people to save more rather than pay more tax. § Housing stock can only improve with constant investment and turnover. § Rich/prosperous being penalised for doing well in life. Policies supporting the less ambitious never turn out well. § No incentive to own or upgrade property will lead to a static housing market. § Passing tax burden to tenants is inevitable.

Tax Commitments based on House Price Levels - Worked Example
Based on Tax Income Numbers for 2004/05

			Tax Income Required Target £	122,896,200,000
		Tax Increment = National Average Gross Salary £		25,000
		Tax per Increment - Multiplier Factor to attain Tax Reqd Target		455

C1	C2	C3	C4	C5	C6
	Estimated	C1/Increment	C2 x C3	C3 x Multiplier	C4 x Multiplier
House Price	No. Of Houses	Tax Increments	Total Increments	Tax Per Property Owned	Total Tax Received
100000	1,000,000	4	4,000,000	1,819	1,819,336,788
150000	1,000,000	6	6,000,000	2,729	2,729,005,181
200000	4,000,000	8	32,000,000	3,639	14,554,694,301
250000	5,000,000	10	50,000,000	4,548	22,741,709,845
300000	3,000,000	12	36,000,000	5,458	16,374,031,088
350000	3,000,000	14	42,000,000	6,368	19,103,036,269
400000	2,000,000	16	32,000,000	7,277	14,554,694,301
450000	1,000,000	18	18,000,000	8,187	8,187,015,544
500000	500,000	20	10,000,000	9,097	4,548,341,969
550000	400,000	22	8,800,000	10,006	4,002,540,933
600000	300,000	24	7,200,000	10,916	3,274,806,218
650000	200,000	26	5,200,000	11,826	2,365,137,824
700000	200,000	28	5,600,000	12,735	2,547,071,503
750000	100,000	30	3,000,000	13,645	1,364,502,591
800000	100,000	32	3,200,000	14,555	1,455,469,430
850000	80,000	34	2,720,000	15,464	1,237,149,016
900000	60,000	36	2,160,000	16,374	982,441,865
950000	40,000	38	1,520,000	17,284	691,347,979
1000000	20,000	40	800,000	18,193	363,867,358
	22,000,000		**270,200,000**		**122,896,200,000**

Assumptions: Minimum House Price is 100,000 and Maximum is 1,000,000

Future Reform

With no income tax to be paid to the government, employees would see a significant increase in their disposable income.
However, the new law requires that employers must now pay the previous 'net' pay as 'gross', and new lower salary levels will now be formed. Of the substantial savings made from employers now having no yearly income tax bill, at least 60% of this saving MUST be allocated to either ;
i) employing more staff or
ii) be evenly distributed as payrises/bonuses.

Image Source:- By The Author

Is it right to expect future generations of naive taxpayers to bankroll the lifestyles of the rich and shameless - even when extortionately lavish sums are involved and brazenly devious practices are undertaken to obtain them?

Background, Facts and Miscellaneous

With public funds, comes the added responsibility for public servants to spend it wisely and in a manner which is in keeping with the general expectations of the millions of taxpayers.

However, with the large sums involved and the guaranteed 'revenue stream' in place, has it come to a point where senior public servants are helping themselves to the loot with little regard to who contributes to the fund, why they do or to how it could have been better spent.

With these public departments being insulated from any external guidelines or authority, has this lack of accountability festered an environment where the decision-makers have become a law unto themselves - self-approving generous contracts, payoffs and pension packages?

• Disguised increases in salary just preceding the retirement age, or an impending redundancy round to maximise the (unfunded) pension schemes based on the final salary level.
• Long term fixed contracts for those in the 'old boys club', even granting them a privilege of the payoff just in case the contract is not renewed.
• Topping up pension pots and accruing as many payoffs as possible by orchestrating their own dismissal/redundancy or in collusion with others. This endless recruitment merry-go-round can somewhat assure a generous retirement package every few years if planned meticulously.
• Rewarding 'early retirement' under the guise of being a cost-cutting measure - in actual fact it is offered purely so that it facilitates roles to be made available for the 'accruing payoffs' system.

Further Background Information:-

∘ Many public sector pension schemes are "unfunded" meaning there is not a sum of money earmarked to pay for each worker's retirement. Instead, each pension is funded from contributions made by today's workers and taxpayers.
2012 figures showed that "unfunded" public sector pension scheme liabilities were equal to £1.2 billion, the equivalent of £33,000 for every household. Research by the *Intergenerational Foundation* in 2012 established that at least 78,186 retired public sector workers are currently receiving pensions worth more than £25,900 a year (based on pensions being paid to former NHS staff, civil servants, teachers and members of the Armed Forces).

∘ The TaxPayers' Alliance (TPA) revealed in 2012 that councils across the UK had a combined pension deficit of £54 billion in 2010-11. This meant that the assets of all 101 local authority pension funds in the UK were dwarfed by their liabilities, creating a deficit which taxpayers are ultimately liable for. Previous TPA research found that the equivalent of £1 in every £5 of Council Tax was spent on employer contributions to the Local Government Pension Scheme (LGPS).

∘ In the 2011/12 financial year alone, it was revealed that more than 100 doctors had retired on NHS-funded pensions of between £78,000 and £111,000 a year, payments that will rise with inflation and are guaranteed for life (in addition to receiving tax-free lump sums of at least £234,000 each). NHS pensions data showed that a total of 2,500 former employees were on retirement incomes worth more than £67,000 a year.

Some of the ingenious practices that have been observed and mastered in this era of prosperity:-

∘ *Nick Johnson*, 57, a council boss who retired because of ill health after being assessed as 'permanently unfit' to work, left with a payoff estimated to be around £300,000 plus a pension of £50,000 a year. But just four months later, he was appointed interim chief executive at another local London authority on a salary of £260,000 a year, though it is not yet known what irrevocable pension contributions agreement is in place.

∘ *Peter Gould*, 54, who'd earned £215,000 a year as chief executive of Northamptonshire County Council, resigned from his post after just seven years receiving a £297,000 lump sum payoff and a guaranteed index-linked pension of nearly £100,000 a year.
His retirement package was agreed under a 'legitimate' contractual agreement.

∘ *Katherine Kerswell*, 49, a former council chief who was given a £420,000 payoff in 2011 was appointed just over a year later by the Coalition government to 'reform' the civil service - on a salary of £142,000. She required just 20 months of service as the £197,000 head of Kent County Council to justify the extortionate payoff plus a £30,000 pension contribution.

∘ The South Lanarkshire Council authority's £120,000-a-year director of education *Larry Forde* took early retirement at the age of 52, when his five-year fixed term contract came to an end. Their former finance director *Linda Hardie* also retired from her post aged 50 with a severance package of more than £500,000 including £106,570 compensation for loss of office and £427,209 towards her pension pot.
Both were employed on controversial fixed-term contracts which were introduced in 2002 and unlike normal council contracts included an entitlement for early-retirement or voluntary severance payments if contracts were not renewed.

∘ Under the 'all but fair' NHS final salary (gold-plated for some) pension scheme, financial circumstances are such that frontline services are being cut in order to maintain this funding agreement. This is not to mention the fact that the lower paid NHS workers have no choice but to subsidise the pensions of managers who may never have even seen the inside of an operating room.
Some of the fortunate NHS managers to reap the benefits include the following cases:-
- Professor *Stephen Smith* (the £247,000 a year chief executive of Imperial College Healthcare Trust): £135,000 pension & lump sum of £405,000.
- *Jan Filochowski* (the £280,000 a year chief executive of West Hertfordshire Hospitals Trust): £135,000 pension & lump sum of £415,000.
- Sir *Ron Kerr* (the £254,000 a year chief executive of Guys and St Thomas' Foundation Trust): A pension pot of £3.06 million.

Image Source:- See Appendix for Sources

Are the (apparently) honourable intentions of 'Quantitative Easing' better served by distributing money evenly amongst the population rather than placing blind faith and trust in a financial system more accustomed to exploiting any wider benefits of a money injection?

Background

Quantitative Easing (QE) is considered to be an unconventional monetary policy, used only to stimulate the national economy when conventional policy has become ineffective. It involves increasing the money supply by flooding financial institutions with (newly created) capital in an effort to promote increased lending and liquidity.

Since the global financial crisis of 2008, both the *Bank of England* and the *US Federal Reserve* have used this QE policy extensively. As of Sep12, the BoE had committed a total of £375bn to QE, however analysts have cited it as a failure noting that lending remained sluggish and inflation stood at perilously high levels.

With the banks' determined reluctance to lend fuelled by their mantra 'debt is good', would consumer spending have been better stimulated by instead injecting this money straight into personal bank accounts, in turn leading to the economic growth so craved?

Facts and Examples

Consider the scenario where in 2008 money expansion took place in such a manner - with £400 billion to be invented and injected into the UK economy, an average payout of approximately £22,000 to every family is instead granted (dependent on type of family). The payment is made subject to strict conditions albeit via a gentlemans agreement:-
• The bulk be actively spent on products and services from UK firms only,
• Cannot be utilised to facilitate the purchase of property which otherwise would not have progressed. Likewise, cannot be used to pay off mortgage arrears,
• Must not be used to clear debt >£5,000. NB: Banks must nullify the payment if original loan was created.
• Must be spent responsibly, in a manner fruitful for the economy and long term personal welfare,
• If personal savings ever exceed £200,000 during the course of a lifetime, then an inflation-adjusted payment could be repaid voluntarily to the BoE.

FOR	**AGAINST**

For the rich, £20K makes no difference but f**k them(!) as they'd likely object to such a blanket distribution of money. § Extensive sums would now not have trickled to the top of the food chain. § Positive adjustment in keeping with a fairer Wealth Distribution ideal. § Immediately alleviates debt worries for those struggling financially. § Higher VAT/Tax income now expected.

Abnormal and uncontrolled wide money distribution can only lead to economical anarchy. § Surge in sales of luxury nice-to-have items (a gentlemans agreement is a fools hope). § Could force foreign firms to adopt similar tactics in refusing to buy abroad too (if UK attempt proved success-ful) - possibly leading to the end of the free global marketplace as we know it.

...and here, take this, it's a rent advance for the next three years. Now, f**k off!

Image Source:- Movie: Mother India (1957) Starring: Nargis & Sajid Khan & Surendra

Did You Know ?

In April 2013, Japan's central bank promised to unleash a massive programme of quantitative easing - worth $1.4tn (£923bn) that will double the country's money supply - in a drastic bid to restore the economy to health and banish the deflation that has dogged the country for more than a decade.

With Japan's total population standing at 127 million, applying this alternative tactic would have instead provided every citizen on average with a Yen spending equivalent of £7,300 each.

With the underclass having bred like rats over the last few decades and the welfare bill becoming unsustainable, the task of stemming this trend has become priority – A mandatory 'Breeding Test' has now been introduced for all parents-to-be to prove that they intend to raise and nurture their child in a loving and responsible manner.

Background, Facts and Miscellaneous

The year is 2018 and with the authorities now tasked with the pressing objective of narrowing the ever widening gap between middle and lower classes as well as the reckless breeding prevalent amongst an irresponsible underclass, it has become evident that radical measures are now deemed necessary to fulfil these satisfactorily.

Having successfully repealed the *Human Rights Act* years earlier, the government has now been given the go-ahead for plans to systematically abort all foetuses conceived by parent(s) who lack any decent moral backbone, personal responsibility or alternatively belong to an 'undesirable' section of society.

The 'undesirable' is loose enough a condition for the government to manipulate quotas such that society maintains a certain balance.

Upon notice of a pregnancy, the doctor is legally obliged to inform authorities of an impending new member of society. However, in order to be admitted, the parents must undertake a psychometric and personality test to help assess their social characteristics, educational background, moral standing and motivation for breeding.

The score is then evaluated and only those who score at least a certain level respective to their social or cultural class, will not be forced to abort their unborn child. Those successful will have their place confirmed into the system.

Discussion Viewpoints:- Racist undertones. § Last of a dying breed - the underclass dying out. § Unfair but necessary manipulation of quotas. § Provoking social unrest. § Brains become sexy.

The Right to Breed: Test Cases

The criteria for a successful pass of eligibility depends largely on personality traits, criminal history, parental ethos, cultural background, childhood experiences, religious inclination(s) and will also require an extensive cross-check on personal relationships with family and close friends.

The following are test cases to illustrate the application of such a 'breeding test' had it been present at that time:-

◦ Cheerio

A 20 year old woman left her 15 month old daughter in a dark, cold, squalid house for a whole week to fend for herself (only being checked on once a day, apparently). She was only discovered when neighbours heard the little girls piercing screams - most likely due to there being no heating or light in the house or the overpowering stench from the dirty nappies strewn across the floors.

Eligibility Test:
What was established was that there was an absent father, a (probable) history of alcoholism and the results from the personality test seemed to indicate a financial motive for having children (drink money). In addition, the c*nt was 3rd Generation Council House residency.

◦ Thank the Lord for Small Miracles

Sanam Navsarka was born to a young single mother who sadly had the natural father inconsiderately walk out on her and her unborn child. The mother would eventually take up with another married man shortly after giving birth, and together tortured *Sanam* to death. A post-mortem examination found 107 injuries on her body, including fractures to all four of her limbs, 36 bruises to her head and neck, 26 to her arms and ten to her abdomen.

Eligibility Test:
The biological parents would most likely have sailed through the personality and parental tests but whether the 'race' quotas would have been exceeded for the 'Pakistan' race for the preceeding 12 months would be largely dependent on the views of the authority in power at the time. Therefore, had a racist party been in power, then it would likely not have been sanctioned for this c*nt from having that poor defenceless little girl.

◦ Father Forgive Me for I Have Sinned

A 24 year old father killed his baby daughter by carrying out 3 seperate cowardly attacks in anger, resulting in fractures of her skull and ribs. The fact that she was just 2 months old when she passed away demonstrated the inherent evil he possessed as well as the depraved individual he must have been, but yet he possessed no criminal history.

Eligibility Test:
There is a likelihood that the parents' background, the strong relationship and clear paternal desire would have concluded that an ideal family environment to raise a young child was evident.
However, discussions with close family and friends would have revealed that the c*nt often displayed an extremely short temper as well as occasional but random bouts of depression. Though these negative trait(s) could be considered part of the human make-up, they could have also have been considered hereditary and depending on any 'Genetics and Eugenics' views the authorities harboured could well have meant an order of 'mandatory abortion' was forthcoming.

◦ Parental Duties

A husband and wife raped their own 13 month old daughter during a supervised visit. Supervised because three children had already been removed from the mother as soon as they were born and also because the father, a registered sex offender, had previously raped his 18 month old nephew while they were babysitting him.

Eligibility Test:
The mother alone and her blase attitude to giving her own children away would have rang alarm bells. The father with previous criminal and paedophile history would have meant a straightforward decline for giving birth. Sexually assaulting, raping and recording the abuse of their own children means they were indeed bonafide c*nts.

Authors Note:

Please note that the author does not advocate nor endorse the use of the word *c*nt*, however, if and when the term is applied correctly against those most deserving of such an accolade, then its the authors' view that no other alternative term will do. In such cases, it ceases to be a derogatory term but that which is most apt.

Image Source:- By The Author (See Appendix for Sources)

With an almost pathological and insatiable craving to grab as much wealth as one possibly can, has the time come to turn the tables on the wealthy. Should we applaud initiatives which unashamedly and stealthily attempt to transfer wealth from the rich back to the people?

Background, Facts and Miscellaneous

In 2006, a UN report discovered that 40% of all wealth is owned by the world's richest 1%. Or even more startling is the fact that 85% of total global assets is owned by the richest 10% of adults. And just to nitpick, half the world's adult population own barely 1% of the global wealth.

These statistics portraying the uneven and grossly unfair distribution are obscene and grotesque in anyones book, yet it's a wonder how things were allowed to get into such a mess.

Capitalism and greed has to take much of the brunt as does the assertion that this distribution of wealth likely maps almost perfectly onto the distribution of the coupled attributes: intelligence, ambition, drive and opportunity. But does it tell the whole story of how extreme wealth manages to trickle itself up to the very top.

As well as the wealthy stubbornly (and being permitted to) safeguarding their fortunes from lawful tax obligations, could the accusation be made that there has been a conscious high-level effort to expedite the transfer of wealth from the middle classes - a plot facilitated via government policy, legislation and premeditated loopholes?

If so, there does seem to be some misguided foresight or a lack of conscience in such policies which promote the accumulation of wealth at the expense of the common people. Even more alarmingly, this widening divide between the elite and the middle/working classes could only lead to long term social revolt or a dystopian future.

With this in mind, should we applaud initiatives which honourably attempt to transfer wealth from the rich straight back to the people?

Progressive Wealth Redistribution

° The 'Modern Conceptual Art' Scheme

In 2042, documents uncovered a scam which took place at the turn of the century. The scheme involved a cabal of individuals who would work together to talk up the value and worth of artistic talent with the view of collectively overvaluing pieces and ultimately selling 'worthless pieces of tatt' at extortionate prices to those who have more money than sense and are considered to be holders of excess wealth.

Curiously, the scheme did not have the intention of making money for those involved on the inside, but rather had the intention of simply stealing from the rich and redistributing it among the wronged demographic of the time, the middle/working classes.

It would transpire that the scheme was concocted up by five friends who were educated at a prestigious private school. The idea was borne out the fact that they all disagreed with the push by the school and its tutors to fulfil the following role upon graduation with the utmost drive: 'To accumulate wealth and a duty to suppress the poor'.

Their grounding and decent morals were only instilled in them by good hands-on parents, who emphasised the importance of a fair and balanced society as well as the futile pursuit of wealth.

The 'five' put their well-meaning plan into action by recruiting select morally-sound influential figures and critics within the Art industry. The final stage involved recruiting a 'public face' for the scam, a person with some knack for Art and who would share their ideals in return for a modest pay packet and adulation. That man was a fellow friend and pupil, a certain *Damien Hirst*.

The culmination of the plan involved the essential icing on the cake. Its important to note that the scheme would have ultimately failed if it indeed provided wealthy individuals with assets which would have continued to accumulate in value, therefore, there had to be a concerted effort to almost devalue the artist and his works overnight.

From around 2008, with the craze for 'Modern Art' at a high, the wheels were put in motion for the 'devaluation' strategy to begin, with many critics tasked with discrediting the work and mainstream publications instructed to ridicule the prices and the buyers. *Hirst* himself was tasked with the 'final nail in the coffin' - making a public statement on the criticism in 2015, where he duly agreed with all that had been protested and delighted in expressing indignation at those who spent so much on cr*p that a two year old wouldn't struggle to recreate.

Within ten years, the market which had appeared out of thin air was dead, and the rich left with unsaleable tosh. A plan perfectly executed - the scam is projected to have netted almost £500 million since inception and had since been distributed via 'charitable' channels.

° The 'Avatar' Project

In 2012, billionaires were given the opportunity for 'immortality' and consequently, a credible reason to justify not giving away their wealth and to hold onto the rewards of a lifetime of toil.

Specifically, they were offered the ability to 'transferring one's individual consciousness to an artificial carrier and achieving cybernetic immortality'. With the emergence and realisation of such technologies, it's no longer just science fiction fantasy - one that is now in their power to make sure that this goal will be achieved in their lifetime. At a price, off course.

Dishonourable Mentions:-

° Tuition Fees: With the recent housing market boom, the Government are fully aware that parents sit on untapped equity in their home, and they will now exploit their powers to tap into this. As a result, caps on University tuition fees were recently relaxed.

° Inheritance Tax: How can the super-rich avoid this by placing property into a 'family trust'?

° Quantitative Easing: The Bank of England admitted in Aug12 that savers were among the biggest losers from its policies and the richest families were the biggest winners - with QE boosting household wealth 'by just over £600 billion' as the value of shares and other assets recovered in the wake of the financial crisis.

° Tax Havens: A recent report ' The Price of Offshore Revisited' by *James Henry* showed that the global super-rich are using loopholes to hide at least £13 trillion from the taxman. The report showed how money was being siphoned into offshore banks instead of being invested at home, where the assets of 'high-net-worth individuals' were being protected by 'professional enablers' taking advantage of gaps in cross-border tax rules.

° Stamp Duty Avoidance: An investment company used a legal loophole to avoid paying stamp duty altogether on an £65 million purchase of the lease of the *Dickens and Jones* Store. The company was controlled by Conservative Party Donor and property magnate *James Ritblat*, and had amongst its many investors, Cabinet Minister *Andrew Mitchell*.

° Corporate Tax Avoidance: Amazon.co.uk accounts revealed that it did not pay any British corporation tax in either 2010 or 2011, despite UK sales of around £2.8 billion in 2010.

Image Source:- Source: By the Author

When middlemen have a vested interest only in what's in it for them and little reserved for their clients, why do we continue to hold so much misguided faith in such an undistinguished profession – Under what circumstances would a broker forsake commission or the bigger picture to instead act in their clients best interests?

Background, Facts and Miscellaneous

With commission being the bread and butter for the majority of a salesman's salary and bonus entitlement, it's no wonder that making the deal is paramount in the mind of a broker.

However, with many placing faith and reliance in the expertise provided by such folk, it's reasonable to expect that opinions forthcoming are unbiased and free of agenda, having only the client's best interests at heart. As romantic as such an understanding sounds, our experience of our fellow man and human nature informs us that the only thing of concern to many in society is the bottom line, and this only.

With this in mind, we still however walk blindly into many a transaction purely on the advice and beckoning of these middlemen, selfishly willing for that move to be made.

Under any of the following scenarios, could it be envisaged that the middleman would wield an honest (yet professionally irrational) opinion:-
• In a self-imploding economy, Estate Agents providing negative housing market predictions;
• A Stockmarket Broker providing a 'SELL' recommendation on an IPO they have been instructed to promote and be rewarded for;
• A Cult Member tasked with god's duty to recruit, whispering in the ear of a young virgin stories of sexual exploitation and abuse instead;
• The Recruitment Consultant steadfastly refusing to encourage an employee with existing promising long term prospects to be pushed into applying for a role with short term monetary gain;
• The Drug Dealer outlining the inevitable downward spiral before enticing with that free sample.

What would have happened, had the (alleged) sequence of events which led to the crash landing of United Airlines Flight 93, not taken place - Would the Commander-In-Chief just have sat back and hoped, against all hope, that it would have landed safely at Washington Airport?

Background

At 10:02am on Sep 11, 2001, United Airlines *Flight 93* crashed into the ground in Pennsylvania. This occurred soon after hijacked passenger jets crashed into the North and South Towers of New York's iconic World Trade Center, as well as the Pentagon.

Flight 93 was the only one of the four hijacked planes not to reach its target, speculated to be the White House, crashing during a valiant courageous attempt by some of the passengers to regain control, killing every one of the 44 souls aboard.

The flight had initially been delayed by about 40 minutes, and this proved to be crucial since this provided its passengers with a communication window allowing them to be informed that a synchronised terrorist attack was underway, highlighting this as likely no ordinary hijacking - leading to the eventual revolt.

However, with the military on full alert at the time and with fighter planes already scrambled, could this version of events be merely a smokescreen.

Facts and Examples

The sequence of events is as follows:-
Around 8:00 am: Scheduled flight departure,
8:42 am: Delayed Flight 93 finally takes off,
8:46 am: Fighter jets scrambled after NORAD alert,
8:46 am and 902am: Planes crash into the towers,
9:30 am: Two F-16 fighter jets scrambled,
9:35 am: Plane crashes into the Pentagon,
10:02 am: Flight 93 crashes in Pennsylvania,
At some point, Dick Cheney had allegedly told Donald Rumsfeld: "*It's my understanding they've already taken a couple of aircraft out.*"

Quote by the President from movie *The Rock* (1995): "These past few hours have been the longest, darkest of my life. How does one weigh human life? One million civilians against eighty-one hostages. We are at war with terror. Fighting a war means casualties and this is the worst call I've ever had to make. Air strike approved."

FOR	**AGAINST**
Never would there be government intervention where the loss of innocent civilians was possible. § All evidence and phone transcripts exist to this day to support the 'brave passengers' theory. § The passengers knew that the plane was to be used as a missile, therefore knew death was inevitable. § Interrupted communications channels meant impossible to verify threat(s).	Not morally wrong if military intervention had taken place. § In such a heightened climate of fear, there could have been no choice to serve an alternate version of events. Self-involvement in the murder of its own civilians may never have been forgiven. § A successful attack on the White House would have been the ultimate publicity coup for the 'cause'.

Guys... quick question, but 'friendly fire' is a good thing right??!!

Be Controversial

In the true-story based film *United 93* (2006), the Title Card states: *"Military commanders were not notified that United 93 had been hijacked until four minutes after it had crashed. The nearest fighter jets were 100 miles away"*. Is it somewhat strange that a US movie would state such 'facts' without it being officially and independently corroborated? Almost has an air of childhood fibbing: "Honestly sir, I was nowhere near him when he tripped over his own foot"!

A persons whereabouts and their social and personal acquaintances will now be stored in a national database using data gathered from their mobile phone - Discuss the impact this will have on criminal activity and police work?

Background, Facts and Miscellaneous

In 2018, news has emerged of an exciting step forward in the area of national and internal security. The *'Mobile Phone Vicinity Wheel'* (MPVW) development encompasses the utilisation of the GPS facility on mobile phones and a revolutionary new scanning function that registers all phones in the immediate vicinity. This information is then uploaded to a national database.

The technology has now become possible because the GPS scanner function is non-intrusive and data storage capacity is no longer an issue.

The primary idea behind this initiative is to provide crime fighters with state of the art data analysis - the key being that GPS co-ordinates can validate whereabouts and associates. This can then help to provide a social contact map for use in a criminal investigation or prosecution case.

With a win-win situation for all law-abiding citizens and for the long term security of the nation, the drawbacks will be significant for those who engage in immoral and criminal activity. With this in mind, discuss the following viewpoints:-

• Will criminals and terrorists be halted and forever be curbed in the majority of their activities;

• The ethical considerations of tracking a persons whereabout and their right to privacy;

• The types of crime disappearing overnight;

• Once established, will it only be a matter of time before third parties be granted access to the database in order to provide bespoke services. Services such as helping out a stalking ex-boyfriend, insider dealing, catching out unfaithful partners, companies delving into the sick days employees have supposedly claimed etc.

The 'Mobile Phone Vicinity Wheel'

◦ The MPVW function scans and only registers mobile phones which have had a presence within a vicinity of 10 yards and for a minimum of 5 minutes. This is so that preferably only family, friends and known associates get registered.

◦ There is but one exception to this condition. If at any point a mobile number has been paired more than five times within the last 365 days and for any amount of time, then that mobile phone and its respective MIC will now always be registered regardless of the vicinity duration.

◦ The function will become default on all phones with opt-out impossible, and more importantly continues to work even when the phone is switched off using its own internal power.

◦ Every mobile phone must be formally registered to the MPVW database, provding the person's full name and their NI number, by the year 2020. The MPVW database will then store these details along with mobile phone numbers/MICs into the master database phone table. Any mobile phone numbers not registered will be automatically deactivated by the mobile providers until further notice.

◦ Periodic uploads to the mobile providers data servers will take place during downtime and after which is then forwarded to the national MPVW database.

MPVW Database Worked Example

Case Scenario:

◦ A single person, *Mr D Naproof*, has been charged with the kidnapping and gang rape of a young woman which took place on the 9 June 2012 between 1:00-3:00am, as there was undeniable DNA evidence against him. The hunt is now on for the other 4 accomplices.

◦ The police have now requested a MPVW database search on whose mobile phone and identity had been in the vicinity of *Mr D Naproof* prior to the kidnapping on 9 June 2012, and the main suspect they hope to prove had significant involvement is a certain *Mr V Tracker*.

◦ A Mobile Phone assigned with an identifier code of '368-465-2329' had been previously registered at source to *Mr Naproof*, and the police detectives are hoping the vicinity wheel results show beyond reasonable doubt that they are known acquaintances and can provide sound evidence for them to be charged, as well as leading to a 'social pattern' linking the other unknown accomplices to have all been in the vicinity of the victim at the time the offence was committed.

Stage A: Master Database Summary 'View'

Inputs:

Mobile Identifier Code (MIC)	368-465-2329 (Mr D Naproof)
As Of Date	11-Jun-12

Output:

Mobile in Vicinity (MIC)	Unique Daily Vicinity Occurrences			
	Last 5 Days	Last 30 Days	Last 12 Months	Last 5 Years
768-765-6878	3	20	200	560
437-687-6568	2	2	2	2
875-375-3136	5	35	400	2400
145-895-8856	1	1	1	1
105-045-0376	25	150	1400	6500
218-843-8284	3	18	20	45
729-479-4280	4	22	250	1300
948-323-2564	7	30	365	1825

Stage B: Drill Down into Database Table

Inputs:

Mobile Identifier Code (MIC)	368-465-2329 (Mr D Naproof)
Drill Down to Pair With:	**218-843-8284 (?)**
Period:	6-10 June 2012

Output:

Mobile Identifier Name (from MIC)	Date	Time
	10-Jun-12	12:39 PM
	09-Jun-12	1:40 PM
	09-Jun-12	**12:20 AM**
Mr V Tracker	08-Jun-12	2:25 PM
	08-Jun-12	1:10 PM
	08-Jun-12	2:32 AM
	06-Jun-12	4:52 PM

Worked Example of the Database in action in the fight against crime:

◦ The Database view finds that *Mr D Naproof* has had lengthy liaisons with 8 persons during 6-10 June 2012.

◦ A drill-down of the date/times from the retrieved MIC's indicate a mobile phone which has a proved connection to the prime suspect, *Mr V Tracker* (the 218-843-8284 MIC which showed in the log).

◦ Subsequent drill-downs and connections should be able to provide the police with enough information to draw up a 'social pattern' to identify the possible culprits as well as a 'movement map' for the said date.

◦ The final verification stage would be to then check whether the mobile phone of the victim had at any point been within range, and thus logged. In this case, the victim will be informed that a list of possible suspects have been drawn up using the database, which will then prompt the victim to provide her mobile phone number to detectives. The Police would then check whether the MIC appeared on any of the View/Drill-Down stages at the respective time of the crime.

◦ Therefore, in this verification stage if the MIC code of the victim was '145-895-8856' and had appeared on one or the other of the suspects log, then this would almost certainly secure a conviction.

If we can no longer rely on society and authorities to effectively aid our children into growing up in an environment which promotes responsible living and appreciating the good life, is a secluded and controlled environment what some of us should strive for?

Background, Facts and Miscellaneous

It can be argued that society has been on an irrecoverable downward spiral for some time now and this soulless, faithless, petty and exceedingly individualistic society is here to stay, further exacerbated by authorities lacking any long term vision, honourable responsibilities or strive.

But what comes of our children who unavoidably can only exhibit characteristics in adulthood which were no different to those nurtured as a child in such an environment - one which does little to encourage moral values, manners or respect for elders. It also becomes increasingly likely that no amount of loving and good upbringing can counteract such decline in successive societies through the generations (the kids are doomed)!

With many folk living in this world being too innocently nice for it, frightened about the world our children are being brought into and becoming totally disillusioned with this state of society and moral decline, has the time come to put our children first and put their environments into our own hands - insulated from the outside world?

Further Discussion Points:-
• Should Mr Walker, Mrs Hunt, Mr Nicholson and the other *Elders* be an inspiration to us all?
• In the movie *The Spy Who Loved Me*, a rich powerful man was convinced that all life on the surface of planet Earth should cease to exist. He planned on wiping the face of the land clean of disgusting, destructive humanity, so that a new world can begin under the sea, a veritable aquatic utopia. Was Bond wrong to ruin his dream?
• Which land should the *League of Shadows* sack?

Image Source:- Movie: The Village (2004) Starring: William Hurt

Napoleon Bonaparte once said;
"History is the version of past events that people have decided to agree upon".

Should we start to question all 'historical facts' in the context of the political and religious climate at the time?

Background

History, we can assume (and as we are rightly entitled to), has been recorded in an unbiased and accurate manner, devoid of the filters and the outright misinformation or disinformation that is routinely introduced into the stream of knowledge.

However, if historians do not question what information is fed to them, then it will leave them open to manipulation - resulting in future generations being recipients of a version of past events that fitted the agenda of the political powers or the dominant religious institutions of that time.

False and inaccurate information could well be disseminated with the sole intent of manipulating peoples minds by creating fear, hate and prejudice thus gathering support for governmental policy/actions.

"God cannot alter the past, though historians can."
~ Samuel Butler (Prose Observations)

Facts and Examples

• It's commonly cited in history school books that America *saved* the world by authorising the use of atomic bombs. Disturbingly, we see little to no questioning on important considerations of i) the moral justification of the attack, ii) the repercussions, iii) destroying two cities instead of one, or even iv) why a lesser populated region was not selected instead.
• Does a 'senseless unprovoked' attack on the US at Pearl Harbour sound better than a 'self-orchestrated' one in order to help justify the forthcoming revenge?
• Official US history (and texts) would have people believe that there were never any US military personnel on the ground during the *secret war*. Lao government statistics however tell a very different history citing 369 Americans killed and 15,861 injured.

Dishonourable Mentions:- Gulf of Tonkin; Blood Libel; Beethoven; Three Wise Men and other religious tales; Government commissioned paintings.

FOR

Top Secret government documents are consciously leaked, and in many cases deliberately altered. This is done so, because *leaks* from such sources are instantly deemed accurate and reliable. § Covering up illegal practices which may have violated international law. § Fictitious tales of courage, with good intention, for maintaining morale and encouraging faith in the cause.

AGAINST

Longer term humane interests are always at the heart of such practices. § Imagine the unrest and turmoil that would have ensued had the truth always been known or reported. § Cover up of illegal practices is undertaken for the accepted greater good, and rightly so because it should not detract from the end goal that was achieved. § High morals and honesty should be present.

Do you think they'll write about our exploits here and we'll be talked about for decades to come ?

Course they will, Atilla. What a silly question !?!!

Wildcard View

If Germany had won the Second World War and with their subsequent world domination under its odious leader, the history books would have no doubt been purged of all the illegal or inhumane activities that took place. There would be very little evidence, if any, of the *holocaust* and any person who makes such outlandish claims would have been written off as a paranoid madman.

After all, we would have read all about zis events in ze school history books, yaah?

Chapter G

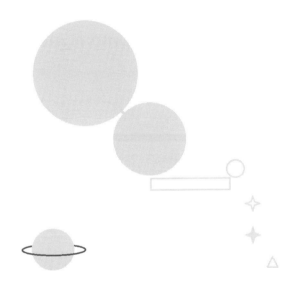

"Live a good life. If there are gods and they are just, they will not care how devout
you have been, but will welcome you based on the virtues you have lived by.
If there are gods, but unjust, then you should not want to worship them.
If there are no gods, then you will be gone, but will have lived a
noble life that will live on in the memories of your loved ones."

- Marcus Aurelius

Were Dinosaurs originally just an experimental test of the Evolutionary Process by the Creator, and made extinct to pave way for 'Species version 1.0', containing the necessary modifications required to spawn a harmonious race?

Background, Facts and Miscellaneous

There are currently two hypotheses that may explain the extinction of Dinosaurs: an extra-terrestrial impact, such as an asteroid or comet, or a massive bout of volcanism. Either scenario would have resulted in the Earth being starved of the sun's energy and the climate change proving catastrophic throughout the food chain.

Now, let's put forward two new theories:-
• Dinosaurs simply stopped mating, due to an increased difficulty or lack of mutual attraction.
• The Carnivore>Herbivore food chain though initially stable, was not in an optimal state, and over time this would prove so with the carnivores overwhelming the herbivore population before eventually devouring each other. With no-one left to eat or copulate with, a slow death ensued.

Should either of these theories prove viable, then could it be pounced upon by the proponents of *Intelligent Design* (those biblically minded and desperate) to propose that the 'Jurassic' age was actually a 'Beta Test' undertaken by the *Creator* to UAT the evolutionary process - to refine the final tweaks of His 'guided in-built evolution process'.

Only once the cell moderations and the necessary environmental adjustments were complete, was a 'human-originating' first living cell put into place, transported to Earth via meteor?

This extrapolation proposes that this new iteration embedded within itself sexual attractiveness, erogenous zones and aesthetically pleasing compatible sexual organs. At an environmental level, plants/trees became wonderfully edible options.

Image Source:- Movie: Jurassic Park (1993)

Should we live righteous, socially responsible lives when readily available biological weapons pose such clear and present danger, particularly when the spiritual afterlife concepts of Heaven/Hell and Reincarnation are unlikely?

Background, Facts and Miscellaneous

Biological weapons are toxic materials produced from pathogenic organisms or artificially manufactured toxic substances that are used to intentionally interfere with the biological processes of a host. These substances work to kill or incapacitate the host and may be used to target living organisms such as humans, animals or vegetation.

Humans have long resorted to any viable means in which to destroy one another and the use of biological weapons has been no exception, from weaponising some of nature's most formidable viral, bacterial and fungal foes to medical science actively employed to seek out and harness nature's most destructive biological agents under the guise of researching potential threats and expanding knowledge for the purpose of formulating pre-emptive treatment to future exposure.

The key word here is nature, that many of these agents occur naturally, and as such, is potentially accessible by anyone who knows where to look.

So, in essence, any terrorist group or corrupt state could utilise such research and underhanded tactics to become a 'world power' overnight. With scientific knowledge and expertise ever-expanding, it doesn't seem infeasible that the pursuit to discover a combination of chemicals producing the most potent fatal bio-weapon would be a futile one, nor perhaps the know-how and capability to increase the lethality of known biological agents by tweaking their genetic structure.

Thus, if world peace and the longevity of humankind is literally hanging by a man-made thread, has the time come to be self-serving and live life to the fullest while we still can?

With so many holes and scientific violations in the widely accepted 'Big Bang' theory, how simple would it be to devise an alternative theory that would answer more questions than it poses?

Background, Facts and Miscellaneous

According to the scientific view, the Universe began expanding over 13 billion years ago in an event termed the 'Big Bang' - a point when space nor time existed yet a singularity which contained all the matter in the Universe and a single unified force (made up of the four fundamental forces), suddenly and with no good reason, started to expand. Long story short, this singularity of zero volume and infinite density would transform itself over time into this wondrous formation of planets, stars and galaxies we call the Universe.

While the most obvious observation of this theory is to question how and why the initial inflation was kick-started, the most pressing concern is how all that matter and energy existed in harmony in the first place, and for how long.

In putting forward this theory, the scientific community have asked us to not do them the disservice of questioning this version of events and accept that 'something came out of nothing', accepting it as a completely random event.

With physicists paying so little regard to their own laws of physics, this Author shall also choose not to be bound by conventional thinking in putting forward a fanciful theory on the origin of the universe. The fundamental law that shall be completely discarded in this instance, is that an object cannot exist wholly within itself, or occupy the same space, at any point in time.

The theory is called 'The Circular Reference Marble' and given its many violations of Physics Law, the author expects over time, equal footing with the famed Big Bang theory. Is he nuts?

The 'Circular Reference Marble' Paradox

Our vast Universe contains many hundreds of galaxies including our very own 'The Milky Way':

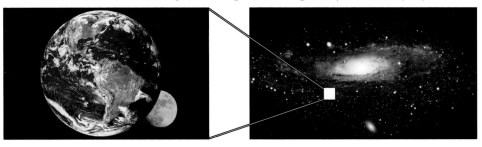

And this entire Universe is contained within a giant glass sphere (with the centre expanding and the outer volume contracting):

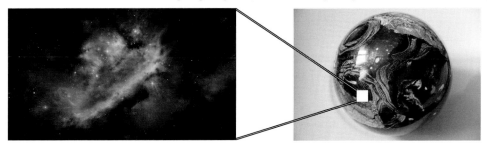

Herein contains the first violation of a fundamental law of Physics, in that this giant glass sphere, the one that contains the Universe sits right here on Earth, nestled innocently and inconspicuously amongst a childs' prized collection of marbles:

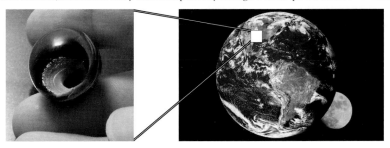

This circular reference effectively advocates no conceivable end of the Universe and that it must have always existed in this state.

Should the dark corners of the internet be contained or should we all be eternally grateful that the undesirable, the immoral and depraved sections of society stay on their side of the fence?

Background, Facts and Miscellaneous

That awkward moment when Mr and Mrs St John-Smythe realise squatters have temporarily taken up residence in their well-to-do neighbourhood, then learning that police had just weeks earlier intervened to evict them from a rundown house in an urban area a safe distance away.

The *Deep Web* is a term coined for World Wide Web content that is not part of the Surface Web (which is indexed by standard search engines), a deep, dark and murky domain of criminality, human filth and depravity.

These sites elect to remain hidden and unsearchable for numerous reasons, many sinister, and only allows itself to be accessed via an anonymising wall and not with regular browsers. However, attaining this privilege is child's play.

With such brazen illegal and immoral conduct taking place under our very noses, one wonders how it can be permitted to function so freely or whether that is indeed the best thing to do.

Discuss the following viewpoints:-
• Should we embrace the fact that those who live underground respectfully do us the courtesy in not infringing upon the internet as we know it?
• Should hackers do the honourable thing and identify, target and disable computer users who utilise anonymity tools for depraved intentions?
• Does the relatively easy access (traditionally required one to mix in such circles) mean it will become an inevitable destination for the tech savvy youngsters of tomorrow, fuelling a generation of scarred or depraved existences?

Image Source:- Movie: The Lord of the Rings: The Fellowship of the Ring (2001) Starring: Ian McKellen

Does every person have the right to live or should we assume the right from those unable to make the decision – Do those children who are severely mentally/physically disabled at birth deserve their parents to have the option of ending their pain and suffering and so not to become the inevitable burden on society and to themselves?

Background

It is currently possible to detect through *amniocentesis* and other tests whether an unborn child will turn out to be physically or mentally handicapped, and to what degree. With such information at hand, abortion remains a choice for women who do not want to take care of such a child or believe it would be cruel to allow their child to be burdened with such handicap.

The year is now 2028 and with risk-free tests available scanning the whole genome of a foetus, the authoritarian government have ruled that abortion or euthanasia will now be automatically bestowed upon a foetus or the infant child as and when a severe disability is diagnosed, without question.

A temporary exception can be made for parents if they are able to show that they can financially and emotionally support their child for the first ten years, after which point custody is transferred back to the government to resume their macabre act.

Facts and Examples

• Under this legislation, 'severe handicap' is classed as those who:- cannot hear or see; cannot feed or care for themselves; severely physically deformed; or those at high risk of death without round the clock care.

• Scientists have recently developed a revolutionary technique that maps the entire genetic code of a baby in the womb, meaning thousands of genetic disorders in unborn babies could be identified without the need for risky and invasive tests. Researchers were also able to identify over 40 'de novo' genetic mutations, mutations which are thought to play a role in complex conditions such as autism and schizophrenia.

• The phrase *life unworthy of life* was a Nazi designation for the segments of populace which had no right to live and thus were to be 'euthanised'. The idea was initiated against those having serious medical problems as they were considered disposable, and culminated in systematically killing all those who were unworthy to live according to Nazi ideologists.

FOR

No parent should see their child suffer. § The truth is most will lead pretty unspectacular lives, have little chance of making a difference and will become a burden to family. § That moment in time your child finally understands their full predicament. § If a parent truly loves their child, then bringing them ill-equipped into this unforgiving world is certainly the wrong choice.

AGAINST

A selfless decision borne out of true love and affection, a love so strong that can beat all the challenges ahead together. § Oh, to witness the smile of a disabled child can brighten the greyest of days and warm the coldest of hearts. § Unfair and immoral to burden a parent with such a choice. § Seeing and hearing is enough to appreciate the beauty and wonder of life.

Anyone there?

Be Controversial

Is the controversial view of Glenn Hoddle a valid one?

"The spirit has to come back again, you have to come back to learn and face some of the things you have done, good and bad. There are too many injustices around. You and I have been physically given two hands and two legs and half decent brains. Some people have not been born like that for a reason. The karma is working from another lifetime. It is not only people with disabilities. What you sow, you have to reap. You have to look at things that happened in your life and ask why. It comes around."

With the advent of DNA resurrection now being possible, should the threat of endangered species becoming extinct now be relaxed. Can we protect the existing populations if we were to utilise this technology to provide the inventory still required to satisfy man's insatiable requirement?

Background, Facts and Miscellaneous

In the 1993 movie, *Jurassic Park*, the science of using preserved DNA to resurrect a long dead species was considered only a fictional possibility. But in 2008, scientists in Melbourne and Texas managed to successfully resurrect genetic material from the Tasmanian tiger - a creature officially declared extinct around 70 years ago.

This was considered to be the first time DNA from an extinct species had functioned within a living host, and has now paved the way for an endless stream of opportunity to revive all manner of extinct species (yes, even dinosaurs)!

Today, the main reasons tigers and elephants are endangered are the illegal hunting for their pelts, meat and body parts (used in medicine) as well as habitat loss. Recent estimates suggest that the black market in ivory is worth more than $12 billion, and thus, around 40,000 African elephants are being killed unlawfully each year.

If the technology was proved, and we were to utilise the 'battery hen' model to facilitate the science community providing sufficient numbers of endangered animals to satisfy consumer demand (by way of artificial DNA generation), could this keep the poachers at bay or make no difference?

Other potentially exciting applications:-
• Spawning an army of super soldiers from the strain of DNA of an exceptionally gifted human.
• In the *Outer Limits* TV episode 'The Shroud', a religious order creates an embryo from DNA found in the *Shroud of Turin*, which they secretly implant into an unsuspecting young woman.

Image Source:- Movie: Gladiator (2000) Starring: Russell Crowe

For an intelligent race, it was incredible naivety and stupidity of the highest order to not acknowledge the manifestations of a discriminatory Dowry system. The misogyny it helped to fester and further exacerbate is now so ingrained into society that India's future now seems bleak, with population decline and devolution inevitable.

Background, Facts and Miscellaneous

In India, the *Dowry* system dictates that a pre-negotiated gift is required by the bridegroom's family in return for 'taking on the burden' of a woman to become their son's bride. Generally, this gift involves the offer of a substantial cash payment, property and/or gold jewellery, which therefore clearly places a great financial burden on those families who have daughters.

With sons being considered as breadwinners, the preferred inheritance avenue and handily the heir to someone else's millions, the practices of selective abortion of female foetuses and infanticide have been rampant through the centuries. So much so that UNICEF have stated that it is now a problem of *genocide proportions*, with 50 million women missing in India because of these immoral acts borne out of discriminatory customs.

Because of these projected trends, the strangely ironic (and somewhat quite poetic) thing is that one day, there will be no offspring left to inherit the family jewels. Unless of course, in a country famous for its repressive sexual customs, there is an impending sexual revolution where ideas such as free love, casual sex and female empowerment become openly encouraged and forced to accept.

With this in mind, is it the downtrodden female that holds the power to save this great nation from falling into disrepair and decay?

Wildcard Question:- Was the Dowry system to this day, the single most effective tool the privileged elite have successfully implemented to achieve both desired ideals; population control and oppressing and stealing from the poor?

The Damage Done: Gender Inequality and the Dowry System

Projection Analysis for the repercussions of the Dowry System in India

Assumptions:-
- In the year 2150, strict anti-dowry laws were finally brought in (and enforced) amidst public acceptance of the self-destructive nature.
- The population is indexed to the year 2000, where it shall be denoted by the index value of 1000.
- The Gender Birth Split over time has been projected by the Author and has taken into account current rates and existing practices and attitudes.
- The Population Depreciation Rate over time has been projected by the Author and has taken into account the likely consequences from a declining female %.

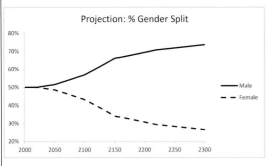

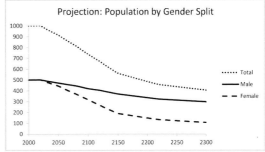

Facts and Statistics:-

° According to the 2011 Census report, the sex ratio in India stood at 914 females per 1,000 males, compared to the 950 to 1000 ratio across the globe. To further put this issue into contrast, the two regions of India which hold deep-lying mysogynistic attitudes, Punjab and Delhi, the child sex ratio was almost 800 females per 1000 males!

° Tens of thousands of girls disappear in India every year (almost 35,000 children were reported missing in India in 2011) and many are sold into exploitation rackets, prostitution, domestic slavery and, increasingly, into marriage in the northern states of India where the sex ratio between men and women has been adversely skewed by the illegal - but widespread - practice of aborting girl foetuses.

° Dowries were outlawed across India in 1961, but the practice is still common, with this specific regulation all but ignored and scarcely enforced. Indian Government statistics for 2001 showed that husbands and in-laws had killed nearly 7,000 women over inadequate dowry payments.

° A UNICEF report said sex selective abortion by unethical medical professionals had grown into a lucrative industry.

Real Life Cases:-

° In Bangalore, 2012, a three-month-old baby *Neha Afreen* was admitted to hospital with a severe head injury, a brain haemorrhage, a dislocated neck and bite and burn marks on her body. Her father is accused of inflicting the injuries on her because he wanted a male child.

° A young Indian mother died and her baby daughter suffered extensive burns after her husband and father-in-law set them on fire as they slept. *Pravartika Gupta*, 25, and 13-month-old *Idika* were attacked at their home in a dispute over a dowry payment.
According to the uncle, the groom's family had continually protested the financial settlement of the union: "They said you are not as good as we are. You must be proud to be our relatives and you must pay."

° Traditionally, unwanted female babies have been fed opium and left to die. Sadly, some are simply sold off as soon as she reaches puberty.

° A 90-year-old Saudi Arabian man is suing the family of his 15-year-old child-bride after she shut herself in her bedroom on their wedding night and eventually fleeing back to her parents' home two days later. The elderly husband is seeking his money back as he claims he paid the parents almost £11,000 for the teenager so they could wed.

Image Source:- by the Author

Illegal drugs are the scourge of the modern world, but what if the war on drugs was finally won?

Background, Facts and Miscellaneous

Drugs are evil and only bring misery... those religiously minded amongst us would question why God would ever create and introduce such a wide varying range of destructive substances onto this wonderful planet of His for us to be easily tempted by, the forbidden fruit that many in society live by, abuse or help attain spiritual enlightenment.

Today, the scourge of drug use is prevalent throughout the world, adversely affecting many peoples lives at one point or another, causing eventual untold misery for those following blindly a path unto self-destruction, for those unable to avoid succumbing to their God-given addictive properties or for those who engage in the lucrative supply and distribution of illegal substances.

But does therein lie the whole point, that it is indeed a divine solution to keeping the unethical, the selfish, the discontented, the insatiable and the socially or mentally inadequate at bay. Or rather, would we wish these personalities to not be preoccupied and instead them be admitted into the mainstream, walking amongst us rather than seeing through the day in the comfort of their own smoke-filled homes or being systematically removed one by one in a hail of gunfire.

Rather than expressing disgust and concern that the war on drugs hasn't yet been won, should we actually be eternally grateful that it looks like it never will be (or maybe, that is the official thinking, that efforts, policies and budgets are optimally tuned to prove ultimately futile).

Speculate and discuss what the aspects of society would be like in 30 years time if the global drugs industry were completely quashed today?

Image Source:- Movie: Bad Boys (1995) Starring: Karen Alexander and Téa Leoni

"Money is King; Live for Oneself; Take no Prisoners"

If this is the ethos the average elite private school wishes to instil into their 'leaders of tomorrow', why do so many well-meaning parents take pride in their children having such a blinkered education?

Background, Facts and Miscellaneous

It is a well known theme that senior and influential career positions have been predominantly filled by those who have enjoyed the benefits of a private education, particularly those from premium establishments such as *Eton, Harrow* etc. If parents are willing to shell out a small fortune on their child's education, the chosen institutions emphasis on rigorous academics and instilling high standards of personal and social responsibility is, presumably, foremost in their thinking.

But a pattern synonymous amongst those in positions of influence and power, one that has been lingering underneath the surface for some time and has become unashamedly more evident in recent times, has been their total disregard for society, an unwavering quest to attain wealth and a guilt-free lack of moral responsibility or ethics.

These characteristics (dishonesty, immorality, uncharitable, unethical, emotional detachment, money-minded etc.) can be quite comfortably levelled against the majority in distinguished professions such as Politicians, Bankers, Judges and Lawyers, Corporate Directors and Journalists.

By consulting statistics showing the proportions made up from those who attended the elite private schools, by the powers of deduction, it would be reasonable to deduce that these principles originated within these establishments, with contagion taking place and spreading them across the breadth and depth of their profession.

If such attitudes are fostered and cultivated by the 'elite educated' demographic, do parents willingly forsake their child's right to flower into a morally responsible, happy and content adult.

Image Source:- Movie: Trading Places (1983)   Starring: John Bedford Lloyd and Susan Fallender

The year is 2027 and a proposal has been submitted for redefining the punishment structure for the Law Courts. The proposal primarily aims to curb and/or sufficiently punish those who habitually commit crime by applying an escalating factor to existing punishment tariffs. Discuss the effectiveness of such a strategy?

Background, Facts and Miscellaneous

With incarceration no longer acting as an effective deterrent to committing crime and with reoffending almost inevitable amongst younger members of society, the festering idea that crime pays and that a life of crime is feasible needs to be eradicated.

A proposal to overhaul the punishment system has been put forward in that there will be a tiered punishment strategy for those who commit subsequent criminal acts thus targeting only the career criminals and those who wish to embark upon such lifestyles. But primarily, the proposal aims to provide a real tangible factor for deterrence - Life Imprisonment.

The proposal draws from one of the most effective deterrents in recent times, and applies an escalating multiplier factor for optimal effect.

Examine the proposal opposite and discuss the effectiveness of such an initiative with regard to crime deterrence and fairness?

For:-
Keeps criminals off our streets for longer. § Prison overcrowding. § Correctly adjusted tariffs means leniency becomes less common. § Would be criminals re-assess the type of life to lead.
Against:-
If faced with a 5th conviction, a criminal is likely to resort to violent acts worthy of a life imprisonment, which otherwise would not have occurred. § Insufficient prison space for potentially vast numbers of lifers. § Petty criminals unfairly punished. § Little incentive to plead guilty. § Punishment should fit the crime.

The 'Five Strikes' Proposal

Background

The 'Three Strikes Law' are statutes enacted by state governments in the United States which mandates state courts to impose 25 years to life sentences on persons who are proved to be habitual offenders of crime.

Specifically, the law significantly increases the prison sentences of persons convicted of a crime who have been previously convicted of two or more violent or serious crimes, and limits the ability of these offenders to receive a punishment other than a life sentence.

The Proposal

A fair 'Five Strikes and You're Out' law combining the basis of the 'Three Strikes Law' together with applying escalating 'multiplying' factors for each subsequent crime. For each conviction, the sentence handed down is subject to a upward revision by a factor dependent on a persons' criminal history.

The factors hierarchy for the final punishment tariff is as follows :-

	Factor
1st Crime	x **1**
2nd Crime	x **1.8**
3rd Crime	x **2.5**
4th Crime	x **5**
5th Crime	**LIFE**. As in LIFE IMPRISONMENT WITHOUT PAROLE.

Conditions:-
- Policy will only kick in once the age of 21 has passed.
- No concurrent sentencing, under any circumstances.
- Crimes will be applied in order of severity.
- Mental condition(s) at the time of the offence may be taken into consideration.

Applied Example

A previously law-abiding person aged 22 is arrested for the theft of a vehicle and dangerous driving which sadly resulted in the death of a pedestrian. The Crown Prosecution Service regards the individual offences seperately, therefore the relatively low level crime of car theft is considered as the 1st Crime, Dangerous Driving as the 2nd Crime and Manslaughter the 3rd Crime.

Assuming the maximum set tariff for the punishments are respectively: Car Theft (2 years), Dangerous driving (5 years) and Manslaughter (10 years) and the maximum sentences are indeed handed down, then the defendant shall be imprisoned for a total of 36 straight years for this misdemeanor (broken down as (1 x 2yrs + 1.8 x 5yrs + 2.5 x 10yrs = 2+9+25 = 36years)).

Upon their release at the age of 58 years old, a conviction of just two more crimes during the remainder of their life will mean an immediate sentence of LIFE imprisonment without the possibility of parole.

In 2048, classified documents uncovered proof that the 'easy credit/de-regulation' policies of the last century and the consequential government bailout programme in 2007 was all part of one big elaborate (lagged) Ponzi scheme - 'lagged' in the sense that the bailout payments had been pre-arranged and assured from the outset.

Background, Facts and Miscellaneous

A *Ponzi Scheme* is a fraudulent investment operation that relays returns to its investors from sources other than any genuine profit earned.

Investment bankers and policy makers of the time had grown frustrated with the depressingly slow transfer of wealth as well as what they considered to be wholly insufficient bonuses, unworthy of their intellectual minds and crafty talents.

With an undying respect and admiration for the *Ponzi* method, their frustrations were further exacerbated by the fact that such a scheme seemed logistically out of bounds to operate, due to it being highly infeasible on a large scale.

Besides, how would one solve the problem of stealing large amounts of money from lowly naive folk who didn't have any in the first place!?!!

The uncovered documents illustrated exactly how such a scheme was discreetly operated on a global scale and how the many hurdles were overcome:-
i) The government and policy makers were consulted in 1990 of the plan to utilise a *Fractional Reserve Banking* model to defraud taxpayers;
ii) Relaxed credit regulations were to pave the way for a housing market bubble. Taxpayers would unwittingly form the lowest tier of the pyramid by way of a cast-iron assurance that all *toxic liabilities* incurred by institutions would be covered;
iii) A complex and heavily traded 'Credit Derivatives' market was designed to be in place, ready;
iv) Because the underlying cash flow was 'virtual', an 'intermediary' must exist for whom the offsetting gain wouldn't be allowed to be written off. Was the evidence always staring us in the face?

The 2007 Global Financial Crisis: The US Banking Bailout

THE PLAYERS

THE LOSERS

Banks and Financial Institutions - The 'Innocent' Party in all this

◦ Instructed to lend as much money as possible via legitimate means, but ideally to those most liable to default on loans.
◦ Relaxed regulations surrounding reserve ratios, lending and credit derivatives will facilitate the maximisation of bad debts and for the scheme to last as long as possible before being allowed to unravel.

Intermediary Institutions - 'In the Know'

◦ Instructed to insure or hold positions in mortgage-backed securities held by the banks and other financial institutions.
◦ By insuring these risky investments, the practice of Banks simply writing off the 'virtual' money on the defaulted mortgages no longer became an option.
◦ With these Credit Derivatives extensively intertwined within the global derivatives market, the institutions exposed to these toxic assets would need to be publicly considered as 'too delicate' to be allowed to fail.
◦ Failure to honour the debts and financial obligations could cause catastrophic losses at the big banks and potentially topple the global financial system.

Home Owners - Unsustainable Mortgage Debtors

◦ The Housing Market would be promoted as a good investment and active encouragement by way of relaxed credit regulations and low interest rates would serve to supplement this. The higher likelihood of mortgage default, the better the chance of being approved zero deposit variable rate mortgages.
◦ A housing bubble would be artificially propped up until the point the 'toxic asset' value is maximised.

Tax Payers - The Bailers Out

◦ The losses incurred by the intermediary institutions, would be covered by an undocumented 'gentlemans agreement' that whatever the amount of losses are, it will be underwritten by the government via the taxpayer.
◦ Taxpayers will, over time, be misled to believe that the bailout was critical to economic harmony.

Further Background:-
◦ Bank of England governor *Mervyn King* claimed the Bank was stripped of its power to regulate banks when Labour came to power in 1997. He said: *"Our power was limited to that of publishing reports and preaching sermons"*.
◦ The problem with 'Virtual Money' - is that you have to one day give it back.
◦ One of the biggest beneficiaries of the 2007 US Government Bank Bailout was the insurance company, AIG Inc, to the tune of almost $180 billion, to cover losses and prevent it from collapse. It would eventually transpire that a considerable proportion of this money was channelled straight back to some of the worlds largest banks, including $12.9 billion to *Goldman Sachs*, $6.8 billion to *Merrill Lynch* and $12 billion to *Deutsche Bank* of Germany.

Image Source:- Source: By the Author

With graduate prospects and the benefits of a university education dwindling by the day, what situation awaits the graduates of tomorrow?

Background, Facts and Miscellaneous

Being a university graduate used to command mutual respect amongst peers and admiration from those who failed to continue onto higher education either through their lack of drive or intelligence. These advantages also extended to career-long benefits such as fast-track career progression, a potentially higher salary over time as well as improved networking opportunities.

However, today, the picture is much different, with the value of a *dime a dozen* Bachelors certificate almost completely diminished and the benefits having been slowly eroded over time, particularly amongst graduates with no recognised qualification or distinguished degree subject.

Additionally, with such advances that IT has provided, it has also paved the way for fewer barriers to entry, job efficiency and automation which in turn has led to an irreversible tide of change in the graduate opportunities landscape.

For the most respected qualified graduates, their situation isn't necessarily ring fenced from adverse circumstances either, therefore, taking into account the following, what marvellous prospects await graduates in 30 years time that justifiably rewards their endeavour, risk, sacrifice and considerable financial outlay, if any?

• IT roles being increasingly outsourced abroad,
• a disappearing manufacturing industry means considerably less engineering opportunities,
• software increasingly automating tasks that were normally the refuge of intelligent graduates,
• due to the cheaper cost of labour, the benefits of healthcare professionals drafted from abroad.

Image Source:- Movie: Casshern (2004) Starring: Akira Terao and Yûsuke Iseya

Could homosexuality one day become the norm rather than the exception?

Background, Facts and Miscellaneous

With trends for homosexuality higher than ever and acceptance increasing year on year (in civilised countries at least), it now no longer holds the same stigma it did as early as 30 years ago. Couple this with the fact that male sperm can now be produced directly from stem cells, the need for heterosexual inclinations are no longer foremost in a person's thinking nor critical to the human race. So, is *gayness* as the norm inevitable? Lets consider the evidence:-

• Is the foundation of marriage only secure in the long term by embracing same-sex unions;

• Men have more in common with each other and a woman's emotional needs can only be fulfilled by other women (Good. Luck. There.);

• Could this sudden emerging boom in homosexuality amongst the masses actually be the divine solution to population control;

• Do gay men know something heterosexual men don't. After all, they're always smiling and happy, even when in a long term union;

• Identical sex drives and converging premenstrual cycles means a more harmonious future;

• At a party, 'ratio' is no longer a concern.

Wildcard Question:-

As the old adage goes: *'Adapt and Evolve to Survive'* For religions to prosper and survive, they must endure and be accommodating of the people and conform to society trends. If homosexuality is looking like it could well become the accepted norm, then will religious institutions go against the word of God and their scriptures and have no choice but to accept it into their doctrine?

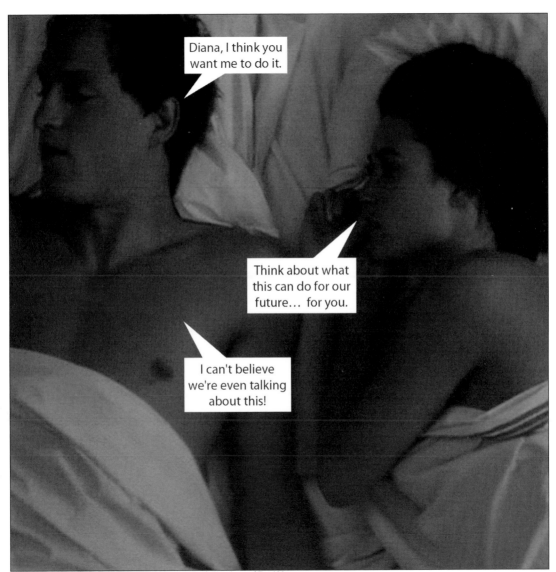

Image Source:- Movie: Indecent Proposal (1993) Starring: Woody Harrelson and Demi Moore

Would a government backed 'cartel' help to curb price rises of items considered essential household expenditure from exceeding inflation?

Background, Facts and Miscellaneous

Please quickly review topic ref:B14 where we explored the concept of 'inflation' and the idea that the actual inflationary pressures on an average household were not being accurately measured.

Here, we explore the same theme but with respect to companies who typically set extortionate price rises for essential items - a proposal to instil a shared vested interest in maintaining the lowest possible price levels and also placing a wider responsibility in having enforced upon them pricing repercussions, one that could signal an end to those yearly inflation busting prices rises.

In 2020, a new fully visible *public cartel* has been put in place, whereby all key items which come under the category of 'essential unavoidable expenditure' will be connected by a formula, one

re-evaluated annually and that which aims to satisfy a minimum profit requirement of 20% and takes into account the underlying fundamentals such as company overheads, tax considerations and wholesale prices. This will provide the pricing benchmark for which companies should align to.

Companies whose price levels exceed above 10% of their respective formula factor, have 3 months to respectfully conform. Failure to conform by this point means that the main premise behind this scheme takes effect, in that the formula must be held true - therefore all other prices can and should be raised in accordance with the violating non-conforming basket item(s). It is this outcome which is expected to place a 'responsible onus' on companies to seriously consider the consequences of their profit-centred actions.

The 'Inflation Cartel' Formula

For the purposes of illustration, we shall assume that there are 3 price categories the government wish to restrict, so that they stay within the confines of reasonable inflation-linked price movements, and these are:-

i) Motor Petrol/Diesel, ii) Gas Utility Prices and iii) Train Fares

The Electricity Price 'Pivot'

Noticeable by its absence, Electricity, does indeed have an important and pivotal part to play. As it is a major cost consideration for businesses/families alike, Electricity shall be used as the index in which to peg these 3 price categories to (this will obviously require nationalising the Electricity Utility companies so that pricing is back in government hands).

Annually, the cartel will then set the Electricity price to a fixed price level which it prematurely assesses will likely result in a break-even situation* at the end of the year. Most importantly, the price will also be subsequently revised each year to take into account price fundamentals as well as taking care not to exceed the measured API inflation rate (see referred topic), so that it can be effectively used as a correctly aligned 'pivot' for the other price coefficients.

* Any profits will be accumulated and offset against any future inevitable losses. In the instance of continuous losses, then these will be covered by any financial penalty levied and the shortfall will need be covered by the taxpayer.
** All participants who conform to the Cartel agreement shall be covered for any losses due to adverse underlying price movements or other factors.

The Cartel Formula

The Formula announced at the outset of each new annum, takes the following form:-

$$E = xP = yG = zT$$

where: E= Price of 1 unit of Electricity, P=Price of 1 litre of Petrol/Diesel, G=Price of 1 unit of Gas, T=Average Demand Weighted Train Fare and x, y and z are the respective coefficients applied to P, G and T in order to equate to matching the Electricity Price (E).

Worked Examples (based on Formula: E=10, x=2, y=3, z=4, therefore Cartel expects prices to conform to: P=5p, G=3.33p T=2.5p)

◦ Scenario A: Gas Price too high/Gas company refusing to comply

Currently, prices are: Petrol=5p, Gas=4p, TrainFare=2.5p
The Gas company has until 31Mar to reduce its unit price level to 3.33p, but refuses to do so.

As a consequence, as well as an additional tax on profits being levied, the cartel formula has to maintain cohesion, therefore the annual formula will be temporarily revised so that it will now be pegged from 1Apr to the new Gas Price standard for the rest of the year - this means that the E, P and T prices need to be raised to match the Gas element of the formula.

In order to satisfy the formula, the other prices will need to adjust upwards by the same proportion for the rest of the year, as follows:-

Gas:	yG=3x4p=12p		
Elec:	E=yG	1xE=12p	New Elec Price=12p
Petrol:	xP=yG	2xP=12p	New Petrol Price=6p
TrainFare:	zT=yG	4xT=12p	New TrainFare Price=3p

◦ Scenario B: Setting a below inflation Electricity Price of 8p

Currently, prices are: Petrol=5p, Gas=3.33p, TrainFare=2.5p
The government realise the strain upon households in this time of austerity, therefore the Electricity price has been set lower than fundamentals allow, with the sole aim of downward pressure on household prices.

As a consequence, for the cartel formula to hold true, the E, P and T prices will all need to be downward adjusted by the companies until the end of the year. The taxpayers will cover all losses borne by the companies as a result of this positive gesture to the economy and society.

In order to satisfy the formula, the other prices will need to adjust lower by the same proportion for the rest of the year, as follows:-

Elec:	E=8p		New Elec Price=8p
Petrol:	xP=E	2xP=8p	New Petrol Price=4p
Gas:	yG=E	3xG=8p	New Gas Price=2.667p
TrainFare:	zT=E	4xT=8p	New TrainFare Price=2p

Image Source:- by the Author

There seems to be widescale cases of systematic baby abduction in recent times. Though misguided and macabre the act of forcing 'involuntary adoption' appears to be, can it be considered the correct course of action in some cases with intentions being totally honourable?

Background

That awkward moment when you see the cutest young child and think how so adorable they are and what untapped potential they possess. And then, their parents turn up and it dawns on you that the child is likely to have a destructive, unloved, pointless and unfulfilled life, as well as inevitably becoming equally as sh*tty as their parent(s), to the detriment of society.

As helpless as we feel, we cannot help but feel a sense of unfairness and injustice that such an innocent child will have an unloving and unfulfilled childhood in store for them, whilst thousands of folk who would provide textbook parenting long to have their own children but are unable to for a number of reasons.

As history has shown, there have been many instances where babies have been forcibly abducted at birth by the very people whom we place total trust in. Though indicating a sinister undertone, is this brave practice of 'involuntary adoption' morally the right stance?

Facts and Examples

In Spain, suspicions still exist that doctors, nurses, priests and nuns were all affiliated in a scheme which stole and sold babies between 1960 and the early 1980s. While the 1,500 open cases vary, a common theme has been the mother being falsely told her newborn has died shortly after birth. The baby is then sold to another couple, and official papers are doctored so this couple would appear as the biological parents.

If proved accurate, could the following hold true:-

i) there seemed to be a misguided duty to mankind to give the children a chance for a better future,

ii) falling trends in the popularity of the Catholic religion meant it was easier to resolve by forcibly placing children into god-fearing homes rather than homes with no such inclination. This also meant little need for a protracted conversion drive.

iii) Occurred in an age where promiscuous living and having children out of wedlock were considered sins against the word and will of the God almighty.

FOR

If such an 'involuntary adoption' procedure was mandatory and a decision based on the parents' character, then it is highly likely that those who wish to carry a baby to 9 months would be those who genuinely wish to be good parents and not those who recklessly do so for selfish or irresponsible reasons. § A generation of loved children can offset the growing scourge of unloved children.

AGAINST

Financial gain is the only driving force behind such practices. § Immoral and scandalous. § A person's standing in society no indicator of the standard of parenting they can provide. § Open to deviant levels of child abuse or criminally controlled supply of children of an age not normally available to Paedophile rings. § Persons normally not suitable for adopting a child could now be.

He will come with us...

I don't f**king think so!!!

Further Facts

In 2013, a three-day-old baby was sold for just £10,000 after his own grandfather told his daughter that her child had died and stole him. Police in Punjab, India, say the grandfather was offered the reward by a hospital nurse and her accomplice who were reportedly involved in a child trafficking ring. The child was later sold to a Delhi-based 'businessman' through a deal arranged on a social network site.

Businessmen around the country are up in arms, in protest that their good name be unfairly allocated.

Image Source:- Movie: Star Wars: Episode I - The Phantom Menace (1999)
Starring: Liam Neeson & Pernilla August

With countless conspiracy theories abound citing Jews as the sinister protagonists of all things bad in this world, and there being an almost global underlying discrimination towards them, are we actually just all being manipulated to this way of thinking - Is there actually a worldwide conspiracy against Jews?

Background, Facts and Miscellaneous

Anti-semitic sentiment, it seems, has been around for longer than one cares to recall and is almost an accepted stance, but why?

Conspiracy theories (or rumours guised as fact) have had origins from the middle ages through to today, even the most outlandish;
• Blood Libel - Consuming the blood of Christian children in rituals,
• World Banking and the US Federal Reserve controlled by a prominent Jewish family dynasty,
• The forged *Protocols of the Elders of Zion*, citing the idea of a socialistic revolution taking place with the aim of Jewish World Domination,
• Claiming the holocaust is a hoax arising from a Jewish conspiracy to present them as victims while helping to advance the interest of Jews.

From a religious point of view, Jews believe themselves to be the only 'chosen ones'. From the perspective of Christianity and Islam, Jews had killed the Christian messiah and also attempted to discredit the divinity of the Islamic bloodline.

This, together with heightened tensions in the middle-east arising from the almost conscience-free policies undertaken by the US-friendly Jewish state of Israel, it's not difficult to understand how such sentiment is growing or has prospered through the centuries.

With Jews being victims of constant persecution and expulsion throughout the ages, is it conceivable that *Higher Order Architects* gathered support against Jews as a smokescreen for continuing their otherwise more sinister intentions?

Further facts, views and discussion points:-

The Protocols
° The famed *Protocols of the Learned Elders of Zion* were a remarkable forgery, purporting to be a series of lectures by the leaders entrusted with the task of achieving Jewish World Domination.
° Supposedly written by an anti-semitic activist, it was first printed in Russia in the late 19th century and eventually led to the anti-Jewish *pogroms* (a form of violent riot, a mob attack directed against minority groups, characterized by violent acts and the destruction of their properties, businesses and places of worship) of the early 20th century.
° In the early 30s, the Nazis started weaving text from the Protocols into their propaganda, presenting them as authentic. Hitler cited from them to help fuel collective support for the persecution of Jews.
° Today, it is still being published in different languages and is even accepted as genuine in parts of the world - at one point even being distributed free by the Saudi government in the 1980s.

The Promised Land
° With no significant conflict existing between Muslims and Jews previously, was it deliberately orchestrated by assigning the piece of land to the Jews that would inevitably provoke, draw criticism and incite hatred?
° Have the senior politicians of Israel actually been 'placed' to deliberately undertake immoral policies and shameless acts against the minority in the region?
° Officially, the stated purpose of the American Israel Public Affairs Committee (AIPAC) is to lobby the Congress of the United States on issues and legislation related to Israel. If indeed, the policymakers of Israel have been 'placed', then could AIPAC merely be the front for maintaining, co-ordinating and supporting the 'plants' and ensuring that two-way dialogue exists utilising this disguised formal 'committee' as the medium?
° Is the (perceived) unwavering US support (providing financial support and a distinct lack of condemnation) for some of Israels' controversial policies actually designed to further stoke the hatred towards Jews (via Israel)?

Adolf Hitler, WWII and the Holocaust
° Was Adolf Hitler indoctrinated with the extremely persuasive 'Protocols' to come up with an answer to '*Endlösung der Judenfrage*'.
° Could the Higher Order Architects (HOA) have engineered the genocide of European Jews by placing their indoctrinated candidate(s) into power. The belief that German strength and superiority was such that this large scale *pogrom* would go unpunished and unchallenged, consequently sweeping across Europe annihilating the estimated 9 million Jews.
° The ensuing conflict meant that the originally intended policy of *Holocaust Denial* became unfeasible, especially if the allies were victorious in battle (See also Wildcard View on the topic 'Written History').
° Could there be a sinister reason behind the apparent late entry of the US to WWII - only once the infrastructure for a mass extermination was in place and underway?
° A recently declassified report by the Justice Department on the secret history of the United States government's Nazi-hunting operation concluded that American intelligence officials created a "safe haven" in the United States for Nazis and their collaborators after WWII. Were the 'safe havens' across the world always assured for the indoctrinated candidate(s)?

Dishonourable Mentions:-
I.G. Farben; Evidence by Fred A. Leuchters; David Irving; Dr Aribert Heim and the surgery waiting room 'Mauthausen';
Honourable Mentions:-
Mermelstein and the IHR; Jean-Claude Pressac; Simon Wiesenthal; Mr and Mrs Klarsfeld;

Image Source:- by the Author

Why in this modern multi-cultural society does an Asian-Indian person receive so much slack and criticism for being a respected artist in the world of Hollywood, almost seeming inevitable as soon as he entered the scene. Could there be some aspect of racial undertones behind the habitual sniping by critics/fans alike?

Background, Facts and Miscellaneous

M Night Shyamalan (MNS) is a talented film writer/director responsible for films like *Unbreakable*.

Recently, he has suffered professionally through a succession of either poorly received efforts or ill-conceived ideas, and his work and his name sadly continues to this day to be ridiculed and almost outcast. Though such privileges are rarely afforded in such an unforgiving industry, this attitude to *MNS* is totally understandable when the criticisms have started to appear after a prolonged and sustained career dip. Sadly, this hasn't been the case, with the sniping being spiteful almost from day dot after his critically acclaimed suspense *Sixth Sense* became a hit, with increasingly personal attacks becoming commonplace and disturbingly, almost acceptable.

Contrary to the obvious route of citing racism, *Hollywood* has actually long embraced the Black community into their circle, onto its big-budget projects and have continually touted them with no (visible) discrimination. Regardless of this apparent indifference, the stance taken by leading industry professionals towards *MNS* seem to suggest there is a stubborn reluctance to 'let the Indian in too', that it is a step too far, that the deal with the devil was already done (by allowing Black people in) and is non-negotiable!

Has the passive and submissive stereotype of the average *Asian Indian* given licence to those associated with the movie industry, free reign to mistreat, abuse and tread all over those *Indians* who dare to make a living above their station, or do *Indians* merely provide an unthreatening avenue for some to focus their racist attitudes on?

Last Chance Saloons

Surely, the genius behind the masterpieces 'Signs', 'Unbreakable' and 'The Village' deserves no less?!??

Mind-Numbing
Review of 'Sixth Sense' by David Keyes
Film Critic at cinemaphile.org
"Here is a movie of long, mind-numbing, tiresome proportions and a brilliant conclusion. No one, however, should be forced to endure all the heartache for five minutes of audacious footage."

Dreary Direction
Review of 'Unbreakable' by Sean Axmaker
Film critic for the Seattle Post-Intelligencer
"A potentially interesting idea deflated by the absurd proclamations of an arch screenplay and smothered under the ponderous gravity of M. Night Shyamalan's dreary direction."

Grasping at Straws
Review of 'Signs' by KJ Doughton
Film critic for Nitrate Online
"Like a one-hit wonder desperately clinging to the pop charts as its lone hit fades into history, M. Night Shyamalan appears to be grasping at straws."

Enraging Nonsense
Review of 'The Village' by Peter Sobczynski
Film critic for The Critic Doctor
"An enraging bit of nonsense that is made all the worse by Shyamalan's apparent delusion that he has created something extraordinary."

A Punching Bag
Review of 'The Happening' by Christian Toto
Film Critic at The Washington Times
"M. Night Shyamalan has morphed from 'the next Spielberg' to a punching bag for critics and audiences alike. The Happening reminds us why."

Gesture of Goodwill
Article 'The Curious Case (and Continued Disgrace) of M Night Shyamalan' by Bill Gibron
"How do you go from "the next Spielberg" to a critical joke in the span of a single decade? How, exactly, do you squander all the cinematic goodwill you've built up over the course of some stellar motion pictures to produce what many consider to be back-to-back-to-back bombs?"

Respect Thy Name
Article 'The Happening sucks OR M Night Shyamalan is a pretentious douchebag' by Morton Malaise
"In the interest of laziness, all future references to the narcissistic prick filmmaker will be expressed as 'MNS', because that last name is a pain to type."

Be Appreciative
Article 'M. Night Shyamalan - This Is Your Final Warning' by Danielle Vintschger
"An open warning to Mr. Shyamalan. Because I have given you so many chances, as have we all, and if Devil sucks, this is the last time I will be disappointed by your work."

Oh boy, I'd hate to be that guy....

The year is 2030 and it has been conclusively proven that there is a consistent link between mobile phone usage and cancer, in that it required around 30 years of cumulative exposure. Could research institutes been well aware of the potential long-term exposure, but deliberately focussed all their efforts into deceivingly proving no direct link?

Background, Facts and Miscellaneous

Mobile phones emit radio frequency energy, a form of non-ionizing electromagnetic radiation. Studies based on past research have shown that in certain circumstances, magnetic fields can affect living cells, however most state that they are very small and cannot harmfully affect living cells.

Official independent research studies from 1995-2010 were, gratefully, unable to show a consistent link between mobile phone use and cancers of the brain, nerves or other tissues in that region. Despite this, the *International Agency for Research on Cancer* (IARC), part of the *World Health Organisation*, recently classified radio frequency fields as *"possibly carcinogenic to humans."*

In 2027, a sudden and unexpected rise in brain cancer incidence amongst patients between the age of 40-50 led to a government-led investigation - and discovered that 99% of sufferers had been regular users of mobile phones for at least 30 years. Further studies proved that it was indeed the cumulative exposure over this longer term which ultimately damaged brain tissue.

Predictably, we are now seeing those adults prevalent to mobile phone exposure from as young as 10 years old being diagnosed with brain tumours at an alarming rate. This sudden pattern coincides with the mass take-up 30 years earlier.

Discussion Viewpoints:- Firms with vested interests funded the research organisations. § 30 year window of astronomical revenue streams to be exploited first. § Would knowing the risk made a difference? ie. We'd have continued anyway!

Cancer Links - Supporting Graphical Evidence

Yearly statistics on all adults aged between the ages of 40-45, have been gathered and monitored to check any rising trends of Brain related Cancer which has been diagnosed in this period. Extensive and common use of the 'mobile phone' came about in the late 1990s and it was not commonplace for almost every child aged between 8-12 to possess their own one as early as the 2005-2010 period.

Based on these new government findngs and official clarification of the Mobile Phone and Cancer links, we have projected the trend for the next 30 years. Therefore, we wholeheartedly conclude that the use of Mobile Phone technology be halted immediately across the western world.

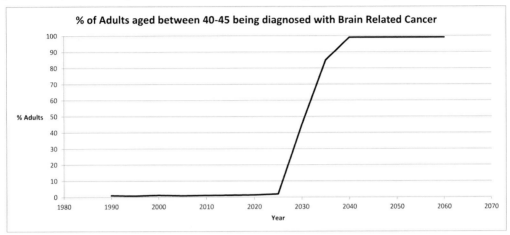

% of Adults aged between 40-45 being diagnosed with Brain Related Cancer

It's good to talk...

Source: By the Author   Image Source: Movie: The Elephant Man: (1980) Starring: John Hurt

Was the recent craze of investing in 'Modern Art' born from the recognition that 'Fine Art' has traditionally been the only safe and reliably lucrative investment area for the super-rich, albeit it being a self-fulfilling prophecy?

Background, Facts and Miscellaneous

A self-fulfilling prophecy (?) - With very few players able to invest at the high-end of *Fine Art* plus any lack of regulation, the ease in which to manipulate the market and falsify transactions can effortlessly allow artificial inflation of legitimate market levels. In other words, it's in the interests of these few to project a view that such investments never sell at a loss or more accurately, that concerted effort is always made to ensure significant gain will be made, even in times of austerity.

Those within the circle are acutely aware that any investment 'tremors' in the Art market could easily have long-term repercussions, wiping hundreds of millions from the personal portfolios of the global super-rich, hence the unwritten rule that *Fine Art* will and shall be propped up at every opportunity, by whatever means.

Modern Conceptual Art is a new beast which reared its head in the Art world as early as the 1950s but has now become a well renowned and respected category. Consequently, the interest in the premium artists (ahem!) of our time has seen the value of their works increase significantly over the years, and thus, so has its desirability as an investment (specially by the not-so-super-rich).

Does recent events suggest however that there could maybe have been an organised conspiracy to fabricate a whole new genre that held the same dynamics as the *Fine Art* market, especially with regard to the self-fulfilling element, but with one marked exception - it allows the not-so-super-rich to get in from the very beginning?

After all, the wealthy live honourably by their only one mantra and that is, 'to get even richer'.

Artists or Con-Artists: Make Your Own Mind Up

Case 1a: 'For the Love of God' by Damien Hirst
A Diamond Encrusted Human Skull - A platinum cast of a real human skull encrusted with over 8,000 diamonds (apparently ethically sourced) worth up to £14 million.

Marketing Spiel: 'For the Love of God' acts as a reminder that our existence on earth is transient. Hirst combined the imagery of classic memento mori with inspiration drawn from Aztec skulls and the Mexican love of decoration and attitude towards death. He explains of death: "You don't like it, so you disguise it or you decorate it to make it look like something bearable – to such an extent that it becomes something else."

Sold: August 2007 for £50 million to an anonymous buyer (sound familiar?).
Purchasers: A consortium which included Hirst himself, reportedly paid the full asking price, in cash, leaving no paper trail.

Case 1b: Damien Hirst vs Picasso
A previous record for a sale dedicated to a single artist was set in 1993 for 88 works by Pablo Picasso himself, which went for a total of £11m (at 2008 prices).

In 2008, the record was shattered when Damien Hirst sold 223 new works for £111m. Such revered works included a bull in formaldehyde adorned with horns, hooves and a disk above its head made of 18-carat gold.
Curiously, Sotheby's didn't charge anything for staging the auction!

Case 2a: 'My Bed' by Tracey Emin
A bed and bedroom objects in an abject state. Artistic talent shone through by the mere fact it included bedsheets stained with bodily secretions and the floor contained carefully selected items from the artist's own room (including used condoms and a pair of knickers with her menstrual period stains). Shortlisted for the prestigious (read discredited) *Turner Prize* in 1999.

Marketing Spiel: By presenting her bed as art, Tracey Emin shares her most personal space, revealing she's as insecure and imperfect as the rest of the world.

Sold: £150,000 to a Mr Charles Saatchi.
Aftermath: Offered to the UK Arts Council for free including all future costs, but was politely refused.
Now installed in a dedicated room in his own home (room reportedly called 'My Bed Room').

Case 2b: 'Two Naked Men Jump Into Tracey's Bed' by Yuan Chai and Jian Jun Xi
A Pillow Fight atop of the pinnacle of Modern Contemporary Art.

Marketing Spiel: "A Couple of Legends"

Status: Video Footage has disappointingly proved elusive.

Robotic doctors/surgeons inside your body... what could possibly go wrong?

Background, Facts and Miscellaneous

A *nanobot* is a device, synthetic or biological, that is able to function on a near atomic level and perform a pre-programmed task.

The day will come when the technology would have advanced so much so that nanobots are routinely called upon to treat a host of medical conditions as soon as they are diagnosed. Decades will then pass before we finally realise the pointlessness of these bots exiting the host, especially when they will be self-powered, can self-navigate and holds within itself multi-purpose arsenal.

Bearing this in mind, the human of tomorrow will conceivably have hundreds of microscopic nanobots rushing around in their veins, waiting around to make corrections and healing cuts, bruises, oncoming diseases and illnesses. What on earth can possibly go wrong!?!!

Classroom Exercises:-

Q1) What possible repercussions could there be if nanobots gained access to the womb? Could they even inflict a premature miscarriage if they self-assessed this new foreign body as having caused the host too much stress and upheaval then deem it an unnecessary risk to endure?

Q2) Could cosmetic enhancements be programmed into the robots, ready to enter a young infant in order to treat them as a blank canvas - making internal and external modifications from within to build to the clients' requirements?

Q3) *The Missing Link*: Has the human race just been Gods' own nanobots incrementally software updated until the version existed capable of navigating itself around the planet and cultivating it ready for habitation by another species?

The year is 2025 and with India's economy at an optimal point to take advantage of its pool of intellectual talent within its borders, the country has initiated 'Order 66' - an instruction ingrained and passed down through the decades for all descendants to obey without hesitation. Discuss the possible success and fallout of such a plan?

Background

Witnessing the eventual economic rot and decline of Uganda resulting directly from the mass expulsion of all people of Indian origin, India, not one to miss a trick, took note. To help achieve eventual global economic superiority, a plan was devised to utilise the lessons learnt but rather to their advantage.

This 'Order 66' was given only to those deemed capable of achieving economic and professional success abroad, instructed to embed themselves into society as irreplaceable employees, accumulate wealth and encourage outsourcing to Indian companies. It was to be discreetly passed down the generations, lying dormant until such a time that the total accumulated wealth, positions and knowledge were such that the turmoil that would ensue from total unrelenting withdrawal would be catastrophic and ideally long term.

Assuming a successful deployment achieving its strategic aims, discuss the economic and global impact of attaining economic superiority in such a manner?

Facts and Examples

In George Lucas' *Star Wars* universe, 'Order 66' was one of a series of contingency orders that the clone troopers of the *Grand Army of the Republic* were trained to obey without hesitation. The order branded the *Jedi Order* as traitors to the Republic and called for their immediate execution without question or hesitation. The issuing of the order by the *Supreme Chancellor* marked the formal beginning of the *Great Jedi Purge*, and signified the rise of the *Galactic Empire*. It was this chief betrayal that led to the downfall of the Republic.

Though this tactic is grounded in the fictional world of a galaxy far far away, it disturbingly held remarkable parallels to the 'Order 66' given to specially selected residents by the Indian authorities.

Both orders assumed the objective of maximising the global and economic standing of the initiator, issued only at the point conditions were in place and deemed at its most advantageous in order to succeed.

FOR	AGAINST
Repatriated funds evenly distributed amongst the Indian population results in a comfortable lifestyle for all. § Sufficient funding now available for an expedited improvement of the country infrastructure, in keeping with its new status. § Accelerated progress at the cost of its rivals. § Western raised women introducing the benefits of equal rights and hair removal. § A run on the banks.	A sudden economic impact on the global economy would be detrimental to all. § A global marketplace no longer accessible for India. § Military engagement by countries perceiving this as an act of aggression. § Upheaval within India from the sudden influx of superior skilled 'immigrants'. § Drastic and outweighing increase of money supply could lead to currency devaluation.

Decree: Order 66
Dated 15 Aug 1966

One must liquidate all financial and physical assets in their current country of residence and transfer forthwith all assets to the Indian Government by a given date. You will then immediately prepare to relocate your family back to India where a guard of honour will await you, generous remuneration for your act of loyalty will be provided and thou shall be restored to a professional position similar to that held previously.

Be Controversial

There is currently a similar initiative already underway in Britain, primed to be exercised in the year 2030, targeting the under classes. The order is passed down successive governments and involves granting the feral and uneducated type to unlimited government support and incentivise reckless breeding. With successive generations of this uneducated lower class in place, ALL benefits and incentives will cease. The immediate aim being that these folk refrain from having children altogether and ultimately all die out.

At risk of a $2 Trillion+ taxpayer funded bailout proposal being publicly chuckled at and then smugly dismissed, were the heads of the large US Banks extremely clever in employing the tactic of 'Pre-meditated Power Placement'?

Background, Facts and Miscellaneous

In the fictional *Star Wars* universe, the Sith Lord engineered himself to be elected as the *Chancellor of the Republic*, granted himself emergency powers which he'd never relinquish as initially pledged, started a war and deceivingly earned himself absolute control on both sides of the war.

He was then able to turn the galaxy against the *Jedi Order* using a deeply embedded meticulously planned military order - an order which fortunately could only be executed by someone with sole unrivalled command and authority.

Assuming the US Banks cartel were aware as early as 2003 the potential catastrophe awaiting them, is it conceivable that they reasoned the only way to avert complete collapse was an external financial injection, one of such large magnitude, that it could only come by way of a government handout. Did they then set into motion an action plan to place *one of their own* into a position of governmental authority, one able to solely facilitate and approve an unprecedented bailout?

Goldman Sachs CEO, *Hank Paulsen*, agreed to become US Treasury Secretary in May 2006. Unchallenged, he went on to orchestrate and oversee the largest corporate bailout in history.

Would the financial elite have taken the risk of allowing an upstanding member of society with unparalleled ethics and incorruptible morals to hold the position of 'Treasury Secretary', when they would inevitably come by, with cap in hand, begging for unprecedented, unlimited and unrestricted financial assistance from the taxpayer?

The US Banking Bailout: A Pictorial Summary

Law-abiding citizens are understandably not answerable to the traditional criminal justice system. However, should a supplementary tier be introduced to try and penalise all those who undertake immoral, idiotic, unethical or irresponsible actions while strategically remaining on the right side of the law?

Background

By definition, law-abiding citizens are completely innocent of any wrongdoing. However, many of us have encountered people in society who behave irresponsibly but sneakily float just within the realm of lawful behaviour, yet some who offend while being unwillingly provoked, being defensive or whose offenses had no adverse impact to society as a whole are punished unduly and mercilessly - bound by a legal system which observes crime only in black and white.

But has the judicial net been cast too tight or must the legal system remain sufficiently slack enough that only those truly guilty of committing or engaging in unlawful crime be punished appropriately.

Should a secondary 'justice' tier be introduced that aims to catch the stragglers, filling a gap that an intolerant society would have otherwise provided. If so, would it be to the betterment of society that law-abiding citizens are susceptible to this secondary set of conventions society now expects them to live by?

Facts and Examples

• Motorway tailgaters be subject to a 5 year jail term. As there seems to be no obvious comprehension of what a braking distance is nor how it varies depending on the speed travelled, they can be deemed of low intelligence therefore removing these lowlifes for this amount of time would do society the world of good;

• Judges who are habitually lenient or not in touch with society's expectations towards wrongdoers, to be handed down a harsh prison sentence themselves;

• Individuals who have been proved to knowingly and systematically engaged in enacting mental abuse upon a loved one or a vulnerable associate over an extended period in order to attain personal benefit in the long term, shall be subject to a stint in a high security mental institution under full psychiatric care;

• Religious 'scholars' who inadvertently incited homegrown terrorism shall be subject to a 6 month prison term with a tailored diet eg. Hindu scholars have a strict menu using only the finest Angus Beef.

FOR

Too easy for many folk to legitimately benefit from unlawful crime. § The current system doesn't legislate in any way for those whose actions indirectly cause harm to others. § A democratically and uniformly chosen set of laws could more effectively tackle societies ills, where unchecked immoral behaviour eventually leads to an inevitable life of crime/dishonesty.

AGAINST

Violates and undermines a civil legal system. § Assuming the possibility to enforce and uphold such measures exist, human rights laws would limit or curb it. § A society whose moral compass have slowly deteriorated through the decades would push through rules contrary to a fair and just society. This would in turn snowball into a system set on targeting the wrong people.

Awww, come on!?!!

Classroom Exercise

On the next occasion you witness a reckless driver pointlessly tailgating at high speed, record your thoughts with respect to the following understandings:-

i) "That idiot will likely cause unnecessary panic for that driver and potentially a fatal accident"
ii) "Why doesn't the driver in front move out of the way leaving the fast lane only for those worthy."
iii) "They've got your number and you've got 5 years b*tch!"

Which one works for you?

If the operation was carried out in the name of Islam, a peaceful religion, why wasn't Sep 911 carried out on a Sunday in order to avoid the murder of innocent civilians - Have gun-wielding anarchists sabotaged the ideology of religion in order to practice legitimately their murderous plans?

Background

On Tuesday Sep 11 2001, 19 militants associated with the Islamic extremist group *Al-Qaeda* committed a series of airline hijackings and suicide attacks against targets in the US. The attacks caused extensive death and destruction and would trigger an enormous US effort to combat international terrorism.

The attacks resulted in the death of 2,996 people, with nearly all of the victims being innocent civilians; only 55 military personnel were among those killed.

Osama bin Laden's declaration of a holy war against the United States, and a fatwa signed by bin Laden and others calling for the killing of American civilians in 1998, are cited as clear evidence of the murderous motivation behind the attacks.

Attacks against civilians are condemned in Islam in no uncertain terms, and anyone who does so shall suffer great torment in the hereafter: "*If someone kills another person, it is as if he had murdered all mankind.*"

Facts and Examples

• More than 90% of the civilians who died in the towers had been at or above the points of impact. The destruction of all three staircases in the North Tower when Flight 11 hit made it impossible for anyone above the impact zone to escape.

• Their bitter rivals, the Christians, consider Sunday a holy day, their day of religious observance.

• The destruction of the Twin Towers caused serious damage to the economy of lower Manhattan and had a significant impact on global markets.

• Among the many victims of 9/11 were several dozen innocent Muslims. Six of these victims were Muslim women including one who, sadly, was 7 months pregnant at the time. The Muslim victims were parents to over 30 children, who were left orphaned without one or both of their parents.

"It is not enough to be a man... you have to become an idea."
~ Henri Ducard, 2005

FOR

Religion is a vehicle that can allow the voice of the bully to be heard and then to overcome. § To be revered as a Martyr rather than a cold-blooded murderer would make mothers so proud. § Distorted extremist views of the scriptures justifies a pro-active approach, encouraging destruction and the murder of non-believers - thereby attracting an unsavoury type into the order.

AGAINST

People only take notice and show concern when a loss of innocent lives take place. Turning building into rubble would get barely a mention in the annals of history had there been a negligible number of lives lost. § Attack was scheduled to take place before 9am Monday, before most workers arrived at their desk. § Mild disruption was intended, not the collapse of the towers.

Let's do this...

Be Controversial

Was it *really* worth destroying both towers?

With one weapon's designated target now to be re-assigned, rather than yet another tower, would it have made more sense as a statement and bragging rights to have destroyed a real symbol of American freedom; the *Statue of Liberty*, the American national monument commemorating the date of the *Declaration of Independence*. Also, there would not have been a single innocent civilian around at that time of morning too!

To help facilitate a fairer distribution of wealth, a new law has been implemented whereby a person's wealth cannot exceed £100million without an annual financial penalty - A tiered 'wealth tax' will be applied annually with the proceeds to be redirected to their chosen charitable causes. Discuss the long term implications?

Background, Facts and Miscellaneous

The year is 2026 and the world is in serious social and economic turmoil having experienced almost 20 years of global depression.

Analysts have concluded that much of the problems have arisen due to wealth retention and accumulation by the super rich, exacerbated by the decreasing supply of money available for circulation amongst the lower/middle classes. Economists are now in agreement that urgent remedial action is necessary to avoid irrevocable socioeconomic problems for future generations - targeting a fairer distribution of wealth as key to a prosperous and booming global economy.

Global law for an '*Excess Wealth Tax* (EWT)' has been passed, which aims to curb excessive wealth by taxing assets above a 'beyond comfortable'

point, such that wealth per person will eventually converge to this point - currently set at £100m.

The idea is that this EWT penalises only negligible levels of wealth - in other words, the penalty should not infringe upon a quality of life (no matter how extravagant or indulgent) while encouraging wealth not to be tied up or held back.

Other perceived benefits are as follows:-
• Discourages the disturbing and pointless pursuit of unlimited wealth amongst the wealthy,
• No longer desire to retain money within a 'privileged' circle, endeavouring to spend randomly rather than this ill-conceived rule of supporting enterprises only having upper class at the helm,
• Good people will strive to succeed even moreso knowing they can help people less fortunate.

Worked Example of the Transfer of Excess Wealth - Over a 25 Year Period

Scenario: At the start of the year 2026, 3 extremely wealthy individuals (with no spouses or children) by the name of Bill, Warren and Mark have a net asset worth of £150m, £800m and £6,000m respectively. The EWT (see 'Tax by Wealth Band' table below) has been implemented and this example charts the erosion of their fortunes over time and the wealth transfer.

Assumptions:-
i) No money gained or spent during the 25 years.
ii) Zero Rate Inflation and Zero Interest throughout the course of the 15 years.
iii) Figures in £millions

Year	Bill			Warren			Mark			Summary Tax Transfer	
	Opening Net Worth	Tax Rate Applied	Closing Net Worth	Opening Net Worth	Tax Rate Applied	Closing Net Worth	Opening Net Worth	Tax Rate Applied	Closing Net Worth	Total Wealth Removed	Cumulative Wealth Transferred
2026	150	5.0%	143	800	12.5%	700	6000	25.0%	4500	1608	1608
2027	143	5.0%	135	700	10.0%	630	4500	25.0%	3375	1202	2810
2028	135	5.0%	129	630	10.0%	567	3375	25.0%	2531	914	3723
2029	129	5.0%	122	567	10.0%	510	2531	25.0%	1898	696	4419
2030	122	5.0%	116	510	10.0%	459	1898	15.0%	1614	342	4761
2031	116	5.0%	110	459	7.5%	425	1614	15.0%	1372	282	5043
2032	110	5.0%	105	425	7.5%	393	1372	15.0%	1166	243	5286
2033	105	5.0%	100	393	7.5%	363	1166	15.0%	991	210	5496
2034	100	0.0%	100	363	7.5%	336	991	12.5%	867	151	5647
2035	100	0.0%	100	336	7.5%	311	867	12.5%	759	134	5781
2036	100	0.0%	100	311	7.5%	288	759	10.0%	683	99	5880
2037	100	0.0%	100	288	7.5%	266	683	10.0%	615	90	5970
2038	100	0.0%	100	266	7.5%	246	615	10.0%	553	81	6051
2039	100	0.0%	100	246	5.0%	234	553	7.5%	512	54	6105
2040	100	0.0%	100	234	5.0%	222	512	7.5%	473	50	6155
2041	100	0.0%	100	222	5.0%	211	473	7.5%	438	47	6202
2042	100	0.0%	100	211	5.0%	200	438	7.5%	405	43	6245
2043	100	0.0%	100	200	5.0%	190	405	7.5%	375	40	6285
2044	100	0.0%	100	190	5.0%	181	375	7.5%	346	38	6323
2045	100	0.0%	100	181	5.0%	172	346	7.5%	320	35	6358
2046	100	0.0%	100	172	5.0%	163	320	7.5%	296	33	6391
2047	100	0.0%	100	163	5.0%	155	296	7.5%	274	30	6421
2048	100	0.0%	100	155	5.0%	147	274	7.5%	254	28	6449
2049	100	0.0%	100	147	5.0%	140	254	7.5%	235	26	6476
2050	100	0.0%	100	140	5.0%	133	235	7.5%	217	25	6500
2026 Asset Worth	150			800			6000			6500	
Tax Payments	50			667			5783				
2050 Asset Worth	100			133			217				

Wealth Tax Tier Structure - Rate applied on asset worth

Wealth Band	Wealth Tax Rate on Excess Assets	Example Tax Liability of annual Wealth Tax Application
<=£100 Million	0.0%	0%
>£100 Million	5.0%	5% Tax if net assets exceed £100 million
>£250 Million	7.5%	7.5% Tax if net assets exceed £250 million
>£500 Million	10.0%	10% Tax if net assets exceed £500 million
>£750 Million	12.5%	12.5% Tax if net assets exceed £750 million
>£1000 Million	15.0%	15% Tax if net assets exceed £1000 million
>£2000 Million	25.0%	25% Tax if net assets exceed £2000 million

Assumptions :-
- Wealth Bands are Inflation-Adjusted. The base year being 2026.
- Wealth Band is Per Person, however will be average adjusted for family units.
For example, if a family of four (two legally married parents and two children) have a net asset wealth of £400m, then there will be a 0% wealth tax applied as the average wealth is £100m.
If however, a parent dies in year 2030, then the average wealth equates to now be £133m, meaning that each person is now in the >£100m wealth band resulting in a 5% annual wealth tax rate in the year 2031.

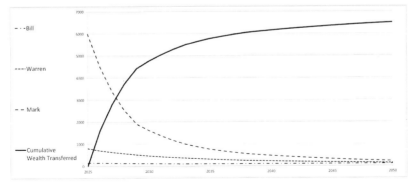

Image Source:- By The Author

Chapter H

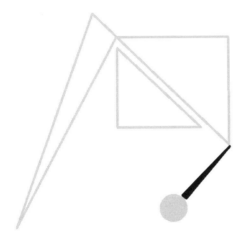

"Being rich and successful is easy. Being a fine man, well, that takes some doing."
- Larivel Dravidayahn

Rather than our passive defeatist attitude as individuals, can a united public front instead better serve as a check on corrupt practices - Should Anarchists be roundly applauded for their unwavering belief in 'people power' and encouraging us all to not passively accept immoral behaviour, in order to achieve a better tomorrow?

Background

Anarchists generally tend to get a bad rep, with many of us law-abiding citizens not wishing to associate ourselves with such irresponsible folk. However, is collective protest the only avenue available to us when our objecting voices are unheard, the politicians fail us or are slow to take action and the corrupt run free.

Could the philosophy of 'turning the tables' be effective in the aim of diverting the power away from the few back into the arms of the people, where it should have resided in the first place perhaps, or alternatively, beckon in a new era where those in power or authority develop an understanding that they are now also answerable to the majority or rather, who they are supposed to primarily serve.

With this in mind, should we start to consider the role of *Anarchists* as unsung heroes with no personal agenda other than to help facilitate progress to a fair and civilised society devoid of greed and corruption?

Facts and Examples

• With disproportionate wages and unmanageable pension levels of council staff already tolerated, the introduction of fortnightly refuse collections and systematic removal of other basic expectations has led folk to grin and bear it as usual (*It is what it is!*). But what if every single resident refused to pay Council Tax ever again unless reasonable conditions were met?
• Having helplessly witnessed the erosion in the value of their pension pots due to fund managers' extortionate annual fees, has led folk to reluctantly accept it (*You have to be in it to win it!*). But what if every holder of stockmarket based pensions pulled their money out with the view of depressing stock prices permanently and putting bankers out on the streets?
• With gay marriages now permitted and sanctioned by the Church, the Christians are left with little other option (*It's all part of Gods plan!*). But what if all Christians threatened defection to rival bible-based faiths should one ever take place in the House of God?

FOR

Worked for the French way back then, and is the thriving (relatively) fair society it is today only because of the courageous actions of the majority to stand up and unite. § Unaccountability will always give way to abuse. § The sense of power and pride one will harbour if undertaking an act of standing up for the better good. § Moral ethics and responsibilities will be governed by society.

AGAINST

Very rarely does hidden agendas not exist. § A state of unchecked anarchy can only lead to lawlessness and an irrecoverable downward spiral when structures/rules are not conformed to. § Backfired (Egypt 2012). § Merely folk who couldn't get a job or refuse to, and now live under the guise of being a social revolutionary activist. Deep down, just a trouble making down and out loser.

Future Reform

On the 1st Jan 2015, every UK citizen has signed a declaration that interest payments will never be paid back to the Banks. Instead, all repayments already made must now be set against the original loan amount (adjusted for inflation) to determine how much really is outstanding, after which interest will still not be charged.

It is envisaged that if the Banks fail to conform to this collective action, not giving in to people power, then it could only result in a systematic crash of the UK and worldwide financial system.

Image Source:- Movie: The Pursuit of Happyness (2006) Starring: Will Smith

The year is 2042 and a major new reform to the prison system is underway - where 'Boredom Capsules' have replaced the typical jail cell establishment and the form of punishment now becoming primarily that of a mental challenge rather than a time-based one. Discuss the effectiveness of such a measure?

Background

There is an overwhelming view that sentencing for convicted criminals are far too soft and in particular that prison conditions are not tough enough to constitute proper punishment or a deterrent to reoffending. The 'insult to injury' in all this is that criminals are increasingly enjoying an existence and creature comforts hardly different from their lives on the outside, one which is fully subsidised by the taxpayer.

After finally freeing itself from the shackles of international human rights laws, a reform of the total prison system has been passed through parliament in order to tackle this disgraceful situation and the shameful lack of justice for victims and their families.

Rather than incarceration being a physical one, it will now strive to become a mentally strenuous ordeal. The idea behind this is that it proves to be such an emotional ordeal that offenders will never wish to endure it again and thus stay away from crime.

Facts and Examples

A new prison system encompassing a 'matrix' style capsule enclosure will now hold each prisoner regardless of their criminality level:-
• The prisoner will be contained within a blacked-out body hugging capsule for 23 straight hours of day with no possibility of moving, nothing to watch, read or anything whatsoever to entertain them,
• The single hour of free time allocated exists only to allow inmates to stretch and limber, and to encourage open conversation amongst inmates about their day.
• Liquefied food is served via an inlet tube with what can only be described as pink meaty slime. Fixed feeding times is suitably complemented with the aroma of spices and herbs piped through just prior. A suction attached outlet pipe exists for liquid and solid waste.
• In order to adhere to medical recommendations due to the nature of the punishment, the prison terms will be significantly shorter (eg. Maximum sentence for Murder shall be 3 years).

FOR

Shorter terms means an opportunity still exists to give life a second more responsible chance. § Could appease the minds of the mentally disturbed. § Criminals given real long hard time to reflect on their actions. § Long term symptoms such as irrecoverable brain damage, in time, becomes another deterrent. § Little possibility of viewing prisoners as being dealt with leniently.

AGAINST

Long term mental effect of an inactive and non-functioning brain over extended periods of time. § Immoral degrading treatment of the human mind, body and soul. § The notion of 'revenge' could fester in the stronger resilient mind and the time to ponder could nurture this further. § Wrong to treat all criminals the same, with time served being the only distinguishing factor.

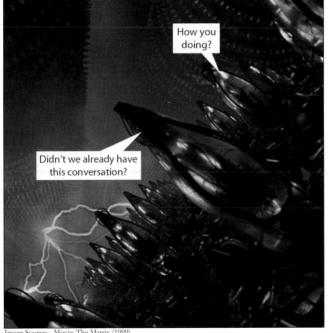

How you doing?

Didn't we already have this conversation?

Be Controversial

Paedophiles are treated much the same way as other inmates but with one slight variation. With boredom being the main reasoning behind such reform, experts have suggested that ambient music would make the day go faster and relax the mind. Therefore, this privilege will be extended to this group only, with music being transmitted into the capsule during lock-up time, resulting in an echoing almost eerie effect - however, it will be littered with the sounds of babies and children screaming in agonising pain.

Image Source:- Movie: The Matrix (1999)

In recent times, increasing awareness is being made of the blight that the 'public school advantage' and 'nepotism' has on Social Mobility, with many distinguished and respected individuals now voicing their concerns. As thankful as we ought to be, should we instead be suspicious of the actual motives behind such initiatives?

Background, Facts and Miscellaneous

There is little doubt that private education has perpetuated class distinctions and inequality, with those educated privately inheriting an unfair advantage over their state school counterparts in entering the fields of business, law and politics.

Though this clearly stands as a barrier to social mobility, with the privileged staying privileged and the poor staying poor, little has ever been done to curtail it nor any concerted effort forthcoming from authorities to create and promote easy networks of access for academically gifted state-educated pupils. Until now, that is.

There has been heightened calls to aim for a meritocratic society, one which puts the most capable into positions where knowledge and wealth can best be created, and an equality in life chances regardless of class or income. Primarily, this has come in the form of trying to break the grip of the public schools and their pupils dominance in senior levels of industry/politics, the introduction of Academies as well as imminent HR laws aiming to identify, curb and root out nepotism.

However, if we were to be overly cynical as to what may lie behind such well-meaning gestures, is it possible that this move (amidst the impending 'changing of the guard') could well be just a ruse to try to maintain and discreetly protect the jobs for the boys policy - albeit preserving it only for the traditional white middle-class?

After all, this is coming in just as there conveniently begins a marked shift in the race demographics of those privately educated, with the proportion of ethnic children rapidly increasing.

The 'Public School Advantage' and the 'Changing of the Guard'

Projection Analysis undertaken in the Corridors of Power (just maybe!)

If such motives are indeed sinister in origin, then at some point, an analysis of current trends to project future scenarios must have taken place in order to flag any possible concerns as well as helping to assess what best form of interception tactic is necessary for 're-alignment'.

This simulation and the projections are based on the following assumptions:
○ Only White and Indian people are assumed to exist in this study.
○ Nepotism does not exist in any form.
○ Consistently over time, 60% of all senior positions in government/industry are those who are privately educated. This is a direct relation to the ratio accepted into the Fast-Track Graduate Trainee programmes, where educational background is considered foremost.
○ There are only 1,000 genuinely 'Senior Positions' considered to be financially rewarding, powerful and influential enough to warrant the accolade. An assumption is made that these primary roles are all made up of Fast-track Graduate Trainees and the level is achieved within 20 years.
○ For the purposes of illustration, we shall assume that there are a 100 graduate trainee positions available every year and 100 of the eldest holding these senior positions retire every year too.
○ The proportion of Indians in Public school will have a starting point of 1% in the year 1991 and will have a conservative estimate of the proportion increasing by 1% every year. This estimate is based on the idea that the IT industry will become ever more stronger and continue to employ the 'tech-smart' Indians at the heart of the business.

Evaluate the following tactical Course of Action:-
Implement a new law effective from the year 2015 whereby a maximum of 50% or 40% of all fasttrack graduate positions can be from the Public School pool (current rate is 60%).
○ In keeping with the suspicion that remedial action is being taken to re-align the demographic distribution of the senior positions (in other words, ensuring a good stock of White people sit at the top table), an assumption is made that all state-educated individuals accepted into the FastTrack Graduate Trainee programmes are all of White origin.

Further Background

The following points seem to not only support the upward trend for all other ethnic origins in public schools to continue as it has been, but more importantly that it will grow at an escalating rate. This would mean that the 'access channels' originally designed with the white middle class in mind, will eventually exist primarily for a larger non-white demographic while the indigenous white middle class will have to fight over the scraps like everyone else.
Unless that is, remedial action is taken now!

○ The demographics of those who occupy the senior/influential positions in industry tend to be consistent with what the private education system have churned out through the decades - a steady reliable stream of aspiring 'White' adults.

○ The public school system are observing ever increasing levels of pupils from different ethnic backgrounds, largely due to varying parental attitudes towards the importance of a good education as well as rising numbers of non-white people in lucrative and well-paid employment. This is also in some part down to the fact that the IT industry have suddenly become extremely powerful, with careers now not only considered safer in the long term but the financial benefits also overshadowing the traditional lucrative professions. It's not hard to argue that the 'brain pool' within such organisation tends to be of Indian origin, and yet another reason why the 'Indian' contingent in public schools are accelerating so rapidly and will continue to do so.

○ It's not far-fetched to suggest folk of Indian origin are extremely more intelligent and harder working than the average English person, and we are now seeing many who possess the necessary prowess exceeding their original mandate and escalating themselves into senior positions.

○ Indians tend to favour a 'keep it in the family' approach to wealth and power.

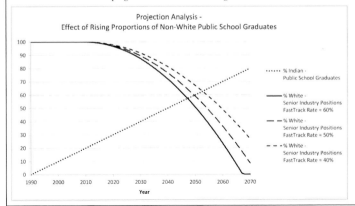

Projection Analysis -
Effect of Rising Proportions of Non-White Public School Graduates

As British Prime Minister, you are instructed to draw up a 'Political Charter' proposing three changes to the legal/judicial system as well as other Home Affairs. Being implemented without legal objection, could such an approach be efficient in meeting the needs of the people?

Background, Facts and Miscellaneous

In 2020, the UK constitution permitted the newly elected Prime Minister to instil three changes to the UK legal/judicial system or Home Affairs. These would be granted immediate unchallenged ratification in the *House of Lords* and will stand for a minimum of 30 years until otherwise revoked.

To ensure that the original honourable purposes of such privileges were adhered to, the laws would need to be perceived by the general public as (possibly) advantageous to the long term security and harmony of Great Britain or at least aimed to halt any disturbing trends observed in society/authority during recent times.

These changes will then be implemented within a year of entering office, by which time an appropriate and adequate support system must have been arranged to be in place.

Classroom Exercise:-
The year is now 2028 and everyone in the room is in a position to become the next PM. Each of you now need to submit to the public domain your Charter, containing the changes to be implemented should you come into power.

Either drawing from personal opinions or selecting 'reform' proposals from this book, complete the three proposal Charter that you consider to have the best combined chance to lead to a better civilised and balanced society.

Once completed, confer amongst yourselves whose Charter best fits its objective. Whoever wins will know not to bother going into Politics!

Bonus Question:- Was the winning Charter the least ethical? If so, discuss as to why.

A Sample 'Change Proposal Charter'

1st Proposal: Tougher Sentencing
○ Reflecting the true nature of the crime and the period of suffering by victim(s).
○ Life means life imprisonment.
○ An eye for an eye, a tooth for a tooth.
○ All financial proceeds from criminal activity confiscated.

2nd Proposal: Immigration Control
○ Points system introduced, where education and career is taken into account.
○ If you have a criminal record, not a chance in hell for entry.
○ Any criminal activity carried out during your 10year work permit means
an instant deportation to wherever you're from, no arguments.

3rd Proposal: Corporal Punishment
○ To curb todays childrens disrespecting attitude and disregard for authority.
○ If you get caned, then you probably deserved it. Tough.

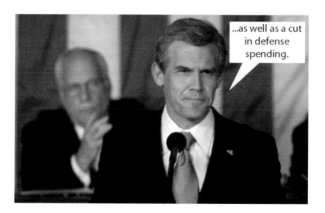

Image Source:- Source: By the Author

'Divide and Conquer' has long been a strategy associated with the all conquering Empires of yesteryear. However, can we look back at recent history and conclude that the strategy is still alive and well, albeit in a more discreet manner?

Background, Facts and Miscellaneous

Rwanda, having close ties and accessibility with their resource-rich neighbours *Congo*, have helped to export diamonds for many years. However, animosity and genocidal conflicts between the *Hutu* and *Tutsi* tribes continue to disrupt the country.

Mounting genetic evidence suggest that these two segregated ethnic rivals were actually artificially formed by Belgian colonists in the early part of the last century, primarily on the basis of their physical characteristics alone.

Today, *Antwerp* is widely considered to be the diamond capital of the world. Coincidence!?!!

The Latin term *dividi et impera* refers to a strategy that gains or maintains power by breaking up larger concentrations of power into chunks that individually have less power than the one imple-menting the strategy. It has been utilised throughout history by empires seeking to expand their territories, and two elements of this strategy are; i) creating or encouraging divisions among the subjects to prevent alliances that could challenge the sovereign, and ii) fostering distrust and enmity amongst local rulers.

Could it be conceivable that this long-standing ethnic conflict was deliberately and callously orchestrated in order that civil unrest remains ever-present, so an internal infrastructure could never form sufficiently enough to uncover the underhand plundering of the regions resources?

Classroom Exercise:- If the British did employ similar tactics in India, what was their motive(s) - to plunder or to hinder economic potential?

Image Source:- TV Series: Seinfeld:Episode 133 - The Wait Out
Starring: Julia Louis-Dreyfus, Cary Elwes, Debra Messing, Jason Alexander and Jerry Seinfeld

If a single religious demographic were to undertake a programme of out-breeding, amidst an underlying customary practice of in-breeding, speculate on and describe the average 'Englishman' of the 22nd century?

Background, Facts and Miscellaneous

There are certain religious communities who wish to spread the word of their religion/culture to the masses via somewhat aggressive means. And there are some so steadfastly adamant that it should be the ruling religion of this land, as well as adorning law as the basis for a new legal foundation and punishment regime, that they have resorted to promoting alternative measures to become the majority, as the current 'conversion' rate doesn't project a desirable trend or time frame.

One alternative measure quite popular, and commonplace amongst a certain religious demographic is the tactic of *out-breeding* - the means to attain a majority by way of birth, conceiving children at a higher average birth rate than all others. Such a tactic would ensure a favourable trend and an inevitable fruition of the original intentions.

A flawless strategy perhaps, however, a considerable spanner in the works comes by way of *in-breeding*, rendering it inherently flawed. The community upholds a traditional custom that family wealth should be strictly kept within the family therefore the quest to have a boy is paramount (girls cannot inherit), but when this is not possible for whatever reason, the age old custom of marrying within the blood family, cousins primarily, is an accepted norm and understandably rife.

This presents a clear oversight, one consciously ignored by religious clerics. Assuming the successful implementation and realisation of this secret *out-breeding* strategy over the course of 100 years, coupled with the practice of rampant *in-breeding*, describe within 20 adjectives, the physical appearance of the average Englishman in 2115?

In, Out, shake the Gene Pool all about

A Projection Analysis probably undertaken by those all-knowing Religious Scholars, sat crowded around a computer screen:-

Let us assume, that there are only two religions in the world, one called *Chrislim* and the other called *Hinju*.
In England, with its population of 10 million, the Hinju's are a minority by a considerable margin, with the religion-divided demographic split Chrislm:80% and Hinju:20%. However, the Hinjus passionately and vehemently wish to change this so they become the majority, whereas the Chrislims are totally indifferent to what proportion believes in their version of 'the truth', and just wish to live in peace and harmony together.

The year is 2015 and the feeling amongst the leading Hinju scholars are that they are deeply unhappy and not content with the current projected trends using their tried and trusted 'conversion' technique, with the current projected trend estimating a 25% minority by 2050. They have now decided on a change of tact, citing an instruction from God himself, urging their followers to undertake their duty to spread the word of their religion by way of Out-breeding the Chrislims. Specifically, this means maintaining a higher birth rate over a considerable period of time so that more children are born into the Hinju religion with this having an additional cumulative effect through the generations such that the majority can be attained quicker, legally and sneakily. The Hinju priests have instructed all couples to be dutiful and have as many children as is physically possible, for the next 100 years.

This simulation and the projections are based on the following assumptions:
◦ All the country's people are assumed to always either be one religion or the other, with no possible atheist choice.
◦ The age distribution is even (eg. as many 20 yr olds as there are 50yr olds). Everyone dies at the age of 70 years old.
◦ All babies are delivered with a 100% success rate with all children living through to 50 years old at least.
◦ The marriage and birth rates have been traditionally the same for both religions through the centuries, at 2 children per couple. Additionally, the male:female split is 50:50 and there is no possibility whatsoever to abort a child once the sex is known.
◦ No benefit cap on the number of children that can be had. On the contrary, the more children the higher and proportionate the amount of financial state support will be, therefore the personal circumstances or the economic climate will not be factors in the projection.
◦ The Chrislims do not veer from their conventions or views towards birth or marriage, despite whatever evidence is presented to them.
◦ People of the Hinju faith are completely comfortable with the practice of *In-Breeding* and is not frowned upon, therefore is heavily widespread. The Chrislims, on the other hand, abhor such practices and would never ever sink so low to retain and to maintain control of the familys' riches.
◦ All women from both religions adhere to the following;
  i)   the average age of women to give birth to their first child is at 22 years old,
  ii) women wait an average of 2 years on average to bear each subsequent child,
  iii) women only marry within their own religion and shall conduct no extra-marital affairs with men of the opposite faith.

Authors Note:		Number of Children per couple			
	Year	2	3	4	5
Original Projection Chart was	2015	20%	20%	20%	20%
considered too convoluted	2030	21%	22%	23%	25%
therefore has been pulled.	2045	23%	25%	27%	31%
	2060	25%	27%	32%	39%
Instead, it is replaced by this	2075	26%	30%	37%	49%
simple worked illustration of	2090	28%	34%	44%	61%
the effect of outbreeding.	2105	30%	37%	51%	76%
	2120	32%	42%	60%	95%

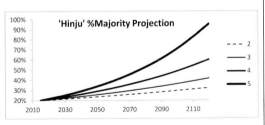

'Hinju' %Majority Projection

Classroom Exercise:
i) Adjust the trends by accommodating an In-Breeding factor of 25% ie. 25% of the Hinju community marry their first cousins. Assume that there are no adverse effects to the purposes of reproduction.
ii) Taking into account the concept of 'inbreeding depression', where the offspring is affected by recessive or disadvantageous physical traits such as genetic disorders or fluctuating facial asymmetry, project some analysis of cumulative defects through four generations of In-Breeding.

With folk in the Science field blindingly dismissive of any spiritual explanation, does a Physicist's stubborn rebuttal of an 'Intellectual Higher Being' prevent them from declaring 'Him' to be the Cosmological Constant?

Background, Facts and Miscellaneous

There's a well-documented human phenomenon called *confirmation bias*, in that if you believe something and something happens to confirm them, you are much more likely to record it and conversely, you are more likely to dismiss, ignore or ridicule evidence that refutes your belief.

Dark Energy (DE) is a mysterious anti-gravitational cosmic force that is believed to have shaped our Universe. Ever since the first evidence emerged, its existence has remained arguably the single biggest unexplained fact about the Universe.

Scientists have attempted to provide sophisticated arguments as to why DE simply couldn't exist, yet recent compelling evidence that DE is at work throughout the entire Universe has soundly put to rest these arguments. Studies of over 200,000 galaxies revealed DE's effects on both the formation and the distribution of stars.

Albert Einstein, applied the equations of his *General Relativity* theory to the cosmos as a whole, and surprisingly it pointed to a universe that was expanding. This flew in the face of the scientific thinking of that time, that the Universe was static. Confronted with this ill-fitting equation, he introduced a fudge-factor to force his theory into producing a static, unchanging universe - known as the *Cosmological Constant*, this factor effectively amounted to a new force at work in the Universe.

A verse in the Holy Bible (*Psalm 139:7-12*) defines *God* as being 'omnipresent'. Since *God* is a spirit, *He* has no physical form - *He* is present everywhere in the Universe and everything is immediately in *His* presence.

Image Source:- Movie: Bruce Almighty (2003) Starring: Morgan Freeman

In 2045, a document unveiling a key strategic move by the 'Higher Order Architects' has been uncovered. Is it possible to reflect on historical events and conclude when and in what form this development turned out to be?

Background, Facts and Miscellaneous

The year is 2045 and a freedom of information request has uncovered a startling revelation, in the form of a highly classified document (shown opposite), revealing a request to a government affiliated entity for a secretive biological research and deployment programme in return for substantial donations and reimbursement.

What has made this to be of utmost concern and of most interest, is because the request was made by a particularly dubious organisation only recently exposed as the legal front for the now widely-accepted *Higher Order Architects*.

Though the existence of an higher echelon is no longer in doubt, what their motivations, influence and true intentions remain so, yet this document has provided an extraordinary insight into their 'plan', intentions and moral code.

Having had this request formally approved and ratified back in 1970 by both the CIA and by certain factions of the US government, discuss whether there is any evidence since to suggest that anything ever came of this proposal?

Further Information:-
• In the late 1940s, US government medical researchers intentionally infected thousands of people in Guatemala with sexually transmitted diseases including gonorrhoea and syphilis without their knowledge or permission. Those infected were then encouraged to pass the infection onto others as part of the study.
• In 1974, National Security Adviser *Henry Kissinger* stated *"Depopulation should be the highest priority of US foreign policy towards the Third World"*.

Extract from the declassified document (Dated 01 Feb 1969):

Donation Pledge
$10 million per annum funding for the next ten years plus share options (on select pharmaceutical companies) granted to the 'research team' in return for their indiscretion, co-operation and understanding.

Primary Directive
An intermediate step required to help expedite our ultimate objective, that is:-
"A better civilised world for the elite race, serviced by intellectually handicapped minions"

Requirement
We have identified the following dangers and concerns that we feel could potentially sabotage and disrupt the application and schedule of our plan. We request a concerted effort by the US authorities to implement an optimal solution in tackling these within the short timeframe we have, as well as to be undertaken in a wholly effective and efficient manner, by whatever means necessary.

Issues to be Tackled
○ The world population is growing increasingly rapidly, particularly and more disturbingly amongst the people of the developing world. The current growth rates would make our future endeavours difficult to implement or likely to succeed.

○ Heroin use tends to only be prevalent amongst the lower classes or criminal elements. But without adequate measures, there is a high probability that this could expand beyond this demographic to become a mainstream pastime for a wider populace. This would render our future minions drug-dependent and largely useless given the addictive nature of the drug.

○ The highly promiscuous and sexually active youth of today are flying in the words of God Almighty and this can only lead to future generations of reckless living with all the disadvantages that this will bring. This will need to be somehow curbed and only those who irresponsibly engage in sexual activity in such a haphazard manner should expect no remorse from our solution.

○ There is increasing evidence that Homosexuality is not an hereditary condition, therefore we can no longer rely on this being addressed by our previous hope that this condition would inevitably die out assuming they did not engage in artificial reproduction methods. Trends indicate that remedial action is well overdue and this 'condition' should be the main focus of our efforts.

○ There is an ever increasing negro population within our borders and they seem to be a people with very little interest in living in a social cohesive society, despite our generosity over the centuries. Our plan to bottleneck this group into contained substandard living conditions with a steady stream of debilitating drugs being allowed in seems to have had little effect on their morale, with many still striving to achieve the 'American Dream'. This, as if it hardly needs mentioning, cannot be permitted in our new world.

Footnote:-
○ To deflect any accusations of wrongdoing or inevitably delay any possible investigations as to the source of this 'fix', then we respectfully suggest that the outbreak occurs a good distance from the confines of our great country. Primarily because the targets mainly reside outside the US anyway but also so that the non-white population be historically recorded as whom to point the blame at through their primitive living and inferior cultures.
○ The tested and pre-approved 'cure' should only be released once these targets have been satisfactorily purged from our society, which we expect to have been fulfilled within 10-15 years. Upon fruition, the global population should be none the wiser as to what actually happened behind the scenes and the world will be primed perfectly for the next stage of our plan.

Image Source:- By The Author

Even when shareholders' best interests are at heart, will company executives sink to any depths to get wealthier?

Background, Facts and Miscellaneous

Modern humans have long had this obscene craving for money and when an opportunity comes up to wring any last cent for themselves, it is rarely, if ever, passed up. The swines!

This behaviour exhibits to such an extent that it has unfortunately infringed on almost every facet of our lives and has even become accepted practice in the world of business where the clamour to offer or receive bribes/commission has become the norm rather than the exception.

The idea that corruption exists at every level of an organisation is indeed widely and openly accepted around the globe yet there have been ever-improving measures to try to curb such practices in light of the growing discontentment amongst the law-abiding society and the unfair consequences on the poorest in society.

Though all's well and good in having watertight measures to eradicate corruption but what if corruptive acts are co-ordinated above the surface and across boardrooms to initiate a perceived legitimate corporate transaction which otherwise would never have taken place - engaging in a mutual unwritten agreement to extort corporate funds to line one's own pocket.

Specifically, when a financial transaction takes place for the transfer of ownership of an entity which is knowingly overvalued by opposing parties. The profitable proceeds (the amount above true market value) will then be allocated to the members in-the-know, thus effectively becoming a completely legal yet fraudulent and systematic theft (at corporate level) of money from the wealthier corporation.

Fictitious Scenarios for the 'Friends with Benefits' scam

RBS Takeover of ABN Amro

The board of Royal Bank of Scotland (RBS) was united in its collective enthusiasm for a £49bn record-breaking bid for the Dutch bank ABN Amro and was naively untroubled by the lack of due diligence that directors were able to conduct before agreeing the deal, according to a 2011 report by the Financial Services Authority.

The City regulator said the size of the deal combined with the lack of visibility on the risks involved made it "a gamble".

A Fictional Scenario:-

With ABN in serious trouble, the head of ABN realised that pro-active action needed to be taken in order to preserve its status and worth.

Therefore, recalling the close friendships with those in seniority at other well-renowned banks, he proceeded to commence a course of action which would be financially rewarding for himself, his friends and ABN shareholders. The conversation went something like this;

ABN Chief: "Fred me ole chum, I need a favour. My bank is in serious doo-doo and is probably worth a fraction of what the market believes".

RBS Chief: "Sure, anything for a banking pal."

ABN Chief: "Ok, basically my share options only kick in if our market valuation is above £45 billion. But realistically, our uncovered exposure on the global housing market means that we are effectively bankrupt. What I'm asking is can you take us over for £45 billion and we will all be handsomely rewarded, especially you and your board buddies."

RBS Chief: "Sure, consider it done... but won't we be at risk then?"

ABN Chief: "Nah... you're too big to fail!"

Impending Takeover of the Worlds Largest Social Network

In 2010, a film 'The Social Network' was released depicting how Harvard student Mark Zuckerberg created the social networking website that would become known as Facebook, but is later sued by two brothers who claimed he stole their idea, and the co-founder who was later squeezed out of the business.

A Fictional Scenario:-

Venture Capitalist: "I want it all, it should be mine!"

Movie Producer: "What should be, and why you telling me this?"

Venture Capitalist: "FaceBook. All that power and money shouldn't be in the hands of that little upstart."

Movie Producer: "O... K..."

Venture Capitalist: "Listen, what's the chance you can rustle up a film that messes with his mind, something which paints him to be a completely unlikeable crook. It's got to make him out to be a social misfit and one that ensures he will never get any true respect."

Movie Producer: "Quite easy. I can also get the marketing and PR boys on it so that it will be a shoe-in Oscar. Though, it will change his life overnight and could tip him over the edge, like in that film 'Trading Places'. "

Venture Capitalist: "Exactly..."

Movie Producer: "You evil man!"

Venture Capitalist: "We got to get all the critics on board too though."

Movie Producer: "No problem, but what if the film is crap?"

Venture Capitalist: "Precisely, most critics haven't got a clue, so they'll praise it."

Movie Producer: "True."

Venture Capitalist: "Internet domination here we come!"

ITV Takeover of Friends Reunited

In 2005, ITV purchased the popular social network Friends Reunited for £175 million. This followed soon after the £330 million sale of a rival social network MySpace to News Corporation.

A Fictional Scenario:-

Friends Reunited Chief: "Mate, I've made a massive mistake and don't know if I can live with the fact I was so greedy."

ITV Chief: "What's up, what could possibly have gone wrong to have you feeling this way?"

Friends Reunited Chief: "Well, you know how popular we were and how valuable we were a while ago, where we literally connected most of the western world with this great idea. And the potential to allow open connectivity between everyone meant our growth potential was huge."

ITV Chief: "Sure, course I do... and you still are aren't you?"

Friends Reunited Chief: "Well, we got greedy and decided to charge if ever anyone wished to contact anyone."

ITV Chief: "You mean 'Unsocial Networking'?"

Friends Reunited Chief: "Yes, exactly. Anyways, this led to other up and coming social network sites to expand their user base massively over the last year using a 'free to use' model. In other words, they have many more active users than we do and we are in a position where we can't reverse this trend. Basically, we are dead in the water and realistically not worth the recent market valuation."

ITV Chief: "Ok, so I'm guessing you want me to short sell on your behalf?"

Friends Reunited Chief: "I like your thinking, but I'm thinking bigger..."

News Corp Takeover of Shine

In 2011, Rupert Murdoch's News Corporation unveiled a £415 million deal to buy the TV production company set up by his daughter. The Shine Group agreed to sell the business to News Corp, with both parties signing a non-binding letter of intent. If the deal is approved, then Shine's chairman and chief executive Elisabeth Murdoch would join her father on News Corp's board.

A Fictional Scenario:-

Elisabeth: "Daddy, do I HAVE to work for a living?"

Daddy Murdoch: "No, of course not pumpkin. While I'm still on this earth, no Murdoch Jr should do a decent days work in their life."

Elisabeth: "Can you buy my company?"

Daddy Murdoch: "Is the Pope Catholic?"

Elisabeth: "I know it means we'd be stealing from the poor, but can you buy it for more than twice its worth?"

Daddy Murdoch: "Sure pumpkin, and I'll even put you on the board. Whose daddy's favourite girl?"

Elisabeth: "I am daddy."

Daddy Murdoch: "Ok, deal done. I have to go honey, got Jeremy Hunt on the other line wanting to discuss his commission. Work, work, work!"

Authors Note:-

The author wishes to reaffirm the fact that these are all fictitious scenarios and have been merely conceived to illustrate the notion that illegitimate transactions are possible.

Do middle-class folk immorally support the 'Bottled Water' industry as way of putting up the proverbial middle finger up at the Third World and the Poor?

Background, Facts and Miscellaneous

Bottled water is drinking water (e.g. distilled, mineral or spring) packaged and distributed in plastic or glass water bottles. In 2008, US sales reached 30 billion bottles despite costing up to $3 a bottle while a similar volume of tap water cost less than a single cent as well as being, well, on tap!

Mineral water is bottled at source from the depths of remote locations such as Argentina, Bulgaria, Nepal and South Africa, and effortlessly transported to the fine folk of developed countries who are too refined to drink free tap water, water that does not require a sun-blazed trek every morning to a well miles away and is readily purified and treated, safe for human consumption.

Meanwhile, in other news, hundreds of millions of people lack access to clean, safe drinking water. And because the logistics of transporting a liquid substance from around the world to those who desperately need it is conveniently considered implausible, infeasible and financially debilitating, well-meaning initiatives are underway to help generate clean safe water sources on land regularly deprived of sufficient rainfall.

Is it just the scourge of *Capitalism* that we observe this ludicrous situation (the preference to distribute water to those who can pay top dollar rather than those desperate and dying of thirst), or is it down to an immoral stance adopted by middle class folk so they can enjoy showing the suffering *Third World* people the luxury of easy access to drinking water provisions but proudly and smugly refuse the offer just because they can?

Could customised dreams be the key to a harmonious and fulfilled existence?

Background, Facts and Miscellaneous

The 2010 masterpiece, *Inception*, put forward the idea of people being able to share a dream space and also the possibility of living alternate lives via lucid dreaming providing individuals with a 'life' different from their own dull dreary ones. Though based in fiction, there are schools of thought which believe that this could conceivably be possible in the distant future.

As unlikely as it is, technological advances cannot be underestimated and neural manipulation shouldn't be discounted. So, assuming the technology became sophisticated enough that dreams could be artificially simulated with pre-defined requirements as well as allowing for fully immersed interaction with multiple individuals plugged in, could this 'alternative existence' ironically revitalise us and give us a new lease of life?

• Unfulfilled career aspirations and untapped potential need no longer be lived in regret.
• An ability to experience and share dream holiday destinations with family and friends scattered around the world can hold loved ones together.
• People may give up on their regular life and engage their alternate lives as being their real one. The startling popularity of *Second Life*® illustrates the feasibility of people actively opting to dedicate themselves to online virtual existences.
• Folks who are paralysed can suddenly be liberated (eg. *Jake Sully* in the 2009 movie *Avatar*).
• Sharing dreams with people in a coma could possibly 'kick' them out of it. Or at least provide family members the ability to engage and share a full life, albeit virtual, with their loved one.
• The most mundane life becomes exciting again.

Image Source:- Movie: Mannequin (1987) Starring: Carole Davis as 'Foxy Roxie' and Christopher Maher as the legend that is 'Armand'

H12	Reform	Left Field

If land and property was reclaimed by the Crown, and then used as a government measure to control inflation and improve economic prospects, could this prove more effective than conventional fiscal and monetary policies?

Background, Facts and Miscellaneous

With Land and Property price levels finally acknowledged as being the primary factor pivotal to the nations wellbeing, economic prospects and inflationary pressures, the authorities have decided to turn their back on conventional 'tried and unpredictable' methods to manipulate its economy and prospects by introducing 'Property Control' with immediate effect. The Bank of England's mandate will now be redirected away from setting or adhering to monetary policy, to now managing the countrys' rental portfolio.

Fundamentally, this means that all Land and Property will be subject to a compulsory acquisition order, so that all land/house/construction domains are now under government control and who will in turn subsequently charge tenants a fair salary/value-weighted ground rent.

As a means of adequately compensating home owners with the 'true' market value, all property price levels will be re-calibrated against the benchmark of '2.5 x Joint Annual Salary'. This should provide real market values for which compensation will be marked against. Owners will have all their % free equity returned to them based on the revised calculation, with the money redistributed from all built up national house mortgage (virtual) debt still outstanding, reallocated as credit. Hence, no mortgage debt now remains unless those who are calculated to be in negative equity.

A fair rent will be calculated annually, at what it perceives will be optimally conducive to a thriving economy. The considerable rental income will go primarily towards building good strong housing and lowering the tax burden for its people.

Government Acquisition of Land and Property

Notes:
- The Government will calculate the rent level based on the revised house price and the Bank of England shall tweak these levels to within +/- 20% depending on the effect it wishes to impact on the economy and affect disposable income.
- Multiple properties cannot be retained immediately after acquisition, where compensation will be paid in full for properties owned and residents must designate which of their properties they wish to reside in.
- Upon acquisition, owners must become tenants or move out. Properties cannot be sublet - guilty offence results in forfeiture of property residence.
- It is envisaged that there will be a considerable number of properties unoccupied therefore area movement and upgrading is unrestricted.

Worked Example
Based on the below example and assumptions, both John and Peter own houses worth £200,000, however, John has paid off £150,000 (75%) over the course of his mortgage, owing the bank a remaining £50,000 on his house whereas Peter has only paid off £50,000 (25%) so far and thus owes them £150,000. Shortly thereafter, the compulsory acquisition order takes place and the government will now need to calculate the equity-based compensation.

John's Case: Johns house has now been valued at £103,226 but he had 75% equity. Therefore, 75% x £103,226 = £77,419 will be credited to his bank account and what was outstanding on the mortgage shall be debited, 25% x £103,226 = £25,806. Therefore his Bank Account now stands at £77,419 - £25,806 = +£51,613.
In summary, John now does not own the property, has no mortgage debt, considerable savings and can remain in the property paying only £6,882 rent per year, a saving of over £6,000.

Peter's Case: Peters house has now been valued at £103,226 but he had only 25% equity. Therefore, 25% x £103,226 = £25,806 will be credited to his bank account and what was outstanding on the mortgage shall be debited, 75% x £103,226 = £77,419. Therefore his Bank Account now stands at £25,806 - £77,419 = -£51,613.
In summary, Peter now does not own the property, has considerably less debt, still no savings and can remain in the property paying only £6,882 rent per year, a saving of over £6,000.

The Banks Case: The net debt for John and Peter has now been reduced from £200,000 to £0.
Under the acquisition, banks have been instructed to reapportion the real hard money accrued over the years in the form of mortgage payments back to the payees in the instance where positive equity compensation needs to be made (John and Peter had made mortgage payments totalling £200,000).
- As John is owed £51,613, this shall be taken from the Banks £200,000 holdings.
- As Peter is owed £0, this shall not affect the Banks remaining £148,387 holdings.
- The remaining £148,387 holdings will be redirected to the Government to either subsidise the tax burden or to settle any remaining compensation claims.

Assumptions:
- Average Mortgage is 15 Years @ 0%, based on a maximum of 4 x Joint Annual Salary.
- Rental amount set by government should be within +/- of this salary/value weighted level.
- Average Annual Salary is based on the median calculation, and is currently a value of £20,000.
- 100 Houses in England, 2 Earning People per House.
- Min Property Value is 110,000 and max value is 200,000.
- Properties and Market Values are evenly distributed.

	Prior to Acquisition			Housing Stock Value Conforming to Joint Salary Multiplier		Post Acquisition: Salary/Value Weighted Revised Market/Rental Value			
No. of Houses	Free Market Value	Yearly Mortgage	Total Market Value Worth	Average House Value	Total House Value	Market Value Per House	Rental Value Per House	Total Market Value	Approximate Yearly Saving
10	110,000	7,333	1,100,000	80,000	800,000	56,774	3,785	567,742	3,548
10	120,000	8,000	1,200,000	80,000	800,000	61,935	4,129	619,355	3,871
10	130,000	8,667	1,300,000	80,000	800,000	67,097	4,473	670,968	4,194
10	140,000	9,333	1,400,000	80,000	800,000	72,258	4,817	722,581	4,516
10	150,000	10,000	1,500,000	80,000	800,000	77,419	5,161	774,194	4,839
10	160,000	10,667	1,600,000	80,000	800,000	82,581	5,505	825,806	5,161
10	170,000	11,333	1,700,000	80,000	800,000	87,742	5,849	877,419	5,484
10	180,000	12,000	1,800,000	80,000	800,000	92,903	6,194	929,032	5,806
10	190,000	12,667	1,900,000	80,000	800,000	98,065	6,538	980,645	6,129
10	200,000	13,333	2,000,000	80,000	800,000	103,226	6,882	1,032,258	6,452

Housing Stock Market Value	15,500,000		8,000,000	8,000,000
Average House Value	155,000		80,000	80,000

Acquisition Adjustment Factor   0.516

Image Source:- By The Author

When the cost-cutting incentives (such as cheaper labour) for 'outsourcing' inevitably erode away, will Western corporations ever be in a position to be able to reverse and reinstate their business/knowledge/skills locally?

Background, Facts and Miscellaneous

Outsourcing is the increasingly common practice of contracting out an internal business process to a third party, rather than staffing it internally. *Offshoring*, on the other hand, is relocating a business function to another country altogether, the driving factor primarily being the substantial financial savings from lower international labour rates.

Todays global economy is such that there is a significant shift in power underway, with the developing world booming while the US/European regions are experiencing a dwindling, and perhaps irreparable, decline in economic harmony.

Assuming the momentum in *offshoring* continued apace throughout much of the 21st century, industries/skill-sets will have all but evaporated in Britain. Furthermore, with such a steady influx of foreign money over the decades and the growing strength of the *Indian Rupee*, the accompanying increase in local salary levels will inevitably take place meaning that *offshoring* costs will no longer remain the economically viable alternative.

Q1) The eventual exodus of British talent, all but shorn of opportunity and the futile point of following careers that are heavily offshored, will mean no local skills exist nor the educational avenues to supplement them. With the cost benefits of *offshoring* having been completely eroded and now an unavoidable financial drain, will it become unviable for many to continue in business? Q2) Will our economies and career opportunities continue in such paths that *India* ultimately offshore all their menial jobs back to the UK?

Should the blame for the disturbing, and remarkably concealed, trend of Church priests engaging in guilt-free sexual abuse of children or uncharacteristic homosexual activity, be levelled at the Church's door?

Background, Facts and Miscellaneous

In the Catholic Church, unmarried men who take Holy Orders and become priests take a vow of celibacy, a formal and solemn oath to never have any form of sexual relations including the self-administered form. In accordance with the *Evangelical Counsel of Chastity*, they willingly relinquish their right to marry in order to devote themselves completely and totally to God and his Church.

By enforcing men of good faith and honourable intentions to strictly adhere to a pledge of life-long celibacy and thus depriving a person from having normal healthy adult relationships, does it contribute to harvesting unparalleled sexual frustrations and unfulfilled emotional attachments, and by not permitting it to be released or fulfilled respectively, would instead manifest itself

to progress to a state of mind so desperate that one blurs the line between depravity, immorality and ones own needs - seeking sexual solace in the arms of the only channels most accessible to them; colleagues and young children.

So, in essence, does the Church actually advocate and encourage good men to turn bad - men who wanted to dedicate their life in the name of God and make the world a better place but instead only served to destroy so many young lives?

Consequently, could the reason why it's apparently concealed amidst a culture of silence be because such is the degraded state of their moral compass on what is acceptable sexual behaviour and standards, that deception is not knowingly being done, as the collective opinion amongst *men of the cloth* is that nothing wrong has occurred?

Perverts of the Cloth

A bastion of righteousness, upholding high moral standards as an inspiration and example to human society

A Cardinal Sin

A senior Vatican cardinal, *Joseph William Levada*, revealed in 2012 how more than 4,000 cases of sex abuse by priests on children have been investigated by the Roman Catholic Church during the last ten years alone.

A Cardinal's Sin

◦ Cardinal *Keith O'Brien*, once Britain's most senior Catholic cleric, admitted in 2012 that allegations that he made inappropriate homosexual approaches to young trainee priests were actually true, admitting that his *"sexual conduct had fallen below the standards expected of a priest, archbishop and cardinal"*.
◦ He has yet to comment on how his behaviour stood against the standards of a cardinal expected within the Church(!)

Twas a good Craic

◦ The Catholic sexual abuse scandal in Ireland is a major chapter in the worldwide Catholic sexual abuse scandal. It included cases of high-profile Catholic clerics involved in illicit heterosexual relations as well as widespread physical abuse of children in the Catholic-run childcare network.
◦ Starting in the 90s, a series of criminal cases and Irish government enquiries established that hundreds of priests had abused thousands of children in previous decades. In many cases, the abusing priests were moved to other parishes to avoid embarrassment or a scandal, assisted by senior clergy.
◦ A government commissioned study, drawing on testimony from thousands of former inmates and officials from more than 250 church-run institutions, found that Catholic priests and nuns had terrorised thousands of boys and girls for decades with chronic beatings, rapes and humiliation. The report characterised rape and molestation as "endemic" in Irish Catholic church-run industrial schools and orphanages.
◦ Father *Brendan Smyth*, who between 1945-89, had sexually abused and assaulted 20 children, some as young as 8 yrs old. As part of a church investigation into *Smyth*, Cardinal *Sean Brady* only reported the information he gleaned to church authorities but not to the police. The church's subsequent failure to deal with him provided an opportunity to abuse more.

Pope Benedict XVI Resigns

◦ In Feb 2013, reports in the Italian media claimed the pope's resignation was linked to a secret 300 page dossier documenting an underground 'gay network' within the clergy.
◦ The concern revolves around the non-observance of the sixth commandment, which forbids adultery, but is linked in Catholic doctrine to the proscribing of homosexual acts.

Surgical Castration

◦ An official investigation into sexual abuse within the Dutch Catholic Church published in 2011, revealed that 10 young boys were castrated in the 1950s, amidst a cover-up and a culture of silence. The surgical removal of testicles was somehow regarded as a treatment for homosexuality but was also a punishment for those who accused clergy of sexual abuse.
◦ After reporting two monks to the police for abusing him in a Catholic boarding home, *Henk Heithuis* was surgically castrated, when he was still a minor.
◦ The investigation headed by *Wim Deetman*, a former Dutch minister, received 1,800 reports of sexual abuse by clergy or volunteers within Dutch Catholic dioceses in the period 1945-1981. The Deetman inquiry also revealed that 800 Catholic clergy and church employees were guilty of abusing children over 40 years.
◦ It found that children in institutional care in the Netherlands, regardless of religious affiliation, were at substantial risk of being sexually abused during the period, including rape, with the molestation rate being 20 per cent.

Pride in Teaching

Richard White, 66, a monk who forced a schoolboy to take part in sex acts was jailed for five years, after evading justice for more than two decades - primarily because monastic authorities hushed the matter up. He was sent to monastic communities across the country during this period, a move designed to supposedly keep him away from children.

Dishonourable Mentions:-
Emanuela Orlandi; Cardinal *Roger Mahony* and Bishop *Thomas J Curry*;

Image Source:- by the Author

In 2046, the Global Council has ratified a legal agreement to implement a compulsory Capital Punishment programme for only the truly sadistic in society. Discuss whether the suggested candidates (see topic 'Devil on Earth') are deserving of such torturous process and at which point would they have felt true remorse and regret?

Background, Facts and Miscellaneous

After decades of unchecked depravity and moral decline, it has been established that the lack of any prospective frightening forms of punishment in recent times has led to moreso increasing levels of immoral and depraved crimes against the fellow man. And with the idea of the existence of a God and 'penance' all but evaporated from the mainstream view, authorities now face the fact that only the introduction of a firm unimaginable form of punishment can curb the disturbing trends in the types of crime currently being observed the world over.

The year is 2046 when the *Global Council*, which oversees international treaties on law and order, have optimised the appropriate capital punishment process for those who fit the criteria of being 'depraved and unworthy of society to tolerate nor reform'. The process has been designed with the aim of achieving the right balance for punishment and to act as an adequate corrective and preventative measure.

It is noted however, that the traditional humane methods have been dispensed with, instead, the most ingenious torture methods that had previously been consigned to history have now been reinstated as a collective, co-ordinated, systematic attack on the mind, body and soul.

The process involves the perpetrator to undergo 7 cumulative stages of torture, each one brought to the brink of death. Critically, the individual is only permitted to expire at the 7th stage and drugs will be employed to ensure survival and consciousness throughout the entire process.

7 Stages of Cleansing: The 'Capital Punishment' Programme for the Morally Corrupt

All perpetrators that satisfy and conform to the tough criteria set out by the Global Council will forcibly undergo an execution programme administered by the authorities, and will take place over the course of 7 days, and no less. Each stage has been designed and ordered to facilitate the subsequent stage(s) and each method will last until they are brought to the very brink of death, with each instance ideally chipping away at their mind and inner soul.

The process is outlined below together with a brief description of what exactly is entailed and its purpose in the line-up :-

1st Stage: Disembowelment (traditionally involved the removal of vital organs from the body)
° A small cut is made across the abdomen to allow a starved rat (with tail clamped) to burrow through the intestines for two hours.
° The patient then has the cavity filled and is provided with antibiotics and drugs to ensure that infection does not set in so that they are in tip-top condition for the rest of the week.

2nd Stage: Catherine Wheel (traditionally involved using a wagon wheel to stretch the victim out and then breaking each limb)
° The 'Lord indeed has Mercy' as only the Collar and Pelvis bones will be smashed during the process. The executioner however can also make a judgement call on whether a mans' testicles will also be crushed if he views their crime as particularly heinous.
° The patient will have any open wounds sealed by having salt rubbed into each one and eventually be provided with mild painkillers.

3rd Stage: Sawing (traditionally involved hanging the condemned person upside down and then slicing them down the middle, starting at the groin)
° The patient shall only be sawed down to the navel (the preceding stages making the procedure less cumbersome). As they are hanged upside down, their brain receives enough blood supply to remain alive and conscious in spite of the pain and severe bleeding.
° Again, the patient will be provided with the necessary support to endure and survive the procedure as well as ensuring they keep the mind at its most receptive to what is taking place on them and what is still yet to come.

4th Stage: Impalement (traditionally involved being pierced with a long stake through the rectum or vagina)
° As a wide opening already exists in the pelvic area, the insertion of the stake should be relatively trouble-free for the patient. The exit shall be where the Collar Bone once stood and has made way for, and the stakes path shall ensure that none of the major organs are infringed.
° The patient now resembles a Spit Roast and therefore any subtle bleeding will be permitted so as to provide a 'sizzling effect' for the next stage.

5th Stage: Death by Burning (traditionally involved a matchstick and affordable petrol)
° The patient shall be basted and then revolved above a roasting fire, much like a spit roast, in order to slowly roast the patient alive.
° Oxygen will be provided throughout as to ensure the patient does not succumb to carbon monoxide poisoning and for a duration just long enough for the skin to lightly detach from the body.

6th Stage: Flaying (traditionally involved removing the skin from the body of a still living prisoner)
° The patient will now have all their skin forcibly and unceremoniously removed from their fully conscious body with every extraction causing untold suffering and despair. The sole purpose of this stage isn't however to cause distress, but rather to facilitate the maximum optimal suffering that can hopefully be achieved in the final stage.
° At this point, it is expected that all patients will have exhibited complete mindful remorse and regret, as well as being in complete agreement of the process endured so far embracing the final stage as the only fitting demise for their soul.

7th Stage: Death by Boiling (traditionally involved water, a fire and a large pot)
° On this 7th Day of Destruction, the skinless body will be slowly immersed into a vat of boiling water.
° Prior to this final hour, the patient will be provided with the effective hallucinogenic drugs so that the experience will be one of 'Hell on Earth'.

With Robotics technology advancing at an alarming rate, it is only a matter of time before a human-like 'companion robot' becomes reality and commonplace - however, does the ability to place him/her 'on standby' at your command lead to it being the optimal life partner?

Background

There is a growing belief within the scientific community that mimicking biological systems could dramatically accelerate the quest for true artificial intelligence. Consequently, the merging of biology and robotics has in recent years, given us *humanoids* who not only look remarkably like humans but can hold conversations and mimic all kinds of human behaviour.

Furthermore, advancements in the medical field have seen the human body merge seamlessly with artificial limbs and foreign organs. And there is even ongoing research by top scientists confident of transferring the human conscience and mind into a robot, paving the way for a 'real' human albeit born in a lab.

With such progressive thinking, a completely realistic and fully working 'companion robot' is inevitably on the horizon, but is it conceivable that such an alternative mechanical 'body' can prove to be no less different and maybe more beneficial than the real thing?

Facts and Examples

• In 2011, high quality stem cells were produced by British scientists in an achievement described as the 'Holy Grail of regenerative medicine'. Crucially, human embryonic stem cells obtained from early stage human embryos are 'pluripotent', meaning they have potential to transform into any kind of body tissue.
• The *Eccerobot* has artificial tendons, muscles and bones, making it move in an eerily human manner.
• The *Ecobot III* contains microbial fuel cells, cow-like stomachs containing bacteria that feed on organic matter, generating electricity to self-power itself.
• The *BioTac* has artificial bone, skin and fingerprints to mimic and even improve upon the sense of touch.
• *Geminoid F*, a robotic female, can talk, sing and produce smiles and enigmatic quizzical expressions, using mechanical actuators underneath her rubber 'skin'.
• In the 'Outer Limits' TV series episode *Valerie 23*, a disabled man has a flawlessly beautiful android companion who develops feelings of jealousy.

FOR

Some people are unable to find or no longer have, a loving companion. § Adverse physical attributes no longer a hindrance to attaining their dream partner. § Women become more appreciative of the 'man' knowing worshipping 'replacements' can be readily ordered. § Disposable love - alternative heads could become possible, of famous celebrities or a bespoke one made of deceased loved ones.

AGAINST

Conversation and sharing experiences with a fellow human being are what makes a loving relationship. § The decline in actively seeking real human companions can become irreparably destructive for the Human Race. § Ethical considerations of loving a 'mechanical droid'. § 'Disposable' nature of a faithful artificial partner. § The human emotion of 'love' receding in our DNA.

This should float your boat honey!

Be Controversial

i) The technology behind organs produced through stem cell reproduction can also be used to produce physically and aesthetically accurate and fully functional female or male genitalia. Would this be the nail in the coffin for a regular human partnership?
ii) If robotics technology is not subject to physical limitations, the possibility of a companion robot with a physical appearance of less than 10 years old can be built to specifications. Could this signal an end to child abuse and other favourite paedophile pastimes?

Image Source:- Movie: Burn After Reading (2008)
Starring: Frances McDormand and George Clooney

The ability to delete age-specific memories has now been realised - Surely, this can only be a good thing?

Background

The year is 2040 and neurologists have unveiled a remarkable discovery, in that the memory portion of the brain is sequenced and has now been completely mapped, in much the same way the DNA genetic code was sequenced 40 years earlier.

They discovered memory was compartmentalised by time period, that is, each memory segment referred to a single 30 day period and conveniently in age order, therefore the respective age periods could be easily identified and mapped. For instance, a 10 year old boy would have 120 segments of the 1200 available, filled with memory data and have them pinpointed.

The privately funded research project has now entered into a commercial enterprise, offering individuals the ultimate mental rehabilitation exercise - the ability to wipe memories cleanly, effortlessly and efficiently. The patient would simply be required to provide the deletion 'time frame' and would undergo a tried and trusted laser 'extraction' technique.

Facts and Examples

A recent case of rehabilitation is as follows:-
A woman was brutally raped at the age of 20 years old, and who three years later is still struggling to move on with her life, her previously bubbly and confident self now feeling depressive and suicidal. She then requests the 6 month period including and following the rape incident to be wiped and the company duly proceeds to 'delete' the specified 6 segments. Today, she has absolutely no recollection of the period and now gratefully has her old life back - out binge drinking and clubbing till the early hours with a smile on her face!

• Researchers at the *University of Minnesota* successfully manipulated the genetic make up of mice in a recent study, causing them to suffer memory loss.
• In the 2004 film *Eternal Sunshine of the Spotless Mind*, a man and woman decide to erase the memory of their failed two-year relationship from their minds to help them get over the break up.

FOR	AGAINST
To improve human well-being - Trauma from accidents, war, childhood etc that still adversely affect everyday lives despite the subjects best intentions to move on. § Bad memories can suppress a sane mind. § Be able to wipe out heartbreak in a heartbeat. § Victims of sexual or child abuse, need suffer no longer. § Success could pave the way for having different memories implanted.	Potentially accidental brain wipe! § Having the presence of mind to know that fulfilling a desire requiring an immoral act can be conducted safely in the knowledge that it can now be easily wiped, primarily absolving one from any feelings of guilt or remorse - the line which has traditionally separated good people from bad. Such a get out clause is akin to the 'confess your sins' loophole.

Oh yeh, I like this idea...

Did You Know ?

The Brain Virus

Andrew Hessel of Nasas' *Singularity University*, suggests that *synthetic biology* could lead to a world where hackers could engineer viruses or bacteria to control human minds. He advocates that cells are living computers and DNA is a programming language, predicting a world where we can 'print' DNA, and even 'decode' it, but warned that viruses and bacteria send chemicals into human brains - and could be used to influence, or even 'control' their host.

Image Source:- TV Series: Seinfeld (The Package) Starring: Jerry Seinfeld

In 2036, a law has passed for the legal 'selective purging' of the population.
Any man or woman at the age of 25 who has not, or looks likely not to, contributed to society in a positive way will be automatically selected for execution.

Background

Due to the age old issues of population control and over-crowding, as well as disturbing trends on the number of people on the wrong side of the law or those not of a good moral standing, the country has seen fit that those such people serve no purpose to the long term success and stability of the country nor are unlikely to contribute in any positive manner.

The law has been passed that those turning 25 years old from the year 2050 onwards will be subject to a vetting procedure to determine their character, morals and psychological state. Coupled with secret information gathered on every person, this will then be used to determine their '*goodness*' factor.

This factor will then be used to determine the 'undesirables', who will then be instantly subject to an execution order, with no right of appeal.

It is expected that by 2080, population will diminish to manageable numbers, crime will fall dramatically and the country becomes the place to be.

Facts and Examples

The algorithm to determine the 'undesirables' involves the analysis of the following factors. A weighting of importance is applied to help determine whether a net positive contribution has taken place or will likely come to pass (a points threshold will represent this):-

• Career: Those in careers greatly positive to society will be granted positive points allocations. Those in Investment Banking, Law or Politics will be granted a zero points allocation;

• Criminal Record: Anyone convicted of a single serious crime or two minor crimes will automatically be designated as 'undesirable' regardless of other factors;

• Parental Qualities: Will be assessed through their childrens personal experience of their upbringing and also school attendance and performance,

• Physical/Mental disabilities: A negative points allocation is allocated to those less fortunate,

• Intellectual and Creative capacities: Positive points are granted though carries a lower importance weight.

FOR	AGAINST
Legitimate excuse for social/ethnic cleansing. § Encourages adherence to law and order. § Promotes the necessity to have positive direction in life from an early age. § Highlights the need for people to give to society rather than take. § Nobody is exempt, even the wealthy or those in power. § Encourages good and responsible parenting. § Social and ethnic cleansing.	Everyone has a right to life. § Sets a precedent for other countries, who could adopt the tactic for disguising unethical genocide. § The privileged, yet again, hold an unfair advantage. § Scope for genuinely good people to be selected. § The expectation that the 'goodness' of a person can be determined, is beyond a mathematical equation. § Unfair pressure on those who mean well.

You're so screwed Biff...

...says the man who thinks 3-D will make a comeback!

Image Source:- Movie: Back to the Future (1985)
Starring: Casey Siemaszko, Billy Zane and Thomas F Wilson

Wildcard View

Tick Tock

If a person has committed two minor crimes at the age of 18, he will be in knowledge of the fact that he is in line for mandatory execution in 6 years time.

Can society afford to have this 'ticking time bomb' with pent up animosity walking amongst us? Can we expect immoral behaviour to be committed in this time, which otherwise would not have occurred had a pending death sentence not been handed down?

Should the premise behind 'Insider Trading' be applied beyond those who work in the financial sector, to all professionals with the power and ability to sculpt and harness policies and decisions with the clear sole aim of guiding prior financial decisions into profit?

Background, Facts and Miscellaneous

Insider Trading is defined as any confidential price-sensitive knowledge and data that can provide an unfair advantage when buying and selling shares of a publicly traded company. In the UK, it has been a criminal offence since 1985 and is currently set out in Part V of the *Criminal Justice Act 1993*, where the definition of 'insiders' refer to only the people who work inside the company that is party to price sensitive information.

Though this offence is confined primarily within the realm of financial markets trading, is this unnecessary restriction justified when, after all, it has already been established and written into law that the offence constitutes acting dishonestly when one is privy to insider information or policies, and is deemed sufficiently serious enough to be worthy of criminal punishment including im-

prisonment. In other words, should the scope and jurisdiction of this offence be widened such that it applies to all individuals of any profession who engage insider information to undertake dishonest conduct for financial gain?

With this legal restriction lifted and the offence now no longer in the sole domain of the *Financial Services Authority* (FSA), determine if there could be sufficient evidence to charge the members and policy makers of the governing Labour Party between the years of 1997-2010 retrospectively with the offence of *Insider Trading* - primarily on the basis of revelations of timely acquired property portfolios amidst a barrage of forthcoming 'house price friendly' policies and a (strangely) stubborn reluctance to curb mass immigration?

The Accused: Politicians   The Charge: Self-fulfilling 'Investment' Prophecies

Evidence: Exhibit A - Trends over time

Year	UK Housing Price	UK Population (000s)	BoE Interest Rate
1995	61,641	57,943	6.57
1996	64,237	58,094	5.89
1997	68,358	58,239	6.56
1998	72,024	58,394	7.21
1999	77,528	58,579	5.33
2000	85,005	58,785	5.98
2001	91,856	58,999	5.08
2002	110,399	59,217	4.00
2003	132,286	59,437	3.69
2004	157,128	59,699	4.40
2005	165,438	60,059	4.65
2006	179,441	60,409	4.65
2007	196,842	60,781	5.52
2008	179,688	61,191	4.63
2009	161,616	61,595	0.63
2010	166,551	62,027	0.50
2011	162,308	62,499	0.50

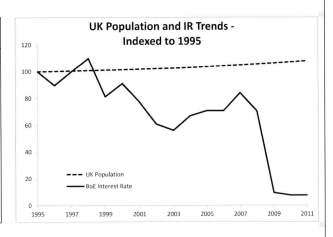

Evidence: Exhibit B - Circumstantial Evidence

Social Housing

According to 2010/11 official figures, in London, where the waiting list for social housing had soared by 60% over the past decade to 362,000, almost half of the lets was handed over to immigrants.

Immigration

During Labour's open door policy, the immigrant population soared by 22%. Studies by the *Migration Observatory* illustrated that over the past two decades, Britain's foreign-born population increased from 7% of the total population in 1993, to a staggering 12% in 2010.

House Prices

UK Chancellor *George Osborne* supposedly made a profit of £450,000 in 2012 by selling a second home that was part paid by the taxpayer. The property was purchased for £445,000 in the year 2000, which since then has seen the average house price more than double.

Interest Rates

With the Bank lending rate at a record low of 0.5% for more than 4 years now, the Bank of England deputy governor *Paul Tucker* suggested in early 2013 that negative interest rates should now be considered. Estate agents and politicians let out collective sighs of relief!

The College Visa Loophole

Each year, Britain admits more than 300,000 young people from outside the EU on student visas. However, in recent years, tens of thousands of them were simply economic migrants seeking a back door into the UK, helped along by complacency by the Labour Party in allowing a loophole to exist and remain for almost a decade.

In 2011, the succeeding Conservative government removed this loophole and closed 460 bogus colleges, sham businesses to facilitate the entry and the visa applications.

Mortgage Lending

In the 1960s and 70s, strict capital reserve and liquidity ratios were applied to banks, and there was sensible rules in place limiting the taking-on of excessive risks in mortgage lending.

These rules were almost completely relaxed soon after Labour came into power in 1997, implementing an wholly inadequate and unfit for purpose *Financial Services Authority* to oversee the monitoring and supervision process for mortgage lending and balance sheet risks.

○ A Politicians Mantra

"I so badly want to make a difference and make a positive change to society... but I want to get paid first"

Image Source:- by the Author

The year is 2020 and with the UK economy collapsing, the concept of 'Fractional Reserve Banking' has been acknowledged as the main cause of such instability. A new concept has been put forward which maintains the FRB system but instead rewards investors accordingly while ensuring a strict control of the money supply.

Background, Facts and Miscellaneous

The new proposal aims to capitalise on this 'creation of money' but rather for the benefit of the saver. In other words, the intention is for wealth in real terms to remain static rather than diminish and for banks to lend responsibly by removing the incentivised factor which encouraged such greed and invited disarray - which in turn would hopefully oversee an eventual return to a natural organic growth of money supply.

The key proponents of the proposal:-
• The basis behind FRB will remain for not to destabilise the global banking system. The key change being that the profits generated (interest) from the money created will be proportionately shared amongst the savers within the bank - the investors whose hard-earned savings make up the capital that the bank is leveraging.
• The primary role of the Bank of England specify on a yearly basis an inflation-targeting *fractional reserve rate* that banks must legally adhere to. Its secondary role is to actively oversee the distinction between real/created money existing within the money supply and ensure that the proceeds from interest repayments are capped at a level which prevents unnatural exponential growth borne out of irresponsible lending.
• Interest on savings no longer take place. The incentive to save is in ensuring their funds are free from the eroding nature of inflation.

Discuss i) whether such a model could be feasible and ii) whether even the banking elite would allow such transfer of their unelected power?

Fractional Reserve Banking: New Approach :-

Worked Example based on the following scenario;

Country has only one Bank of which it has 4 account holders (Persons A-C and Loanee D) which have deposits totalling £100,000 (this represents the total UK Money Supply at Year 0). For the purposes of illustration, we shall assume the interest rate on saving is 0%.
Case: An account holder (Loanee D) takes out a loan for £80,000 in Year 1 (Interest Only Loan at 10% over 5 Years).

Fractional Reserve Rate	20%	Lending Rate	0%	Commencing Money Supply	£100,000
Maximum Loan Liability	£80,000	Borrowing Rate	10%		

See accompanying Figure for Breakdown of Account Movements over Time

Fractional Reserve Banking Model

The Fractional Reserve Rate is only used to determine the proportion of deposits that it must hold back. Under this model, the Banks stand to gain 100% of all 'profit' from the loans and mortgages it can successfully grant.

	Loan Book				Individuals Bank Account				Banks Own Account		
	Total Loan Liability	Loan Interest Payable	Loan Repayment		Total Account Balance	Interest Redirected from Loans	Cumulative Balance		Total Account Balance	Interest Redirected from Loans	Cumulative Balance
Year 0	£0	£0	£0		£100,000	£0	£100,000		£0	£0	£0
Year 1	£80,000	-£8,000	£0		£92,000	£0	£92,000		£0	£8,000	£8,000
Year 2	£80,000	-£8,000	£0		£84,000	£0	£84,000		£8,000	£8,000	£16,000
Year 3	£80,000	-£8,000	£0		£76,000	£0	£76,000		£16,000	£8,000	£24,000
Year 4	£80,000	-£8,000	£0		£68,000	£0	£68,000		£24,000	£8,000	£32,000
Year 5	£80,000	-£8,000	-£80,000		£60,000	£0	£60,000		£32,000	£8,000	£40,000
Year 6	£0	£0	£0		£60,000	£0	£60,000		£40,000	£0	£40,000
		-£40,000				£0	£60,000			£40,000	£40,000

Proposed New Banking Model

The Fractional Reserve Rate now also becomes key to determining the allocation of the interest received on loans.
In this case, since the rate is 20%, then 20% of all interest received from loans will go to the Bank providing the loan and the remaining 80% will be allocated proportionately among ALL its savers dependent on the savings held (as of close the previous year).
However, this redirection of interest is subject to a cap set by the Central Bank (eg. Any interest payments generated from loans which can only be redirected to savers if the benefit does not exceed a 40% annual return. All excess monies above this amount would either be redirected to Central Bank to alleviate public spending or just 'deleted' as easy as the loan was 'created'.

	Loan Book				Individuals Bank Account				Banks Own Account		
	Total Loan Liability	Loan Interest Payable	Loan Repayment		Total Account Balance	Interest Redirected from Loans	Cumulative Balance		Total Account Balance	Interest Redirected from Loans	Cumulative Balance
Year 0	£0	£0	£0		£100,000	£0	£100,000		£0	£0	£0
Year 1	£80,000	-£8,000	£0		£92,000	£6,400	£98,400		£0	£1,600	£1,600
Year 2	£80,000	-£8,000	£0		£90,400	£6,400	£96,698		£1,600	£1,600	£3,302
Year 3	£80,000	-£8,000	£0		£88,698	£6,400	£94,886		£3,200	£1,600	£5,114
Year 4	£80,000	-£8,000	£0		£86,886	£6,400	£92,959		£4,800	£1,600	£7,041
Year 5	£80,000	-£8,000	-£80,000		£84,959	£6,400	£90,908		£6,400	£1,600	£9,092
Year 6	£0	£0	£0		£90,908	£0	£90,908		£8,000	£0	£9,092
		-£40,000				£32,000	£90,908			£8,000	£9,092

Summary Comparison of Account Movements

Under the traditional FRB system, the banking system have within 5 years attained 40% of the money supply, literally out of thin air. If the loan had been at mortgage levels and repaid over 25 years, it would become evident how personal wealth would be diminished in real terms and how the theory that FRB allows for a systematic transfer of wealth from savers to bankers could well hold true.

Under the proposed reform, the savers are rewarded for their investments and the bankers considerably less so (though still managing to attain 9% out of nothing). This seismic shift in 'incentive' could well be either the catalyst for a responsible banking system or a self-imploding one over the long term.

	Initial Account Deposits			After Loan Period of Traditional FBR Ends			After Loan Period of New Proposal Ends	
	Opening Balance	% Real Worth		Closing Balance	% Real Worth		Closing Balance	% Real Worth
Person A	£10,000	10%	Person A	£10,000	10%	Person A	£13,637	14%
Person B	£20,000	20%	Person B	£20,000	20%	Person B	£27,273	27%
Person C	£30,000	30%	Person C	£30,000	30%	Person C	£40,910	41%
Loanee D	£40,000	40%	Loanee D	£0	0%	Loanee A	£9,088	9%
Banks Own Account	£0	0%	Banks Own A/C	£40,000	40%	Banks Own A/C	£9,092	9%
	£100,000	100%		£100,000	100%		£100,000	100%

Quotes Through the Ages

"The modern banking system manufactures money out of nothing. The process is perhaps the most astounding piece of sleight of hand that was ever invented. Banking was conceived in iniquity and born in sin. Bankers own the earth. Take it away from them, but leave them the power to create money and control credit, and with the flick of a pen, they will create enough money to buy it back again. Take this great power away from the bankers and all the great fortunes like mine will disappear, and they ought to disappear, for this would be a better and happier world to live in."

Though this quote is attributed to a certain Sir Josiah Stamp, Director of the Bank of England during the 1920s, apparently no such speech took place and should more likely be attributed to a person whose agenda is to change the fundamental financial system the modern world lives under. However, there are certainly some truths in this statement and for this alone, it is being included here in its entirety.

"If my money has been loaned 10 times, then I'm correct in assuming you are using my money to work for you. In fact, I am the one giving you a loan! I now no longer want interest on my savings, I want 90% of all interest you receive on loans you have commissioned and leveraged with my money."
~ A Savers' Rant at a Banker, May 2019

Further Discussion Points:-

- With an overpowering onus to now save money, what long term effect would this penalty for spending have on the economy and the housing market as a whole?
- With savings now tracking inflation, does the stockmarket become less attractive?

The Stockmarket has long been abused by the powerful and wealthy - Has the time come to restore a level playing field by introducing a two tier system, one extended window in which all information must be submitted and a lagged one for actual trading?

Background, Facts and Miscellaneous

The underlying premise of why the Stockmarket is such a popular investment area is because, in theory at least, it is a fair and efficient market.

The *Efficient Market Hypothesis* (EMH) maintains that all stocks are perfectly priced according to their inherent investment properties, the knowledge of which all market participants possess equally. The EMH would suggest that an *Informationally Efficient Market* (IEM) is a given, where any new information about a firm is known with certainty and immediately priced into that stock.

However, those who beat the market are those who rely on it not being a pure market, with unexpected information the main factor behind volatile price movements. This has given way to open and rife abuse, especially in the form of insider dealing and the systematic trickling of news.

Understandably, this would be great if the average investor benefitted from these short term fluctuations, but frankly they don't - that would just be too overly generous and wholly immoral of your typical Capitalist to permit occurring. Only professional investors, and by this we do not mean those allocated to passively manage your pension funds and stock investments (despite quite happily exploiting stock holdings without your knowledge, to short or day trade), are able to react and profiteer before the information is absorbed and finally factored into the price.

With such themes in practice, is it time to make the Stockmarket a truly fair and efficient one again, one without the scourge of unfactored news or insider information - discuss the merits of the proposal for a limited trading window?

Proposal: Distinct and Separated Windows for 'Announcements' and 'Trading Activity'

Let's assume the conspiracy has merit, and that news/information pertaining to a particular company stock or industry's prospects are filtered at a high-level and then systematically dripfed to market participants in a controlled manner. A pre-defined order which looks to maximise return over the short term while being careful not to draw attention that such manipulation is present.

Case:- A Stockmarket traded Company 'Acme Inc' and the forthcoming trickle of good and bad news

'Acme Inc' is currently trading at 100p on the UK stockmarket before the trading week starts. There are two pieces of information expected to have a large effect on its share price, to be released seperately during the course of the week, one positive and the other negative. The important thing to consider here is that the net cumulative effect once both items are absorbed is expected to be 0%.

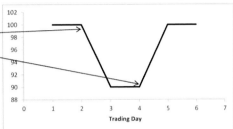

Analysts estimate of factored price		% Move	Price
Information A:	Profits Warning	-10%	90p
Information B:	Job Cuts	+10%	110p
Information A+ B:		0%	100p

Under a typical scenario, the professional investor would be afforded the privilege of knowing the sequence and timing of these information releases beforehand, whereby the bad news is released in sufficient time (day 2) before the offsetting good news is (day 4).
By shorting or trading the stock during this week, the 'insider' could generate a potential 20% profit from essentially, what is an unmoved share price.

The Overhaul:- (Mon-Wed) Information Window | (Thur) Order Submission and Price Calc | (Fri) Trading Window

A complete overhaul of the trading week is necessary in order to distinguish company information from the opportunity to benefit from and exploit the inefficiencies, to minimise the trading opportunities regularly opening up for the stockmarket 'professionals'. The following provides a breakdown of windows and the permitted activities that take place:-

Information Release Period Mon - Wed	Order Submission Period Thur 8am - 2pm	Order Fulfillment & Opening Fair Price Thur 2pm - 5pm	Trading Day Friday
· All company information required to be in the public domain must be disclosed during this 3 day window only. · Additionally, all credible rumours which appear in officially endorsed financial media outlets (eg. Newspapers, magazines, websites etc) must be addressed with honesty. · The period must be strictly adhered to, and the company/industry/government must apply their best effort to trying to ensure that any traded stock related information is released during this.	· All market participants have this window to absorb information and news that has been released. · All orders for buying/selling company stock during the 'Order Fulfillment' period must be submitted, and which must take the form of: i) Market Order: Guaranteed fulfillment of sale/purchase quantity at the closing price (which will be equal to the opening price of the 'Trading Day' period as after hours trading is no longer permitted), or ii) Fixed Price Orders: Fulfillment only if orders can be matched at specified price, or iii) Quantity Orders: Fulfilled quantities at any price, but preferably with parties who have opted for the same order type and secondly, executed in an orderly process beneficial and conducive to upward pressure on the underlying share price.	· Buy/Sell orders matched and executed. · Best effort made to fulfill all (reasonable) 'Fixed Price' and 'Quantity' orders. · 'Market' orders are immediately confirmed but the executed price confirmed only at end of day. · Full market transparency present and available to all. · A panel of independent expert financial price analysts follow a designated method to revise and confirm a new 'fair' and 'efficient' new 'opening price' for Fridays 'Trading Day'. This method ensures that the supply and demand pattern of orders is heavily weighted, as well as the likely sentiment taken by market participants towards the new information/news just released.	· Market opens with share prices opening at the new revised financially assessed 'fair' opening price. · Unfulfilled Market Orders executed first and foremost before the free market price is permitted to float (liquidity is assumed). · Regular trading conventions will then ensure throughout the rest of the working day. Trading cannot resume again until the following Thursday/Friday.

Now, under such a proposal, the case study above would have yielded a completely different yet fair outcome, and this would suggest the market is more 'informationally efficient' than it had been.

A worked example of this case would propose that items 'Information A and B' would have been released during Mon-Wed, and the calculated 'fair' and 'efficient' opening price for Friday trading would have been approximately 100p. The Hypotheses holds?

417

Synthetic Biologists have discovered that a delicate 'ecosystem' must be preserved within human DNA to generate a normal life form. Confined by this rule in applying genetic modifications on humans, will our world soon be scattered with superheroes and villains?

Background

Synthetic Biology is a promising new branch of biological research, which endeavours to apply principles of engineering to biological problems in order to create or modify these systems with specific new properties. Fuelled by the rapid and advancing progress of DNA synthesis techniques, synthetic biology could offer unprecedented opportunities and unlimited potential to improve our lives and our capabilities.

Initiatives such as the *Human Genome Project* which cracked the human DNA code, now mean that every individual can now be biologically identified and classified by trait and ancestry, as well as critically, paving the way for making the effective modification of the human species feasible. In other words, the ability to manipulate human DNA code such that one can now pick and choose attributes for life, is almost upon us.

This chance to play God and exploit the untapped benefits for humankind should bear great caution, but will nevertheless, proceed gung-ho with none.

Facts and Examples

The year is 2080 and after many failed and ethically indefensible attempts to re-engineer a human being, biologists have discovered that an extraordinarily complex verification process is at work, one that the entire compiled DNA sequence must authenticate before the normal biological creation process can commence. This highly ingenious, yet naturally occurring equivalent of a *checksum algorithm* has been collectively interpreted by scientists as natures way of ensuring the delicate human ecosystem is in balance and stable.

Though this was a major setback for the biological terrorists, they have managed to discover a way to fool the check by utilising the *yin-yang* concept.

It has been ascertained that a compatible human DNA structure can only successfully permit external manipulation if it balances the positive attributes granted to a person with ones of equal and offsetting negative worth. Therefore, conceivably, humans will soon couple superhuman abilities with disabilities.

FOR	AGAINST
The majority of humanity would select beneficial attributes rather than destructive or malicious ones. § The multiple orgasm, now available for men. § Honorary membership of the X-Men. § Plenty of redundant and seemingly pointless body parts that can easily be forsaken. § The relatively fast improvements could speed up our natural evolution. § An eye for a bionic eye.	A fight to the death will ensue, meaning that the world population will converge to a much lower population. § Hereditary defects may lie dormant, invoked only by successive generations of genetically modified DNA. § Though the human reproduction process always reverts the DNA code to normal, disposing of any modifications, evolutionary theory may resolve this perceived 'flaw'.

Oh-ho! Wow!

Wahoowww... simply impressive!

He's the one... Ok, lets wheel him out there then.

Wildcard View

Now, lets assume the technology proves to be unrestricted and any modification can be made, as well as having a 50:50 chance of being passed down, could the following prove a blessing for our race:-

i) Females belonging to the lower classes or specific races having their child-rearing facilities written out of their DNA;
ii) A complete immunity to illness, disease and pain;
iii) Engineering a super-man, one with super strength, invulnerability and at the governments command.

Image Source:- Movie: Bachelor Party (1984)
Starring: Michael Dudikoff & Tom Hanks & Adrian Zmed

Could the Evolutionists explain how and why did the male-female separation occur, and at what point in the human evolutionary process did it take place (your answer must conform to the 'unguided' argument)?

Background, Facts and Miscellaneous

According to the *Theory of Evolution*, billions of years ago, chemicals randomly organised themselves into a self-replicating molecule. This spark of life, that simplest life form, through the processes of mutation and natural selection, has been shaped into every living species on the planet.

Although the theory is now widely accepted as to how life on earth originated, it is still outrightly refuted by *Creationists* on the grounds that not only does it leave no room for a supernatural creator, but the notion that such sophisticated design and complexity arose from completely random and naturalistic processes seems totally implausible. Nevertheless, despite many unexplainable gaps in the Evolution theory, it's likely to gain irreversible momentum as Science begins to slowly and inevitably unravel the mysteries.

One aspect of the theory which is given very little consideration is how exactly did males and females come to be, after all, cells were already ably equipped to self-replicate and/or multiply.

With the sexual organs, the reproduction system (womb) and processes universally consistent throughout the 'mammalian' branch of the *Tree of Life*, it stands to reason that this two tier male-female design must have evolved and satisfactorily matured at some evolutionary point prior to the 'tetrapods' branching off. If this were not true, then this would leave very little room to manoeuvre in which to explain how the reproduction roles of the different sexes came to be identical under independent random paths.

With no 'intelligent tinkering', how and why was the male-female mutation deemed necessary?

The Thinking Process: Sometime around 4,000,000,000 BC

With an in-built readiness to adapt to its surroundings and to increase its propensity to survive, it's somewhat reasonable to assume that there is some kind of conscious thinking present and in occurrence.

Scenario A: The Thinking Cell

"Ok, now I know I have no preconception of the notion of 'fairness', but it doesn't seem fair that I'm doing all the work in endlessly regenerating. I'm going to go ahead and tweak my own DNA code to store a revolutionary two-tier reproducing variation, and henceforth call myself a Tetrapod."

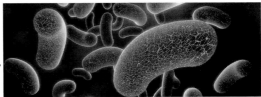

Scenario B: Coincidental Natural Selection

"We're going to just plod along and hope at some point in our evolutionary cycle, two distinct variations and a common reproductive process prevails, where the genetic mutations of two types of reproductive organs and systems are selected naturally and they coincidentally bear remarkably indistinguishable similarities throughout our entire branch millions of years from now."

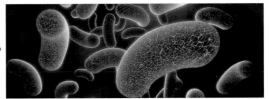

Scenario C: Intelligent Tinkering

God:"I need to constrain the reproductive process so that multiple fission is no longer a possibility. Otherwise, I'm going to have to deal with a 'population issue' much earlier than I ever envisaged."

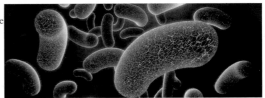

Scenario D: Random Events

"Being a random unguided process, I may accidentally stumble upon radiation which tweaks my genetic code that makes my cell structure dominant over others. As I have no defined path ahead of me, I do not care to speculate for what repercussions there may be down the line, or whether it could result in us branching off."

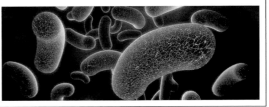

Image Source:- By the Author

Is the deregulation of the food commodity derivatives markets and the consequential boom in prices, all part of a bigger plan?

Background

By mid-2008, international food prices had skyrocketed to their highest level in 30 years. This, coupled with the global economic downturn, pushed millions more people into poverty and hunger.

Closer analysis showed the price surge followed a concerted strategy by the major investment houses to speculate on the food/commodity derivatives markets. With lingering suspicion that market cycles are purposely co-ordinated to accumulate wealth for the few, could it be conceivable that this cycle is the first to strategically coincide with the overall *master plan*.

Is this 'starve the poor in the African nations forcing the majority to die out' policy the final phase of the *Higher Order Architects* master plan - which had previously prioritised the recovery of wealth and land through both the 'Capitalism' initiative and 'Transfer of Wealth' schemes. Success would pave the way for the land to be cultivated primarily as farmland to serve the remaining global population.

Facts and Examples

• Observers have noted that should such high price levels continue then disastrous consequences await the poorest especially those living in the third world.
• Limits (designed to prevent manipulation and distortion) on how much certain agricultural commodities could be traded by non-commercial players, were suddenly relaxed in 2000. This deregulation led the way for the creation of commodity funds that allowed speculators to invest in agriculture for the first time.
• Between 2005-2008, the US regulatory authorities expanded futures trading limits on agricultural commodities and proposed full regulatory exemption for index and pension funds (the real gamechanger).
• Poor countries import large quantities of rice, wheat and maize. Recently, this became increasingly unaffordable as food prices have since risen sharply.
• *Christine Haigh* of the *World Development Movement* said: "Financial speculation is fuelling food price spikes and Goldman Sachs is the No 1 culprit."

FOR

Makes complete sense as a *three birds with one stone* final stage - lowering the world population/growth rate; solving the food shortage crisis; resolving the third world 'problem'. § The inability to self-sustain/progress has meant that some third world nations forsake their right to a place in a better new world. Therefore, ethical considerations of such measures can be comfortably ignored.

AGAINST

Speculation occurs in every part of a free market economy, eventually. Pure paranoia to suggest an agenda, a higher one at that, is behind such policies. § Rising populations will inevitably lead to food shortages and as such, price trends reflect this. § Unethical and unspeakably immoral, that is beyond even the harshest ethics-free bankers. § There is no master plan or architects!

The FAO (UN Food and Agriculture Organisation) Food Price Index is a measure of the monthly change in international prices of a basket of food commodities. It consists of the average of five commodity group price indices (representing 55 quotations), weighted with the average export shares of each of the groups for 2002-2004.

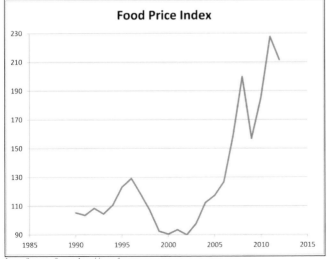

Food Price Index

Did You Know ?

Approximately a billion people around the globe suffer from malnutrition or starvation, made worse by poor weather.droughts and food price speculation. Meanwhile in other news, strict EU imposed quota restrictions have forced fisherman to throw away or discard almost a million fish every year. When suggested that the dead fish instead be provided for free to the poor around the world, an EU spokesperson stated "Don't be stupid".

(NB: Totally fabricated quote)

Image Source:- Source: http://www.fao.org

Have we all unwittingly accepted the prophesised 'Mark of the Beast', in the form of the smartphone (And should the duel between Google® Android and Apple® iOS concern every person on this planet)?

Background, Facts and Miscellaneous

Within the Bibles' Book of Revelations, lies a prophecy about the coming of an anti-Christ, whose followers will be deceived into accepting a *'mark of the beast'*. It is proclaimed that those bearing the mark will be betrayed by the ruling elite and will feel the wrath of the God almighty, therefore his goal is to win the worship and allegiance of every person on earth.

And he causeth all, both small and great, rich and poor free and bond, to receive a mark in their right hand, or in their foreheads: And that no man might buy or sell, save he that had the mark, or the name of the beast, or the number of his name: Here is wisdom. Let him that hath understanding count the number of the beast: for it is the number of a man; and his number is 666.

~ Revelation 13:16-18

Many speculations exist as to what the *mark* will constitute of, but technological advancements have been cited as a highly plausible method, with the technology already existing to create an implantable device that can be used as an identifier and a means to buy and sell.

With the advent of mobile technology over the last 20 years, have many of us already unwittingly accepted it - the mobile smartphone?
• The future world population will all own a smartphone and will hold these GPS-enabled (possibly carcinogenic) devices in the right hand,
• A cashless society with the use of the phone as the payment device will become inevitable,
• Every phone has a number, one which will be associated with that person their entire life.
• Users will follow either *Android* or *iOS*.

Further Background Information:-

Book of Revelations

And I saw as it were a sea of glass mingled with fire: and them that had gotten the victory over the beast, and over his image, and over his mark, and over the number of his name, stand on the sea of glass, having the harps of God.   Revelations 15:2

And the first went, and poured out his vial upon the earth; and there fell a noisome and grievous sore upon the men which had the mark of the beast, and upon them which worshipped his image.   Revelations 16:2

And the beast was taken, and with him the false prophet that wrought miracles before him, with which he deceived them that had received the mark of the beast, and them that worshipped his image. These both were cast alive into a lake of fire burning with brimstone. Revelations 19:20

The 'New World Order' conspiracy theory

There is the notorious conspiracy theory that a powerful group of individuals have been manipulating the course of global events for centuries as part of a plot to take control of the world and establish a *New World Order.*

This theory could well have arisen from the 'single global government' idea apparently foretold in the Bible's Book of Revelations, and some theorists such as *Pat Robertson* have pounced on this claiming that the formation of such a NWO is the work of Satan himself.

In Jan04, Pope John Paul II launched one of the most important diplomatic initiatives of his papacy when he called for a new international order. In his homily, the Pope said the new world order he wanted "would be able to provide solutions to the problems of today... based on the dignity of human beings, an integrated development of society, solidarity between rich and poor nations, and on the sharing of resources and the extraordinary results of scientific and technological progress."

Apple® and the Smartphone

The Cult of Apple :-

According to a BBC documentary series, neuroscientists ran a magnetic resonance imaging (MRI) test on Apple devotees and discovered that images of the technology company's brand stimulated the same parts of the brain as images of a deity do for religious people.

The Sea of Glass :-

The newly released Apple® smartphone, the IPhone 5, comprises of an aluminium and glass body to help the 'retina' screen achieve its impressive resolution. No doubt rival smartphone manufacturers will soon follow and embed this 'sea of glass' effect to their products too.

Adam and the apple :-

Of every tree of the garden you may freely eat; but of the tree of the knowledge of good and evil you shall not eat, for in the day that you eat of it you shall surely die.   Genesis 2:16,

The Number of the Beast

Vicarius Filii Dei

A well known conspiracy theory cites that the head of the Roman Catholic Church will one day actually be the Anti-Christ. This is further underpinned by the strange coincidence that the latin interpretation for the 'substitution for the son of god' (VICARIUS FILII DEI) having the rather dubious honour of the sum of the roman numeral letter substituions equalling the number of the beast, as shown below.

It doesn't quite help in quietening the conspiracy nuts out there when the very same words are (apparently) inscribed upon the mitre of his holiness, the Pope.

V	I	C	A	R	I	U	S		F	I	L	I	I		D	E	I		
5	1	100			1	5				1	50	1	1		500		1	=	**666**

The Maths

Now, if we take the main components of this 'mark of the beast' theory together with the ludicrous assumption that he who adorns the title of VICARIUS FILII DEI is the anti-christ, and apply some numerical substitutions for the alphabet, we arrive at a similarly surprising conclusion:-

H	O	L	Y		B	I	B	L	E								=	90
8	15	12	25		2	9	2	12	5									
M	A	R	K		O	F		T	H	E		B	E	A	S	T	=	144
13	1	18	11		15	6		20	8	5		2	5	1	19	20		
N	E	W		W	O	R	L	D		O	R	D	E	R			=	174
14	5	23		23	15	18	12	4		15	18	4	5	18				
V	I	C	A	R	I	U	S		F	I	L	I	I		D	E	I	=	165
22	9	3	1	18	9	21	19		6	9	12	9	9		4	5	9		
A	P	P	L	E		I	O	S									=	93
1	16	16	12	5		9	15	19										
																		666

Classroom Exercise

Just to appease the 'Apple' nuts out there, you may wish to apply a similar numerical exercise on either of the following statements;

Statement 1:
"Lucifer - Roman Catholic Church - New World Order - Google Android - Rapture"

Statement 2:
"When the Anti-Christ - NWO - Google Android occur, an Armageddon will commence."

Supplementary Figures

Breakdown of Tier/Bucket based Tax Calculation

NOTE: % Tax Applied per Bucket is as follows ; Tax Bucket Number x Incremental Tax Rate % x Multiplier Factor
Tax Bucket Number is each incremental salary range above the Tax Free Allowance

Taxable Income by Tier/Bucket		0	0	0	0	1	2	3	4	5	6	7	8	9	10	11	Check Salary Sum
		0%	0%	0%	0%	6%	13%	19%	26%	32%	39%	45%	52%	58%	65%	71%	
		4,745	6,001	7,001	8,001	10,001	12,001	15,001	20,001	30,001	50,001	70,001	100,001	200,001	500,001	1,000,001	
		6,000	7,000	8,000	10,000	12,000	15,000	20,000	30,000	50,000	70,000	100,000	200,000	500,000	1,000,000	3,000,000	
Salary Tier	A	5373	0	0	0	0	0	0	0	0	0	0	0	0	0	0	Correct
	B	6000	501	0	0	0	0	0	0	0	0	0	0	0	0	0	Correct
	C	6000	1000	501	0	0	0	0	0	0	0	0	0	0	0	0	Correct
	D	6000	1000	1000	1001	0	0	0	0	0	0	0	0	0	0	0	Correct
	E	6000	1000	1000	2000	1001	0	0	0	0	0	0	0	0	0	0	Correct
	F	6000	1000	1000	2000	2000	1501	0	0	0	0	0	0	0	0	0	Correct
	G	6000	1000	1000	2000	2000	3000	2501	0	0	0	0	0	0	0	0	Correct
	H	6000	1000	1000	2000	2000	3000	5000	5001	0	0	0	0	0	0	0	Correct
	I	6000	1000	1000	2000	2000	3000	5000	10000	10001	0	0	0	0	0	0	Correct
	J	6000	1000	1000	2000	2000	3000	5000	10000	20000	10001	0	0	0	0	0	Correct
	K	6000	1000	1000	2000	2000	3000	5000	10000	20000	20000	15001	0	0	0	0	Correct
	L	6000	1000	1000	2000	2000	3000	5000	10000	20000	20000	30000	50001	0	0	0	Correct
	M	6000	1000	1000	2000	2000	3000	5000	10000	20000	20000	30000	100000	150001	0	0	Correct
	N	6000	1000	1000	2000	2000	3000	5000	10000	20000	20000	30000	100000	300000	250001	0	Correct
	O	6000	1000	1000	2000	2000	3000	5000	10000	20000	20000	30000	100000	300000	500000	1000001	Correct

Total Tax Received by Tier/Bucket		0	0	0	0	1	2	3	4	5	6	7	8	9	10	11
		0%	0%	0%	0%	6%	13%	19%	26%	32%	39%	45%	52%	58%	65%	71%
Salary Tier	A	0	0	0	0	0	0	0	0	0	0	0	0	0	0	0
	B	0	0	0	0	0	0	0	0	0	0	0	0	0	0	0
	C	0	0	0	0	0	0	0	0	0	0	0	0	0	0	0
	D	0	0	0	0	0	0	0	0	0	0	0	0	0	0	0
	E	0	0	0	0	65	0	0	0	0	0	0	0	0	0	0
	F	0	0	0	0	130	195	0	0	0	0	0	0	0	0	0
	G	0	0	0	0	130	389	486	0	0	0	0	0	0	0	0
	H	0	0	0	0	130	389	973	1297	0	0	0	0	0	0	0
	I	0	0	0	0	130	389	973	2593	3242	0	0	0	0	0	0
	J	0	0	0	0	130	389	973	2593	6483	3890	0	0	0	0	0
	K	0	0	0	0	130	389	973	2593	6483	7780	6808	0	0	0	0
	L	0	0	0	0	130	389	973	2593	6483	7780	13615	25934	0	0	0
	M	0	0	0	0	130	389	973	2593	6483	7780	13615	51867	87526	0	0
	N	0	0	0	0	130	389	973	2593	6483	7780	13615	51867	175051	162085	0
	O	0	0	0	0	130	389	973	2593	6483	7780	13615	51867	175051	324169	713173

Summary Tax Income

Tax Income per Salary Tier	No of Taxpayers	Total Tax Income
-	1,440	-
-	1,160	-
-	1,590	-
-	2,950	-
65	2,760	179,031
324	3,650	1,183,455
1,005	4,950	4,974,860
2,788	6,000	16,727,917
7,326	4,090	29,964,934
14,458	859	12,419,549
25,156	410	10,313,866
57,897	300	17,369,073
171,356	89	15,250,704
420,967	16	6,735,467
1,296,224	6	7,777,344
	30,270	122,896,200

Fractional Reserve Banking: New Approach
Supplementary Tables for Worked Example

	Fractional Reserve Banking Model: Individual Account Movements over Time										MONEY SUPPLY
	Person A Amount	Person A % Worth	Person B Amount	Person B % Worth	Person C Amount	Person C % Worth	Loanee D Amount	Loanee D % Worth	Bank Acc Amount	Bank Acc % Worth	MONEY SUPPLY
Year 0	£10,000	10%	£20,000	20%	£30,000	30%	£40,000	40%	£0	0%	£100,000
Year 1	£10,000	10%	£20,000	20%	£30,000	30%	£32,000	32%	£8,000	8%	£100,000
Year 2	£10,000	10%	£20,000	20%	£30,000	30%	£24,000	24%	£16,000	16%	£100,000
Year 3	£10,000	10%	£20,000	20%	£30,000	30%	£16,000	16%	£24,000	24%	£100,000
Year 4	£10,000	10%	£20,000	20%	£30,000	30%	£8,000	8%	£32,000	32%	£100,000
Year 5	£10,000	10%	£20,000	20%	£30,000	30%	£0	0%	£40,000	40%	£100,000
Year 6	£10,000	10%	£20,000	20%	£30,000	30%	£0	0%	£40,000	40%	£100,000

	Proposed New Banking Model: Individual Account Movements Over Time										MONEY SUPPLY
	Person A Amount	Person A % Worth	Person B Amount	Person B % Worth	Person C Amount	Person C % Worth	Loanee D Amount	Loanee D % Worth	Bank Acc Amount	Bank Acc % Worth	MONEY SUPPLY
Year 0	£10,000	10%	£20,000	20%	£30,000	30%	£40,000	40%	£0	0%	£100,000
Year 1	£10,640	11%	£21,280	21%	£31,920	32%	£34,560	35%	£1,600	2%	£100,000
Year 2	£11,321	11%	£22,642	23%	£33,963	34%	£28,772	29%	£3,302	3%	£100,000
Year 3	£12,046	12%	£24,091	24%	£36,137	36%	£22,613	23%	£5,114	5%	£100,000
Year 4	£12,816	13%	£25,633	26%	£38,449	38%	£16,060	16%	£7,041	7%	£100,000
Year 5	£13,637	14%	£27,273	27%	£40,910	41%	£9,088	9%	£9,092	9%	£100,000
Year 6	£13,637	14%	£27,273	27%	£40,910	41%	£9,088	9%	£9,092	9%	£100,000

Projection Analysis for the repercussions of the Dowry System in India

DATA

Starting Indian Population   1000

Gender Birth Adjustment Factor	Population Depreciation Factor		Population by % Gender				Population by Sex		
		Year	Male	Female		Year	Total	Male	Female
1	1	2000	50%	50%		2000	1000	500	500
1	1	2010	50%	50%		2010	1000	500	500
1	1	2020	50%	50%		2020	1000	500	500
1.01	1.03	2030	51%	50%		2030	971	490	481
1.01	1.03	2040	51%	49%		2040	943	481	462
1.01	1.03	2050	52%	48%		2050	915	471	444
1.02	1.04	2060	53%	47%		2060	880	462	418
1.02	1.04	2070	54%	46%		2070	846	453	393
1.02	1.04	2080	55%	45%		2080	814	445	369
1.02	1.05	2090	56%	44%		2090	775	432	343
1.02	1.05	2100	57%	43%		2100	738	420	318
1.03	1.05	2110	59%	41%		2110	703	412	291
1.03	1.05	2120	60%	40%		2120	669	404	265
1.03	1.06	2130	62%	38%		2130	631	392	239
1.03	1.06	2140	64%	36%		2140	596	381	214
1.03	1.06	2150	66%	34%		2150	562	371	191
1.01	1.03	2160	67%	33%		2160	546	363	182
1.01	1.03	2170	67%	33%		2170	530	356	173
1.01	1.03	2180	68%	32%		2180	514	349	165
1.01	1.03	2190	69%	31%		2190	499	343	157
1.01	1.03	2200	69%	31%		2200	485	336	149
1.01	1.03	2210	70%	30%		2210	471	329	141
1.01	1.03	2220	71%	29%		2220	457	323	134
1.005	1.015	2230	71%	29%		2230	450	320	130
1.005	1.015	2240	71%	29%		2240	444	317	127
1.005	1.015	2250	72%	28%		2250	437	314	123
1.005	1.015	2260	72%	28%		2260	431	310	120
1.005	1.015	2270	72%	28%		2270	424	307	117
1.005	1.015	2280	73%	27%		2280	418	304	113
1.005	1.015	2290	73%	27%		2290	412	301	110
1.005	1.015	2300	74%	26%		2300	406	298	107

Public Schools: Projection Analysis Data

	Projection Analysis - Effect of Rising Proportions of Non-White Public School Graduates											
	Based on Assumption that 60% of Senior Positions are Privately Educated											
	Public School Educated Graduates		% School/Race Origin of Fastrack Trainee Programme			Summary Race Demographic of Fastrack Trainee Programme		Summary Race Demographic of Fastrack Trainee Programme (Lagged by 20 Years)		Summary Race Demographic of Senior Industry Positions		
Year	% White	% Indian	State School - White	Public School - White	Public School - Indian	White	Indian	White	Indian	White	Indian	% White
1970	100	0	40	60	0	100	0	100	0	1000	0	100%
1975	100	0	40	60	0	100	0	100	0	1000	0	100%
1980	100	0	40	60	0	100	0	100	0	1000	0	100%
1985	100	0	40	60	0	100	0	100	0	1000	0	100%
1990	100	0	40	60	0	100	0	100	0	1000	0	100%
1995	95	5	40	57	3	97	3	100	0	1000	0	100%
2000	90	10	40	54	6	94	6	100	0	1000	0	100%
2005	85	15	40	51	9	91	9	100	0	1000	0	100%
2010	80	20	40	48	12	88	12	100	0	1000	0	100%
2015	75	25	40	45	15	85	15	97	3	991	9	99%
2020	70	30	40	42	18	82	18	94	6	967	33	97%
2025	65	35	40	39	21	79	21	91	9	928	72	93%
2030	60	40	40	36	24	76	24	88	12	874	126	87%
2035	55	45	40	33	27	73	27	85	15	805	195	81%
2040	50	50	40	30	30	70	30	82	18	721	279	72%
2045	45	55	40	27	33	67	33	79	21	622	378	62%
2050	40	60	40	24	36	64	36	76	24	508	492	51%
2055	35	65	40	21	39	61	39	73	27	379	621	38%
2060	30	70	40	18	42	58	42	70	30	235	765	24%
2065	25	75	40	15	45	55	45	67	33	76	924	8%
2070	20	80	40	12	48	52	48	64	36	0	1000	0%

Child Abuse, Rehabilitation and the Legal System - Recent Examples

Chemical Castration

Chemical castration involves a man taking hormones that suppress the production of testosterone, leading to a decreased sex drive. The drug is already mandatory for child sex offenders in Poland, Russia and certain U.S. states.

It was reported in 2012, that around 100 paedophiles had been chemically castrated under a Government scheme to stop them reoffending. The sex offenders volunteered to take drugs designed to stifle their libido during a pilot experiment at HMP Whatton in Nottinghamshire. The drug reduces their testosterone levels to that of a prepubescent boy for a three-month period. The medication is intended for use on those with compulsive or impulsive urges to offend and those who have difficulties controlling sexual arousal, intrusive sexual fantasies or urges, sadism or other 'dangerous' tendencies such as necrophilia.

Parental Care

A husband and wife, Felicia and Cody Beemer, from Ohio, were accused of raping their own 13-month-old daughter during what was supposed to be a supervised visit at a children's service center, and recorded it on a cellphone - which also contained 532 images of child bestiality. Cody, 23, pleaded guilty on charges of rape, gross sexual imposition and four counts of pandering obscenity involving a minor. It had also emerged that he had previously raped his own 18-month-old nephew while they were babysitting him, which was also taped on the phone.

Sex, Drugs and Mack'rell

A child rapist, Darren Mackrell, attacked three young children in a 'truly abhorrent' way. He pleaded guilty to raping the children he had drugged and forced to sexually abuse each other while he watched in a six-hour ordeal. The two boys aged eight and ten years old, and a girl, nine, were lured to his flat were drugged with cannabis, amphetamine and Viagra before he abused them.

Depraved C**ts

A man and a woman, from Gravesend, Kent, were arrested after a one-month-old baby boy was raped and battered so badly that his heart stopped. The baby's horrific injuries were said to have included a sexual injury and internal wounds, a broken arm, a broken collarbone, punctured lungs and severe bruising, and reportedly, all of his ribs were also fractured.

To Breed

Robin Malka, a predatory paedophile, hatched a 'twisted and depraved' plan to father his own victims and feed his sexual obsession with children. He believed having sex with babies was 'natural and beautiful'!

Out of Touch

Two men, Roshane Channer and Ruben Monteiro, were each given a sentence of just forty months after they admitted raping an 11 year old schoolgirl. While the Judge David Farrell QC agreed their crimes were 'abhorrent', he agreed she may have been a 'willing participant' and looked 14 years old!

Papa don't Preach

A prominent Saudi Arabian preacher who raped his 5-year-old daughter before torturing her to death has been spared a death sentence or even a lengthy prison term after agreeing to pay "blood money" to the slain girl's mother. Fayhan al-Ghamdi, a former drug addict, was charged with brutally raping and torturing 5-year-old Lama al-Ghamdi to death. According to a medical report, the little girl had been tortured with whips, electric shocks and an iron and had broken arms, a broken back and a fractured skull. According to social worker Randa al-Kaleeb, the young girl had been raped "everywhere." Hospital staff told the girl's mother that her "daughter's rectum had been torn open and the abuser had attempted to burn it closed."

Poetic Justice served by a True Hero

On his eighth birthday, Robbie Middleton, was tied to a tree, doused in petrol and set on fire. It left him with third-degree burns to 99 per cent of his body and no-one expected him to survive. But in a story of staggering courage, Robbie lived and would endure 200 operations and endless therapy to repair the burns. Tragically, he was to die just weeks short of his 21st birthday from a cancer which doctors blamed on the original injuries. In a harrowing 17-minute video made just before he died, he named the man he believed had torched him in Texas, back in 1998. And he also claimed that he had been raped by the same person, a 13-year-old neighbour called Don Collins, two weeks before being set alight. The terrible act was, Robbie alleged, a way of ensuring his silence. His accusations have since opened the way for Collins to be charged with murder.

Appendix and References

Though all the reference sources have been tracked for each topic, special thanks go to the following online resources and books for providing initial topic pointers or trusted cross-referencing mediums:-

dailymail.com	For information, not opinions
cracked.com	First port of call for anything
wikipedia.org	Invaluable but needs triple cross-referencing
howstuffworks.com	Premium educational research site
about.com	Providing information on almost anything
imdb.com	Movie and Actor information

Aside from these sources of research, education and opinion, specific information sources used for each topic and any further supplementary information or research pointers are listed below, in topic order.

Question Topic:A1:-
References:
"religion." Encyclopædia Britannica. Standard Edition. Chicago: Encyclopædia Britannica, 2012
www.sikhphilosophy.net/spiritual-articles/685-14-good-reasons-why-society-needs.html

Further Information and Scribble Notes:
en.wikipedia.org/wiki/Thuggee
www.rustylime.com/show_article.php?id=2392
The Goa Inquisition by Christian Historian Dr. T. R. de Souza
www.vgweb.org/unethicalconversion/GoaInquisition.htm

Question Topic:A3:-
References:
www.aboutanimaltesting.co.uk/animal-testing-cosmetics.html
www.ehow.com/info_8487412_pros-cons-animal-testing.html
www.ehow.com/info_8077283_arguments-against-animal-testing-cosmetics.html
www.howtodothings.com/fashion-and-personal-care/a3435-how-to-make-perfume.html
www.guardian.co.uk/world/2010/dec/31/animal-testing-cosmetics-industry-europe
www.aboutanimaltesting.co.uk/quick-statistics-on-animal-testing.html
www.independent.co.uk/news/science/animal-testing--the-facts-and-the-figures-6262642.html

Further Information and Scribble Notes:
www.peta.org/features/top-five-shocking-animal-experimentation-facts.aspx

Question Topic:A4:-
References:
listverse.com/2009/09/05/10-bizarre-cases-of-identity-theft/

Further Information and Scribble Notes:
Dishonourabe Mentions:- W-9095, W-8BEN, W-8888 forms;

Question Topic:A5:-
References:
www.esquire.com/features/answer-fella/chicken-or-egg-solved-0611#ixzz1pn6UlYlj
en.wikipedia.org/wiki/Chicken_or_the_egg

Further Information and Scribble Notes:
The Correct Answer (Apparently) ;
In 2006, a team made up of a geneticist, a philosopher and a chicken farmer found the correct answer: The egg came before the chicken. The reason for this is simple – the genetic material of a living being does not change during an animal's lifetime. This means that an animal can't simply mutate into another animal but it has to give birth (or lay an egg) for a genetic mutation to occur. The egg was probably laid by a bird similar to a hen but not actually a hen.
Professor John Bookfield, an evolutionary geneticist from University of Nottingham agreed: "The living organism inside the eggshell would have had the same DNA as the chicken it would develop into, not the DNA of his parents."
The British organization of chicken farmers – Great British Chicken - also agrees: "Eggs were around long before the first chicken arrived. Of course, they may not have been chicken eggs as we see them today, but they were eggs."
articles.cnn.com/2006-05-26/tech/chicken.egg_1_chicken-eggs-first-egg-first-chicken?_s=PM:TECH

Question Topic:A7:-
References:
pandyablog.dailymail.co.uk/2011/10/international-aid-simply-props-up-third-world-corruption.html
www.worldinterestingfacts.com/human/the-most-corrupted-political-leader-in-the-world.html

Further Information and Scribble Notes:
www.dailymail.co.uk/news/article-2107280/Nigerian-state-governor-funded-international-playboy-lifestyle-50million-fraud-rose-humble-roots-working-London-DIY-store.html
www.bbc.co.uk/news/world-asia-india-17471359
www.bbc.co.uk/news/world-south-asia-12769214
www.bloomberg.com/news/2012-08-28/poor-in-india-starve-as-politicians-steal-14-5-billion-of-food.html

Question Topic:A8:-
References:
www.guardian.co.uk/commentisfree/2010/jun/08/cuts-armed-services-fantasy-enemies
www.guardian.co.uk/world/2003/may/09/nuclear.northkorea

Further Information and Scribble Notes:
Future Reform case: If the US spends 500Bn on the military in total for the period 2000-2005, then 100Bn must be paid to the UN in 2006.
Wildcard: Like any government budget, to keep them maintained and rolling over, it must be seen to be spent. Even when it can't be allocated, it will either be spent on needless equipment, intitiatives or corruptive practices and schemes.
www.guardian.co.uk/commentisfree/2010/jun/08/cuts-armed-services-fantasy-enemies

www.sipri.org/databases/milex
www.economist.com/blogs/dailychart/2011/06/military-spending
www.cepr.net/documents/publications/military_spending_2007_05.pdf
www.dailymail.co.uk/home/moslive/article-2152676/HMS-Queen-Elizabeth-Its-taller-Nelsons-Column-generates-energy-power-5-500-homes--does-Britain-really-need-super-sized-3-5bn-aircraft-carrier.html

Question Topic:A9:-
References:
www.independent.co.uk/news/uk/crime/lawyers-defend-crossexamination-of-dowler-family-2302969.html

Further Information and Scribble Notes:
Extract from the website of Lindeman & Alvarado;
lindemanalvarado.com/Criminal-Defense-Overview/Child-Sexual-Assault-Internet-Solicitiation-of-a-Minor.shtml
CHILD SEXUAL ASSAULT & INTERNET SOLICITATION OF A MINOR
At the law firm of Lindeman & Alvardo, our team of experienced criminal defence attorneys represent clients charged with a full range of sex crimes in which children were the alleged victims, including: Child sexual assault, Child sexual abuse or molestation, Indecency with a child, Possession of child pornography (kiddie porn) and Internet stalking or sexual solicitation of a minor
www.dailymail.co.uk/news/article-2152736/Family-man-died-threesome-awarded-3million--doctors-didnt-warn-extreme-physical-activity.html
www.dailymail.co.uk/news/article-2223422/Speeding-driver-Shehzad-Munir-killed-father-hit-speeds-155mph-showing-attempt-win-girlfriend.html

Question Topic:A10:-
References:
history.howstuffworks.com/african-history/african-diamond-trade2.htm
ngm.nationalgeographic.com/ngm/data/2002/03/01/html/ft_20020301.1.html

Further Information and Scribble Notes:
diamondfacts.org/
en.wikipedia.org/wiki/Cubic_zirconia
www.dailymail.co.uk/news/article-2135369/Charles-Taylor-trial-Found-guilty-arming-Sierra-Leone-rebels-exchange-blood-diamonds.html

Question Topic:A11:-
References:
"diplomatic immunity." Encyclopædia Britannica. Standard Edition. Chicago: Encyclopædia Britannica, 2012.
www.answers.com/topic/diplomatic-immunity
www.dailymail.co.uk/news/article-2086573/Dozens-diplomats-pocketing-thousands-pounds-hardship-payments-working-far-flung-holiday-hotspots.html
www.independent.co.uk/news/uk/crime/murder-rape-assault-the-secret-crimes-of-londons-diplomats-408170.html

Further Information and Scribble Notes:
www.avert.org/age-of-consent.htm

Question Topic:A12:-
References:

en.wikipedia.org/wiki/Taxation_in_the_United_Kingdom
elitechoice.org/2011/03/14/worlds-most-expensive-offerings-from-luxury-brands/
www.marketoracle.co.uk/Article18924.html

Further Information and Scribble Notes:
www.fastcompany.com/1594734/design-crimes-the-worlds-most-expensive-bottled-water
www.audioholics.com/reviews/transports/high-definition-dvd-players-hd-dvd-blu-ray/lexicon-bd-30-blu-ray-oppo-clone/oppo-inside-lexicon-outside-1
Amazon.com customer reviews on the Denon AKDL1 dedicated link cable from DVD to AV Receiver (www.amazon.com/Denon-AKDL1-Dedicated-Link-Cable/dp/B000I1X6PM/) include ;
Matthew Sidor 'seadour' states "Transmission of music data at rates faster than the speed of light seemed convenient, until I realized I was hearing the music before I actually wanted to play it, or before I even realized I was in the mood for them"
Lord Sandwich states "This amazing product significantly improved my transfer speeds, so much so that my packets now arrive at their destination before they're sent. In fact, I haven't even typed this review yet."

Question Topic:A13:-
References:
truth11.com/2009/12/01/nazi-connections-to-flouride-in-americas-drinking-water/
onespeedbikerpolitico.blogspot.nl/2010/05/debunking-fluoride-use-by-nazis.html
books.nap.edu/catalog.php?record_id=11571#description
www.ncbi.nlm.nih.gov/pmc/articles/PMC1449416/#r3
www.dentalhealth.org/tell-me-about/topic/sundry/fluoride/
www.sonic.net/kryptox/politics/lead20s.htm
www.insidetime.org/articleview.asp?a=626&c=dental_treatment_in_prison
Mixson J, Eplee H, Feil P, Jones J, Rico M. Oral health status of a federal prison population. J Public Health Dent. 1990;50:257–261 www.ncbi.nlm.nih.gov/pubmed/2391675
Salive ME, Carolla JM, Brewer TF. Dental health of male inmates in a state prison system. J Public Health Dent. 1989;49:83–86   www.ncbi.nlm.nih.gov/pubmed/2785210

Further Information and Scribble Notes:
www.greaterthings.com/Lexicon/F/Fluoride.htm
cclitgirl.hubpages.com/hub/Should-You-Buy-Fluoride-Toothpaste
- Scientific conclusions currently have a stance that fluoride toothpaste and correctly fluoridated water, are of great benefit to dental health, helping to reduce tooth decay, and causes no harmful side effects to general health.
- In 2006, a U.S. National Research Council committee reviewed health risks associated with fluoride in the water, unanimously concluding that the maximum contaminant level of 4 mg/L should be lowered.

Question Topic:A14:-
References:
www.digitaltrends.com/opinion/whats-the-next-big-thing-in-entertainment-after-3d/
en.wikipedia.org/wiki/3D_film

Further Information and Scribble Notes:
With this overhaul of all the equipment, is this the AV industry's last hurrah to fleece consumers?

Question Topic:A15:-
References:
Article from the The Daily Telegraph, "Death toll from hospital bugs hits new high" by Laura Donnelly 15Aug09
www.telegraph.co.uk/health/healthnews/6034988/Death-toll-from-hospital-bugs-hits-new-high.html
news.bbc.co.uk/2/hi/health/1035679.stm

Further Information and Scribble Notes:
www.patient.co.uk/health/MRSA.htm
www.dailymail.co.uk/health/article-2311636/Pair-newborn-babies-died-killer-bug-new-400m-University-Hospital-North-Staffordshire-hospital-people-neonatal-ward-failed-wash-hands.html

Question Topic:A16:-
References:
Article on Judge Wapner vs. Judge Judy:
www.metnews.com/articles/reminiscing091103.htm
www.squidoo.com/judge-judy-tv-show

Further Information and Scribble Notes:
www.americanbar.org/content/dam/aba/migrated/dispute/essay/syndicourtjustice.authcheckdam.pdf
She's not even a real judge, yet is operating in a legal capacity; Public ridicule could be waiting for litigants; Bringing down the already maligned legal profession;

Question Topic:A17:-
References:
www.businessweek.com/technology/content/oct2010/tc20101021_425496.htm
www.telegraph.co.uk/news/worldnews/middleeast/iran/9298488/Flame-virus-most-powerful-espionage-tool-ever-UN-warns.html
en.wikipedia.org/wiki/Year_2000_problem
www.securelist.com/en/analysis/174405517/The_contemporary_antivirus_industry_and_its_problems?
www.pcworld.com/article/130455/is_desktop_antivirus_dead.html

Further Information and Scribble Notes:
2038bug.com/
www.securitynewsdaily.com/1166-ten-scariest-computer-viruses.html
www.hendersonpress.com/local-news/item/710-todays-computer-viruses-threats-going-ballistic

Question Topic:A18:-
References:
www.weenc.com/support-files/livingyouroptimallife.pdf
Honourable Mentions: Dominique Strauss-Kahn; Silvio Berlusconi; George Best;

Question Topic:A19:-
Further Information and Scribble Notes:

www.guardian.co.uk/law/2012/jul/07/longer-prison-sentences-cut-crime
www.dailymail.co.uk/news/article-2155353/The-harrowing-footage-Ive-seen-Judge-slams-thug-punched-sex-assault-victim-30-times-20-minutes-attack-caught-CCTV.html
'Taking the bible oath in court. As a significant number of people don't believe in the bible/religion an alternative law is put forward that anyone found guilty of lying in court will have to forfeit 33% of their assets at the time of the original offence.
- Encourages criminals to employ sinister scare tactics instead.
- Jury has faith that correct facts are in their domain.

Question Topic:A20:-
References:
www.uknetguide.co.uk/Homes_and_Gardens/Article/Foreign_property_ownership_in_London-106351.html
www.guardian.co.uk/business/2011/aug/30/home-ownership-fall-mid-80s-levels

Question Topic:A21:-
References:
www.dailymail.co.uk/news/article-482122/Migrants-sending-1m-child-benefits-home-Eastern-Europe-EVERY-month.html
www.dailymail.co.uk/news/article-1374920/Afghan-asylum-seeker-lived-1-2million-house-escapes-jail-despite-admitting-30-000-benefit-fraud.html
www.dailymail.co.uk/news/article-1293730/Somali-asylum-seeker-family-given-2m-house--complaining-5-bed-London-home-poor-area.html
www.dailymail.co.uk/news/article-1288801/BUDGET-2010-Tax-credit-cuts-freezing-child-benefit-hit-ordinary-families.html

Further Information and Scribble Notes:
www.dailymail.co.uk/news/article-2297796/The-single-mother-benefits-2-5million-Belgravia-mansion-wants-pay--And-mystery-VERY-elusive-fashion-boss-husband.html

Question Topic:A22:-
References:
christianity.about.com/od/denominations/p/christiantoday.htm
www.religioustolerance.org/chr_deno.htm
www.adherents.com/misc/WCE.html
christianity.about.com/od/denominations/p/christiantoday.htm

Further Information and Scribble Notes:
panthic.org/articles/5348
www.guardian.co.uk/world/feedarticle/9892642
articles.philly.com/2012-01-18/news/30639498_1_mosque-rival-factions-board-members
www.dailymail.co.uk/news/article-2150076/Vatican-leaks-scandal-Pope-Benedicts-butler-Paolo-Gabriele-arrested-leaked-documents.html

Question Topic:A23:-
References:
www.comicvine.com/superman/4005-1807/

Further Information and Scribble Notes:
www.comicbookmovie.com/superman_movies/news/?a=46795

Question Topic:A24:-
References:
www.dailymail.co.uk/health/article-2149557/Found-The-breakthrough-discovery-gene-key-production-sperm-male-Pill.html

Dialogue Transcript of Typical Household:
Tracey: "Well, you know what they say 'Once you go black...' "
Sharon: "...you don't go back"
Cue cackling...
Michael: "Bitch, when you go black, we don't fu*king want you back"

Question Topic:A25:-
References:
zenplease.com/the-importance-of-distressing-and-relaxation/
www.grandmascraftguides.com/Family_Corner/
www.guardian.co.uk/money/2011/apr/16/four-day-working-week
A report from the Chartered Institute of Personnel and Development;
www.dailymail.co.uk/health/article-2045309/Stress-Top-cause-workplace-sickness-dubbed-Black-Death-21st-century.html

Further Information and Scribble Notes:
Today, its become evident that the family unit is not being considered as important by the people as it used to be and this has become a huge social problem. The family life adds a sense of responsibility in your personality which lacks in those people who have not had a very nice family life.
neweconomics.org/press-releases/shorter-working-week-soon-inevitable-forecasts-think-tank130210
www.dailymail.co.uk/news/article-2122509/Half-unhappy-failing-balance-work-family-life.html
www.dailymail.co.uk/news/article-2299486/Your-working-life-laid-bare-Six-jobs-12-pay-rises-125-days-sick--office-romance.html

Question Topic:B1:-
Further Information and Scribble Notes:
Its perceived that the main beneficiaries of this reform would be young persons with little parental guidance or support. Being shown an active interest in their future careers by alternative role-models, encouraging them to become somebody if the right dedication and direction is given to it.

Question Topic:B2:-
References:
www.thedailybeast.com/articles/2010/09/19/childless-by-choice-why-some-women-dont-want-kids.html
www.westminster.edu/staff/kpark/park/syllabi.html

Further Information and Scribble Notes:
www.dailymail.co.uk/news/article-2145687/Number-babies-born-ethnic-minorities-surpasses-whites-U-S-time.html
www.bbc.co.uk/news/magazine-10786279

Question Topic:B3:-
References:
www.defra.gov.uk/wildlife-pets/pets/dangerous/

www.ukandspain.com/dangerous-dogs/
www.dailymail.co.uk/news/article-2064664/How-cats-snatched-streets-gangs-deadly-dogs-tear-pieces--sport.html

Further Information and Scribble Notes:
www.direct.gov.uk/en/HomeAndCommunity/InYourHome/AnimalsAnd-Pets/Dogs/DG_180098

Question Topic:B4:-
References:
worldofweirdthings.com/2009/11/17/what-your-doctor-doesnt-want-you-to-know/

Further Information and Scribble Notes:
"Why Animals Don't Get Heart Attacks, But People Do!" by Dr Matthias Rath
www.articlesbase.com/non-fiction-articles/diabetes-management-the-drug-company-conspiracy-127362.html
www.mnwelldir.org/docs/editorial/pharm.htm
www.bbc.co.uk/news/magazine-16165605

Question Topic:B5:-
References:
www.direct.gov.uk/en/Pensionsandretirementplanning/StatePension/index.htm
www.moneysavingexpert.com/savings/state-pensions

Further Information and Scribble Notes:
The report highlighted that the £70,000 profit (from the rise in the value of the FTSE 100) a saver made in contributions between 1994 and 2009, £46,000 in was taken by the financial services industry in charges.
www.dailymail.co.uk/news/article-2075735/High-hidden-charges-City-fees-leaving-pensioners-savers-worse-off.html

Question Topic:B6:-
References:
law2.umkc.edu/faculty/projects/ftrials/conlaw/beararms.htm
www.opposingviews.com/i/arguments-against-gun-control
www.guardian.co.uk/news/datablog/2011/jan/10/gun-crime-us-state
www.nraila.org/news-issues/fact-sheets/2012/nra-ila-firearms-fact-card-2012.aspx
www.telegraph.co.uk/news/worldnews/northamerica/usa/8134804/Buy-a-truck-get-a-free-AK-47-used-car-dealership-launches-unusual-promotion.html
www.justfacts.com/guncontrol.asp;
Book: Firearms and Violence: A Critical Review. By the Committee to Improve Research and Data on Firearms and the Committee on Law and Justice, National Research Council of the National Academies. Edited by Charles F. Wellford, John V. Pepper, and Carol V. Petrie. National Academies Press, 2005. Pages 56-57

Further Information and Scribble Notes:
www.nraila.org/news-issues/fact-sheets/2012/right-to-carry-2012.aspx
www.dailymail.co.uk/news/article-2131352/Verna-Deann-McClain-Nurse-shot-Kayla-Marie-Golden-ripped-baby-son-arms.html
A country without an army - how long before an unanswered invasion?

Question Topic:B7:-
References:
www.dailymail.co.uk/debate/article-2124941/UK-house-prices-Market-heading-crash.html
www.lloydsbankinggroup.com/media1/economic_insight/halifax_house_price_index_page.asp

Question Topic:B8:-
Nod to: BBC's Bellamy's People at the Hartwell Street Mosque

Further Information and Scribble Notes:
www.englishbaby.com/forum/LifeTalk/thread/196712

Question Topic:B9:-
References:
www.dailymail.co.uk/news/article-1339142/Asylum-seeker-Aso-Mohammed-Ibrahim-let-girl-12-die-stay-UK.html
www.guardian.co.uk/law/libertycentral/2010/dec/28/human-rights-act-aso-mohammed-ibrahim
www.guardian.co.uk/society/2001/jan/07/socialcare

Further Information and Scribble Notes:
A Brilliant for/against discussion in the UK Independent Paper;
www.independent.co.uk/news/uk/crime/the-big-question-are-prison-sentences-too-lenient-and-does-the-system-need-changing-1706866.html
news.bbc.co.uk/1/hi/uk/1169457.stm
www.thestar.co.uk/news/local/torched-teenager-south-yorks-killer-s-lenient-sentence-challenged-1-5600065
www.cps.gov.uk/news/fact_sheets/unduly_lenient_sentences/

Question Topic:B10:-
References:
vaccines.procon.org/
vaccines.procon.org/sourcefiles/vaccineinjurytable.pdf
www.dailymail.co.uk/health/article-2121781/Could-swine-flu-vaccine-cause-narcolepsy-Scientists-probe-link-drug-increase-cases.html
www.netdoctor.co.uk/health_advice/facts/childhoodvaccinations.htm
www.vaccinesuncensored.org/autism.php
www.buenosairesherald.com/article/88922/gsk-lab-fined-$1m-over-tests-that-killed-14--babies
news.sky.com/home/world-news/article/16142354

Further Information and Scribble Notes:
- Vaccines can be either prophylactic (to prevent or improve the effects of a future infection by any natural or wild pathogen) or therapeutic (eg. vaccines to fight cancer).
- It's claimed that the WHO admitted that vaccine manufacturers routinely release potential flu pandemics into the population, by the covert use of vaccinating patients with vaccine containing flu viruses that have never attacked man or have not done so for decades.
- GlaxoSmithKline (GSK) was fined following the death of 14 babies during illegal laboratory vaccine trials conducted in Argentina between 2007 and 2008. The charges included experimenting with human beings as well as falsifying parental authorizations so babies could participate in vaccine-trials.
"Any deaths in the study have been thoroughly and independently investigated, and it has been concluded that none of the deaths were related

to the vaccine they were given," a GSK said in a statement.
"ANMAT has also concluded that there was no causality between the administration of the vaccine and the deaths that have occurred in the study."
Future Reform:
Vaccines are fully tested over the long term before it can be granted a license to distribute.   Heavy fines to offset all profits from a particular vaccine which produces the same adverse effect in >30% of patients, in order to deter Pharm companies to put profits before patient care.

'www.dailymail.co.uk/health/article-2127238/Universal-vaccine-tackle-90-cent-cancers-tested-humans-time.html
www.vaccineriskawareness.com/Swine-Flu-Epidemic-H1N1-Vaccine-Deaths-and-Injuries
www.thedailytell.com/2010/05/gates-foundation-donates-7-8-million-to-research-global-initiatives/
www.dailymail.co.uk/health/article-2073137/Boy-slept-19-HOURS-day-reaction-flu-jab.html
Anfrew Wakefield against the drug vaccine companies: www.thedaily-bell.com/1089/Dr-Andrew-Wakefield-on-the-AutismVaccine-Controversy-and-His-Ongoing-Professional-Persecution.html

Question Topic:B11:-
References:
www.newsmonster.co.uk/paranormal-unexplained/mediums-really-do-talk-to-the-dead-claim-top-scientists.html
www.afterlife101.com/HESL.html
www.articlesbase.com/metaphysics-articles/clairvoyance-and-medium-ship-absolute-bullshit-the-future-is-not-ours-to-see-3625034.html

Further Information and Scribble Notes:
What if Gary Schwartz is right? by Robert Todd Carroll
www.skepdic.com/essays/schwartz.html
How Psychic Scams Work: Don't Get Conned! By Christoph Reilly
christophreilly.hubpages.com/hub/How-psychic-scams-work
The Stargate Project.

Question Topic:B12:-
References:
www.bbc.co.uk/ethics/honourcrimes/crimesofhonour_1.shtml
www.guardian.co.uk/politics/2010/sep/01/tony-blair-diana-relationship-fayed
www.dailymail.co.uk/news/article-495189/Embalming-Diana-illegal-needed-Paris-heat.html
www.historylearningsite.co.uk/royal_prerogative.htm
www.dailymail.co.uk/news/article-146022/Diana-wanted-wed-doctor.html

Question Topic:B13:-
References:
www.bbc.co.uk/news/magazine-15196517
www.telegraph.co.uk/news/uknews/2072030/Cushy-prisons-see-doz-ens-trying-to-break-in.html
www.dailymail.co.uk/news/article-2002870/British-prisons-Make-inmates-work-contribute-wages-crime-victims.html

Further Information and Scribble Notes:
¬ In Jun08, the then Justice Secretary disclosed that 37,000 inmates

eligible to be released early declined to apply for the perk between 1999 and 2006. Even more surprisingly, between 2003 and 2008, 42 individuals were detected attempting to break INTO prisons.
¬ For minor crimes, one must be a persistent offender in order to receive a custodial sentence.
¬ Prisoners perks have included free telephones, TV and entertainment consoles in their own cells, cable/satellite television in most areas for recreational use, cash bonuses for good behaviour and conjugal visits.
¬ Victims or their immediate relatives are permitted at any time to participate in the 'rehabilitation' ritual themselves (where video cameras ARE allowed).
Dishonourable Mentions:- Rapin Osathanondh; Amos Moobeng and PlayStations; The Preddie's;

Question Topic:B14:-
References:
www.bbc.co.uk/news/business-17365137
www.ons.gov.uk/ons/rel/cpi/cpi-rpi-basket/2012/index.html
www.economicshelp.org/blog/54/inflation/how-is-inflation-calculated/

Further Information and Scribble Notes:
news.goldseek.com/JohnBrowne/1256796480.php
www.dailymail.co.uk/news/article-2137103/One-households-squeezed-travel-costs-soaring-prices-mean-families-spend-10-income-transport.html

Question Topic:B15:-
References:
www.christiancourier.com/articles/133-the-big-bang-theory-vs-gods-word
big-bang-theory.com/
biblicalworldviewacademy.org/1247/major-problems-with-the-new-world-translation/

Further Information and Scribble Notes:
www.religionfacts.com/big_religion_chart.htm
www.bbc.co.uk/religion/religions/judaism/history/abraham_1.shtml

Classroom Exercise:
- W, son of god, had special powers and did good in the world.
- Fearing X, the king ordered all first born sons to be killed.
- Y was born on the 25 Dec.
- Z had a friend called Mary Magdalene.
Fill in the missing variables of W,X,Y,Z with the following values;
Jesus; Moses; Hercules; Mithra;

Question Topic:B16:-
References:
www.dailymail.co.uk/news/article-2130461/Austerity-whats-Spanish-King-Juan-Carlos-slammed-27-000-elephant-hunting-trip-countrys-economy-teeters-brink.html
www.dailymail.co.uk/news/article-2212319/Prince-Charles-earns-1m-estates-people-dying-just-years-thanks-medieval-law.html
www.dailymail.co.uk/news/article-2154152/Saudi-Royal-Princess-Maha-Al-Sudairi-does-5m-runner-Paris-hotel.html
www.freemalaysiatoday.com/category/opinion/2012/06/08/royal-flap-over-unwise-spending/

Further Information and Scribble Notes:
As the Duke of Cornwall, Charles has several little known rights and powers, including the right to veto Westminster legislation. One of these is Bona Vacantia - from the Latin meaning vacant land - the right to claim the estates of people who die without heirs in the county.
The Duke of York recently secured a 75-year lease on a Crown Estate property, the 30-room Royal Lodge in Windsor Great Park, for just £1m according to reports. Under the terms of the lease he can pass the property to his daughters to live in rent-free until the lease expires.
www.dailymail.co.uk/news/article-2150894/Corruption-probes-launched-Duke-Yorks-15m-home-deal.html
www.telegraph.co.uk/news/uknews/theroyalfamily/5750689/Royal-family-members-offered-cut-price-deals-on-properties.html
news.uk.msn.com/the-big-question/the-big-question-should-the-monarchy-be-privatised.
www.dailymail.co.uk/news/article-2218614/Prince-Charles-letters-Labour-ministers-stay-private-preparations-King.html
www.thecrownestate.co.uk/estates-map/

Question Topic:B18:-
References:
"artificial intelligence ((AI)) ." Encyclopædia Britannica. Standard Edition. Chicago: Encyclopædia Britannica, 2012.
en.wikipedia.org/wiki/Skynet_(Terminator)

Further Information and Scribble Notes:
www.dailymail.co.uk/sciencetech/article-2239077/Would-plane-pilot-Tests-begin-generation-civilian-aircraft-controlled-REMOTE.html
In the Outer Limits TV eposode 'The Tipping Point', A programmer who claimed someone was out to get him mysteriously vanishes after trying to download some software from the company's mainframe. His replacement finds out there is a secret project, called Prometheus, to create a universal language that will allow any computer to instantaneously talk to any other computer. If instantaneous communication between millions of computers can be achieved the computers may act as neutrons within the brain in which non-thinking computers merge into a thinking intelligence - the tipping point. When this happens someone will be able to rule the world by using computers.

Question Topic:B19:-
References:
www.independent.co.uk/news/science/fertility-landmark-as-scientists-make-sperm-from-stem-cells-2332157.html

Further Information and Scribble Notes:
www.guardian.co.uk/lifeandstyle/2009/jul/09/women-men-better-off-without
www.everseradio.com/bethany-brings-us-top-five-all-female-utopias-dystopias/
www.bbc.co.uk/news/health-15181015
www.dailymail.co.uk/sciencetech/article-2129200/Could-cure-AIDS-horizon-Genetically-engineered-human-stem-cells-hunt-kill-HIV-inside-body.html

Question Topic:B20:-
References:
alexandrakinias.wordpress.com/2010/10/29/a-tribute-to-aisha-ibrahim-

dhuhulow-1995-2008/
www.amnesty.org/en/for-media/press-releases/iran-death-stoning-grotesque-and-unacceptable-penalty-20080115
news.bbc.co.uk/1/hi/7708169.stm
news.uk.msn.com/world/articles.aspx?cp-documentid=154079952

Further Information and Scribble Notes:
Since it's slower than other forms of execution it is considered a form of execution by torture.
2004 case of sister stoned for being raped but brother let off free.

Question Topic:B21:-
References:
www.cia.gov/library/publications/the-world-factbook/geos/af.html

Further Information and Scribble Notes:
- Repatriation. eg. the destruction is apportioned to be 70% USA and 30% Russia therefore these countries will take in the respective proportion of refugees.
- Allow the Taliban and the drug warlords to fight over the rock and rubble Afhganistan has now been turned to.

Question Topic:B22:-
References:
areuonsomething.com/features_hip-hop.html
www.uncoached.com/2008/09/24/the-10-most-successful-and-some-pathetically-comical-white-rappers-of-all-time/

Further Information and Scribble Notes:
www.mtv.com/bands/h/hip_hop_week/2006/emcees/
www.listology.com/list/mtvs-22-greatest-voices-music
www.rollingstone.com/music/lists/100-greatest-artists-of-all-time-19691231
Honourable Mentions:- Everyday Normal Guy;

Question Topic:B23:-
References:
www.usatoday.com/tech/products/2009-12-23-virtual-retail-sales-avatar_N.htm
www.popsci.com/science/article/2010-11/real-sale-virtual-property-nets-half-million-dollars

Further Information and Scribble Notes:
en.wikipedia.org/wiki/Virtual_good
news.bbc.co.uk/2/hi/technology/7575902.stm
techcrunch.com/2007/06/20/virtual-goods-the-next-big-business-model/
www.dailymail.co.uk/news/article-2258877/Chinese-father-hires-virtual-hitman-kill-son-online-games--job.html

Question Topic:B24:-
References:
science.howstuffworks.com/environmental/earth/geophysics/h2o.htm
science.nasa.gov/earth-science/oceanography/ocean-earth-system/ocean-water-cycle/
Booklet: "Was Life Created" by the Watch Tower Bible and Tract Society of Britain. 2010

Question Topic:B25:-

Further Information and Scribble Notes:

- Inconsiderate drivers who consider themselves above decent etiquette,
- How much have your life have you given up to be stuck in traffic jams ?
See also: GQ article by XXXX, "".

Question Topic:C1:-

References:

www.msnbc.msn.com/id/38434537/ns/technology_and_science-space/t/
asteroid-could-threaten-earth/
www.dailymail.co.uk/sciencetech/article-1298285/Massive-asteroid-hit-
Earth-2182-warn-scientists.html
www.dailymail.co.uk/sciencetech/article-1301493/Scientists-plan-Nasa-
mission-land-asteroid-possible-collision-course-Earth.html

Question Topic:C2:-

References:

www.dailymail.co.uk/news/article-474974/The-real-price-2-chicken.html
www.dailymail.co.uk/news/article-2131927/Our-shrinking-foods-How-
manufacturers-making-everyday-products-smaller-keeping-prices-same.
html
www.peta.org/issues/animals-used-for-food/chickens.aspx

Question Topic:C4:-

References:

au.ibtimes.com/articles/337787/20120507/cashless-society-promotes-
tyranny-ibtimesau-ibtimes-com.htm
www.vanguardngr.com/2012/05/cashless-society-why-ceos-should-pay-
more-attention-to-information-security/
www.bloomberg.com/news/2012-03-29/visions-of-a-cashless-society-
echoes.html
www.dailymail.co.uk/sciencetech/article-2131858/How-mobile-phone-
turned-credit-card--mean-end-small-cash-payments-5-years.html

Further Information and Scribble Notes:

www.dailymail.co.uk/news/article-2137106/Your-card-details-stolen-air-
Information-robbed-radiowave-thanks-new-contactless-technology.html

Question Topic:C5:-

Further Information and Scribble Notes:

www.lovesceneonline.com/celebritygossip/top-10-non-celebs-
%E2%80%93-beyond-the-z-list/
www.macmillandictionary.com/buzzword/entries/structured-reality.html
www.dailymail.co.uk/femail/article-1015638/My-despair-generation-
ambition-talentless-celebrities.html

Question Topic:C6:-

References:

www.infinite-energy.com/iemagazine/issue12/coldfusion.html
pesn.com/2011/07/03/9501862_Cheap_Cold_Fusion_to_Save_World_
Billions/

Further Information and Scribble Notes:

Cold Fusion is a theoretical form of energy source where energy is
generated when hydrogen interacts with various metals, the reaction
creating excess heat and transmutation products.
 Theoretically, cold fusion devices can produce so much heat, more than
can be accounted for by chemical means, and therefore must be generated by a nuclear source. But cold fusion is unlike the potentially dangerous 'nuclear power' as no radioactive materials are used therefore
none of the dangerous radiation associated with conventional nuclear
reactions are produced.
¬ Being the most abundant element in the universe, and found in water,
an energy source from hydrogen is clean, with no carbon dioxide emissions. Also, metal is recyclable when spent.
¬ Transmutation occurs when one element is transformed, or transmuted, to another element. Research shows that radioactive materials
can be transmuted to benign elements, promising a path to ridding the
planet of radioactive waste.
¬ Cold fusion energy generators will not need to be connected to an
electrical grid, therefore small and portable power units can provide
energy on-demand in any location. When access to water means access
to fuel, a new kind of freedom can empower people and communities.

Question Topic:C7:-

References:

www.npia.police.uk/en/8934.htm
www.nytimes.com/2009/08/18/science/18dna.html
news.bbc.co.uk/1/hi/uk/8037972.stm

Further Information and Scribble Notes:

www.parliament.uk/documents/post/postpn258.pdf
www.dailymail.co.uk/news/article-1322426/Alan-Newton-cleared-rape-
awarded-18-5m-compensation.html

Question Topic:C8:-

References:

www.drinkaware.co.uk/facts/drink-driving
www.direct.gov.uk/en/TravelAndTransport/Roadsafetyadvice/
DG_195019
drugdrive.direct.gov.uk/getcaught.shtml

Further Information and Scribble Notes:

www.dailymail.co.uk/news/article-2222645/Teenager-jailed-killing-friend-
car-crash-driving-Halloween-party-high-ecstasy-cannabis.html
www.dailymail.co.uk/news/article-2229811/Trauma-father-son-Kyle-
Griffith-reunited-time-20-years--boy-killed-driver-Stephen-Freye-snorted-
70-lines-cocaine-just-SIX-DAYS-later.html

Question Topic:C9:-

Further Information and Scribble Notes:

news.bbc.co.uk/2/hi/uk_news/4012797.stm
www.dailymail.co.uk/news/article-2209675/State-pension-double-120bn-
just-20-years-making-higher-economic-output-Israel-Czech-Republic.
html

Question Topic:C10:-

References:

Paper "The Evolution of Speed in Athletics: Why the Fastest Runners
are Black and Swimmers White"
A. Bejan E C Jones & J D Charles. Int Journal of Design & Nature. Vol.
5 No. 0 (2010) 1-13

www.constructal.org/en/art/THE_EVOLUTION_OF_SPEED_IN%20ATHLETICS.pdf
www.livescience.com/10716-scientists-theorize-black-athletes-run-fastest.html

Further Information and Scribble Notes:
"Why black athletes are the fastest runners" by Emma Lindsey
Daily Express Newspapers, 8 Sep 2000
www.jonentine.com/reviews/Daily_Express_9_8_2000.htm
"Why Black Athletes Dominate Sport And Why We're Afraid To Talk About It." by Jon Entine
www.jonentine.com/taboo.html

Question Topic:C12:-
References:
www.intothyword.org/pages.asp?pageid=53501

Further Information and Scribble Notes:
christiananswers.net/q-dml/dml-y001.html

Question Topic:C13:-
References:
www.bbc.co.uk/news/world-europe-13038095
news.bbc.co.uk/2/hi/middle_east/5411320.stm

Question Topic:C14:-
References:
timeforchange.org/are-cows-cause-of-global-warming-meat-methane-CO2
www.independent.co.uk/environment/climate-change/cow-emissions-more-damaging-to-planet-than-co2-from-cars-427843.html
environment.about.com/od/globalwarming/a/greenhouse.htm
www.religionfacts.com/hinduism/overview.htm

Further Information and Scribble Notes:
articles.cnn.com/2010-03-24/tech/meat.industry.global.warming_1_climate-change-greenhouse-gas-emissions-meat?_s=PM:TECH
Further info;
- As well as not eating beef, should Hindus go that little step further and avoid all dairy products altogether (see Jainism).

Question Topic:C15:-
References:
www.imdb.com/title/tt1182345/
en.wikipedia.org/wiki/Human_cloning
In the Outer Limits TV eposode 'Feasibility Study', An entire community is transported to another world as an experiment to see just how feasible it would be to breed humans into a perpetual race of slaves.

Further Information and Scribble Notes:
www.dailymail.co.uk/sciencetech/article-2175374/Russian-research-project-offers-immortality-billionaires--transplanting-brains-robot-bodies.html

Question Topic:C17:-
References:
www.direct.gov.uk/en/governmentcitizensandrights/yourrightsandresponsibilities/dg_4002951

news.bbc.co.uk/1/hi/uk/946400.stm
www.hrla.co.uk/
www.liberty-human-rights.org.uk/human-rights/human-rights/the-human-rights-act/index.php
news.uk.msn.com/the-big-question/should-the-human-rights-act-be-axed-6
www.dailymail.co.uk/news/article-2063439/Child-rapist-used-human-rights-fight-deportation--struck-again.html
www.telegraph.co.uk/news/uknews/immigration/8901430/Criminal-babyfathers-dodge-deportation.html
www.dailymail.co.uk/news/article-2049811/Rapist-killer-foreign-criminals-using-Human-Rights-Act-fight-deportation.html
news.softpedia.com/news/Top-6-The-Most-Severe-Human-Right-Violations-Around-the-World-63112.shtml
www.dailymail.co.uk/news/article-2316026/Convicted-drug-dealer-abandoned-children-allowed-stay-Britain-girlfriend.html

Further Information and Scribble Notes:
www.dailymail.co.uk/news/article-2065880/Britains-notorious-drug-baron-told-Stop-running-300m-empire-prison.html
www.dailymail.co.uk/news/article-2072835/These-human-rights-rulings-bonkers--thats-equalities-chief.html
www.dailymail.co.uk/news/article-2042198/Another-3-terrorists-dodge-deportation-using-Human-Rights-Act.html

Question Topic:C18:-
References:
www.telegraph.co.uk/finance/financialcrisis/9334170/How-Greece-has-got-itself-in-this-mess.html
www.guardian.co.uk/news/datablog/2012/oct/16/tax-biggest-us-companies-uk

Further Information and Scribble Notes:
www.dailymail.co.uk/news/article-2192352/Government-push-petrol-taxes-UP-motorists-afford-think-tank-claims.html
www.bbc.co.uk/news/business-13798000
en.wikipedia.org/wiki/Taxation_in_the_United_Kingdom
www.dailymail.co.uk/news/article-2027698/Ever-wondered-tax-REALLY-pay-Even-basic-rate-taxpayers-forced-hand-40p-pound.html
www.immortaltechnique.co.uk/Thread-How-much-tax-do-you-really-pay
www.guardian.co.uk/news/datablog/2012/oct/16/tax-biggest-us-companies-uk
www.dailymail.co.uk/news/article-2233280/Tax-Amazon-die-Plea-John-Lewis-boss-level-playing-field-foreign-multinationals-paying-little-tax-Britain.html
www.dailymail.co.uk/news/article-2271633/Were-proud-help-firms-make-billions-avoiding-tax-accountants-tell-MPs.html

Question Topic:C19:-
References:
www.myfinances.co.uk/pensions/2011/10/28/ftse-100-directors-pay-rises-by-49-per-cent-in-just-one-year

Further Information and Scribble Notes:
Here's What The Wall Street Protesters Are So Angry About' by Henry Blodget
www.businessinsider.com/what-wall-street-protesters-are-so-angry-

about-2011-10

According to the 'Executive Excess 2006, the 13th Annual CEO Compensation Survey from the Institute for Policy Studies and United for a Fair Economy' in the US, CEO pay has tripled since 1990, while the average production worker has had their pay increased by just 4%.

The 'Executive Excess 2008, the 15th Annual CEO Compensation Survey from the Institute for Policy Studies and United for a Fair Economy' in the US, illustrated that CEO pay is now 350x the average worker, up from 50x from 1960-85.

An excellent article 'Help the rich to save the poor' by Mark Steel in the Independent newspaper 17Jan2007:

www.independent.co.uk/opinion/commentators/mark-steel/mark-steel-help-the-rich-to-save-the-poor-432424.html

simonhughes.org.uk/en/article/2011/527413/simon-hughes-condemns-obscene-pay-rises-for-top-executives

www.dailymail.co.uk/news/article-2083827/The-12m-tax-mystery-Tony-Blairs-earnings-soar-42--pays-315-000-HMRC.html

Question Topic:C20:-

References:
www.independent.co.uk/news/business/analysis-and-features/trading-psychology-theyll-do-it-for-kicks-ndash-until-trading-kicks-them-back-777312.html
www.hrmreport.com/article/Business-ethics-is-inextricably-linked-to-the-current-financial-meltdown/
www.dailymail.co.uk/news/article-2174785/HSBC-scandal-Britains-biggest-bank-let-drug-gangs-launder-millions--faces-640million-fine.html
www.dailymail.co.uk/news/article-2072730/RBS-warned-Fred-Shreds-leadership-FIVE-YEARS-banks-failure-says-damning-report.html
www.dailymail.co.uk/news/article-2114829/Greg-Smith-resignation-letter-Goldman-Sachs-exec-quits-firms-toxic-culture.html
www.dailymail.co.uk/sciencetech/article-2107293/Wealthy-likely-lie-cheat-break-law.html
www.dailymail.co.uk/news/article-2134739/Bankers-receiving-Himalayan-pay-packages-despite-poor-performance--says-senior-Bank-England-executive.html

Further Information and Scribble Notes:
www.dailymail.co.uk/news/article-2102316/Ive-changed-mind-banks-brutish-institutions-run-brutes.html
www.dailymail.co.uk/news/article-2198628/Taxpayer-backed-Lloyds-facing-fine-City-watchdog-launches-probe-claims-paid-huge-bonuses-staff-mis-sold-financial-products.html

Question Topic:C21:-

References:
www.archives.gov/research/jfk/warren-commission-report/

Further Information and Scribble Notes:
www.dailymail.co.uk/news/article-2236766/Clint-Hill-Jackie-Kennedys-bodyguard-reveals-decades-guilt-49th-anniversary-JFKs-assassination.html

Question Topic:C22:-

References:
en.wikipedia.org/wiki/List_of_wars_and_anthropogenic_disasters_by_death_toll

cambodiangecko.com/cambodian-genocide-facts-timeline/

Question Topic:C23:-

Further Information and Scribble Notes:
listverse.com/2009/04/13/10-christ-like-figures-who-pre-date-jesus/

Question Topic:C24:-

References:
www.foxnews.com/world/2012/06/12/un-climate-organization-wants-immunities-against-charges-conflict-interest/
johnosullivan.wordpress.com/2012/06/14/un-climate-scientists-plead-for-immunity-from-criminal-prosecution/
en.wikipedia.org/wiki/Stephen_Schneider
www.nytimes.com/2010/07/20/science/earth/20schneider.html?_r=0

Further Information and Scribble Notes:
"Once a hypothesis has been set up, do everything in your power to prove it wrong. Only if you can't prove it wrong can you begin to prove it right."
healthland.time.com/2012/01/13/great-science-frauds/#scientist-rogues-gallery-2
www.dailymail.co.uk/sciencetech/article-2085814/Scientists-falsify-data-research-published-whistleblowers-bullied-keeping-quiet-claim-colleagues.html
www.dailymail.co.uk/sciencetech/article-2130184/Forget-global-warming-Scientists-discover-glaciers-Asia-getting-BIGGER.html
www.env-econ.net/2008/02/global-watming.html
www.dailymail.co.uk/sciencetech/article-2217286/Global-warming-stopped-16-years-ago-reveals-Met-Office-report-quietly-released--chart-prove-it.html
www.dailymail.co.uk/sciencetech/article-2125714/Legal-loophole-let-billionaires-BUY-planets-human-settlers-arrive-snap-Moon.html

Question Topic:C25:-

References:
www.bls.gov/opub/ted/2000/feb/wk3/art03.htm
www.jobsite.co.uk/career/advice/women_at_work.html
www.dailymail.co.uk/news/article-2069965/Stressed-angry-How-modern-female-boss-bully.html
www.telegraph.co.uk/family/4600556/House-husbands-Are-you-man-enough.html
www.telegraph.co.uk/family/9039858/Breadwinning-wives-lead-to-more-househusbands.html

Further Information and Scribble Notes:
www.dailymail.co.uk/femail/article-1061416
www.dailymail.co.uk/femail/article-2130291/Why-women-moral-especial-ly-theyre-30.html

Question Topic:D1:-

References:
www.bbc.co.uk/health/treatments/healthy_living/nutrition/healthy_alcohol.shtml

Further Information and Scribble Notes:

www.dailymail.co.uk/sciencetech/article-2082808/New-drug-lets-drink-getting-drunk-wake-hangover--youre-rat.html
www.dailymail.co.uk/health/article-2085320/Drinking-DOES-make-feel-happy-Alcohol-triggers-endorphins-brain.html
www.dailymail.co.uk/sciencetech/article-2152903/New-version-canna-bis-plant-developed-scientists-looks-smells-like-real-thing--wont-leave-users-high.html

Question Topic:D2:-
References:
www.fbi.gov/about-us/cjis/ncic/ncic
www.independent.co.uk/news/uk/thousands-of-people-who-disappear-without-trace-1427685.html
www.independent.co.uk/news/uk/home-news/the-missing-each-year-275000-britons-disappear-1801010.html
www.skepdic.com/aliens.html

Further Information and Scribble Notes:
In the US, the number of active missing persons cases is more than 110,000.
Believers are also convinced that there is a government and mass media conspiracy to cover up the alien activities, making it difficult for the abductees to prove or validate their account.

Question Topic:D3:-
References:
www.director.co.uk/ONLINE/2010/12_10_bribery-act-corruption.html
www.telegraph.co.uk/news/worldnews/europe/greece/7880108/Ex-Greek-ministers-friends-and-family-spend-20-million-euros-in-taxpayers-money-on-sex-lines.html
www.telegraph.co.uk/finance/newsbysector/banksandfinance/4932325/Sir-Fred-Goodwin-could-face-legal-action-over-pension-in-weeks.html
www.dailymail.co.uk/news/article-2122241/Crumbs-Andrew-Lansley-Department-Health-blew-100-000-tea-biscuits-THREE-MONTHS.html
www.dailymail.co.uk/news/article-2176290/Taxpayers-lose-Lloyds-branch-sell-Co-op-buys-600-1bn-bank-offered-year.html
www.bbc.co.uk/news/uk-20096414

Further Information and Scribble Notes:
www.dailymail.co.uk/news/article-2092408/Smartphones-kept-officers-beat-How-80m-efficiency-drive-backfired.html
www.dailymail.co.uk/news/article-2091616/University-State-Piaui-buys-2k-educational-sex-toys-using-state-funds.html
www.guardian.co.uk/football/2012/may/10/bebe-manchester-united-portuguese-police
www.standard.co.uk/lifestyle/london-life/the-french-connection-is-our-banking-crisis-a-parisian-problem-7961902.html
www.dailymail.co.uk/news/article-2228701/Putin-sacks-Russian-de-fence-minister-Anatoly-Serdyukov-60m-corruption-scandal.html
www.dailymail.co.uk/news/article-2229908/Andrew-Mitchell-defends-giving-160million-Rwanda-day-job.html

Question Topic:D4:-
References:
www.gmc-uk.org/about/role.asp
www.dailymail.co.uk/news/article-1379115/A-sad-day-press-freedom--Incompetent-doctors-secret-GMC-hearings.html

www.telegraph.co.uk/health/healthnews/9076442/Doctor-barred-after-20-years-of-sex-abuse.html
www.guardian.co.uk/society/2004/apr/24/NHS.uknews

Further Information and Scribble Notes:
www.alexanderharris.co.uk/News/AHNewsComments/Pages/GMChear-ingrulesgynaecologistisfittopractice.aspx
www.livingfoods.co.uk/pages/articles/doctor-diagnoses-the-general-medical-council-with-dementia.php
www.guardian.co.uk/society/2011/jul/26/gmc-too-lenient-poor-doctors-mps

Question Topic:D5:-
References:
www.guardian.co.uk/money/2011/jul/22/smartphones-hacked-zeus-malware
www.informationweek.com/news/231001685

Further Information and Scribble Notes:
- In the UK, identity fraud in itself is not a crime, although profiting from it is.
- Technology already exists to request other information during online transactions, other than that which is already printed on the card itself.
www.cracked.com/funny-4179-credit-cards/
www.dailymail.co.uk/news/article-2188381/My-7-000-just-vanished-How-slip-finger-cost-life-savings.html

Question Topic:D6:-
References:
www.sparknotes.com/lit/lion/section11.rhtml
www.sparknotes.com/lit/lion/section9.rhtml

Further Information and Scribble Notes:
www.dailymail.co.uk/news/article-2204263/Growing-married-parents-important-good-education-escaping-poverty.html

Question Topic:D7:-
References:
www.haverford.edu/engl/engl277b/Contexts/gender_and_religion_in_ker.htm

Further Information and Scribble Notes:
www.dailymail.co.uk/news/article-2155265/Indian-untouchable-lynched-village-strongman-breaking-strict-caste-rules-touching-hand-pump-heatwave.html

Question Topic:D8:-
References:
en.wikipedia.org/wiki/Disinformation
www.jimkarpen.com/wikipedia-lies.html
www.telegraph.co.uk/news/uknews/1575346/Lies-damn-lies-and-counterknowledge.html

Further Information and Scribble Notes:
www.ehow.com/how_2216484_avoid-false-information-internet.html
www.usatoday.com/news/opinion/editorials/2005-11-29-wikipedia-edit_x.htm

Libyan Lies - www.zimbabwemetro.com/?p=29617

Question Topic:D9:-
References:
www.vatican.va/roman_curia/congregations/cfaith/documents/rc_con_cfaith_doc_20000626_message-fatima_en.html
en.wikipedia.org/wiki/Three_Secrets_of_Fatima

Question Topic:D10:-
Further Information and Scribble Notes:
www.bbc.co.uk/news/uk-england-south-yorkshire-20761726

Question Topic:D11:-
References:
en.wikipedia.org/wiki/Somatic-cell_nuclear_transfer
en.wikipedia.org/wiki/Devolution_(biology)
www.dailymail.co.uk/sciencetech/article-489653/Human-race-split-different-species.html
science.howstuffworks.com/environmental/life/genetic/human-cloning.htm
www.dailymail.co.uk/sciencetech/article-2299423/Brain-scans-predict-criminal-likely-reoffend.html

Further Information and Scribble Notes:
In the Outer Limits TV eposode 'Replica', A biogeneticist illegally clones his comatose wife.

Question Topic:D12:-
Further Information and Scribble Notes:
www.dailymail.co.uk/news/article-2142064/Half-men-obese-2040--cost-treating-related-illnesses-reach-320bn.html
www.dailymail.co.uk/health/article-2151962/Britains-obesity-crisis-NHS-spending-16m-year-200-fat-leave-home.html
news.uk.msn.com/uk/nhs-overcrowded-and-short-staffed
www.dailymail.co.uk/news/article-2216550/Booze-toll-baby-boomers-Their-alcohol-abuse-costs-NHS-825m.html
www.dailymail.co.uk/health/article-2317068/Woman-beaten-boyfriend-REFUSED-NHS-funding-rebuild-shattered-nose-barely-breathe.html
Alternative Future Reform:
Alternatively, should the NHS still be available to all and sundry. However, even with the NHS in financial disarray, the service are permitted by law to treat but are also free to make restrospective charges to the patient on the care received. The cost of the bill will be dependent on the percentage of accountability attributed to the patient, based on the opinion of the doctor(s) and previous medical history. The law will back up this initiative by legally placing owned property as collateral.

Question Topic:D13:-
References:
www.space.com/15395-asteroid-mining-planetary-resources.html
www.lifeslittlemysteries.com/2385-asteroid-mining-space-law.html
www.bbc.co.uk/news/science-environment-17827347
www.registerguard.com/web/business/27962774-41/space-asteroids-company-anderson-fuel.html.csp

Further Information and Scribble Notes:
The 18th was the Century of Chemistry, the 20th of Physics and the

21st will be the Century of Biology, but could well be the Century of Cosmology.
In the movie 'Alien', the ill-fated Nostromo is heading back to Earth with twenty million tons of mineral ore in her hold.

Question Topic:D15:-
References:
www.prospectmagazine.co.uk/magazine/no-kidding/
www.nytimes.com/2008/09/15/world/asia/15brainscan.html
www.wired.co.uk/magazine/archive/2009/06/features/guilty?
www.dailymail.co.uk/news/article-2240397/Councils-using-lie-detector-tests-root-benefits-cheats.html

Question Topic:D16:-
References:
answers.yahoo.com/question/index?qid=20090310130005AAzwQn0

Honourable Mentions:
http://www.dailymail.co.uk/news/article-2154729/Patrick-Drum-Convicted-felon-34-fatally-shot-sex-offenders-left-note-saying-planned-killings.html
Dishonourable Mentions:
http://www.dailymail.co.uk/news/article-2302976/Predatory-paedophiles-twisted-depraved-plot-breed-daughter-sexually-abuse-her.html
http://www.dailymail.co.uk/news/article-2148624/Paedophiles-raped-11-year-old-girl-block-flats-sentences-doubled-trial-judge-gave-just-years-prison.html
http://www.dailymail.co.uk/news/article-2156013/Couple-raped-daughter-supervised-visit-recorded-sex-abuse-nephew-18-months-cellphone-contained-532-images-child-bestiality.html
http://www.dailymail.co.uk/news/article-2174031/400-sex-convicts-freed-rape-Soft-justice-anger-offenders-strike-again.html
http://www.dailymail.co.uk/news/article-2191101/Darren-Mackrell-Southampton-man-guilty-raping-children-drugged.html
http://www.digitaljournal.com/article/342697
http://www.dailymail.co.uk/news/article-2069467/Man-woman-arrested-month-old-baby-raped-battered.html
http://www.dailymail.co.uk/news/article-2092193/Nigel-Leat-Bosses-did-teacher-paedophile-sickening-order.html
http://www.dailymail.co.uk/news/article-2114924/Don-t-let-Final-moments-girl-raped-murdered-abducted-way-home-school.html
http://www.dailymail.co.uk/news/article-2114341/One-paedophiles-chemically-castrated-controversial-prison-experiment-crush-sex-drive.html
http://www.paltelegraph.com/columnists/peter-eyre/4403-the-deeply-upsetting-story-of-hollie-greig
http://www.dailymail.co.uk/news/article-2218450/Will-horrifically-burned-victim-convict-killer-grave-Man-named-attacker-video-died-cancer-caused-wounds.html
http://www.dailymail.co.uk/news/article-2218998/Colin-Cooper-Sadistic-paedophile-terrorised-victims-snarling-dogs-Nazi-horror-stories-forced-eat-flesh-pigs-head.html
http://www.dailymail.co.uk/news/article-2224573/Three-doctors-collaborated-abuse-Savile-helping-select-child-patients-rape.html
http://www.dailymail.co.uk/news/article-2229227/Parents-girl-raped-babysitter-14-sent-prison-fail-bid-thrown-jail.html

Wildcard View:-

Is there a connection between Paedophiles who engage in satisfying sexual desires with young children and that of the age of their first sexual experience.

eg. Paedophiles who desire girls as young as 8 are also men who had their first consensual sexual encounter at a young age and with a girl around the ages of 7-10.

eg. Paedophiles who desire boys as young as 8 are also practising heterosexual men who had their first homosexual encounter (consensual or not) at a young age and with another young boy of similar age.

Question Topic:D17:-
Further Information and Scribble Notes:
www.dailymail.co.uk/news/article-2064297/Intars-Pless-Latvian-drink-drive-killer-revealed-axe-murderer-knew-about.html
www.dailymail.co.uk/news/article-2088354/Victor-Akulic-Lithuanian-child-rapist-allowed-UK-brutally-rapes-woman.html
www.dailymail.co.uk/news/article-2109800/In-country-people-work-hard-pay-people-don-t-want--We-don-t-understand-say-parents-Malaysian-bad-Samaritan-riot-victim.html
www.dailymail.co.uk/news/article-2128690/Illegal-immigrant-subjected-mother-hour-machete-rape-ordeal-children-filmed-jailed-14-years.html
www.dailymail.co.uk/news/article-2144788/Free-roam-streets-protect-human-rights-100-foreign-criminals-month.html

Question Topic:D19:-
Further Information and Scribble Notes:
www.popularmechanics.com/technology/gadgets/news/2078467
mpkv.academia.edu/PratikButtePatil/Papers/309646/Technological_Advancements_and_Its_Impact_on_Humanity
inventors.about.com/od/timelines/a/twentieth.htm
www.futuretechnology500.com/
timprosserfuturing.wordpress.com/2008/04/15/how-long-can-technological-advancement-keep-speeding-up/
Cloud Computing (A solution to copyright infringement and other digital offences): Deleting all Mp3's etc and scanning for child porn using metadata on known images
www.dailymail.co.uk/sciencetech/article-2254412/Anger-Google-Musics-scan-match-feature-swaps-explicit-songs-clean-versions.html

Question Topic:D20:-
References:
www.thisismoney.co.uk/money/mortgageshome/article-2193459/Repossession-sales-cheating-taxpayer.html
www.dailymail.co.uk/news/article-2061552/Young-buyers-trapped-homes-Bought-property-peak-years-ago.html
www.estateagenttoday.co.uk/news_features/Gap-between-auction-and-estate-agent-prices-widens

Question Topic:D22:-
References:
www.dailymail.co.uk/news/article-2134739/Bankers-receiving-Himalayan-pay-packages-despite-poor-performance--says-senior-Bank-England-executive.html
www.hurriyet.com.tr/english/world/11343277.asp
www.guardian.co.uk/world/2009/apr/01/g20-summit-protests

Further Information and Scribble Notes:
www.guardian.co.uk/money/2006/dec/06/business.internationalnews
www.dailymail.co.uk/news/article-2068875/Mervyn-King-warns-mortgage-rates-likely-soar-tells-banks-slash-bonuses.html
www.dailymail.co.uk/news/article-2086557/JPMorgan-staff-220k-EACH-bonuses-bank-returns-record-profits.html

Question Topic:D23:-
References:
"French Revolution." Encyclopædia Britannica. Standard Edition. Chicago: Encyclopædia Britannica, 2012.

Question Topic:D24:-
References:
www.futuretimeline.net/21stcentury/2039.htm

Further Information and Scribble Notes:
Full immersion virtual reality
www.futuretimeline.net/21stcentury/2039.htm
Computers are now sufficiently advanced and miniaturised that billions of them can be implanted within the brain. Advances in neuroscience, in parallel with these and other developments, have led to a new form of simulation known as full immersion virtual reality. By the end of this decade, it has been successfully demonstrated in a human volunteer.*
Though still in its early stages, and yet to become fully mainstream, this technology provides astounding realism and detail. Users now have the option of actually "being" in a game environment and experiencing its graphics, audio and other effects (e.g. tactile feedback) in a manner that is largely indistinguishable from the real world.
This breakthrough has been achieved through exponential trends in computing over the previous decades – including a billionfold improvement in processing power and price performance, combined with a 100,000-fold shrinkage of components and circuitry.*
For the first time, human brains are actually being merged with computer intelligence. Rather than viewing games on a screen, users can now experience the program from within their own nervous systems, as though it were an extension of their mind. A simple, minimally invasive procedure inserts nanobots (blood cell-sized devices) into their bodies. These microscopic machines are self-guided towards the neurons in their brain respon-sible for visual, auditory and other senses. Here, they remain in a dormant state, but in close proximity to the brain cells.
When the user wishes to experience a simulated reality, the nanobots immediately move into place, suppressing all of the inputs coming from the real senses and replacing them with signals corresponding to the virtual environment. If the user decides to move their limbs and muscles as they normally would, the nanobots again intercept these neurochemical signals – suppressing the "real world" limbs from moving, and instead causing their "virtual" limbs to move within the game. This means a user can be sitting in a fixed position, while experiencing a high degree of activity and movement.

Question Topic:D25:-
Further Information and Scribble Notes:
www.dailymail.co.uk/news/article-2197369/The-paedophiles-aged-136-children-15-convicted-sex-offences-youngsters-2011.html
www.koreaittimes.com/story/4414/has-internet-changed-our-lives-better-or-worse

www.pcworld.com/article/194081-3/10_things_the_internet_has_killed_
or_ruined_and_5_things_it_hasnt.html
www.dailymail.co.uk/news/article-2220485/Children-spend-hours-online-
day-world-2D-warns-scientist.html
www.dailymail.co.uk/news/article-2234956/Internet-porn-rape-suspects-
aged-TEN.html
www.dailymail.co.uk/news/article-2311534/Rapist-14-hooked-porn-
websites-Judge-links-Scots-teenagers-obsession-online-sex-sites-
attack-year-old.html

Question Topic:E1:-
Further Information and Scribble Notes:
www.chrisspivey.co.uk/?p=7469

Question Topic:E2:-
References:
www.newscientist.com/blogs/shortsharpscience/2011/02/nano-particles-
could-help-deli.html
www.naturalnews.com/028887_vaccines_Bill_Gates.html
news.bbc.co.uk/1/hi/health/8674380.stm
The Free Lance-Star - Jul 1, 1964:
news.google.com/newspapers?nid=1298&dat=19640701&id=GW4QAA
AAIBAJ&sjid=8YoDAAAAIBAJ&pg=6088,178239

Question Topic:E3:-
References:
en.wikipedia.org/wiki/Carbon_credits
www.telegraph.co.uk/finance/businesslatestnews/6686057/European-
Climate-Exchange-chief-Patrick-Birley-defends-the-carbon-trading-
system.html
climateandcapitalism.com/2011/03/08/europes-carbon-market-scam/

Further Information and Scribble Notes:
www.nytexaminer.com/2012/08/the-carbon-credit-hoax/
www.bloomberg.com/apps/news?pid=newsarchive&sid=aXRBOxU5K
T5M

Question Topic:E4:-
References:
en.wikipedia.org/wiki/Corporate_ethics
saltycurrent.blogspot.co.uk/2011/10/corporate-ethics-xigris-example.html

Further Information and Scribble Notes:
www.dailymail.co.uk/news/article-2134850/Rupert-Murdoch-quit-chair-
man-News-Corp-lax-ethical-culture-major-shareholder-groups-demand.
html

Question Topic:E5:-
References:
carm.org/cults
answers.yahoo.com/question/index?qid=20091017100807AAHDyJE
listverse.com/2007/09/15/top-10-cults/
history1900s.about.com/od/1970s/p/jonestown.htm

Further Information and Scribble Notes:

www.neatorama.com/2011/01/28/the-best-cults/
www.dailymail.co.uk/news/article-2129032/Rebecca-Musser-reveals-
seven-years-sexual-violations-married-Warren-Jeffs-father-Rulon-FLDS-
church.html
www.cracked.com/article_18885_5-people-who-started-religions-just-
to-get-laid.html
www.xenu-directory.net/
www.xenu-directory.net/topics/scn-vs-udhr.html

Question Topic:E6:-
References:
RSA Commission on Illegal Drugs, Communities and Public Policy -
2005 Paper The Supply of Drugs in the UK
www.drugscope.org.uk/Resources/Drugscope/Documents/PDF/
Good%20Practice/supply.pdf
UNODC World Drug Report 2010
www.unodc.org/unodc/en/data-and-analysis/WDR-2010.html
Home Office Statistical Bulletin - Drug Offenders in England and Wales
2004
webarchive.nationalarchives.gov.uk/20110220105210/rds.homeoffice.
gov.uk/rds/pdfs05/hosb2305.pdf
www.thesun.co.uk/sol/homepage/news/3569446/Nearly-half-of-convict-
ed-drug-dealers-are-avoiding-jail-because-of-soft-justice.html

Further Information and Scribble Notes:
www.cps.gov.uk/legal/d_to_g/drug_offences/
www.dailymail.co.uk/news/article-2233313/Grieving-Diana-Hardings-
courtroom-denounciation-drug-dealer-jailed-daughters-ecstasy-death.
html

Question Topic:E7:-
References:
www.nature.com/news/2010/100721/full/466432a.html
www.control-mosquitoes.com/
www.britishecologicalsociety.org/about_bes/press/press_releases/
macquarie.php
"ecosystem." Encyclopædia Britannica. Standard Edition. Chicago:
Encyclopædia Britannica, 2012.

Further Information and Scribble Notes:
Paper: Turning the Tide: The Eradication of Invasive Species:
www.issg.org/pdf/publications/turning_the_tide.pdf
From the movie 'Terminator' :
John Connor sends his younger friend, Kyle Reese (who just happens to
be his actual father), 45 years back in time where he would subsequently have sexual intercourse with Johns mother (resulting in the
conceiving of the same said John Connor) - who would of course not
have given birth to him had an alternative reality John Connor not sent
Kyle Reese across.
Mosquitos can carry any number of deadly diseases including malaria,
dengue fever, yellow fever and encephalitis.
www.dailymail.co.uk/news/article-2233414/Galapagos-Islands-Ecuador-
drops-20-tons-poison-bid-wipe-rats.html

Question Topic:E8:-
Further Information and Scribble Notes:
www.businessweek.com/magazine/content/10_19/b4177056214833.htm

not4attribution.blogspot.nl/2012/07/hans-and-eva-rausing-from-archive.html

www.telegraph.co.uk/news/worldnews/africaandindianocean/angola/1313517/Mitterrand-who-cannot-escape-justice.html

www.theaustralian.com.au/news/mitterrand-legacy-under-heavy-scrutiny/story-e6frg6to-1111117156815

www.telegraph.co.uk/news/worldnews/europe/france/9212536/Pippa-Middleton-French-aristocrat-sorry-over-Paris-gun-joke-row.html

www.dailymail.co.uk/news/article-2155612/British-envoy-Edward-Werner-daughter-Pamelas-death-Peking.html

www.msnbc.msn.com/id/13715925/ns/business-corporate_scandals/t/enron-founder-ken-lay-dies-heart-disease/

www.telegraph.co.uk/news/worldnews/asia/china/9201253/Neil-Heywood-mystery-Bo-Guagua-the-student-playboy-who-earned-contempt-of-tutors-and-forced-Chinese-diplomats-into-pleading-his-case.html

Question Topic:E9:-
References:
www.parenting.com/article/teach-spirituality-kids?
www.guardian.co.uk/education/2012/jan/15/free-schools-creationism-intelligent-design
wiki.answers.com/Q/What_is_the_role_of_a_parent

Further Information and Scribble Notes:
Today, there exists great debate on which of the competing origin theories should be taught in school, but with creationism now ruled out of the science curriculum, it seems the children of tomorrow are reliant on the apatheistic argument that morals are already present in human society.
www.dailymail.co.uk/news/article-2149075/The-thousands-Britons-don-t-moral-compass-One-admit-bad-people.html
www.dailymail.co.uk/news/article-2202083/Nottingham-rapist-Joseph-Moran-jailed-years-branded-pathological-liar.html
www.dailymail.co.uk/news/article-2312657/A-generation-unruly-toddlers-Schools-Minister-says-Nursery-children-arent-taught-manners.html
idebate.org/debatabase/debates/education/house-would-teach-creationism-schools

Question Topic:E10:-
Further Information and Scribble Notes:
www.cracked.com/article_18955_6-crackpot-conspiracy-theories-that-actually-happened.html

Question Topic:E11:-
References:
en.wikipedia.org/wiki/Virtual_reality
news.bbc.co.uk/2/hi/technology/3485918.stm

Further Information and Scribble Notes:
www.dailymail.co.uk/health/article-2132418/Computer-game-tackles-depression-teenagers-using-fantasy-game.html
www.dailymail.co.uk/sciencetech/article-2136077/Can-playing-Call-Duty-make-better-driver-Shoot-em-ups-actually-IMPROVE-visual-attention-circuits-brain.html
www.dailymail.co.uk/news/article-2222803/SnowWorld-Groundbreaking-experiment-virtual-reality-treats-wounded-soldiers-pain.html
www.dailymail.co.uk/sciencetech/article-2235313/We-technology-Science-Six-Million-Dollar-Man-inches-closer-advance-mind-control-computers.html

Question Topic:E12:-
References:
www.zdnet.com/blog/btl/the-top-five-reasons-why-windows-vista-failed/10303

Further Information and Scribble Notes:
www.itwire.com/2012-06-01-13-40-03/browse/c-level/56422-exponential-growth-versus-linear-thinking
www.dailymail.co.uk/sciencetech/article-2311740/New-mobile-phone-battery-charge-SECOND.html

Question Topic:E13:-
Further Information and Scribble Notes:
money.uk.msn.com/investing/articles.aspx?cp-documentid=153970828
Pension Statements are received yearly from the age of 22 to to help people keep track of their life, and their life compared to the society in general.

Question Topic:E14:-
References:
genealogy.about.com/cs/geneticgenealogy/a/nature_nurture.htm

Further Information and Scribble Notes:
www.dailymail.co.uk/news/article-2204144/Cristian-Fernandez-The-sad-past-boy-13-tried-adult-killing-2-year-old-brother.html
Nature endows us with inborn abilities and traits and Nurture takes these genetic tendencies and molds them as we learn and mature.
TV Episode 'Outer Limits - Resurrection', tells the story of how after extinction, a single human is cloned from a single strand of hair.

Question Topic:E15:-
Further Information and Scribble Notes:
www.cracked.com/article_19790_6-tiny-mistakes-that-almost-ended-world_p2.html
www.dailymail.co.uk/news/article-2204151/Declassified-documents-1980-US-planned-fight-nuclear-war.html
www.bbc.co.uk/news/magazine-17026538
www.hnn.us/articles/132788.html
www.dailymail.co.uk/news/article-2218288/Cuban-Missile-Crisis-Robert-Kennedys-notes-reveal-US-invasion-plans-brought-WWIII.html

Question Topic:E16:-
References:
Article: 'Smarty Plants' by Emma Bayley. BBC Focus Magazine Apr07
www.wired.com/underwire/2008/06/the-happening-s/
io9.com/5016361/the-happening-is-the-biggest-intelligent-design-movie-of-the-year
www.popularmechanics.com/technology/digital/fact-vs-fiction/4268571

Further Information and Scribble Notes:
science.jrank.org/pages/5773/Red-Tide.html

Question Topic:E17:-
References:
www.castlecover.co.uk/historic-home-utility-prices/

www.decc.gov.uk/en/content/cms/statistics/energy_stats/prices/prices.
aspx

inflationdata.com/inflation/inflation_rate/historical_oil_prices_table.asp
www.independent.co.uk/news/the-great-jobs-divide-that-splits-britain-
while-salaries-in-privatised-utilities-rise-by-74-1171279.html
21stcenturysocialism.com/article/the_privatisation_scam_02064.html
www.telegraph.co.uk/finance/newsbysector/energy/oilandgas/8583543/
Scottish-Power-chairman-has-pay-package-doubled.html
www.politics.co.uk/reference/water-regulation-and-ofwat
www.dailymail.co.uk/news/article-2125261/As-hosepipe-ban-begins-
water-bosses-pocketed-huge-bonuses.html
www.pcs.org.uk/en/news_and_events/facts-about-civil-and-public-
services/the-truth-about-privatisation.cfm

Further Information and Scribble Notes:
Case Study :-
Giles and Delroy both have a young family, consisting of a housewife
and 10yr old twins. Giles lives in a 3-bed terraced house in Peckham
while Delroy lives in a similar style house in Kensington. While Giles
only earns $20,000 a year, Delroy is enjoying a $300,000 salary. In
2013, the utility and travel companies formally announce a 30% above
inflation hike in prices and the regulators step in to ask people to buy
more fleece adorned clothing.

With the new reduced levels of disposable income, of whose children
wishes they were old enough to start a riot ?

Be Controversial: Could there be an even more sinister reason to
privatise: The Utility companies are now a cartel where the prices are
controlled by the government still with the aim to keep prices artificially
high and increasing. Increasing fuel costs would lead to elderly people
cutting down on heating, eventually dying at a faster rate as a result.
The government then see the realisation of their long term plans and
cleans up, taking the inheritance tax and any unclaimed inheritance.

tutor2u.net/economics/revision-notes/a2-micro-privatisation-deregula-
tion.html
en.wikipedia.org/wiki/Tax_per_head
news.bbc.co.uk/2/hi/business/5049176.stm
www.moneywise.co.uk/cut-your-costs/household-bills/the-shocking-
truth-about-energy-prices
www.rmtbristol.org.uk/2006/11/   The Times: November 29, 2006
"Ticket price rises make rail travel 'preserve of the rich" by Ben Webster,
Transport Correspondent
www.dailymail.co.uk/news/article-2131992/Hard-pressed-families-
spending-filling-petrol-tank-weekly-food-shop.html
www.dailymail.co.uk/news/article-2233109/Power-firms-profits-surge-
38-goes-QUARTER.html
www.dailymail.co.uk/money/news/article-2300051/British-Gas-bosses-
pocket-16m-gas-electricity-bills-roof.html
en.wikipedia.org/wiki/Guilds_of_Ankh-Morpork#Thieves.27_Guild
John Wiseman or whatever his name is. Double Cross

Question Topic:E18:-
References:
www.science20.com/news_articles/daf16_aging_gene_governs_lifes-
pan_humans
www.dailymail.co.uk/sciencetech/article-2175374/Russian-research-pro-
ject-offers-immortality-billionaires--transplanting-brains-robot-bodies.html

In the Outer Limits TV eposode 'The Balance of Nature', A doctor develops the technology to reverse aging and disease.

Further Information and Scribble Notes:
www.dailymail.co.uk/health/article-2056433/Forever-young-drug-allows-
people-grow-old-gracefully-soon-reality.html
www.dailymail.co.uk/sciencetech/article-2107236/You-CAN-live-forever-
-long-flatworm-say-scientists.html
www.dailymail.co.uk/news/article-2161869/Top-doctors-chilling-claim-
The-NHS-kills-130-000-elderly-patients-year.html
Further Discussion Viewpoints:-
¬ Should it be commercialised instead - If you can afford it, then why not
reap the fruits of your labour and enjoy wealth, family, and your grandchildren. Let people choose when to die when they are tired of life.
¬ Population control is a problem as it is, and medical funding should be
allocated to keeping the younger healthier and alive. The elderly have
had their cake and should accept their elapsing time.
¬ People should instead look to die younger and make the most of the
time they have self-pledged.

Question Topic:E19:-
Further Information and Scribble Notes:
What-If Scenario -
What if Religions adopted a single overriding principle for the basis for
entering hell or heaven; That one must not cause physical/mental/sexual
hurt to others.

Question Topic:E20:-
References:
en.wikipedia.org/wiki/Sharia_law
dcfnfb.blogspot.nl/2010/11/ten-facts-about-sharia-law-islamic-law.html

Further Information and Scribble Notes:
www.answering-islam.org/Authors/Arlandson/top_ten_sharia.htm
www.islamreview.com/articles/sharia.shtml
wikiislam.net/wiki/Islam_and_Pedophilia
www.news24.com/World/News/Fury-as-victim-14-forced-to-marry-
rapist-20120628
www.dailymail.co.uk/news/article-2271682/Divorce-cases-settled-Shar-
ia-religious-courts-landmark-High-Court-ruling.html
www.dailymail.co.uk/news/article-2236787/British-businesswoman-
jailed-months-Dubai-taxi-tryst-despite-DNA-evidence-showing-did-sex.
html
www.dailymail.co.uk/news/article-2277942/Dubai-father-killed-daughter-
8-torturing-hot-irons-stun-guns-naughty-sentenced-death.html

Question Topic:E21:-
References:
Left Behind in the Labor Market: Recent Employment Trends Among
Young Black Men'
Paul Offner and Harry Holzer, Georgetown Public Policy Institute
www.brookings.edu/es/urban/publications/offnerholzer.pdf
When my child does not do well in school' by Ms Carolyn Kee
news.sma.org.sg/4302/Child.pdf

Further Information and Scribble Notes:
Level Driven School Classes - So the less mentally able are not intimi-

dated and can study amongst similar intelligence groups, hopefully in the knowledge that they can excel in a level group.
www.football365.com/faves/7884196/Where-Are-The-Middle-Class-Footballers-
www.dailymail.co.uk/news/article-2234425/So-thats-genius-Einsteins-intelligence-unusual-features-brain.html

Question Topic:E22:-
References:
jaygary.com/templebomb.shtml
www.truthnet.org/islam/Islam-Bible/10Islam-Israel-Jerusalem/IslamIs-raelJerusalem.htm
realtruth.org/articles/090710-004-middle.html

Further Information and Scribble Notes:
Further Question:
Could 'Oil' be just a smokescreen for the Western world to have an active legitimate interest in the Middle East, and hence reluctance to develop alternative sources of power.
en.wikipedia.org/wiki/War_of_Ezekiel_38-39
en.wikipedia.org/wiki/Knights_Templar

Question Topic:E23:-
References:
en.wikipedia.org/wiki/Top_Gear_challenges
www.guardian.co.uk/news/datablog/2011/jul/12/bbc-spending
In a letter dated 11Nov2008, in a response to a 'N Smith' an email reference 'request-3991-4b122bc5@whatdotheyknow.com', the BBC refuses to disclose the costs inclusive of salaries/expenses in relation to the Top Gear program.
See: www.whatdotheyknow.com/request/top_gear_production_costs

Further Information and Scribble Notes:
¬ Supercar shootout on a road trip to Italy,
¬ Clarkson tried to avoid being caught in missile lock from an WAH-64D Apache attack helicopter in a Lotus Exige.
¬ Taking the Bugatti Veyron to its top speed of 253mph.
¬ Snipers shooting at presenters while driving a Porsche and a Mercedes.
¬ Racing back from Italy in a Veyron - against a little plane.

Question Topic:E24:-
References:
en.wikipedia.org/wiki/Vigilante

Further Information and Scribble Notes:
www.dailymail.co.uk/news/article-2169135/Fathers-suicide-note-reveals-killed-drug-dealer-blamed-sons-ecstasy-death.html
www.dailymail.co.uk/news/article-2178626/Battered-face-pensioner-Joe-Carter-82-chased-burglars-beaten-home.html
www.dailymail.co.uk/news/article-2177048/Savannah-Dietrich-Teen-faces-jail-lashing-Twitter-naming-boys-sexually-assaulted-her.html

Question Topic:E25:-
A Cautionary Tale: Adapted from the movie 'True Romance' (1993)
Please note, the Author does not wish to employ derogatory terms but is reluctantly required to do so here;

The Scenario: Two Indian persons were overheard in deep, heated conversation with one under duress and the other behaving in a threatening manner. The two individuals were respectively, a slightly dark fellow named 'Mohan' who was from South India, and 'Rajesh' who was a paler skinned version originally from North India, and below is the transcript of their actual conversation:

Mohan: "You're North Indians, right?"

Rajesh: "Yeah, we're North Indians."

Mohan: "You know... I read a lot, especially about things about history. I find that shit fascinating. Here's a fact I don't know whether you know or not, but North Indians were spawned by honkies."

Rajesh: "Come again?"

Mohan: "No, it's... it's a fact. Yeah. You see, North Indians have white blood pumping through their hearts. If you don't believe me, you can look it up."

Mohan: "Hundreds of years ago, you see, the White English conquered North India. And the White English are honkies.
You see, way back then, North Indians were like, uh, the darkies from Southern India. They all had dark skin and good looks.
But, uh, well... then the White English moved in there, and... well, they changed the whole country. They did so much fucking with North Indian women, that they changed that whole bloodline forever.
That's why... dark skin and good looks became olive skin and mediocre looks. You know, it's absolutely amazing to me... to think that to this day, hundreds of years later, that North Indians... still carry that honkie gene."

Rajesh: "Now, this..."

Mohan: "No, I'm quoting history. It's written. It's a fact. It's written."

Rajesh: "I love this guy."

Mohan: "No. Your ancestors are honkies. Huh? Hey. Yeah.
And... And your great-great-great-great-grandmother... fucked a honkie. Yeah. And she had a half-honkie kid. Now, if that's a fact, tell me, am I lying? Cause you... you're part hummus. Huh? Hey, hey, hey."

Rajesh: "You're an eggplant. That's beautiful."

Classroom Exercise:-
Adapt this fictitious example by reverting to another historic period, the 13th-16th centuries, when the 'Moghuls' conquered much of India. And the Moghuls are Muslim.

Further Information and Scribble Notes:
www.dailymail.co.uk/news/article-2297776/SATURDAY-ESSAY-Why-Left-epic-mistake-immigration.html
www.dailymail.co.uk/news/article-2305675/Former-UK-Border-Agency-chief-Tony-Smith-says-immigration-control.html

Question Topic:F1:-
References:
www.independent.co.uk/news/world/politics/top-un-official-says-it-is-not-fit-for-purpose-7536442.html

Further Information and Scribble Notes:
In the Outer Limits TV eposode 'Monster', The CIA experiments to use telekinesis as an assassination tool.
www.dailymail.co.uk/news/article-2133201/Dr-Richard-Holmes-Suicide-riddle-weapons-expert-worked-David-Kelly.html
www.dailymail.co.uk/news/article-2086700/Iran-says-U-S-assassination-nuclear-scientists.html
Chavez socialist revolution - Declines oil to the US and a fairer price. Then Chavez gets Cancer soon after.
venezuelanalysis.com/analysis/1027

Question Topic:F2:-
References:
www.direct.gov.uk/en/HomeAndCommunity/Gettinginvolvedinyourcommunity/Charities/Startingacharity/Isstartingacharitytherightchoice/DG_066537
www.charity-commission.gov.uk/FAQS/Running_a_charity/default.aspx
www.telegraph.co.uk/news/religion/7229874/Tony-Blairs-faith-charity-pays-six-figure-salaries-to-top-officials.html
www.dailymail.co.uk/news/article-2083822/Carla-Bruni-sleaze-scandal-giving-millions-pounds-Aids-charity-money-close-male-friend.html
www.independent.co.uk/news/uk/home-news/city-pay-culture-has-spread-to-charities-union-says-1817725.html

Further Information and Scribble Notes:
www.usatoday.com/news/washington/2010-03-12-senators-charity-expenses_N.htm
www.dailymail.co.uk/news/article-2127929/Great-charity-revolt-800-furious-charities-say-Osbornes-budget-lose-millions.html
www.cpexposed.com/
www.dailymail.co.uk/news/article-2132999/Mandy-Smith-WAG-sister-mystery-250-000-missing-sick-childrens-charity.html
www.dailymail.co.uk/news/article-2198927/It-s-obscene-political-stunt-Save-The-Children-equate-British-families-starving-poor-Africa.html
www.dailymail.co.uk/news/article-2092425/Haiti-shaming-aid-zealots-How-donated-billions-INCREASED-poverty-corruption.html

Question Topic:F3:-
References:
www.nationmultimedia.com/opinion/Cyber-warfare-is-the-new-threat-to-the-global-orde-30203813.html
news.uk.msn.com/features/articles.aspx?cp-documentid=156437856
selil.com/archives/649

Further Information and Scribble Notes:
voices.yahoo.com/the-increasing-human-dependence-computers-1360477.html
www.dailymail.co.uk/sciencetech/article-2299999/REVEALED-The-Nato-bunker-deep-Netherlands-forest-hackers-brought-worlds-internet-biggest-cyber-attack.html

www.dailymail.co.uk/news/article-2295948/Black-Dragon-cyber-criminal-tried-hack-UN-computers-steal-6-5million-carbon-credits-jailed-years.html
www.dailymail.co.uk/news/article-2299999/Global-internet-slowdown-biggest-cyber-attack-history.html

Question Topic:F4:-
References:
uk.askmen.com/top_10/entertainment/top-10-signs-the-devil-exists.html
www.dailymail.co.uk/news/article-2067326/Just-254m-nest-egg-Rich-bankers-pocket-huge-lottery-jackpot-1-ticket.html
www.dailymail.co.uk/news/article-2082640/How-year-old-Adolf-Hitler-saved-certain-death--drowning-icy-river-rescued.html
DeathRow Stats - www.tdcj.state.tx.us/stat/executedoffenders.htm

Further Information and Scribble Notes:
www.dailymail.co.uk/news/article-2181595/Shaurya-abuse-Monster-parents-tortured-little-boy-physically-deformed-face-jail.html
www.thesun.co.uk/sol/homepage/news/3714448/HIV-monster-Nkosinati-Mabanda-gets-four-years-jail.html
www.dailymail.co.uk/news/article-2104792/Nikitta-Grender-trial-Boy-friends-cousin-Carl-Whant-guilty-rape-killing-pregnant-teenager.html
crime.about.com/od/murder/p/gein.htm
www.dailymail.co.uk/news/article-2173138/Arturo-Martinez-I-forgive-man-raped-killed-daughter-10-wife-Las-Vegas-home-invasion.html
www.dailymail.co.uk/news/article-2205493/Burglar-punched-heavily-pregnant-woman-s-stomach-11-TIMES-woke-ransacking-bedroom.html
www.dailymail.co.uk/news/article-2114924/Victoria-Tori-Stafford-trial-2012-Final-moments-girl-8-raped-murdered-Woodstock-Ontario.html
www.dailymail.co.uk/news/article-2222298/Tragedy-left-Innocent-baby-carried-away-home-mother-siblings-slaughtered.html

Question Topic:F5:-
References:
www.computerworlduk.com/news/it-business/3303046/accenture-pays-64m-to-settle-kick-back-case/
www.computerworlduk.com/news/it-business/3339678/rbs-steps-up-it-expenditure-as-losses-double/
www.dailymail.co.uk/news/article-2136675/9m-waste-High-Court-doesnt-work--So-spend-9-5m-new-one.html

Further Information and Scribble Notes:
www.dailymail.co.uk/news/article-1287229/Lord-Savilles-Bloody-Sunday-Inquiry-spent-34m--just-computers.html

Question Topic:F6:-
References:
Article Name: "The Horrifying American Roots of Nazi Eugenics " by Edwin Black
hnn.us/articles/1796.html
www.evilbible.com/Murder.htm

Further Information and Scribble Notes:
en.wikipedia.org/wiki/Eugenics
www.dailymail.co.uk/news/article-2100067/Did-U-S-university-plan-create-intellectually-superior-race-children-repopulate-Britain-World-War-Two.html

news.bbc.co.uk/2/hi/health/1952449.stm

Question Topic:F7:-
References:
www.economist.com/blogs/banyan/2011/05/sri_lankas_war
en.wikipedia.org/wiki/20_July_plot
en.wikipedia.org/wiki/Politics_of_Sri_Lanka

Further Information and Scribble Notes:
en.wikipedia.org/wiki/Sri_Lankan_Civil_War
www.dailymail.co.uk/news/article-2239058/Was-Yasser-Arafat-really-
poisoned-Israel-Body-exhumed-8-years-death.html

Question Topic:F8:-
References:
www.dailymail.co.uk/news/article-2177445/Backlog-migrants-
276-000-growing-border-chiefs-struggle-deal-rising-number-cases.html
www.dailymail.co.uk/news/article-2144788/Free-roam-streets-protect-
human-rights-100-foreign-criminals-month.html
www.dailymail.co.uk/news/article-2177165/Home-Office-let-250-foreign-
criminals-deported-stay-UK-letting-judge-decide-fate.html
www.huffingtonpost.co.uk/jonathan-davis/britains-problem-with-
imm_b_977990.html
www.guardian.co.uk/commentisfree/2012/apr/28/news-corporation-
governments

Further Information and Scribble Notes:
- In 2012, the UK Home Office are faced with an an enormous backlog
of 276,000 immigration cases. These are made up of 3,900 foreign
offenders released by the courts to protect their 'human rights', 150,000
foreign workers and students believed to still be in the country even
after being refused visa extensions and 101,000 untraced asylum and
immigration cases.
- It was revealed in 2006 that 1000 foreign prisoners had been released
between 1999 and 2006 without even being considered for deportation.
- In 2011, over 250 foreign criminals including killers, paedophiles, rapists and a terrorist were allowed to stay in the country on human rights
grounds without government lawyers challenging their court cases.
These unchallenged cases have increased five-fold in the past three
years.
www.dailymail.co.uk/news/article-2224386/Fears-new-immigration-
surge-Bulgarians-Romanians-Britain-borders-open.html

Question Topic:F9:-
References:
people.howstuffworks.com/intelligent-design.htm
en.wikipedia.org/wiki/Victor_J._Stenger
mukto-mona.net/new_site/mukto-mona/Articles/brent_meeker/
id_cheap_poly.htm

Question Topic:F10:-
References:
www.trueconspiracies.com/
business.financialpost.com/2012/08/24/debunking-the-biggest-conspira-
cy-theories-in-finance/
www.dailymail.co.uk/news/article-2131192/Interest-mortgages-How-
million-Britons-sitting-time-bomb.html

Further Information and Scribble Notes:
Q2. Are textbooks in on the conspiracy. Why do they nevre suggest that
having no position in the market IS a position, but insist that an investment must be moved around and never extracted (feeding the demand
required in order to realise a reasonable peak).

Question Topic:F11:-
References:
humanorigins.si.edu/resources/intro-human-evolution

Further Information and Scribble Notes:
www.lifeslittlemysteries.com/2269-aliens.html
www.dailymail.co.uk/sciencetech/article-2157644/Why-aliens-look-like-
DNA-universal-constant--making-humans-ET-closer-cousins.html

Question Topic:F12:-
References:
Wildcard View:- Sex is one of the most marvellous wondrous experiences in life. Yet, it's only great if it's with someone new and there's a
mutual animal attraction at that moment in time. Otherwise, it really is a
cumbersome chore with no lasting gratification.
www.top10stop.com/lifestyle/top-10-reasons-for-divorce-and-marriage-
breakdowns-stats-from-the-us
www.iguides.org/articles/articles/832/1/Importance-of-Marriage-to-
Society/Page1.html
www.dailymail.co.uk/news/article-2145925/Women-beat-men-adultery-
stakes-Ladies-2-3-secret-lovers-affair-compared-1-8-blokes.html

Further Information and Scribble Notes:
Image 1 removed: Scene from Internal Affairs (1990) starring Richard
Gere. Scene when John Kapelos walks in on the pair, Caption: "Oops,
sorry. Can I get either of you a cup of coffee or a digestif perhaps"
Image 2 removed: Scene from Friday (1995) starring Chris Tucker and
Ice Cube. Scene with Smokey and Craig on the front porch, Caption:
"Erogenous zones are all over our bodies. God put them there for me
and you. Take advantage man, take advantage."

That beautiful stranger that goes by the name of 'Greta':
"It should really be 10 passes. I wanna be 60 and take comfort in the
fact that I'd have covered all demographics."

Famous joke :- Bigamy: One wife too many. Monogamy: Same problem.
debatepedia.idebate.org/en/index.php/Debate:_Marriage_is_outdated
www.dailymail.co.uk/news/article-2083692/Why-men-ALWAYS-cheat-
love-partners-dont-want-leave-them.html
him.uk.msn.com/sex-and-dating/are-men-hardwired-to-cheat

Question Topic:F13:-
Further Information and Scribble Notes:
en.wikipedia.org/wiki/Zakat

Question Topic:F14:-
References:
www.dailymail.co.uk/sciencetech/article-2155322/Rising-populations-
driving-Earth-irreversible-tipping-point--scientists-global-government.
html

Further Information and Scribble Notes:
Wildcard View: If it continued on its present path, is it possible for Great Britain to descend to such a degree, that the majority of the population become classified under v), therefore being marked for selection - if so, would it be such a bad thing?

Question Topic:F15:-
References:
starwars.wikia.com/wiki/Chosen_One
movies.uk.msn.com/features/the-phantom-menace-was-it-that-bad

Question Topic:F16:-
References:
england.shelter.org.uk/campaigns/why_we_campaign/Home_owner-ship_issues
Future Reform; Alternatively, mortgage lending will be completely overhauled and tightened such that mortgages will only be provided at a maximum of 5 x Joint Salary. Additionally, rent is controlled at a maximum of 30% above the actual mortgage payment (regardless of whether it is interest-only or repayment).
This means that tenants can benefit from low interest rates and that mortgages are only authorised for those who have the means to pay back such a large sum.

Further Information and Scribble Notes:
'January 7, 2011 "Property wealth gap widening" By Daniel Thomas, Property Correspondent www.ft.com
www.ft.com/intl/cms/s/0/5de50358-1a88-11e0-b100-00144feab49a.html#axzz1uT6WFkAR
www.dailymail.co.uk/news/article-2104726/Fears-50p-tax-working-income-revenue-collected-falls-rich-make-plans-avoid-higher-rate.html
www.dailymail.co.uk/news/article-2109685/Mansion-row-causes-coali-tion-rift-deal-tax-2-million-homes-stalls.html

Question Topic:F17:-
References:
www.dailymail.co.uk/news/article-1382411/Council-chief-retired-ill-health-earning-1m-consultant.html
www.dailymail.co.uk/news/article-1138502/For-7-years-8217-service-council-boss-gets-whopping-100-000-pension.html
www.dailymail.co.uk/news/article-2202567/Kent-County-Council-chief-Katherine-Kerswell-wins-142-000-civil-service-post-gets-420-000-pay-off.html
www.rutherglenreformer.co.uk/rutherglen-news/rutherglen-local-news/2012/08/29/another-council-boss-set-for-golden-good-bye-63227-31714404/
www.taxpayersalliance.com/home/2012/04/research-54-billion-black-hole-council-pension-schemes-revealed.html
www.dailymail.co.uk/news/article-2160422/Doctors-Strike--100-000-pen-sion-deals-1m-property-portfolios.html
www.telegraph.co.uk/news/politics/9254676/80000-public-sector-pen-sions-get-more-than-the-average-worker.html
www.telegraph.co.uk/health/healthnews/8933107/NHS-managers-to-receive-3-million-pension-pots.html

Further Information and Scribble Notes:

Wildcard view:- Have councils just learnt a trick or two from the govern-ment. Raising taxes from the bottomless pit that are the people, to fund their own pockets.
www.dailymail.co.uk/news/article-1296373/Town-halls--5bn-pensions-thats-quarter-council-tax.html
www.dailymail.co.uk/news/article-2129033/The-54bn-pensions-ticking-time-bomb-drive-council-tax.html
www.dailymail.co.uk/news/article-2136404/The-5trillion-burden-state-sector-pensions-Laid-bare-time--180-000-facing-family-Britain.html
www.dailymail.co.uk/news/article-2171737/Report-warns-council-pen-sions-ticking-time-bomb-million-draw-generous-payouts.html
www.tuc.org.uk/extras/publicsectorpensions.pdf
Post-Completion:
www.dailymail.co.uk/news/article-2248046/Sherwood-Park-Community-Primary-Schools-entire-governing-body-forced-resign-spending-6-000-public-funds-headteachers-farewell-BBQ.html
www.dailymail.co.uk/news/article-2236793/Parade-BBC-chiefs-hit-pay-jackpot-MPs-fury-executive-gets-670-000--wanted-quit.html

Question Topic:F18:-
References:
www.investopedia.com/terms/q/quantitative-easing.asp
www.bbc.co.uk/news/business-15198789
www.ons.gov.uk/ons/rel/wellbeing/measuring-national-well-being/house-holds-and-families/art---households-and-families.html#tab-Families
en.wikipedia.org/wiki/Quantitative_easing
www.guardian.co.uk/business/2013/apr/04/japan-quantitative-easing-70bn

Question Topic:F19:-
References:
www.time.com/time/magazine/article/0,9171,2111250-1,00.html
www.dailymail.co.uk/news/article-2104660/Two-London-babies-parent-abroad.html
www.dailymail.co.uk/news/article-2190972/Bingeing-mother-left-baby-week-Jail-20-year-old-child-starving-cot.html
www.dailymail.co.uk/news/article-1114502/Pictured-The-dark-cupboard-toddler-died-107-injuries-locked.html
www.dailymail.co.uk/news/article-2218981/Father-jailed-fracturing-month-old-baby-daughters-skull-squeezing-hard-ribs-popped-horren-dous-attack.html
www.dailymail.co.uk/news/article-2156013/Couple-raped-daughter-supervised-visit-recorded-sex-abuse-nephew-18-months-cellphone-contained-532-images-child-bestiality.html

Question Topic:F20:-
References:
www.guardian.co.uk/money/2006/dec/06/business.internationalnews
www.dailymail.co.uk/sciencetech/article-2175374/Russian-research-pro-ject-offers-immortality-billionaires--transplanting-brains-robot-bodies.html
news.uk.msn.com/the-big-question/the-big-answer-death-tax-is-indefensible
www.dailymail.co.uk/news/article-2192822/Even-recession-rich-richer-Savers-hit-70bn-printing-money-helps-rich-admits-Bank-England.html
www.dailymail.co.uk/news/article-2122476/The-Minister-utter-hypocrisy-Tory-attacked-tax-dodgers-invested-firm-did-just-that.html
www.dailymail.co.uk/news/article-2125790/Amazon-faces-probes-

paying-penny-company-tax-UK-2-years.html
www.dailymail.co.uk/news/article-2271633/Were-proud-help-firms-make-billions-avoiding-tax-accountants-tell-MPs.html
www.dailymail.co.uk/news/article-2177168/Tax-Justice-Network-Super-rich-elite-deprive-taxman-13trillion-using-cross-border-rules-hide-wealth.html

Further Information and Scribble Notes:
- extreme wealth brings unhappiness and the loss of appreciation of life!
- hopes of the instructed are better than the wealth of the ignorant.
truth-out.org/buzzflash/commentary/item/17669-five-facts-about-america-s-pathological-wealth-distribution
www.dailymail.co.uk/sciencetech/article-2056276/The-5-000-000-iPad-2-crusted-dinosaur-bones-gold--actually-bought-one.html
www.dailymail.co.uk/news/article-2239504/As-prices-Damien-Hirsts-works-plummet-pity-credulous-saps-spent-fortunes-tosh.html
www.dailymail.co.uk/news/article-2124244/Damien-Hirst-Tate-Modern-2012-Gift-shop-sells-36-800-plastic-skull.html
www.dailymail.co.uk/news/article-2081519/Damien-Hirsts-army-assistants-insults-art-says-David-Hockney-joins-Order-Merit.html
www.dailymail.co.uk/news/article-2224413/Art-critic-quits-modern-art-self-reverential-industry-focused-celebrities-money.html
Honourable Mentions: Candy's £65m flat; Encourage Drug Use of the wealthy.

Question Topic:F21:-
Further Information and Scribble Notes:
www.dailymail.co.uk/news/article-2148414/Facebook-IPO-Were-investors-misled-REALLY-worth.html
www.dailymail.co.uk/femail/article-2144745/The-1-3m-wine-hoax-How-man-sold-cheap-Napa-plonk-worlds-finest-vintage--fooled-industry-elite.html
www.dailymail.co.uk/news/article-2067723/Middle-class-boy-set-robot-program-financial-advice-investors-pocketed-1-5m.html

Question Topic:F22:-
References:
www.globalresearch.ca/index.php?aid=5626&context=va
www.npr.org/templates/story/story.php?storyId=1962910
Book: 'The Rough Guide to Conspiracy Theories' by James McConnachie and Robin Tudge

Question Topic:F24:-
References:
www.tomslatin.com/reflections-on-the-downward-spiral-of-modern-society/

Further Information and Scribble Notes:
www.dailymail.co.uk/news/article-2041639/Dream-home-The-floating-city-future-life-sea.html
notcoming.com/reviews/spywholovedme/
www.dailymail.co.uk/sciencetech/article-2096928/Google-Earth-removes-gridlike-pattern-sparked-lost-city-Atlantis-rumours-map.html

Question Topic:F25:-
References:
Paper: 'Government Manipulation and Distortion of History' by Louis

Wolf, Director of Research, Covert Action Quarterly
www2.iath.virginia.edu/sixties/HTML_docs/Texts/Scholarly/Wolf_Distortion_01.html
National Security Archive: The Atomic Bomb and the End of World War II. Edited by William Burr - 202/994-7000
www.gwu.edu/~nsarchiv/NSAEBB/NSAEBB162/index.htm
whatreallyhappened.com/WRHARTICLES/lieofthecentury.php
www.preservingourhistory.com/Laos.html

Further Information and Scribble Notes:
- Battle of Chamkaur, 1,000,000 Mughal Warriors vs 48 Sikh Warriors lasted 14-15 hours.
- General Gordon's Last Stand.
www.dailymail.co.uk/news/article-2146719/Anger-SNP-rewrite-history-New-school-curriculum-downplays-role-British-Empire.html

Question Topic:G1:-
References:
science.nationalgeographic.co.uk/science/prehistoric-world/dinosaur-extinction/
dinosaurs.about.com/od/dailylifeofadinosaur/a/dinomating.htm
dinosaurs.about.com/od/dinosaurevolution/a/creationists.htm

Further Information and Scribble Notes:
www.ucmp.berkeley.edu/mesozoic/cretaceous/cretaceous.php
www.dailymail.co.uk/sciencetech/article-2297594/Were-dinosaurs-killed-comet-New-analysis-suggests-smaller-faster-space-rock-sparked-mass-extinction.html

Question Topic:G2:-
References:
biology.about.com/od/biotechnologycloning/a/biological-weapons.htm
science.howstuffworks.com/bioweapon.htm

Further Information and Scribble Notes:
Stockpiles of the deadly Smallpox exist around the world in laboratories, however it is not known how many secret stockpiles exist nor how secure they are held.
www.dailymail.co.uk/news/article-2299661/Medicines-stockpiled-alert-biological-war-strike-UK.html
www.dailymail.co.uk/sciencetech/article-2101437/Editor-science-journal-says-ready-publish-details-lethal-man-flu-complete-form.html
www.dailymail.co.uk/news/article-2295811/Russia-accuses-Syrian-rebels-killing-25-banned-chemical-weapons.html
www.dailymail.co.uk/sciencetech/article-2172406/Jurassic-Park-Petri-dish-Scientists-recreate-500-million-year-old-bacteria-lab--possibly-wrong.html

Question Topic:G3:-
References:
science.howstuffworks.com/dictionary/astronomy-terms/big-bang-theory7.htm

Further Information and Scribble Notes:
www.dailymail.co.uk/sciencetech/article-2168557/Higgs-boson-Scien-

tists-God-particle-40-year-search-momentous-day-science.html
www.worldinterestingfacts.com/nature/largest-star-ever-known-in-the-universe.html

Question Topic:G4:-
References:
thenextweb.com/insider/2012/10/08/mail-order-drugs-hitmen-child-porn-a-journey-into-the-dark-corners-of-the-deep-web/

Further Information and Scribble Notes:
www.guardian.co.uk/technology/2009/nov/26/dark-side-internet-freenet
www.dailymail.co.uk/news/article-2232582/School-groping-surge-blamed-net-porn-Third-sixth-form-girls-abused-classmates.html

Question Topic:G5:-
References:
christiananswers.net/q-sum/q-life032.html
www.dailymail.co.uk/health/article-2155666/Scientists-soon-screen-unborn-babies-3-500-genetic-disorders-raising-fears-increase-abortions.html

Further Information and Scribble Notes:
en.wikipedia.org/wiki/Life_unworthy_of_life
listverse.com/2010/01/18/top-10-extraordinary-people-with-disabilities/

Question Topic:G6:-
References:
www.newscientist.com/article/dn13928-tasmanian-tiger-dna-lives-again.html
ecological-problems.blogspot.co.uk/2010/09/why-are-elephants-endangered.html
www.huffingtonpost.com/2010/11/22/tiger-extinction-tigers-c_n_786659.html
www.dailymail.co.uk/sciencetech/article-2295146/Back-dead-nearly-Scientists-create-living-embryo-extinct-frog-gives-birth-MOUTH.html

Further Information and Scribble Notes:
www.dailymail.co.uk/news/article-2265402/Adventurous-human-woman-wanted-birth-Neanderthal-man-Harvard-professor.html
in.answers.yahoo.com/question/index?qid=20090813071040AAyzNaH
www.allaboutwildlife.com/endangered-tigers-facts

Question Topic:G7:-
References:
www.dailymail.co.uk/news/article-2125007/Maternity-ward-mix-babies-leaves-parents-claiming-boy-theirs.html
www.dailymail.co.uk/indiahome/indianews/article-2128393/Battered-baby-dies-Afreen-gives-fight-life-brutalised-father-born-girl.html
www.dailymail.co.uk/indiahome/indianews/article-2148350/Female-foetuses-Beed-fed-dogs-hide-evidence.html
www.bbc.co.uk/news/magazine-20938125
www.dailymail.co.uk/femail/article-1276902/Britains-hidden-gendercide-How-Britains-Asians-copying-Indian-cousins-aborting-girls.html
www.dailymail.co.uk/news/article-2258385/Saudi-girl-15-barricades-bedroom-married-90-year-old-groom-huge-dowry.html

Further Information and Scribble Notes:

Wildcard Questions:-
i) Gold as Indian Dowry as stupid as diamonds as engagement presents. A custom promoted by its respective interested organisations.
ii) India has EXISTING legislation that prohibits the dowry system. Why do the authorities not impose it?
Surrogate Mothers from India as solution to women around the world who are unable to have children but don't mind a daughter:

www.dailymail.co.uk/news/article-2218381/Indian-wife-dies-baby-daughter-suffers-horrific-burns-husband-set-slept-dowry-dispute.html
www.dailymail.co.uk/news/article-2139708/The-designer-baby-factory-Eggs-beautiful-Eastern-Europeans-Sperm-wealthy-Westerners-And-embryos-implanted-desperate-women.html
www.dailymail.co.uk/news/article-2311800/Five-year-old-girl-raped-days-kidnapped-neighbour-Delhi-paedophile-crime-month.html
www.guardian.co.uk/commentisfree/2012/may/23/dowry-deaths-big-fat-indian-wedding
www.soroptimistinternational.org/blog/post/437-indias-70-million-missing-women-female-feticide

Question Topic:G8:-
Further Information and Scribble Notes:
www.wikihow.com/Understand-Why-People-Use-Drugs
www.dailymail.co.uk/news/article-2109073/Kathryn-Fuller-Pleads-guilty-drug-charges-Uganda.html

Question Topic:G9:-
References:
Wildcard Questions:-
1) Does it say more about human nature that people strive to ensure their children adopt this ethos, and them proudly displaying unwavering loyalty to it?
2) Should the schools double their rates in return for the disservice they do society?
3) Are people aware of the social chasm on the horizon, and only by displaying these traits will they see their children on the 'elite' side rather than that of the servicing minions.
¬ Private Schools tend to harvest acquisitive attitudes towards wealth and power.
¬ Fatcats are all privately school educated, so is that where the underlying issue is.
¬ Infamous war generals and dictators have been privaely educated.

Further Information and Scribble Notes:
www.guardian.co.uk/education/2009/jul/19/private-schools-life-privilege-pupils
news.bbc.co.uk/1/hi/education/4514156.stm
www.independent.co.uk/news/education/education-news/private-school-dominance-of-top-jobs-is-morally-indefensible-says-gove-7733437.html
www.dailymail.co.uk/news/article-2235719/Britain-run-private-school-elite-study-shows.html
www.timeshighereducation.co.uk/408584.article
www.dailymail.co.uk/news/article-2305548/Shamed-bank-boss-told-slice-25m-pension-HBOS-trio-face-boardroom-ban.html
www.dailymail.co.uk/news/article-2304274/Catastrophic-failures-HBoS-grandees-Bombshell-report-calls-City-ban-reckless-bankers-lumped-taxpayer-28billion-bill.html

Question Topic:G10:-

References:
www.aclu.org/racial-justice_prisoners-rights_drug-law-reform_immi-grants-rights/10-reasons-oppose-3-strikes-youre-

Further Information and Scribble Notes:
www.dailymail.co.uk/sciencetech/article-2312418/Are-crooks-really-criminally-minded-Abnormal-brain-activity-means-offenders-control-behaviour.html

Question Topic:G11:-

References:
www.dailymail.co.uk/news/article-2138650/I-failed-banking-collapse-Sir-Mervyn-King-says-shouted-warnings.html
dailybail.com/home/the-hammer-gets-hit-by-a-tree.html
www.nytimes.com/2009/03/16/business/16rescue.html?_r=0
biz.thestar.com.my/news/story.asp?file=/2009/3/9/
business/3436727&sec=business
usatoday30.usatoday.com/money/industries/banking/2010-07-24-gold-man-bailout-cash_N.htm

Further Information and Scribble Notes:
www.dailymail.co.uk/debate/article-2048016/Why-euro-bailouts-biggest-Ponzi-scheme-ever.html
www.rollingstone.com/politics/news/why-isnt-wall-street-in-jail-20110216

Question Topic:G12:-

Further Information and Scribble Notes:
Wildcard Question:-
With prospects and benefits dwindling by the day, will many of todays Universites be confined to the scrapheap, hence the desperate clamour to make as much money as they possibly can (via fees and student volume) while the Bachelors Degree is still perceived as a valuable posession?

www.guardian.co.uk/education/2012/nov/07/graduate-job-prospects-decline
www.independent.co.uk/student/career-planning/getting-job/the-futures-still-bright-graduate-career-prospects-may-not-be-as-bleak-as-jobseek-ers-think-2021131.html
www.dailymail.co.uk/news/article-2086771/Richard-Wilson-Dispatches-How-humans-replaced-machines.html
www.dailymail.co.uk/news/article-2086652/Bosses-new-London-Route-master-bus-fly-Poland-hire-drivers-turning-Britons.html
www.dailymail.co.uk/news/article-2104986/Shocking-truth-graduate-unemployment-chance-work-school-leaver-GCSE.html
www.dailymail.co.uk/news/article-2229587/Value-university-education-falls-Graduates-degree-earn-22-decade.html
www.dailymail.co.uk/news/article-2304096/Graduate-physics-PhD-31-fell-death-block-flats-taking-job-centre-qualified-for.html

Question Topic:G13:-

Further Information and Scribble Notes:
www.dailymail.co.uk/debate/article-1349951/Gayness-mandatory-schools-Gay-victims-prejudice-new-McCarthyites.html
www.dailymail.co.uk/sciencetech/article-2127260/Why-having-sex-real-ly-IS-best-thing-Gene-mapping-finally-proves-mating-best-way-evolve-

self-reproduction.html
www.dailymail.co.uk/health/article-2133371/Huge-rise-IVF-single-gay-mothers-law-requiring-father-figure-removed.html
www.dailymail.co.uk/femail/article-2190065/The-woman-wants-abolish-sex-Genetics-expert-urges-embrace-future-virgin-births-women-AND-men-sex-marriage-redundant.html
www.dailymail.co.uk/news/article-2052431/The-world-population-approaching-perfect-storm-swells-15bn-2100.html
www.dailymail.co.uk/sciencetech/article-2081260/Infertility-break-through-scientists-grow-sperm-outside-body.html
www.dailymail.co.uk/news/article-2306755/Church-England-allow-responsible-gay-couples-relationships-blessed-priest.html

Question Topic:G14:-

Further Information and Scribble Notes:
www.dailymail.co.uk/news/article-2083316/Petrol-set-hit-1-40-litre-summer--matched-inflation-20-years-just-83p.html
www.dailymail.co.uk/money/bills/article-2283902/Inflation-cuts-value-money-67-30-years--prices-everyday-goods-like-bread-milk-beer-rise-far-faster.html

Question Topic:G15:-

References:
www.thedailybeast.com/articles/2012/04/11/spain-s-baby-snatching-scandal-focuses-on-nun-s-alleged-role.html
www.nytimes.com/2011/07/07/world/europe/07iht-spain07.html?pagewanted=all
www.dailymail.co.uk/news/article-2128929/Elderly-nun-accused-baby-snatching-Spanish-hospitals-trafficking-ring.html
www.dailymail.co.uk/news/article-2314239/Grandfather-sells-day-old-baby-Facebook-telling-daughter-child-dead.html

Further Information and Scribble Notes:
At one infamous Madrid clinic called San Ramón, it was reported in the Spanish media that staff kept a dead newborn in the freezer to prove to mothers that their babies had died.

www.bbc.co.uk/news/world-latin-america-18733415
www.guardian.co.uk/world/2012/mar/28/spain-stolen-babies-reunited-mother
www.dailymail.co.uk/news/article-2229289/Take-children-care-say-MPs-despite-20-rise-death-Baby-P.html
www.dailymail.co.uk/news/article-2237063/Seven-couples-try-adopt-children-fall-wayside-More-22-000-parents-rejected-social-workers.html

Question Topic:G16:-

References:
www.nytimes.com/2010/11/14/us/14nazis.html
www.abovetopsecret.com/forum/thread308865/pg1
Book: 'The Rough Guide to Conspiracy Theories' by James McCon-nachie and Robin Tudge

Further Information and Scribble Notes:
en.wikipedia.org/wiki/American_Israel_Public_Affairs_Committee
en.wikipedia.org/wiki/Final_Solution
usc.news21.com/madeline-story/expert-analysis
news.bbc.co.uk/1/hi/world/7857753.stm
www.dailymail.co.uk/news/article-2149734/Why-people-hate-Jews-

Shocking-GCSE-religious-studies-question-set-Britains-biggest-exami-
nations-board.html

Question Topic:G17:-
References:
Reviews:
www.cinemaphile.org/reviews/1999/thesixthsense.html
www.seattlepi.com
www.nitrateonline.com/2002/rsigns.html
www.criticdoctor.com/petersobczynski/thevillage.html
whatwouldtotowatch.com/2008/07/07/not-much-happening-here/
www.popmatters.com/pm/post/127773-the-curious-case-and-continued-
disgrace-of-m-night-shyamalan/
mortonmalaise.blogpeoria.com/2008/06/16/the-happening-sucks-or-m-
night-shyamalan-is-a-pretentious-douchebag/
www.mamapop.com/2010/09/mnight-shyamalan-final-warning.html

Further Information and Scribble Notes:
www.firstshowing.net/2008/what-happened-to-the-great-m-night-
shyamalan/

Question Topic:G18:-
References:
cellphones.procon.org/
www.cancer.gov/cancertopics/factsheet/Risk/cellphones
www.careministries.cc/general-health/are-mobile-phones-dangerous-to-
our-health.htm
www.lef.org/magazine/mag2007/aug2007_report_cellphone_radia-
tion_01.htm

Further Information and Scribble Notes:
An excellent article by Geoffrey Lean 21Sep08;
www.independent.co.uk/news/science/mobile-phone-use-raises-child-
rens-risk-of-brain-cancer-fivefold-937005.html
Children and teenagers are five times more likely to get brain cancer if
they use mobile phones, startling new research indicates. The study,
experts say, raises fears that today's young people may suffer an
"epidemic" of the disease in later life. At least nine out of 10 British
16-year-olds have their own handset, as do more than 40 per cent of
primary schoolchildren. Yet investigating dangers to the young has been
omitted from a massive £3.1m British investigation of the risks of cancer
from using mobile phones, launched this year, even though the official
Mobile Telecommunications and Health Research (MTHR) Programme
- which is conducting it - admits that the issue is of the "highest priority".
Despite recommendations of an official report that the use of mobiles
by children should be "minimised", the Government has done almost
nothing to discourage it.
Professor Lennart Hardell of the University Hospital in Orebro, Sweden
told the first international conference on mobile phones and health
that "people who started mobile phone use before the age of 20 had
more than a five-fold increase in glioma", a cancer of the glial cells that
support the central nervous system. The extra risk to young people of
contracting the disease from using the cordless phone found in many
homes was almost as great, at more than four times higher. Those who
started using mobiles young, he added, were also five times more likely
to get acoustic neuromas, benign but often disabling tumours of the auditory nerve, which usually cause deafness. At 20 the danger diminishes
because then the brain is fully developed. Indeed, he admits, the hazard
to children and teenagers may be greater even than his results suggest,
because the results of his study do not show the effects of their using
the phones for many years. Most cancers take decades to develop,
longer than mobile phones have been on the market.
news.uk.msn.com/uk/no-hard-evidence-of-mobile-damage-4
www.dailymail.co.uk/news/article-2134382/Risks-biggest-technological-
experiment-history-species-Calls-research-links-using-mobile-phones-
brain-cancer.html

Question Topic:G19:-
References:
www.dailymail.co.uk/news/article-2138678/Iconic-Scream-painting-
fetches-whopping-119-million-auction.html
www.dailymail.co.uk/news/article-2138715/Cezanne-watercolour-mas-
terpiece-sells-12million.html
www.metro.co.uk/news/49229-rothko-painting-sells-for-record-36-8m
www.dailymail.co.uk/news/article-2217383/Eric-Clapton-sells-Gerhard-
Richter-painting-record-21-3-million--11-years-buying-paintings-just-
1-9-million.html
www.dailymail.co.uk/femail/article-2050113/Kate-Moss-yoga-statue-
sells-577-000-Sotheby-s.html
www.dailymail.co.uk/news/article-2146436/Empty-sculpture-stand-blank-
canvas-main-attractions-invisible-art-exhibition.html
www.theartwolf.com/articles/10-most-expensive-photographs.htm

Further Information and Scribble Notes:
www.damienhirst.com/for-the-love-of-god
www.telegraph.co.uk/culture/art/artsales/3560707/Damien-Hirst-sale-
makes-111-million.html
www.dailymail.co.uk/news/article-480729/Did-Damien-Hirst-really-sell-
diamond-skull-50m.html
en.wikipedia.org/wiki/My_Bed
www.dailymail.co.uk/news/article-2190504/No-thanks-Nation-turns-
Tracey-Emins-bed-30-million-art-gift-snub.html
www.dailymail.co.uk/news/article-2311727/Mishka-Henner-puts-images-
Google-Streetview-prostitutes-display-gallery.html

Question Topic:G20:-
References:
electronics.howstuffworks.com/nanorobot.htm

Further Information and Scribble Notes:
www.microscopemaster.com/nanobots.html
curiosity.discovery.com/question/nanorobots-can-be-used-for
www.dailymail.co.uk/sciencetech/article-2129200/Could-cure-AIDS-
horizon-Genetically-engineered-human-stem-cells-hunt-kill-HIV-inside-
body.html
In the 'Outer Limits - 'The New Breed' TV episode, a scientist who's trying to find a way to repair damaged cells develops robots of microscopic
size - with which a lab assistant secretly injects himself in hopes of
curing his cancer.

Question Topic:G21:-
References:
starwars.wikia.com/wiki/Order_66

Further Information and Scribble Notes:
In return, the recipients and family line would receive unrivalled yet undocumented financial and underground support to enable them to eventually ingrain themselves to senior levels and invaluable and untenable positions of organisations and government, achieving considerable economic rewards.
Also provided financial assistance to relocate and integrate successfully.

Question Topic:G22:-
References:
en.wikipedia.org/wiki/Palpatine
www.reddit.com/r/FanTheories/comments/zt9l8/the_real_reason_emperor_palpatine_created_the/
www.bearishnews.com/post/524
www.nytimes.com/interactive/2009/02/04/business/20090205-bailout-totals-graphic.html?_r=0

Further Information and Scribble Notes:
www.nytimes.com/2009/08/09/business/09paulson.html?

Question Topic:G23:-
Further Information and Scribble Notes:
ethicsalarms.com/rule-book/unethical-rationalizations-and-misconceptions/

Question Topic:G24:-
References:
"September 11 attacks." Encyclopædia Britannica. Standard Edition. Chicago: Encyclopædia Britannica, 2012.
en.wikipedia.org/wiki/September_11_attacks#Casualties
islam.about.com/od/terrorism/a/Muslim-Victims-Of-9-11-Attack.htm

Further Information and Scribble Notes:
¬ Al-Qaeda was headquartered in Afghanistan and had forged a close relationship with the country's ruling Taliban militia, the ultraconservative political and religious faction. The faction took its name from its membership, which consisted largely of students trained in madrasahs (Islamic religious schools).
¬ Less working people and less security, therefore logistically, weekdays was the worst choice.
www.guardian.co.uk/world/2002/aug/18/usa.terrorism

Question Topic:G25:-
Further Information and Scribble Notes:
www.dailymail.co.uk/news/article-2007057/Mega-rich-prosper-austerity-Britain-500-000-dollar-millionaires.html
www.dailymail.co.uk/news/article-2135901/Nice-work-The-extraordinary-perks-Britains-fat-cats-including-25k-clothes-allowance--300k-private-jet-fees-100k-private-school.html

Question Topic:H1:-
References:
www.dailymail.co.uk/news/article-2134688/3-000-town-hall-staff-earn-100-000-hundreds-figure-salaries-despite-cutbacks.html

Question Topic:H3:-
References:
www.standard.co.uk/comment/comment/breaking-the-grip-of-the-public-schools-7737182.html
www.totalpolitics.com/blog/45433/academies-will-struggle-to-break-public-schools-grip-on-top-jobs.thtml

Further Information and Scribble Notes:
www.guardian.co.uk/commentisfree/2011/apr/10/social-mobility-debate-cohen-johnson
www.dailymail.co.uk/news/article-2085444/Clegg-plans-end-grip-old-school-tie-business-jobs-making-applications-anonymous.html
www.dailymail.co.uk/news/article-2184009/Universities-accused-social-engineering-drawing-plans-favour-pupils-poorer-backgrounds.html
www.dailymail.co.uk/news/article-2171806/Social-engineering-lead-class-war-Governments-social-mobility-tsar-admits.html
www.dailymail.co.uk/news/article-2235719/Britain-run-private-school-elite-study-shows.html
www.dailymail.co.uk/news/article-2152968/Thousands-middle-class-students-WILL-lose-university-equality-drive-warns-UCAS-chief.html
www.dailymail.co.uk/news/article-2259299/One-Britons-non-white-2050-minority-groups-grow-prosperity-status.html
www.nwtimes.com/news/local/govt-and-politics/new-anti-nepotism-law-may-transform-local-government-employment/article_55a4a533-e1fc-56f4-8cb7-cb17663e5901.html
www.dailymail.co.uk/news/article-2150265/The-banker-IT-director-company-boss-Prince-Harrys-school-photo-shows-classmates-gilded-educations.html
Post-Completion:
www.dailymail.co.uk/news/article-2244306/University-personal-statements-scrapped-unfair-state-school-pupils.html

Question Topic:H4:-
Further Information and Scribble Notes:
www.dailymail.co.uk/news/article-2125336/Ban-cane-schools-led-discipline-childrens-behaviour.html

Question Topic:H5:-
References:
history1900s.about.com/od/rwandangenocide/a/Rwanda-Genocide.htm
www.bbc.co.uk/news/world-africa-11108589
worldnews.about.com/od/africa/a/hututsiconflicthistory.htm
en.wikipedia.org/wiki/Divide_and_rule
www.telegraph.co.uk/news/worldnews/africaandindianocean/rwanda/3536709/Congo-Hutus-and-Tutsis-will-always-kill-each-other.html

Further Information and Scribble Notes:
Wildcard View:
¬ The Projex. Making them self-implode. Drugs, then the guns in the ghettos of the US.
¬ West planted bombs against the Shiite to ignite a civil war so they self-implode.
¬ Supporting Israel blindly to wind-up the palestines so conflict remains.

sundayposts.blogspot.com/2008/09/should-britain-apologise.html
www.dailymail.co.uk/news/article-2135369/Charles-Taylor-trial-Found-guilty-arming-Sierra-Leone-rebels-exchange-blood-diamonds.html

dawn.com/2013/03/04/hunting-down-shias-societys-deafening-silence/

Question Topic:H6:-
Further Information and Scribble Notes:
www.dailymail.co.uk/news/article-2145687/Number-babies-born-ethnic-minorities-surpasses-whites-U-S-time.html
www.dailymail.co.uk/sciencetech/article-2295824/100-000-year-old-skull-shows-signs-inbreeding-adds-evidence-theory-ancestors-regularly-practised-incest.html
en.wikipedia.org/wiki/Inbreeding

Question Topic:H7:-
References:
BBC Knowledge Magazine Article "Dark Energy" by Robert Matthews. Sep2011, Issue 19
news.bbc.co.uk/2/hi/science/nature/6156110.stm
www.dailymail.co.uk/sciencetech/article-2280975/Have-dark-matter-Scientist-leading-2bn-space-experiment-says-results-set-release.html
www.theopedia.com/Omnipresence_of_God

Question Topic:H8:-
References:
www.dailymail.co.uk/sciencetech/article-2077232/Scientist-created-deliberately-created-Armageddon-bird-flu-virus-lab-says-publish-details.html
www.alternet.org/newsandviews/article/658903/u.s._gov._secretly_infected_thousands_of_guatemalans_with_stds/
www.msnbc.msn.com/id/39456324/ns/health-sexual_health/t/us-apologizes-guatemala-std-experiments
www.infoplease.com/ipa/A0762136.html
en.wikiquote.org/wiki/Talk:Henry_Kissinger

Further Information and Scribble Notes:
www.dailymail.co.uk/health/article-2134863/Anti-depressants-harm-good.html
www.dailymail.co.uk/sciencetech/article-2271532/Genetically-modified-version-herpes-virus-block-spread-ovarian-breast-cancer.html

Question Topic:H9:-
References:
www.guardian.co.uk/business/2011/dec/12/rbs-abn-amro-fsa-report
www.telegraph.co.uk/finance/newsbysector/banksandfinance/8933151/Royal-Bank-of-Scotland-collapse-the-10-questions-the-FSA-must-answer.html#
www.channel4.com/news/articles/arts_entertainment/media/why+itv+failed+friends+reunited/3012562.html
www.independent.co.uk/news/media/tv-radio/shine-agrees-to-newscorp-takeover-2221546.html

Further Information and Scribble Notes:
www.telegraph.co.uk/finance/newsbysector/mediatechnologyandtelecoms/electronics/8850041/Chairman-steps-down-at-scandal-hit-Olympus.html
www.bbc.co.uk/news/world-asia-india-16137127
compliancesearch.com/compliancex/jail-sentence/paul-allen-ex-mortgage-ceo-sentenced-to-prison-for-3b-fraud-2/
economictimes.indiatimes.com/news/international-business/jpmor-gan-ceo-jamie-dimon-confronted-over-2-billion-trading-loss/articleshow/13162694.cms

Question Topic:H10:-
References:
en.wikipedia.org/wiki/Mineral_water
www.britishbottledwater.org/vitalstats.html
www.finewaters.com/Bottled_Water/index.asp
www.lenntech.com/applications/drinking/faq/drinking-water-faq.htm
thewaterproject.org/how-to-give-clean-water.php

Question Topic:H11:-
Further Information and Scribble Notes:
en.wikipedia.org/wiki/Inception
www.psychologytoday.com/blog/mental-mishaps/201007/inception-the-science-creating-dreams

Question Topic:H12:-
Further Information and Scribble Notes:
en.wikipedia.org/wiki/Land_reform_in_Zimbabwe

Question Topic:H13:-
References:
en.wikipedia.org/wiki/Outsourcing
news.cnet.com/The-end-of-Indias-offshore-dominance/2010-1022_3-5668292.html

Further Information and Scribble Notes:
www.virtualemployee.com
www.outsourcing.com/content.asp?page=01b/articles/index.html
www-cs-faculty.stanford.edu/~eroberts/cs181/projects/offshoring/impact.html

Question Topic:H14:-
References:
catholicism.yoexpert.com/catholicism-general/why-is-there-a-requirement-of-celibacy-for-catholi-1755.html
www.dailymail.co.uk/news/article-2283190/Pope-resigns-Claims-blackmail-sex-parties-secret-report-cardinals.html
www.dailymail.co.uk/news/article-2117574/Dutch-Catholic-Church-castrated-10-boys-1950s-effort-purge-homosexuality.html
www.dailymail.co.uk/news/article-2075070/Tens-thousands-children-victims-child-sexual-abuse-hands-paedophile-priests-Netherlands-1945.html
www.dailymail.co.uk/news/article-2151911/Was-girl-murdered-snatched-Vatican-sex-parties.html
www.dailymail.co.uk/news/article-2082037/Paedophile-monk-paid-schoolboy-50p-time-sexually-abused-locked-up.html
www.dailymail.co.uk/news/article-2097643/Vatican-investigated-4-000-cases-child-sex-abuse-10-years-U-S-cardinal-reveals.html
www.dailymail.co.uk/news/article-2287430/Cardinal-Keith-O-Brien-admits-sexual-misconduct-facing-Vatican-inquiry.html
boingboing.net/2013/02/01/catholic-priest-child-sex-abus.html
www.latimes.com/news/local/la-me-0201-mahony-curry-20130201,0,3889565.story
en.wikipedia.org/wiki/Roman_Catholic_Church_sexual_abuse_scandal_in_Ireland

news.bbc.co.uk/1/hi/northern_ireland/8567868.stm

Further Information and Scribble Notes:
www.guardian.co.uk/world/2010/sep/15/paedophile-priests-active-church-role

Question Topic:H15:-
References:
www.tdcj.state.tx.us/stat/executedoffenders.htm

Further Information and Scribble Notes:
www.environmentalgraffiti.com/news-12-most-exorbitant-and-vicious-execution-methods-worlds-history?

Question Topic:H16:-
References:
BBC Focus Magazine Issue 247 "Rise of the Biobots" by Duncan Graham-Rowe
www.dailymail.co.uk/sciencetech/article-2128115/Living-doll-Geminoid-F-convincing-robot-woman--facial-expressions-talks-sings.html
www.dailymail.co.uk/sciencetech/article-2070938/The-Holy-Grail-regenerative-medicine-British-researchers-create-stem-cells-potential-human-therapy.html
www.dailymail.co.uk/sciencetech/article-2221344/Humanoid-robots-day-friends-perform-surgery-beat-humans-football.html

Further Information and Scribble Notes:
www.dailymail.co.uk/sciencetech/article-2073936/Could-hackers-develop-virus-infect-human-mind.html
www.dailymail.co.uk/sciencetech/article-2108209/Russian-entrepreneur-aims-transplant-human-mind-robot-body-10-years.html

Question Topic:H17:-
References:
www.dailymail.co.uk/sciencetech/article-2073936/Could-hackers-develop-virus-infect-human-mind.html
www.upi.com/Science_News/2005/07/14/Scientists-reverse-memory-loss-in-mice/UPI-91421121386246/

Further Information and Scribble Notes:
www.thedoctorweighsin.com/the-neurobiology-of-memory-manipulation/
www.guardian.co.uk/science/2013/apr/02/obama-brain-initiative-fight-disease

Question Topic:H19:-
References:
www.out-law.com/page-11115
lexicon.ft.com/Term?term=insider-trading
en.wikipedia.org/wiki/Demography_of_the_United_Kingdom
www.dailymail.co.uk/news/article-2285004/Paul-Tucker-Bank-chief-raises-prospect-base-rate-BELOW-zero-bid-kickstart-spending.html
www.dailymail.co.uk/news/article-2130095/Calls-British-people-given-priority-social-housing-queue-revealed-foreigners-HALF-properties.html
www.dailymail.co.uk/news/article-2132012/Immigration-boom-Labour-changed-face-Britain-faster-major-country-Italy-Oxford-experts-reveal.html
www.dailymail.co.uk/news/article-2236790/Osborne-400-000-profit-

second-home-claimed-expenses-say-neighbours.html
www.dailymail.co.uk/debate/article-2196055/London-Metropolitan-University-crisis-Visas-sham-courses-bogus-students.html
www.guardian.co.uk/business/2012/may/06/shout-rooftops-bank-dereg-ulation-leads-to-disaster

Further Information and Scribble Notes:
www.guardian.co.uk/news/datablog/2010/jun/26/non-eu-immigration-uk-statistics
www.telegraph.co.uk/news/uknews/1563934/The-Labour-Partys-dec-ade-in-power-reviewed.html
www.dailymail.co.uk/news/article-2249851/Primary-school-thirds-chil-dren-speak-English-second-language-gets-100-pass-rate-exams.html
www.ems.bbk.ac.uk/faculty/wright/pdf/oxrep
www.dailymail.co.uk/news/article-2296190/BUDGET-2013-Osborne-bets-house-helping-HALF-A-MILLION-families-buy-new-homes-aston-ishing-130bn-pledge-bankroll-mortgages.html
www.dailymail.co.uk/news/article-2287903/Romania-boasts-secret-deal-UK-benefits-migrants-ministers-plan-ID-cards-free-NHS-care-curb-welfare-tourism.html

Question Topic:H20:-
References:
en.wikipedia.org/wiki/Fractional_reserve_banking

Further Information and Scribble Notes:
www.dailymail.co.uk/news/article-2138650/I-failed-banking-collapse-Sir-Mervyn-King-says-shouted-warnings.html
www.positivemoney.org.uk/
economix.blogs.nytimes.com/2011/01/13/what-goldman-sachs-failed-to-acknowledge/

Question Topic:H21:-
References:
www.investopedia.com/articles/basics/04/022004.asp
www.investopedia.com/terms/i/informationallyefficientmarket.asp
www.independent.co.uk/news/uk/home-news/insider-dealing-what-is-it-who-does-it-why-do-they-do-it-what-happens-if-they-get-caught-and-what-is-being-done-to-stop-it-david-bowen-offers-a-laymans-guide-1412888.html

Further Information and Scribble Notes:
www.dailymail.co.uk/money/news/article-2168242/Barclays-release-details-Bank-England-man-says-led-Libor-rigging.html
'agiven' = 'a given'

Question Topic:H22:-
References:
www.livescience.com/10715-synthetic-biology-great-promise-potential-peril.html
www.ia-sb.eu/go/synthetic-biology/synthetic-biology/about-synbio/

Further Information and Scribble Notes:
www.bbc.co.uk/news/science-environment-17436365
www.economist.com/node/16163154
In the Outer Limits TV eposode 'Unnatural Selection', A young couple elect to use a new technique to genetically enhance their unborn baby.

In the Outer Limits TV eposode 'Descent', A mild-mannered professor becomes bold and powerful after he injects himself with primitive DNA.

Question Topic:H23:-
References:
www.conservapedia.com/Origin_of_life
science.howstuffworks.com/life/evolution/evolution.htm
en.wikipedia.org/wiki/Evolution

Further Information and Scribble Notes:
Theory of Evolution has a number of unsatisfactory explanations behind the theory, specifically the idea that :-
i) Chicken or Egg, ii) Cell complexity, iii) Catch-22 situation with regards to the existence of Oxygen
www.answersingenesis.org/articles/nab/hasnt-evolution-been-proven
voices.yahoo.com/differences-between-eutherians-metatheri-ans-11757844.html
www.nytimes.com/2013/02/08/science/common-ancestor-of-mammals-plucked-from-obscurity.html?pagewanted=all&_r=0
www.icr.org/article/5137/361/

Question Topic:H24:-
References:
www.independent.co.uk/news/business/news/goldman-bankers-get-rich-betting-on-food-prices-as-millions-starve-8459207.html
www.telegraph.co.uk/foodanddrink/foodanddrinknews/9776144/Cost-of-food-not-going-to-stop-rising-warns-UK-chief-scientist.html
www.fao.org/worldfoodsituation/wfs-home/foodpricesindex/en/
www.globallabour.info/en/2008/07/financializing_food_deregulati.html
www.dailymail.co.uk/news/article-1296068/Trading-death-Rapacious-bankers-making-fortunes-forcing-price-food-leaving-millions-starve.html
www.independent.co.uk/life-style/food-and-drink/news/north-sea-fisher-ies-madness-2137103.html

Further Information and Scribble Notes:
According to the United Nations, 2012 prices were more than twice as expensive than a decade earlier, even after adjusting for inflation.

Question Topic:H25:-
References:
www.guardian.co.uk/world/2004/jan/02/catholicism.religion
www.digitaltrends.com/computing/apple-causes-religious-reaction-in-brains-of-fans-say-neuroscientists/
www.aloha.net/~mikesch/666.htm
www.666mark-of-the-beast.net/
www.rapturechrist.com/Mark.htm
www.markbeast.com/satan/lucifer-satan-devil.htm
www.carlg.org/engmarkofthebeast.html
www.av1611.org/666/biochip.html
en.wikipedia.org/wiki/Vicarius_Filii_Dei
www.dailymail.co.uk/news/article-2220002/Mobile-phones-CAN-cause-brain-tumours-court-rules-landmark-case.html

Further Information and Scribble Notes:
www.dailymail.co.uk/sciencetech/article-2145908/Beware-iCloud-Snoop-ing-software-lets-police-read-iPhone-real-time-knowing.html
www.newstatesman.com/blogs/nelson-jones/2011/10/steve-jobs-apple-religious
thedoggstar.com/articles/robot-agenda-mark-beast/
www.godonthe.net/evidence/rapture.htm
After The Rapture, God will begin executing judgments against unbeliev-ers, during a period called the Tribulation. At the end of the Tribulation all nations will attack Israel, and Jesus Christ will physically return, lead-ing the armies of heaven. At the Battle of Armeggedon they will destroy everyone who is not a believer. Then Satan will be bound, and Jesus will set up the Millennial Kingdom, headquartered in Jerusalem. Jesus and the saints will rule over the nations of the Earth for a thousand years. During this period there will be people born who are not loyal to Christ. However, it usually will not be obvious. Therefore, at the end of the thousand-year period, God will release Satan and let him tempt those who inhabit the Earth. A large group will take up arms against the Lord and be defeated. Then, Christ will judge all who have ever lived, giving rewards to some and punishment to others. Those who were ""de-stroyed"" will be cast into the Lake of Fire, i.e., Hell. After that, God will destroy heaven and Earth because they have been polluted by sin. He will create a new heaven and a new Earth, put those who were saved on the new Earth, and rule it forever."